# Fiscal and Monetary Reforms in India

# Fiscal and Monetary Reforms in India

*Editor*

***K R Venugopal***

**I.K. International Publishing House Pvt. Ltd.**

NEW DELHI • BANGALORE

*Published by*

I.K. International Publishing House Pvt. Ltd.
S-25, Green Park Extension
Uphaar Cinema Market
New Delhi–110 016 (India)
E-mail : info@ikinternational.com
Website : www.ikbooks.com

ISBN 978-81-89866-23-5



10 9 8 7 6 5 4 3 2

Reprint 2011



Published by Krishan Makhijani for I.K. International Publishing House Pvt. Ltd., S-25, Green Park Extension, Uphaar Cinema Market, New Delhi–110 016 and Printed by Rekha Printers Pvt. Ltd., Okhla Industrial Area, Phase II, New Delhi–110 020.

*Dedicated to*

***Prof. K Venkatagiri Gowda***

***Smt. Savithri Venkatagiri Gowda***

# Preface

Dr. K Venkatagiri Gowda obtained his Bachelor's and Master's Economics from the University of Mysore and Ph.D in Economics from the London School of Economics. He began his career as a Lecturer with the University of Mysore, where he went to become Reader. From 1967 to 1983, he worked as Professor and Chariman of the Department of Economics in Bangalore University. He had specialisation in Monetary Economics and International Finance.

His works have been internationally acclaimed as definitive and path breaking in the area of Monetary Economics, International Finance and Planning. He published the following books: Fiscal Policy and Inflation (1959), Appreciation of the Indian Rupee (1960), Keynes-Triffin Plans for International Liquidity (1961), European Common Market and India (1962), Commonwealth Common Market (1963), International Currency Plans and Expansion of World Trade (1964), Euro-Dollar Flows and International Monetary Stability (1979), A Plan for Eradication of Black Money and Black Wealth (1983), Perestroika and Glasnost for India (1988), Democracy in Deficits (1995), New Dimensions for Indian Planning (1995), Economic Performance of the Government (1997).

Professor Gowda was an incisive man par excellence. His economic analysis on the budget was greatly valued by the economists and administrators in the country. He was invited by the Government of U.S.A. to deliver lectures on "Oil Crisis" in U.S. Universities.

He represented the Bangalore South Constituency (from BJP) in the Lok Sabha during 1991-96. As a Member of Parliament, his contribution to the economic policy was substantial. I was closely associated with Prof. Gowda for nearly three decades. I had the opportunity to be his Doctoral Pupil from 1986-89. I used to have long and frequent discussions with him. He possessed an uncanny analytical ability and a perfect command over English. Prof. Gowda received Lord Leverhulme Special

Research Award, London School of Economics. In 1983, he received the Karnataka Rajyotsava Award.

He was a great scholar and perfectional, known for his sincerity and honesty. His scholarship, frank opinions and expertise in economics was always appreciated by the prime ministers of our country. His five decades of crusade to bring about economic reforms in our country will never go unnoticed in the annals of our history.

The present book is a collection of memoranda of Professor Gowda mostly addressed to the Late Hon'ble Prime Minister Sri P V Narasimha Rao and the present Hon'ble Prime Minister Sri Manmohan Singh, during 1991-96.

The articles in the book are on topics like Fiscal Structure, Industry Policy, Bank Restructuring, Exchange Rate of Rupee, Gold policy, Inflation Management, Deficit Financing, Liquidity Crisis, Oil Fueled inflation, Oil Exploration, Oil Crisis, Privatisation of Insurance, Foreign Capital Inflows, Foreign Investment, IMF and its Conditionalities, Foreign Exchange Reserves, Public Expenditure, Budget, Disinvestments, Buyoncy of Indian Rupee, Inflation Trap, Subsidies for food and fertilizers, MNCs, Trade deficits, Public Borrowing, External debt, Short and Long Term Capital Flows, Banking Policy, Deregulation of Interest Rates, Convertibility, Liberalization, Industrial Sickness, Export-Import Strategies, NRI Investments, Subsidies, Industry and Agriculture Growth, Debt Crisis, Wage Freeze, etc.

The observations made by him are very critical and useful. They are of special interest to postgraduate and research students, academic planners and policy makers and statesmen.

The book comprises 114 articles, which provide solutions to myriad economic problems in our country. This great personality left us on 5th July 2004 at the age of eighty-one. This book is brought out in the memory of my beloved Professor K Venkatagiri Gowda.

***Venugopal K R***

# Acknowledgements

I wish to place on record my deep debt of gratitude to Sri M.C. Jayadeva, who has been a constant source of inspiration. His gentle encouragement and taste for perfection have been the key to my growth and success in my career. Moreover his timely suggestions and counseling have been of immense help to me.

I am also grateful to Prof. S. Lakshmana Reddy, Prof. N.R. Shetty, Prof. P. Sreenivasa Kumar, Justice N. Rama Jois, Sri. N. Krishnappa, Prof. K. Mallikarjun Chetty, Prof. H.N. Shiva Shankar, Prof. N. Srinivasan, Prof. L.M. Patnaik and Prof. M. Venkatachalappa for encouraging me to bring out this book in the present form. I sincerely thank Sri. K.P. Jayarama Reddy, Sri T.G. Girikumar, Sri P. Palani, Sri M.G. Muniyappa, for their support in preparing this book.

I express my gratitude to Sri K. Narahari, Sri Y.K. Raghavendra Rao, Sri P.R. Ananda Rao, Justice T. Venkataswamy, Prof. Y.V. Somayajulu, Sri Sreedhar Sagar, Sri N. Nagabhusan, Sri Prabhakar Bhat, Prof. K.V. Acharya, Sri Khajampadi Subramanya Bhat, Sri V. Nagaraj, Sri Dinesh Kamath, Sri D.M. Ravindra, Sri Jagadesh Karanath, Sri N. Thippeswamy, Sri H. K. Mohan Kumar, Sri Sudhir, Sri V. Manjunath, Sri N Dinesh Hegde, Sri Nagendra Prasad, Sri Sripad, Sri K. Thyagaraj, Smt. Savithri Venkatagiri Gowda, Smt. Karthyayini V. and Smt. Rukmini T, my well wishers for inspiring me to write this book. I thank Dr. P. Deepa Shenoy, Sri K.B. Raja, Sri K. Suresh Babu, Smt D.N. Sujatha, Sri K.G. Srinivasa, Smt. S.H. Manjula, Smt Suraiyya Taranaum, Smt. Vibha L. for their assistance.

I am indebted to Tejaswi Venugopal, T. Shiva Prakash, T. Krishna Prasad and Lakshmi Priya K. for their help. I thank L. Nalini and G. Hemalatha for neat composing the book.

*Venugopal K R*

# Contents

Prof. K Venkatagiri Gowda

Dr. Venugopal K R, Prof. K Venkatagiri Gowda,
Smt. Savithri Venkatagiri Gowda

**Prof. K Venkatagiri Gowda, His Excellency S M Krishna, Prime Minister Dr. Manmohan Singh, Hon'ble Minister Mallikarjuna Kharge**

**Hon'ble Prime Minister Dr. Manmohan Singh, and Prof. K Venkatagiri Gowda**

**Hon'ble Prime Minister Dr. Manmohan Singh, Dr. Venugopal K R, Prof. K Venkatagiri Gowda**

**Indian Economist Forum 1991-92**

**Prof. K Venkatagiri Gowda, family and friends**

# 1

# Public Borrowing and Fiscal Accountability

The Finance Minister who has had vast experience in the area of financial management, is reputed for springing pleasant surprises. In the Union Budget for 1994-95, he set limits on how much the Government can borrow from the Reserve Bank of India. He had announced that the budget deficit broadly defined as the borrowings from the Reserve Bank of India will be limited to Rs. 6,000 crore and at no time it be allowed to go higher than Rs. 10,000 crore for more than 10 days. This position was generally maintained. As of May 13, 1994 the net Reserve Bank credit to the Government stood at Rs. 10,366 crore, Rs. 840 crore less than the level at the same time in 1993.

Lately the Finance Minister has taken a decision to let the public hold treasury bills. This idea to broad base the holdings of Government debt has long been felt. But the authorities cold shouldered it. The transactions in 91 and 364 days treasury bills are now being routed through the National Stock Exchange (NSE). In doing it, the Finance Minister has given the Reserve Bank more powers of manoeuvre. Not only that, he has gone a step further on the road to investing Indian fiscal policy with some degree of accountability.

Redesigning the monetary system does not generate strong positions in the same way as cuts in subsidies and hikes in tax rates though they are useful in the task of maintaining macro-economic stability. Till 1992, the Reserve Bank of India used to absorb nearly all of the government's short term debts. Every rupee borrowed by the government from Reserve Bank added a rupee to the stock of money. This resulted in inflation. In 1993-94 the treasury bills came to be auctioned and the Reserve Bank had no longer to underwrite the entire fiscal deficit as a major part of it was held by the scheduled commercial banks and state-owned financial institutions. This had the effect of reducing the inflationary impact of the deficit though it did not eliminate it altogether. Commercial banks hold the securities as statutory reserves. The liquidity they surrender to acquire government debt is more than made up by the enhanced credit expansion of new reserves permit. Keeping the fiscal deficit inflation neutral involves draining the economy of that amount of liquidity which the deficit creates. This means selling government securities to the public which has no means of independently creating liquidity. The Reserve Bank can achieve this by conducting open market operations on the National Stock Exchange.

This strategy has enlarged the scope of monetary policy. Besides this going public with the national debt imposes far greater fiscal accountability than legislative measure could even achieve. The Members of Parliament angling for constituency development on public funds will have to subordinate their demands to what the public can lend. The government debt will have to compete with the private investment demands. If, however, the market borrowings do not satisfy the government's need for money, the government can go back to the Reserve Bank of India and the captive banking sector. If the public is to be allowed to hold government debt there should be legislation to impose cuts on such tendencies. The effects of the deficit can be dampened with the help of economic instruments. But are they effective in the face of political constraints?

Admittedly borrowings from the Reserve Bank of India cause an equal expansion of money supply. A monetary expansion causes a rise in the price level in the same proportion in accordance with the mechanism underlying the Classical Quantity Theory of Money. Furthermore, as per the reformulated Quantity Theory of Money given by Don Patrikein, a rise in money supply, the price level being hold constant, generates a real balance effect which releases additional demand which in turn, causes a rise in the price level. A rise in the price level removes there all balance effect and in consequence demand stops rising and the price level also stops rising. The price level reaches a real equilibrium where it remains stable unless it is again disturbed by monetary expansion. In the case of public borrowing also inflation is possible. If the public lends money which they would have spent on consumption, there is no net inflationary effect. What the government spends is equal to what the public refrained from spending. There is no net rise in spending and so there is no rise in the price level. If the public tends what they would have saved after meeting their consumption requirement and if the government spends this money there is net rise in spending and a rise in the price level. In the absence of information about the source of money which the public uses to buy government debt, no inference can be drawn about whether public borrowing to meet government expenditure is inflationary or not.

There are two methods of financing the budget deficit; money financing and debt financing. Money financing is definitely inflationary as it causes a rise in money supply which causes a rise in the price level in the same proportion. But modern fiscal theorists hold the view that debt financing is more inflationary than monetary financing. Their logic is this: Public borrowing involves interest payment to the debt holders. The larger the public debt the larger the interest payment. This involves a rise in non-plan expenditure. This initially reduces the fiscal deficit which is inflationary. Thus an increase in fiscal deficit has a bearing on future government expenditure, because of higher repayment liabilities and interest payments. The importance of this indicator is such that today just the interest obligations on past borrowings of the government make up 35 percent of the centre's revenue expenditure. This is a major reason why the government is unable to reduce its non-plan expenditure. This is the reason for the rise in the fiscal deficit. Though the direct budget deficit i.e., government's borrowings from the Reserve Bank has so far been kept within the stated limits, the fiscal deficit has been increasing. Against the target of 4.7 percent of GDP for 1993-94 the actual fiscal deficit for the year has turned out to be as high as 7.3 percent. The Finance Minister wants it be brought down to 6 percent of GDP in 1994-95. This year the position is serious, because though the borrowings from the Reserve Bank have been contained in the new dispensation, there has been a sharp rise in the government's borrowings from the commercial banks. Statistics available for April 1994 show that there has been a massive increase of Rs. 9492 crore in the credit released by the commercial banks to the government. The magnitude of this increase can be judged from the fact that total credit by commercial banks to the government during the whole of 1993-94 was Rs. 27000 crore. During April 1993, there was a decline of Rs. 235 crore in the commercial bank credit to the government which worked out to a percentage reduction of 0.3 percent. In comparison the increase was 9.3 percent in April 1994. Official figures are not available for the subsequent months.

In view of this it is not enough to reduce borrowings from the Reserve Bank of India and to resort to public borrowings. Public borrowing may, of course, increase the degree of fiscal accountability but it does not free the economy from the danger of an inflationary surge. The need for public accountability can be minimized and the inflationary surge can be held in check if there is a constitutional limit imposed on public borrowings. This will discipline the government and its various departments in their expenditure commitments and expenditure programmes and check their fiscal profligacy. This, of course, is a political instrument beyond the powers of the Finance Ministry. This instrument only the Parliament can wield. Will it? It should if it is serious about resolving the escalating fiscal crisis.

# 2

# Forecasts About The Indian Economy

In the post-budget months this year the predictions made by the Western Agencies about the future course of the Indian economy and the business behaviour are both optimistic and pessimistic. There are two think-tanks and they have predicted opposite growth paths for India. The US think-tank WEFA an offshoot of the Wharton Econometrics has recently predicted that India's real GDP will grow at 6.3 percent in 1995-96 and 6.5 percent in 1996-97. In their opinion growth rate will be fueled by a rise on private consumption of 6.5 percent in 1995-96 and there would be an inflow of foreign direct investment of $ 2 billion. The picture this agency predicts is rosy and cheering.

But there has been a recurring reference to political uncertainty in the media. This has lately come to be perceived as the single most important determinant of the goings-on in the stock market or the halting progress in the inflow of foreign direct investment. The latest in the series is the growth forecast by the London based Economist Intelligence Unit in its latest quarterly report. This anticipates political instability in India as a dampener of the investment scenario. It also predicted in its last quarterly report that India's risk rating is lower than that of China even though it rated Indian economic policies to be more risk conducive than those of China and Pakistan. But they emphatically pointed out that political risk was higher in China. In the latest quarterly report they have warned against the growing political risk in India.

The Finance Minister has gone on record predicting a growth rate of 5.5 percent. But the Economist Intelligence Unit (EIU) for the first time predicts a less than 5 percent growth rate. This is sweet music to those who have been warning about the slow pace of economic reforms. According to the EIU growth will be constrained by the slow growth in consumer demand as a result of higher interest rates, disruption to production caused by the 1996 elections and devaluation of the rupee. It warns about the rupee reaching a level of Rs. 42/- to a US dollar (as against the current rate of Rs. 31.37). It also predicts the possibility of current account deficit increasing due to a deluge of imports and a large outflow of funds if the current political stability persists. If these predictions materialize the warning could become a relief.

The EIU predicts a decline in private consumption as a result of higher interest rates, disruption to production caused by the forthcoming 1996 elections to the Parliament and devaluation. This prediction needs close examination. This examination holds a mirror to the grave pitfalls in the forecasting made by the EIU.

## GROWTH PROSPECTS

In his Budget for the 1995-96, the Finance Minister has designed a "two track strategy" for growth. The critics of the Finance Minister were quick to conclude that the new awareness about the poor is a consequence of the unfavourable experience for the ruling party at the Assembly polls. There is some truth in this assertion. The elaborate spelling out of each and every anti-poverty and pro-poor programme in his budget speech definitely reflects the realization by the Finance Minister that his policies have to be marketed better both to the masses and his party. At the same time, there is evidence of a broad consensus on the economic reform programme among the Opposition parties particularly those in power in different States and this has given the Finance Minister the confidence to proceed on his charted course.

Is there something new in the two-track strategy? The Finance Minister himself answers it by saying that "the task of lifting the age-old burden of poverty in our society is daunting, but we are on the right track. We must preserve with our two-track strategy of accelerating growth, investment and modernization on the one track and strengthening anti-poverty programmes on the other".

The question that arises is this. Are the two tracks parallel tracks which do not meet or do they meet and interact so as to accelerate the growth process? In fact, they do meet and interact as otherwise they will have to be conceived of as two independent agents of growth. Immediately after the Keynesian Revolution R.F. Harrod and P.A. Sammuelson built trade cycle models incorporating the multiplier and the accelerator and explained the upswing and the downswing. When there is a rise in the marginal propensity to consume the value of the multiplier rises and for any given investment the level of income rises higher. This causes a rise in investment as per the acceleration coefficient. And the interaction between the multiplier and the accelerator cause a rise in income. This interaction was subsequently incorporated into the growth models by R.M. Goodwin and H.J. Johnson. The poverty alleviation programmes cause a rise in the marginal propensity to consume and the value of the multiplier, this cause a rise in investment to a degree depending on the acceleration co-efficient and the interaction between the two accelerates the rate of economic growth. The Finance Minister's two-track strategy appears meaningful if it is understood in this light.

The critics of the Finance Minister have accused him of "rediscovering the poor" afresh. When the Finance Minister launched India into the market-friendly policies in 1991 he was clear about the position of those who create wealth as well as the under privileged in the new system. "We must restore to the creation of wealth its proper place in the development process. For, without it, we cannot remove the stigma of object poverty, ignorance and disease. But we cannot accept social misery and inequity as unavoidable in the process of creation of wealth. The basic challenge of our times is to ensure that wealth creation is not only tampered by equity and justice but is harnessed to the good of removal of poverty and development for all". A reference again to the earlier budget speech would absolve the Finance Minister of the accusation of "rediscovering the pon", because of electoral reverses. He had the candour to admit that his budget proposals came under the influence, albeit marginally, of the political factors. Though he reduced the rural development expenditure in his second budget in

1992, by February 1993 he had increased the outlay for the Department of Rural Development (the development dealing with anti-poverty programme) by 62 percent to take it to Rs. 5010 crore. That year, the allocation for the Jawahar Rozgar Yojana too was increased to Rs. 3,306 crore (up from Rs. 2,046 crore the preceding year) with the objective of creating 1100 million man days. The provision for rural water supply was raised from Rs. 460 crore and Rs. 740 crore. Enhanced provisions were made and outlays for other social sector like education (up 37.6 percent) and health (up 60 percent) were increased. The process saw a continuation in 1994 when the allocation for rural development went up by another 40 percent to a level of Rs. 7,010 crore. A fresh allocation of Rs. 1,200 crore was made for a new employment assurance scheme and the allocation under the Jawahar Rozgar Yojana was gain raised to Rs. 3,885 crore. In the 1995-96 budget the allocation for rural development has been raised from Rs. 7,010 crore to Rs. 7,700 crore. Similarly, the increase under other head of social spending has been raised marginally despite the budget preceding the general elections. The Finance Minister does not seem to agree with those analysts who feel that the election results reflect a rejection of the new economic policies, particularly in the face of the contradictory evidence that comes through the endorsements by the Governments in the States. Instead, the message that seems to have gone home is that reforms per se are not bad but the support base for the reforms is still very narrow.

The emphasis of the Finance Minister this year on the two-track strategy reflects the desire to reach out directly to the 700 million people who are outside the purview of the market. But he is constrained by the existing system. Having raised social spending and anti-poverty programme allocation in the last two years the Finance Minister has concluded that simply increasing budgetary allocation for social sectors and poverty programmes is not enough. Instead, the requirement is to revamp delivery systems and administrative structures for such programmes to make them much more accountable and responsive to the beneficiaries for whom the schemes are intended. But the fiscal deficit comes in the way of doing more than this on the second track. Containment of the fiscal deficit is the only anti-inflationary tool. The other track of the two-track strategy of accelerating growth, investment and modernization continues without any let or hindrance. The budget continues with the process of lowering excise and customs duties aimed at making the Indian industry competitive and growing. The expected higher levels of industrial production are expected to contribute more revenue for the Government and help it to reduce the fiscal deficit. There is optimism that this would be the result of the taxation exercise. Many changes have been made in the excise rules and regulations aimed at plugging the loop holes in revenue. The expectation of buoyancy in tax revenues depends on this also.

The benefits of reforms have not spread evenly among the 250 million of Indians who constitute the upper middle class and who are supporting the ongoing economic reforms. Within this group there are those who grasped the early opportunities provided by the market economy and who have improved their living standards. The others feel that the benefits of reforms are bypassing them. It is necessary to respond to their feelings and to devise policies meant to improve their lot.

The Indian economy is looking up and the rate of economic growth is bound to grow. In July 1991, when the economic reform programme was initiated, the London Economist published a report captioned "The Tiger Unchained" meaning thereby that the economy was unshackled by bureaucratic controls and licensing procedures. The *Economist* of January 1995 was a special on India titled "The Tiger Steps Out", it mirrored India very comprehensively. It said "After 4 decades of suffocation and a couple of years of post-adjustment gloom, Indian business is bouncy. The business confidence index compiled by the National Council of Applied Economic Research went from optimistic to ebullient in 1994. Corporate projects in the first half of 1994-95 were up by 102% .....". The Asian Tigers are leaping forward on the high road to economic growth. The Indian Tiger, more buoyant and more dynamic, will leap forward faster.

This is not to argue that there are no distortions or shortcomings in the Indian economy under the management of the present Finance Minister. There are innumerable structural and institutional rigidities and imperfections which impede rapid progress despite the dynamism built into it. Even so, there is a remarkable turnaround since the dark days of 1991, when India was a damsel in distress. The critics harp on unemployment, poverty and inflation. They talk as if inflation is a new phenomenon, poverty is a new emption and external debt is a new scourge accumulated since 1991. This is to present a distorted picture of reality. In February 1995, 13 'eminent' economists published a statement attributing inflation, unemployment, poverty etc., to the economic reform programme. Obviously, they forgot to attribute the earthquake in Kobay in Japan to the Indian economic reforms. After the Budget for 1995-96 was presented one of them living in South India resiled and paid compliments to the macroeconomic competence of the Finance Minister. These drawingroom cassandras, as the Finance Minister chooses to characterize them, have failed to provide viable alternatives. In fact, they expect the Finance Minister to do away with the ills accumulated over 48 years since Independence. This, indeed, is a tall order. The mechanism is working. The structural and institutional rigidities inherent in the system have rendered the working of the mechanism slow. We cannot expect miracles overnight.

The Budget for 1995-96 assumes that the income and corporation taxes would rise by 20 percent. Since prices are assumed to rise by 8 percent growth is assumed to be 7 or 8 percent. Union excise duties are assumed to rise by 16 percent after taking changes in rates into account. In other words, a real growth of atleast 8 percent is assumed. In the case of customs duties, import growth of 17 percent seems to have been estimated assuming that there is no devaluation. Thus all these figures point to a GDP growth of 7 to 8 percent i.e., a rise from the 1994-95 figure of 5.3 percent. Such a rise implies an industrial growth rate of 12 percent. The budget is expected to provide the stimulus for the rate of growth to rise to this level.

A lot depends on agricultural growth which in turn depends in favourable monsoons. It is estimated that the monsoons this year will be favourable so that the rate of agricultural growth will rise generating higher incomes for the farm families. This higher income is to be used to improve their standard of living, healthcare, sanitation and the housing facilities and the consumption standards in general. This provides an added stimulus to growth through the acceleration mechanism. The prophets of doom have a blinkered view of the future of the Indian economy. All evidence points to a buoyant economy brimming with the dynamism. This is as it should be after the initial years of the economic reform programme.

# 3

## Decline of Foreign Capital Inflow

Statistical evidence, of course, shows that there is a decline in the inflow of foreign capital into India. The forex reserves had started dwindling because of the reduced capital inflow after November 1994. This had started putting pressure on the dollar rupee exchange rate off late. Between April 1994 and November 1994 the foreign exchange reserves excluding gold and SDRs increased by around 30 percent from $ 15.083 billion to $19.496 billion. But during the next four months the reserves increased by only around 2.3 percent to $ 20.954 billion. In fact during the current financial year, the reserves had taken a further dip. On April 21, 1995, the reserves had depleted by around $460 million. This put pressure on the dollar exchange rate which went up sharply in recent days. In April 1995 the rupee had depreciated to the average rate of Rs.31.60 per US dollar. The market circles feel that with the widening trade deficit the rupee would depreciate further.

Until 24th May 1995, the Government was reluctant to give permission to repatriate Euro-Issue proceeds to India as it would increase the money supply which would give a further upward push to the rate of inflation. But in a move to book the sagging forex reserves the Ministry of Finance decoded on May 24, to permit Indian companies to bring their Euro-Issue proceeds back to India as foreign currency deposits with banks and public financial institutions. This was required to give a boost to the stock market which has remained continuously at a bottom level because of the prevailing liquidity crunch in the country which would affect industrial growth this year. It was argued that if the repatriation of the Euro-Issue proceeds could help in ameliorating the situation the Government must permit the same. It is said that if the rate of inflation came down to less than 8 percent and remained at that level for four consecutive weeks the Government would allow the repatriation along with the conversion into Indian currency. The Ministry further said that the repatriated money would only be converted into Indian rupee as and when the expenditure for the approved end uses are incurred. This decision would help to boost the dwindling forex reserves.

The prediction of reduction in the inflow of foreign capital is not invalid. It is likely to slow down in 1995-96 for several reasons: (a) National elections are due early in 1996 and there is a perception in international capital markets of a political uncertainty; (b) devaluation of the rupee is expected since the havala market premium has risen and this creates the fear of a capital loss; (c) the international climate is not conducive to inflow of foreign capital after the collapse of the Mexicon Peso and the rising interest rates in the US. The last factor is reinforced by the warning administred by the IMF Managing Director Mr. Camdessus. Speaking to the representatives of the co-financing institutions in Washington on May 26, 1995 he said that world growth has now close to its long term trend rate and he expected most industrial countries to experience sustained growth and developing countries to maintain 6 percent growth a year if policy improvements are maintained. But he mentioned two key risks— the instability and misalignments of exchange rates among currencies and "a sharper than expected slow down in capital flows to emerging market economies today. He said that the IMFs projections include a further weakening of these capital flows following their rapid growth in the early 1990s, partly as a result of the recovery in the industrial economies. "But the risk is that there could be a much sharper fall-off, perhaps triggered by financial crisis in one or two countries but threatening growth prospects much more widely", Mr. Camdessus said. He emphasized that this risk was vividly illustrated by Mexico's financial crisis and its spill over effects which reached many countries in the Western hemisphere, he further said. This risk as well as the exchange rate instability were partly the result of globalization of financial markets. But he warned that the answer to this situation is not reversion to exchange rate controls or less open markets but in improving economic policies at the national level as well as stronger international monetary co-operation at the global level through the IMF. Mr. Camdessus noted that a number of policy lessons could be drawn from the Mexican experience vis-à-vis capital flows. The Mexican crisis displayed all too clearly how suddenly market assessments of a country's situation can turn around when a country lowers its guard and allows its economic policies to weaken.

Mr. Camdessus referred to the market economies in general that too those whose policies are weak and not at all to India. It would be wrong to draw a parallelism between Mexico and India. The Mexican crisis is the country's own making, having devalued the Peso contrary to its earlier promise and not having been in a position to take suitable follow up action. Some economists have gone to the extent of attributing the London bank failure to adventurism, both unwanted and unwarranted, in globalization. If what they say is correct, nationalized or communist economic must be better. But that is not to be. It has caused the disintegration of the entire nation a super power at that.

Be that as it may, it would be idle to pretend that what happened in Mexico will happen in India and to blame the "useful toils of the Finance Minister. The investments in Mexico were of a short term variety liable to shift without notice. These investments were made mostly in consumer goods industries. Mexico had a massive current account deficit of 8 percent of GDP. The rate of inflation was high and surging. The weakness of the fiscal-monetary policies made the foreign investors shift their capital abroad. In about two weeks, the foreign exchange reserves declined from $ 27 billion to 7 billion. This in sharp contrast with the situation in India; the rate of inflation is 8.5 percent at present and is expected to fall further; the current account deficit is 0.5 percent of GDP and even if it goes upto 1.0 percent of GDP because of the surge in imports there will be no danger to the economy. The credit rating agencies have rated India very high.

# 4

# Foreignisation of Public Sector Companies

The people of this country have become alarmed at the report that the government is contemplating the sale of share of public sector companies to foreign investors as part of the disinvestment policy. This is nothing short of what I call foreignisation of domestic companies.

Already, the Government of India has been following a policy of disinvestment in public sector companies as a method of covering the budget deficits a process which is called privatisation. This can be welcome as the control of these companies will be in Indian hands. But foreignisation is bound to be resisted by the people of the country as it lends credence to the opposition charge that the Government is pursuing a policy of sell out of foreign interests. The proposal regarding foreignisation has been reportedly made by Shri G.V. Ramakrishna, Chairman of the Securities and Exchange Board of India (SEBI) and this proposal is reportedly being examined by a high level committee headed by Mr. V. Krishna Murthy, Member of the Planning Commission. The Finance Ministry is in favour of this move as it is likely to bring in foreign exchange. It is felt that instead of borrowing from the multilateral financial agencies and the international capital market agreeing to their conditionality prescriptions which may be found to be harsh at times, the Government can use the public sector shares to earn foreign exchange. There is no precise estimate of the quantum of foreign exchange that can be mobilized in this manner as it depends on the percentage of shares to be sold to foreigners and their response to it.

It is the Government's perception that the shares of public sector companies will be in great demand considering the fact that anybody from any country can invest in them. The Government's stand is that it will retain control over these undertakings by keeping a majority of the shares with it i.e., 51 percent of equity. This implies that upto 49 percent of equity can be disinvested. What the precise percentage of disinvestment should be is to be decided by the Krishna Murthy Committee. The Chairman of the SEBI has not made any commitment regarding the precise percentage of shares to be disinvested. But the Krishna Murthy Committee has to take a decision about it. What the precise amount of shares for disinvestment should be, the Committee can decide on the percentage of share to be disinvested depending on the Government's requirement of foreign exchange. Initially the Committee may not recommend more than 10 percent of the shares for disinvestment in favour of foreign investors.

It is the contention of the Government spokesman that when the Government decides to retain control over the company by keeping 51 percent of the shares to itself, it matters little whether the balance of 49 percent of the shares is made over to foreigners, NRIs or the Indian investors. It is generally believed that some of the public sector units can compete with the private firms over the market value of the shares. There is no reason why the shares of certain companies where disinvestment is contemplated should be quoted lower than the shares of other strong companies. Even some of the loss-making public sector units are intrinsically strong and are likely to commend a good price in the share market.

The process of disinvesting in the shares of public sector companies may not be immediate. In India, the process of disinvestment began only in 1991-92. The Government disinvested equity worth Rs. 3,000 crore. If this disinvestment process comes to pass the first batch of industries whose shares are to be disinvested involves 31 companies including SAIL and ITI. In the second round the industrial units in the energy and petroleum sectors will figure. And the process will continue until disinvestment is complete.

At present many public sector units are unviable and loss making. They subsist on budgetary support which is a burden on the tax payer. In this case privatization is necessary and is understandable. This is a case of the Government and the private sector jointly managing the industrial units. But foreignisation is fraught with grave risks. Even though the Government keeps the majority of the shares under its control 51 percent, leaving balance 49 percent in the hands of foreigners, there may crop up problems in the running of the units. If the voice of the foreign shareholders is not heard, they may demand return of their investment funds in foreign exchange. As the foreign exchange they paid while buying the shares will have been used up by the Government in settlement of the foreign balances, the Government will be hard put to it to find the resources of the magnitude invested by the foreigners. In this event, the Government will have to submit tamely to the commanding voice of the foreign minority share holders or to raise loans in the international capital market for the purpose agreeing to the harsh conditionality prescriptions imposed by the international financial institutions. What the Government tried to avoid coming in through the front door, it has to allow through the back door. Or, in the alternative, it has to sell the majority of the shares to the foreign investors keeping the minority shares in its hands. As a minority shareholder the Government of India will have no voice. Holding minority shares is worse than selling the company to the foreign investors.

Even if the Government keeps the majority shares, it may turn out that it will have to sell the majority shares to the foreign investors in order to avoid borrowing from the international capital market to be able to return the share amount to the foreign investors in the event of their demanding it. In this event, the investment policy, employment policy and the pricing policy will be determined by the foreign partners and will be imposed on the Government of India which will be in an unenviable position of helplessly accepting these policies. These are problems, which sooner or later will crop up to the discomfiture of the Government. For this reason, the Government should have second thoughts about selling shares of public sector companies to foreign investors as part of its disinvestment policy. It is true and truth always hurts that the Indian bureaucracy, unduly fond of foreignisation, may recommend policies intended to handover the leading sectors to foreign interests.

But the Government should not display avidity in accepting them uncritically.

If the country is short of foreign exchange, its expenditure must be minimized in all possible ways of which there are many. It must reduce the balance of payments gap by means of import compression and export promotion and also by reduction of the magnitude of budget deficits. What can be said in favour of privatization cannot be said with equal fervour in favour of foreignisation. The Government would do well to beware of those who advise foreignisation of public sector companies as this amounts to a real sell out to foreign sector companies as this amounts to a real sell out of foreign interest which the majority of Indians cannot tolerate.

# 5

## The Silver Import Policy : Is it Viable?

The Union Finance Minister, in his speech presenting the Union Budget for 1992-93 on 29-02-1992 proposed a Gold Bond Scheme under which the non-resident Indians and other nationals who have stayed abroad for over six months to bring in 5 kg of gold after paying customs duly. Under this scheme upto August 31, more than 42 tonnes of gold imports have taken place in just 5 months as against the annual target of 35 tonnes. More than Rs. 100 crore have been collected by way of duty as against the annual target of Rs. 75 crore.

Encouraged by the success of the scheme the Government is presently reported to be working out a scheme to allow import of silver on the lines of gold, excise duty exemption to a sizeable section of this tiny sector and liberalisation of the baggage rules. The details of the silver import scheme are said to be at an advanced stage of finalization.

The Government seems to be in an illusion in supposing that the success which attended the gold import policy will also attend the silver import policy. The case of gold import is different from the case of silver import. Gold is a precious metal recognized as an important component of foreign reserves of the Central Banks all over the world. Even the International Monetary Fund has recognized it as such. But silver does not enjoy this status. Silver is used as an industrial material and as material used in the manufacture of jewellery for use especially in the rural sector and tribal area. It is nowhere used as a component of foreign reserves. Furthermore, it does not normally enhance the social status of the owners in the same way as gold. Silver jewellery is, by and large, unacceptable by the lenders as security. These factors make silver a commodity distinct and separate from gold in international and interpersonal transactions.

The excise duty exemption and liberalisation of baggage rules are unlikely to encourage the import of silver to India. In the case of gold, those who bring in gold to India can sell it to the black money barons at a premium and make a sizable profit. This is a device to launder black money into white. But the demand for silver on the part of the black money barons cannot be much as the appreciation in its value is marginal unlike the appreciation of the value of gold. As the demand for silver domestically is not as big and persistent as the demand for gold, import of silver is not a profitable enterprise. For this reason silver import is unlikely to be considerable. Even the bulkiness of silver militates against its import on a large scale.

If silver is imported on any large scale, it entails a large scale expenditure of scarce foreign exchange reserves. Those who bring in silver have to buy it in the foreign markets by using foreign exchange in their possession. This reduces the inflow of foreign exchange to the Reserve Bank of India. This will not be compensated by the inflow of silver as silver is not reckoned as a component of foreign reserves. In the case of gold the Reserve Bank of India issues gold bonds tenable for a certain period and gets gold in exchange. This gold becomes part of foreign reserves. The Reserve Bank cannot issue silver bonds in order to get silver in exchange, for silver is not part of its foreign reserves. Even if the Indians who visit foreign countries bring in silver the demand for it is not as strong and persistent as the demand for gold. Therefore, to allow import of silver enthused by the success of the gold import policy is to assume away the problem. The Government should ponder over the proposed silver import scheme before implementing it.

# 6

# Problems of External Debt

India's external debt has posed two problems to the authorities: (a) its bulging volume and (b) the preponderance of the short-term debt. While the former has imposed a heavy repayment obligation and servicing, the latter has created the problem of repaying maturing debt almost every year. The Government of India last week adopted certain guidelines meant to cap the external debt and to reduce the short-term component of the total external debt.

The new guidelines have certain features: (a) proposals for loans of more than $ 15 million will be considered only if they are for more than seven years against the earlier maturity period of three years; (b) applications for raising external loans of less than $ 15 million will be cleared by the Government if they are for a period of at least three years; (c) the ceiling for the total value of external commercial borrowing in 1994-95 will be $ 3.5 billion which has gone up from the earlier $ 2.5 billion in 1993-94. (d) priority would be given to the borrowing for infrastructure projects and the approvals one granted would be valid for only 6 months. Thus extending the period of maturity for loans of more than $ 15 million under (a) above will shift the structure of India's external debt will lengthen the maturity schedule of the debt and reduce the shorter duration and quick repayment loans. This is a welcome move but the raising of the limit on the total value of external commercial borrowing under (c) above from $ 2.5 billion to $ 3.5 billion is inadvisable even if it is invested in infrastructure projects which involve large amount of funds and even if the debt-equity norms have been relaxed for such projects. Foreign direct investment in 1993-94 was just $ 800 million. This was less than the external commercial borrowing approvals of $ 2.5 billion for that year. In all probability the aggregate of foreign direct investment and capital mobilized through Global Deposit Receipts (GDRs) will be less than $ 3.5 billion proposed for 1994-95.

At present interest rates abroad are lower than those prevailing in India. The Indian companies are attracted towards borrowing abroad. This route is particularly attractive because of the temporary unattractiveness of the GDR route on account of the discounts on Indian equity quoted abroad. Though the international credit agencies have pushed India to the bottom half of the credit-worthiness, this does not constitute any constraint on the Indian companies raising capital abroad. But the need of the hour is to discourage and reduce the quantum of external commercial borrowing. It can be asserted that India's external debt crisis of 1991 is due to the preponderance of short-term debt in the aggregate external debt.

The World Debt Tables published recently by the World Bank records the size of India's external debt and the size of external commercial borrowing component of total debt. India's external debt at the end of 1993 was 37 percent of GNP compared to 28 percent at the end of 1990. But the debt servicing ratio (debt servicing as a percentage of export earnings) declined from 1990 onwards mainly because of improved export performance. Furthermore, the share of short-term debt (of less than one year maturity) has declined from over 10 percent at the end of 1990 to 4 percent at the end of 1993. The large stock of short-term debt aggravated the balance of payments crisis of 1991. Seen in this perspective the reduction in the stock of short-term debt is commendable.

But what is causing concern is the stock of debt owed to private creditors. As per the World Debt Tables of the World Bank the total debt owed to private creditors was $ 22.4 billion at the end of 1990. By the end of 1993 this stock rose to $ 27.4 billion. This increase in the debt of $ 5 billion owed to private creditors was about 40 percent of the $ 13 billion increase in total debt during the same period. In a similar manner the disbursements of private loans from abroad have increased. They were of the order of $ 3.2 billion in 1990 and they rose to $ 4.1 billion in 1993. In 1992 they declined to less than $ 2 billion. But India needs more external debt from private creditors in recent years. This means that the external debt is poised to grow at a rapid rate constituting a danger to the viability of the balance of payments.

Admittedly, the shift of the maturity schedule towards long term debt carries a heavier interest burden as the rate of interest on long term debt is higher than on short term debt. But the advantage of the shift towards long term debt is that it avoids the need for repayments of short term debt almost every year. The short-term debt carries a lower rate of interest which, of course, is an advantage but it has to be repaid almost every year. This is an irrevocable obligation causing embarrassment to the Government when it finds it hard to find resources to repay short-term debt. This constitutes a danger. Seen in this perspective the shift of the maturity schedule of external debt in favour of long term debt, despite the higher interest cost, is a decided advantage. In view of this, the shift in favour of long term debt by reducing the volume of short-term debt is commendable. There is also need to cap the external debt which at present, is of the order of $ 92 billion. This is already high and if the debt accumulates at the present rate, there is the danger of the debt trap opening itself up to gulp India. The external debt of Mexico is of the order of $ 120 billion and the debt service ratio is 33 percent. In the case of India the external debt is $ 92 billion and the debt service ratio is 27 percent. That is the case of India both of these are lower than those of Mexico is a poor consolation. In view of this there is need to place an upper limit on external debt. Action is urgently necessary in this regard.

# 7

# An Alternative Budget : An Exercise in Bubble Blowing

The Finance Minister is faced with the unenviable task of presenting a Budget which would help him to reach the goals of macroeconomic stabilisation. India is at present plagued by balance of payment deficit and the soaring rate of inflation. But there is some cause for comfort on the balance of payments front. The buoyancy in export growth, negative growth in imports, uptrend in foreign exchange reserves and a stable rupee against US dollar and Japanese Yen have put India's balance of payments in a comfortable position. The latest monthly economic report showed that the foreign exchange reserves soared to $ 10.49 billion in January 1994 and sufficient to meet the country's four months' import requirements. But the continuation of this improvement cannot be taken for granted. On the domestic side, the annual rate of inflation stood at 8.2 percent for the week ending January 22, 1994 as compared to 7.6 percent a year ago. It is expected that after the hikes in the prices of LPG cylinder, sugar, wheat, rice and the possible rise in the passenger and freight rates the rate of inflation would be pushed up to the double-digit zone. It is in this context that the Budget has to be prepared.

The most important variable that needs to be tackled is the fiscal deficit. In 1993-94 the Finance Minister was not so obsessed by it or by the burgeoning revenue deficit. But this year he cannot ignore them. The programme of fiscal consolidation launched in 1991 was waylaid during 1993-94. While liberalisation and deregulations proceeded apace fiscal consolidation was sidelined in fact, if not in theory. The revenue deficit has grown alarmingly to over Rs. 20,000 crore and the Government has gone deep into the internal debt trap. The increase in the deficit is due to the sudden surge in revenue expenditure with receipts remaining virtually stagnant. The non-monetisation of the budgetary deficit has helped to bring the monetised deficit down thus helping to curb the rate of inflation somewhat. But this is achieved by increasing the borrowing by the Government thereby pushing up both the fiscal and revenue deficits.

In 1993-94 it was sought to reduce the fiscal deficit to 4.7 percent of CDP. But it has become clear that the fiscal year will end up with a fiscal deficit of 6 percent of CDP. It would have been even higher but for the fact that the inflationary surge has pushed up the CDP in nominal terms. The hikes in the administered prices of various essential commodities, of course, help to bring in some revenue.

The World Bank in its report, "India: 1993 Country Economic Memorandum "States". These are a few aspects of the 1993-94 budget that raise questions about its contribution to sustainable fiscal adjustment. The tariff and excise duty rate cuts being introduced for 1993-94 are expected to result in a reduction in the tax-CDP ratio. The lower tax-CDP ratio is not sustainable, and will have to be reversed. About a third of the expenditure reduction budgeted for 1993-94 is to come from lower investment spending which has already been constrained excessively. Measures to improve fundamentally government savings performance must be accorded high priority in the near term. This will require determined actions to broaden the tax base and to contain recurrent expenditures. The Report further suggests that "a number of expenditure measures are required also to strengthen government saving. Desirable steps would include: Price increases and improved targeting to reduce subsidies, elimination of budgetary support to loss-making public sector enterprises; phasing out of investments in non-infrastructure PSEs; more vigorous action to contain the government wage bill; and continued restraint in defence spending. Other reforms are needed to improve the composition effectiveness and efficiency of government spending." Action along these lines has already been initiated with the recent administered price increases and the proposed cuts in the budgetary support to PSEs.

The Finance Minister is under pressure to increase capital expenditure in order to improve the growth performance of the economy. At the same time he is also under pressure to increase allocation for social and welfare sectors. The latter is necessary because elections to the three South Indian State Assemblies towards the end of 1994 are scheduled and the Government is determined to emerge successful in all the three. This expenditure cannot be sustained if the Finance Minister is serious about reducing the fiscal deficit to even 5.5 percent of CDP unless revenue mobilisation is attempted more seriously than was possible in 1993-94. Herein lies the problem. The Finance Minister is committed to cutting tariff and reducing the tax rates. But he cannot afford to do so if revenues are not buoyant enough. This underlines the need for increasing revenue by means of structural adjustments in the tax base and tax rates. The recent hikes in administered prices will not lead to any reduction in the fiscal deficit. In fact there is a possibility of the fiscal deficit increasing despite the hikes in administered prices.

A team of economists, under the aegis of the Preparatory Committee for Alternative Economic Politics (PCAEP) have proposed an alternative Union Budget 1994-95 with intent to increase tax revenues necessary to reduce the fiscal deficit. Under the tax proposals made in the alternative budget tax collections under direct taxes will increase to Rs. 75,000 crore against the 1993-94 budget estimate of Rs. 19,700 crore. The major chunk of direct taxes are proposed to be mobilised in the form of income taxes which are to account for Rs. 47,000 crore compared to the 1993-94 Union Budget estimate of Rs. 9,500 crore. In what they call an "alternative to the Fund-Bank dictated budget" income tax collections are sought to be raised by bringing more "black" incomes into the tax net. It is estimated that both black and white income of the top five percent of the households in the country is of the order of Rs. 3,00,000 crore. Assuming a ten percent tax rate on this income the tax yield would be of the order of Rs. 30,000 crore. The balance of Rs. 17,000 crore is sought to be mopped up by reducing the income tax exemption limit to Rs. 15,000 per annum besides eliminating all deductions relating to savings except those for Provident Fund and Public Provident Fund. The economists being of left-of-centre orientation justify these measure on the ground that the middle and elite classes pay very little direct taxes. The budget document states that "the middle class is fooled into believing that it needs to : demand lower direct tax rate" At the same time, they are forced into paying hefty sums by way of "invisible" indirect taxes and price hikes on administered items such as diesel and LPG cylinders. The economists seek to expand the number of tax payers in the country to 40 million comprising less than five percent of the population. At the same time, they also call for keeping the marginal tax rate within a maximum limit of 60 percent.

They estimate that corporate taxes will yield Rs. 15,750 crore. Besides, the wealth tax on property and corporate shares would yield another Rs. 7,000 crore. This in contrast to the provision of only Rs. 10,500 crore and Rs. 200 crore respectively. Under these accounting heads in the Union Budget for 1993-94. According to them corporate tax revenues can be boosted through levying these collections on gross profits, which would include gross revenues net of workers' salaries and expenses on raw materials. Higher managerial remunerations are thus not to be allowed as deductible costs "since they would not be treated as workers' incomes". As per this definition gross profit for 1993-94 is projected at Rs. 63,300 crore. An average of 25 percent tax on this amount realises Rs. 15,750 crore. As per taxes on property it is estimated that there were around 4.4 million households in the country; the market price of those holdings averaged about Rs.11.5 lakh. Assuming a 1 percent tax or Rs. 11,500 per household the collection would be Rs. 5,000 crore. Thus the alternative budget proposals seek to enhance direct tax collections to Rs. 75,000, the revenue from indirect taxes are slated to fall from the 1993-94 Budget estimate of Rs. 58,000 crore to Rs. 46,000 crore. It is argued that lower indirect taxes would result in a fall in prices of basic and intermediate goods and get reflected in favour final product prices and higher "real" incomes. The alternative budget seeks to raise the Centre's expenditure on key growth areas and social services. Capital expenditure alone is to go up by Rs. 44,800 crore from the provision of Rs. 29,000 crore in the Union Budget for 1993-94. These proposals contained in the alternative budget which have received undue media publicity needs to be examined.

There is no dispute about the need to reduce the fiscal deficit and through it to attain macroeconomic stability. The inflation rate is high and is poised to rise further. This can be brought down to the tolerable level by reducing the fiscal deficit. This task is possible by raising the tax revenue and/or reducing government expenditure. The alternative budget proposals are aimed at raising the revenue yield considerably. If they are practicable and yield the projected revenue this nation should be greatful to the economists for making the proposals. But it is easier said than done. It is obvious on the face of it that these economists have not taken into account the ground realities. They are just excessively euphoric about the success of their proposals. According to them the direct tax collections will yield Rs. 75,000 crore against the estimated yield of Rs. 19,700 crore in the 1993-94 budget. This means that the additional yield would be of the order of Rs. 55,000 crore. If this is realised there will not only be a reduction of the fiscal deficit but in actual fact there will be a fiscal surplus and the inflation rate will be brought down considerably. The income tax revenue is estimated to be of the order of Rs. 47,000 crore against the estimated revenue of Rs. 9500 crore. This means that there will be an additional revenue realisation of Rs.37,500 crore. This is sought to be achieved by taking both black income and white income. The sum of these two incomes of the top 5 percent of the population is estimated to be about Rs. 3,00,000 crore. If this income is taxed at 10 percent the revenue yield will be Rs. 30,000 crore.

The estimates of black income and black money holdings are too numerous to recount here. The black income and black assets are hidden from the tax officers' view and there is no way of ascertaining their magnitude. The economists have not made clear how they arrived at the figure of Rs. 3,00,000 crore as the sum of both white income and black income. If black income can be identified and the earners of this black income can be asked to disclose their income the task of levying a tax on their income is very easy. But how to identify them is a problem that defies any easy solution. In the absence of any mode of identification of the black income earners and in the absence of any mode of assessing the magnitude of black income, the estimate of the yield of income tax can be said to be an exercise in sweet day dreaming.

The economists state that Rs. 17,000 crore can be mopped up by reducing the income tax exemption limit to Rs. 15,000 per annum. The exemption limit has gone on rising and in the 1993-94 budget it was fixed at Rs. 28,000. At present there is a widespread and persistent demand for raising it to Rs. 48,000 per annum. Admittedly an argument can be advanced for bringing more and more people within the tax net in order to garner more and more revenue. But to reduce it to Rs. 15,000 per annum is bereft of logic and warying in concern for the poor and the destitute sections of society. Under the proposal a man earning about Rs. 15,000 per annum or above Rs. 1,250 per month is liable to pay the tax. Even the class IV employees in Government service and private establishments get Rs. 2,000 per month or Rs. 24,000 per annum. At a time when the prices of essential commodities, fuel, house rents are rising relentlessly it becomes difficult even for a family earning Rs. 24,000 per annum to make both ends meet. In this situation to argue for lowering the income tax exemption limit to Rs. 15,000 per annum would be grossly unfair and inequitous.

The economists propose the elimination of all deductions relating to savings. A growing economy is faced with a 'savings gap' meaning that there is an excess of investment over savings. This situation exacerbates inflationary forces. This calls for increasing the savings ratio. This can be done by providing incentives to savings. If the concessions to savings are removed the savings ratio falls enlarging the excess of investment over savings and this releases fresh inflationary forces which are hard to arrest. The need of the hour, therefore, is to increase the savings ratio, to reduce the savings gap. It must be recognized that larger savings mean larger investment and larger investment means higher rate of economic growth.

The other direct taxes including corporate taxes, wealth and property taxes were estimated to yield Rs. 10,700 crore in the 1993-94 budget. But under the alternative budget proposals they are expected to yield Rs. 22,750 crore i.e., an excess of Rs. 12,750 crore. The corporations depend, for their investment programmes, on internal resources. They can be built up by reducing the corporate tax rate to 40 percent. Many corporations which find even this too high are clamouring for a lower tax liability. When this is the case, unless the tax rate is raised about 60 percent it is humanly impossible to get the targeted revenue. The proposal to levy corporation tax on gross profits is bound to be resisted by the corporations. Why should we have tax on the gross profits from which should be deducted several items of expenditure? They ask and they are not unreasonable. At present high managerial expenses are not taxable. But the economists argue, quite correctly, that managerial remuneration should not be allowed as deductible costs since they would not be treated as workers' incomes. But the corporations have to deduct the managerial remuneration from their gross income and the remuneration has to be fixed the liability falling on the managers receiving the remuneration.

The case for reducing the corporate tax rates is very strong indeed. India would face competition from the companies of the industralised world and the newly industrialised Asian Tigers. For example, the USA, Germany, Finance, Korea, Taiwan have corporate tax rates which are below the rates prevailing in India where they range from 51.75 percent to 57.5 percent. The USA has tax rate of 34 percent, Germany 36 percent, France 34 percent, Korea 22 to 34 percent, and Malaysia 35 percent. This enables the companies operating in these countries to plough back more capital for modernisation and technological upgradation. India has a major disadvantages which must be immediately removed. The corporate tax rates in India should be reduced to 40 percent to begin with and subsequently to 30 percent. Given this presumption, the alternative budget proposals regarding corporate taxation cannot realise their revenue target.

There is also need to rationalise the capital gains tax. At present foreign investment attracts 30 percent tax on short-term capital gains and 10 percent tax on long-term capital gains. Corresponding rates for Indian companies are 40 percent on short-term and 30 percent on long-term capital gains. There is need to have parity between capital gains tax on domestic and foreign investment.

The economists make proposals about indirect taxes also. The Union Budget for 1993-94 estimated the indirect tax revenue at Rs. 58,000 crore but the economists estimate it to be Rs. 46,000 crore i.e., a fall of the order of Rs. 12,000 crore. This fall is to be accounted for by the lower rates of indirect tax they have proposed. It is their contention that lower indirect taxes lead to lower prices and this helps to bring down the rate of inflation. But this contention ignores several factors on which the prices of goods and the rate of inflation depend.

In the Union Budget for 1993-94 the Finance Minister reduced the excise duties with intent to reduce the final market prices of several commodities. But even though tax rates were reduced the market prices did not fall as the manufacturers refused initially, at any rate, to pass on the benefit of lower tax rates to the consumers in the form of lower prices. The Government, therefore, was constrained to administer a stern warning to the manufacturers that unless the lower taxes are passed on to the consumers in the form of lower prices, the concessions would be withdrawn. It must be remembered that unless, following the reduction of indirect taxes and prices of goods are reduced, the expected rise in real income will not come about.

The fall in prices depends on several other factors also. A fall in the prices of taxed goods will initially lead to a rise in real income. If the demand for the goods has a price elasticity greater than unity the demand for these goods rises. This generates excess demand for these goods and causes a rise in their prices. It is also possible that the enhanced real income will be spent on other goods in which case the excess demand for them results causing a rise in their prices. In this case the fall in the prices of the original set of goods may be offset by a rise in the prices of latter set of goods leaving the general price level unchanged. Further, the behaviour of the prices of the taxed goods themselves depends on the monetary assumption underlying the analysis. If the supply of money is held constant, a fall in the prices of goods following the reduction of excise duties generates a real balance effect. On the assumption that demand is a function of real balances a rise in real balances causes a rise in demand and therefore a rise in prices to the earlier level. If, on the other hand, the supply of money is reduced the real balance effect will not emerge to generate excess demand and a rise in prices to the old level. This means that the fall in the prices of goods following a reduction of excise duties will eventuate when there is a fall in the supply of money at the same time. But in India the supply of money is expanding and so this will not allow the prices to fall ultimately though there may be an initial fall in prices following a reduction in excise duties. Under the alternative budget proposals there is a decline in the indirect tax collections far larger than the decline under the 1993-94 budget proposals. This means that the reduction in the rates of indirect taxes under the alternative budget proposals is greater than under the proposals contained in the 1993-94 budget.

The economists propose a rise in the capital expenditure of the Union Government on the key growth areas and social services to Rs. 44,800 crore against the 1993-94 budgeted amount of Rs. 29,000 crore. This means that the capital expenditure will have to rise by Rs. 15,800 crore. The rise in capital expenditure especially in the area of infrastructure is necessary to rise the rate of economic growth. Despite the fact that private investment has been allowed in many areas including infrastructure, which were hitherto reserved for the public sector the response from the private sector has been lukewarm. This is due, in part, to inadequate infrastructure. Infrastructure development should receive priority. This would substantially contribute to the generation of gainful employment to a large number of people as well as provide a demand stimulus arising out of enhanced income generation. This is necessary even if the fiscal deficit remains high at 5.75 percent of CDP. The impact of inflation will be compensated by the gains in overall economic growth.

Another area where, as the alternative budget proposals suggest investment is necessary is the area of human capital formation. The Prime Minister has suggested that the expenditure on education in the Ninth Plan which begins in 1997 will be raised to 6 percent of the total outlay from the present 3.7 percent. This is a belated recognition of the fact that investment in "human capital" is not only an overwhelming social priority but makes economic sense as well. A US study cites how between 1930 and 1960 nearly a quarter of the increase in that country's CDP was attributed to higher education of its labour force. For the liberalisation of the economy in India, a trained and skilled workforce is a precondition. The experience of the Asian Tigers is relevant in this context, Japan, for instance, made primary education compulsory a hundred years ago. Indeed, it has been calculated that if the average period which children spent in school in India was increased by a year, it would raise the CDP by a fifth, a far cheaper and more effective method than boosting output by conventional means.

The basic philosophy of the Government is to open up the Indian economy to foreign competition. But it is necessary to ensure that domestic industry is not at a disadvantage. For this purpose, a level playing field is necessary. The level playing field must encompass the harmonisation as well as the availability of inputs, finance and infrastructure facilities for a healthy competition between indigenous companies and MNCs. The 1993-94 budget introduced certain distortions by changing the customs duties and these distortions have hurt domestic industry and they have to be corrected. Foreign companies by taking advantage of the liberalised import trade regime have resorted to dumping their goods in the Indian market. This calls for the adoption of anti-dumping duties and enhancement of duties where dumping prices are so low that without tariff protection the domestic industry cannot have a level playing field against imports. The time limit for the levy of anti-dumping duties needs to be reduced in order to prevent excessive damage to domestic industry, in areas where international prices dip steeply (not due to dumping) by as much as 25 percent a regulatory duty needs to be imposed for a specific period during which the domestic industry adjusts itself. These measures are not included in the alternative budget prepared by the economists.

Every political party in the country is found to be preparing a budget which is considered to be an alternative to the Union Budget. Each of these budgets is built on the ideology of the party concerned. Each party knows for certain that if and when it comes to power it will not be in a position to implement its own proposals. In like manner a certain group of economists has proposed an alternative budget without realising that if and when they become Finance Ministers they will not be able to implement them. They seem to have forgotten that while it is easy to propose, it is difficult to implement. Their idea seems to be to gain media publicity of a transistory duration without realising that before long they and their proposals pass into the limbo of history. Their main idea seems to be to confuse the public. They consider it their achievement if they succeed in doing it.

The alternative budget proposal by the group of economists and analysed above is in the same group. The proposals contained therein have ignored the ground realities. This can legitimately be called an exercise in bubble blowing and the bubbles disappeared into thin air seconds after they were forcefully blown. Their sinister desire to embarrass the Prime Minister and the Finance Minister went hopelessly in vain.

# 8

# Multinationals in Oil Exploration

The New Industrial Policy of the Government of India projects a positive approach to direct foreign investment. At the same time, the Government is bedeviled by the continuing foreign exchange crisis which is averted by external borrowing. Taking advantage of these two positions the oil multinationals are seeking approach to exploit the proven oil fields of the country. They are averse to new discoveries.

These oil multinationals include the TOTAL Group of France which has acquired in depth knowledge of Indian off-shore reserves of oil. This knowledge it acquired in its capacity as consultant to the Oil and Natural Gas Commission (ONGC) for the past 15 years. The World Bank has been pressurizing the Government to accept such offers but so far the Government has successfully spurned them for valid reasons.

The Government has evolved a policy in the matter of oil exploration. It is to ask the multinationals to submit bids for oil exploration and enter into production sharing joint ventures with public sector oil companies in the event of their discovering commercially exploitable reserves. However the multinationals have been luke warm in their attitude towards this risky and challenging job. Now they have started demanding licensing rights over the country's vast proven reserves of black gold as a parallel exercise to the Government's fourth round of international competitive bidding for exploration of oil and natural gas. The last date for submitting tenders is 15-4-1992.

If the Government gives an indication to hand over large oil fields to multinationals through bilateral negotiations, the other multinationals will lose interest in the fourth round of bidding for oil exploration and will lobby for their share in the discovered reserves. In this tricky situation the risky job of oil exploration will be left to the ONGC and Oil India Limited (OIL). These organisations will then be discovering oil for the benefit of the multinationals who will only pump it up.

The foreign multinationals are avid about developing oil fields that are discovered. TOTAL has been looking for direct investment in India for exploration, development are production of oil and gas. In this context TOTAL proposed in November 1990 a technical evaluation agreement in respect of three areas: the Cambay Gulf, the cutch off-shore and the Sanchor Depression in order to negotiate a production sharing contract and carry work on a fast track basis. The TOTAL is currently studying the blocks offered for bids within the fourth round. Even as late as November 1991 TOTAL expressed its interest in the development of already discovered hydrocarbons fields under agreement to be negotiated with ONGC.

In a similar manner Chavron of the US in January 1992 expressed a desire to develop a discovered field in the off-shore Bombay or Cambay basins. It has said that this project meshes with India's new economic strategy since (1) Chavron will supply the necessary foreign exchange to complete the development, thereby relieving the ONGC of this burden; and (2) it will increase India's domestic oil production and reduce oil imports. It has further stated that according to their assessment the Neelam and Ghandar fields would be ideal projects since the estimated reserves would justify the required technical and financial investment. It has further stated that it does not have details on the Panna and Mukta fields to assess their potential but they would not rule it out. The Dutch multinational, Shell, has also made a similar offer to the Government of India.

It was the World Bank which as early as May 1990 mounted pressure on the Government to open up the ONGC's prized fields. The Bank alleged that an "irrecoverable loss" of 75 million tonnes had occurred from the Bombay High and found fault with the ONGC for this loss. The Bank noted that additional reserves required could be secured if exploitation in basins such as Bombay off-shore or the Gulf of Cambay are opened to international companies or to joint ventures between India and international companies.

The allegations of the World Bank are not refused by the ONGC. Its Chairman (Mr. S.L. Khosla) has proposed the concept of build, operate and transfer for development of proven reserves by multi-nationals. This proposal is an unviable one as it hands over the oil development task to the multinationals. It is true that the discovery of reserves is risky and challenging and it is expensive also. The foreign multinationals are weary about discovering the reserves and they expect the ONGC to invest in discovering the reserves and then transferring the fields to them for pumping. The ONGC has neither the resources nor the technical expertise necessary to discover the reserves. Even if it has been why should it invest in discovering the reserves and then handing over the fields to multinationals? Discovery should be the task of the multinationals themselves.

It is true Indian oil bill is rising and at present it is of the order of Rs. 14,000 crore. This is a burden on India's balance of payments. Oil exploration and oil production are necessary to reduce India's oil bill. But that should not be the reason for the ONGC investing in the risky and challenging business of discovering the reserves and then handling over the fields on a platter to the multinationals for pumping oil.

India should be careful about the intentions of the multinationals. They should be permitted to enter the business if they undertake the task of discovering the reserves also besides, thereon, unearthing the reserves. Their demand amounts to India accepting their philosophy: "heads I win; tails you lose". India needs foreign capital and technology in oil exploration but the offer made to the multinationals should be total discovering and producing.

# 9

# The Reduction of Fiscal Deficit by using the Sale Proceeds of Public Sector Equity Per Se is not Anti-Inflationary

Inaugurating the Economic Editors' Conference in New Delhi on 20-9-1994 the Finance Minister gave a glowing account of the performance of the Indian economy globally and sectorally. Inflation has come down to 8.29 percent; the fiscal deficit will not exceed 6 percent of GDP as targeted in the Budget for 1994-95, the rate of GDP growth would be 5 percent; investment boom is in the offing; industrial sector has registered a growth of 7 percent, the balance of payments deficit is of the order of $ 0.8 billion, the external debt as a proportion of GDP has declined from 40 percent to 35 percent and the foreign exchange reserves are comfortable. All these are, of course, well taken.

It is in the area of disinvestment of public sector equity that there is some confusion. In 1993-94 the Government sold equity worth Rs. 5,600 crore to the public; in 1994-95 the Government declared its intention to sell equity-worth Rs. 5,700 crore in order to reduce the fiscal deficit and also in order to reduce the burden of domestic debt. The interest burden of domestic debt has reached staggering heights and this being an item of non-plan expenditure has made it difficult for the Government to reduce the fiscal deficit. Disinvestment is intended to reduce both. It reduces the interest burden because to the extent that disinvestment is undertaken, the quantum of Government borrowing falls causing a fall in the interest burden. This helps to reduce the fiscal deficit. Furthermore, given the technical inflexibility of Government expenditure, the funds obtained from disinvestment operations are used to meet Government expenditure and this obviates the necessity of increasing the fiscal deficit and also, to that extent, it contributes to the actual reduction of the fiscal deficit. The Finance Minister adumbrated a bolder programme of disinvestment in public sector equity in order to reduce the interest burden of internal debt. It is necessary to bear in mind, at this stage, that the World Bank is opposed to the sale of public sector equity in order to reduce the fiscal deficit as the proceeds of the sale of public sector equity are not current revenues. Fiscal deficit can be reduced by reducing Government expenditure or by increasing revenues. But the sale proceeds of public sector equity are not part of current revenues.

The reduction of fiscal deficit is necessary to reduce the rate of inflation. At present the fiscal deficit has been targeted at 6 percent of GDP. The Finance Minister holds that though in the current fiscal year the target would be reached because of the buoyancy of tax revenues, it has got to be brought down further in the long run.

The World Bank which earlier disfavoured the sale of public sector equity has subsequently come round to the view that they could be sold. According to it, the Indian authorities should try additional resource mobilisation such as acceleration of disinvestment of public sector shares or further expenditure cuts to ensure that the fiscal deficit target is met and inflationary expectations are dampened. While the reduction of the fiscal deficit is necessary to reduce the rate of inflation, the effectiveness of reducing the fiscal deficit through the sale of public sector equity has to be examined.

Other things being equal a surplus budget is contractiory while a deficit budget is expansionary. Though it is normally held that a balanced budget keeps the price level constant, as per the celebrated Haavelmo Theorem, as balanced budget, which has a multiplier effect of equal to unity, is inflationary even on the assumption of a linear consumption function. Quite apart from this special case it can be argued that a reduction in the budget deficit will have a contractive effect on the rate of inflation.

In macroeconomic analysis taxes are a leakage from the income stream while Government expenditure is an injection into it. Given the expenditure, an increase in tax revenue increases the leakage, reduces aggregate demand and helps to bring down the price level. This, of course, is a simple and commonsense proposition. But in the context of disinvestment in public sector equity we have to answer the question whether the revenue realised from the sale of public sector equity can be regarded as constituting a leakage from the income stream in the same way as tax revenues can be so required.

In the context of inflation it is necessary to increase the leakage from the current income stream. But the sale proceeds of public sector equity do not constitute leakage in this sense. To take a hypothetical case. Let us assure that the tax system is targeted to yield Rs. 10,000 crore and the tax yield is inflexible. Let us assume that the planned expenditure of the Government is Rs. 20,000 crore. There is a deficit of Rs. 10,000 crore. This obviously is inflationary. The remedy for this situation is a reduction of the deficit. Assuming that both the tax revenue and Government expenditure are inflexible, the country has to face the inflationary danger. If the Government sells equity worth Rs. 5,000 crore and uses the sale proceeds to finance expenditure the budget deficit, of course, falls to Rs. 5000 crore. Can this be expected to reduce the rate of inflation and to mitigate the inflation danger? Since the sale proceeds of equity are not current revenue, they do not represent a leakage from the income stream and so the aggregate demand remains unaffected by the tax side. In the past investment was made by the Government in public sector equity from out of its savings. In the current period, the public buys these shares from out of their savings. To the extent that they purchase these shares, there will be a reduced flow of funds to the other investment channels. The sale proceeds are used to meet a part of the deficit left uncovered by current revenues. If the deficit remains at Rs. 10,000 crore, it will be inflationary. But now the Government deficit is reduced to Rs. 5,000 crore and it is financed by money creation. To that extent it is inflationary. The balance of the deficit left uncovered by tax revenue and money creation is covered by the utilisation of sale proceeds of public sector equity. This is regarded as constituting a reduction of the deficit and is held to be anti-inflationary. But the sale proceeds are to be construed as constituting a net addition to aggregate demand in the current period. The Government deficit is reduced, of course, but the aggregate demand is not reduced and so the rate of inflation does not come down.

To the extent that the use of the sale proceeds of equity are used to finance Government expenditure the volume of Government borrowing in the current period falls causing a fall in the interest burden which again causes a fall in the Government deficit the following year. To this extent, the use of sale proceeds from public sector equity to finance the deficit reduces the fiscal deficit and is thus anti-inflationary. But this is only an indirect consequence. But there is no direct effect on aggregate demand and on the rate of inflation. The use of sale proceeds from disinvestment in public sector equity, of course, reduces the burden of internal debt; reduces the burden of interest payment in the following year. But the reduction of the fiscal deficit per se brought about by the utilisation of the sale proceeds from public sector equity does not reduce aggregate demand and so does not reduce the rate of inflation whatever be the other consequences, it may have. This point needs to be borne in mind by those who assert that the reduction of the fiscal deficit by using the proceeds from the sale of public sector equity reduces the rate of inflation. This is not so.

# 10

## Indian Rupee in Turmoil

The Indian rupee which is in turmoil, has started to create problems for the authorities. Several industrial houses want the rupee to be devalued while the Reserve Bank Governor maintains that the rupee is stable. It cannot be denied that the rupee has slided gently in relation to the US Dollar. What is it due to? What does it portend? These questions need to be answered in the right perspective.

The currencies of several countries have become shacking in recent weeks. Their exchange rates are unstable some are rising and the others are falling. It is difficult to say what is going to happen tomorrow. There is the fear that stability may receive a hard knock.

It is the U.S. dollar that deserves the title "International Currency". It continues to be so since the establishment of IMF. Despite its rise and fall, it has its own importance in the currency markets. But there are other currencies, which pose a challenge to its supremacy. The German D-Mark the Japanese Yen constitute a challenge to the US dollar. Due to exchange rate fluctuations between the Yen, D-Mark and the currencies of the European Union these countries had evolved an exchange rate system, which would prevent instability caused by the international flow of capital. But these currencies have become weak in the face of the strong D-Mark. Capital is moving from the countries where the interest rate is low to countries where it is high. The pound sterling, the French France, the Italian Lira and the Swedish Kroner have all become off-coloured. Even the Japanese Yen is strong and its value is rising. The US dollar is losing its importance in the face of the buoyancy of these currencies. Its value is falling when compared with Yen, Swiss France and D-Mark. It is the responsibility of the Central Banks of the countries to guard against the instability of the exchange rates of their currencies. But they have found it difficult to discharge this responsibility. The pressure on the US dollar is immense. The Federal Reserve System is contemplating raising of the interest rate in order to prevent the outflow of capital. It is its expectation that the owners of Capital may repatriate their capital to the US Capital market because of a higher interest rate. At the same time it is also feared that because of this step the prices might rise, the cost of production might rise, the competitiveness of US goods might decline and in consequences, recession might set in. In the attempt to solve one problem there is the fear of occasioning another.

What is the reason for this state of affairs? Many have begun to wonder whether the other countries will go the way of Mexico whose currency Peso faced a crisis in the aftermath of the economic liberalisation programme; whether the capital that left the shores of Mexico has begun to destabilise the exchange rates of the other currencies or whether it is due to the failure of the Barings bank and whether people have lost faith in the stability of currencies or whether it is due to Germany and Japan increasing their exports while restricting their imports thus causing payments deficits in those countries. It is not possible to assign any definite reason for the currency muddle immediately. It takes time. It can be done in the face of unfolding events.

In the context of international interdependence a change in the country will have its repercussions on all other countries. The question is whether it will have its effects on India. We cannot avoid on escape from these repercussions. At the same time it cannot be forgotten that there are several reasons accounting for our predicament. But the international events do not have much effect on the Indian rupee. The internal factors have caused instability. For many years India's external payments position was most unfavourable. As the payments were in excess of receipts it became necessary to raise external loans to cover the current account deficit. In this context in July 1991 there was two-step devaluation of the rupee. The rupee dollar exchange rate which was Rs. 20 = $ 1 became Rs. 30-50 = $1 in 1993. In actual fact the value of the rupee was not so low as this. Many knowledgeable persons felt that the value of the rupee was lowered excessively. If the value of the rupee is lowered below its actual level, it will occasion inflation. Even so, the devaluation of the rupee promoted exports by making them cheap. Despite liberalisation of imports the trade deficit was not as big as before. Seen in this perspective it can be argued that the new exchange rate of the rupee was the realistic one.

It was felt that the rupee was on strong and stable foundations. Owing to the incessant inflow of foreign capital, there was the danger of the rupee appreciating. In this event Indian exports, instead of becoming cheaper to foreigners, would be costlier in which case Indian exports would fall. In order to keep the rupee dollar exchange rate stable, the Reserve Bank of India continued to intervene in the foreign exchange market and to purchase the incoming dollars.

During the past two years the rate of inflation has risen to the double-digit zone. At present the rate of inflation is 11.5 percent and it is expected to go up to 12 percent though according to the Finance Ministry it will fall to 7-8 percent by mid - 1995. This means that the rupee has suffered depreciation. When its purchasing power declines, it affects the exchange rate also and this must fall as per the purchasing power parity calculations. Otherwise it adversely affects export growth. In this context there is a controversy about the devaluation of the rupee. The cases for and against devaluation has been advanced. There is a danger in the expectation of devaluation of the rupee. The exporters who earn dollars and the companies which raise dollars deposits in foreign capital markets will possibly keep their dollar earnings and deposits abroad. They may think that if they brought these dollars to India after the rupee is devalued they will get more rupees than they would get if they brought them before devaluation. When the inflow of dollars falls its value rises. Under the present circumstances there is the possibility of dollars flowing out. The foreign exchange dealers might accentuate this trend. For these reasons, the exchange value of the rupee has fallen. The rupee dollar exchange rate is over Rs. 32 per dollar. It had earlier touched the Rs. 32-15 limit.

There is a school of thought which holds that the Reserve Bank of India should purchase rupees in exchange for dollars in order to raise the value of the rupee. In the meanwhile, as the value of the dollar has plummeted in the currency markets, it can be argued that the value of the rupee has relatively risen. Any move in any direction seems unnecessary.

However, one thing is certain. The rupee will not be and shall not be devalued. The current account deficit is just 1 percent of GDP. Even if it worsens India has ample forex reserves to cover it. The effect of devaluation on exports is uncertain while its effect on imports is to increase their value. As 45 percent of imports are for producing goods for the export market devaluation which has the effect of raising the prices of imports will raise the cost of production of exports. This may outset any favourable effect of devaluation on exports. Hence devaluation of the rupee is unwarranted and even dangerous. It must be observed that the reduction of customs and excise duties in the 1995-96 budget has made Indian exports competitive. This is indeed an alternative to devaluation.

The international currency experience at present is confusing in the extreme. Exchange rates are fluctuating holding out the threat of currency transfers across national borders in pursuit of safety, security and profitability. If this tendency is left unchecked international capital movements will become inflammatory upsetting macroeconomic stability the world over. Such inflammatory capital transfers have to be checked by means of an international agreement about the measures to be adopted to do it. Tobin tax, ban on such capital transfers, short-term capital gains tax etc.

The European Exchange Rate Mechanism (ERM) is in disarray due to the speculative manner on the currency exchanges rather than to the exposure of deep-seated economic disequilibria whether in Spain or Portugal. Within a week almost all the European currencies received a severe battering vis-à-vis the D-M. There is too much of short-term investment funds criss-crossing the currency markets of Europe. The rupee had also to experience the kind of volatility which currency speculation creates in an otherwise stable regime of near convertibility. The slide in the rupee on March 3 to a low of Rs. 32-15 per dollar was not due to a transitory spent in the demand for dollars as India was receiving dollar remittances. Even the expectation of inflation ruling at 12 percent cannot explain the slide of the rupee to that extent. The villain of the piece was the speculative factor of the operators in the Indian exchange market anticipating devaluation of the rupee. This is an example of how speculative forces can disrupt the stability of the exchange rate despite the strong fundamentals of the rupee. But the turmoil in the exchange market was due to the uninterrupted course of double-digit inflation and the consequent erosion of the competitiveness of Indian exports. When exporters and the corporations parking GDR proceeds do not bring dollars home, importers can face a situation of excess demand for dollars causing a depreciation of the rupee. This situation continues unless the speculative forces stop on the Reserve Bank of India releases its dollar reserves. This possibility is remote.

India is holding over $ 20 billion of forex reserves. These can be better utilised by investing abroad. With portfolio investment, Indian companies can acquire controlling interest in such ventures. Though portfolio investment siphons off money from the economy, it does not contain inflation caused by supply factors. Inflation is due to excess demand in the economy. For an economy to sustain a GDP growth of 7-8 percent inflation should be ideally placed at 6 percent. It is hoped that the growth projections and the projection about the rate of inflation will be realised.

The rupee should not be made fully convertible. It has been losing ground against some strong currencies in recent weeks. Exchange market sources were quick to point out that the slide was due mainly to a panic reaction to the sudden rise in demand for the dollar. If corporate demand can lead to a slide of this magnitude, the market could behave considerably worse if greater convertibility is allowed. Therefore, convertibility of the rupee on capital account should not be attempted unless the rate of inflation is brought down to the "safe" level and unless the hot money component of foreign capital is removed.

# 11

# Controlling the Volatility of Short Term Capital

India's forex reserves have been bulging causing concern for the monetary authorities. As on March 8, 1995 they stood at $ 20.1 billion. These have set off monetary expansion, which is of the order of 20 percent against the targeted figure of 15 percent. This is the primary cause of inflation in the Indian economy. The capital inflow into the country during the current financial year in the form of direct and portfolio investment is of the order of $ 3.00 billion. In a developing economy like India which is labouring under shortage of capital, capital inflows are welcome. But it is their volatile character and their built in instability that are causing concern. In the current year the Government of India adopted several measures to remove all the volatile elements from the reserves like the short-term liabilities.

Capital inflows have exchange rate and monetary implications. If the capital inflows are not taken into reserves by the Reserve Bank not intervening in the market, the exchange rate appreciates with adverse consequences on the rate appreciates with adverse consequences on the rate of growth of exports and on the balance of payments. If the capital inflows add to the net foreign exchange assets of the Reserve Bank, the supply of money expands exacerbating inflation.

The Reserve Bank of India cannot afford not to take the capital inflows into the reserves and to abstain from intervening in the exchange market to buy up the inflowing dollars. If it abstains from a policy of intervention, the rupee appreciates in the foreign exchange market. The Reserve Bank cannot afford a policy of non-intervention because of the upward pressure on the exchange rate. If it intervenes in the foreign exchange market, it buys up the following dollars, which add to the reserves, which expand the supply of money. Thus the Reserve Bank of India is in a dilemma. If the rupee is allowed to appreciate, there will not be monetary expansion as the incoming dollars will not add to the forex reserves; if the rupee exchange rate is held stable by a policy of buying up the dollars, the forex reserves swell causing a rise in the monetary growth which serves to exacerbate inflation. The Reserve Bank of India has opted for a policy of buying up dollars which helps to keep the exchange rate stable at Rs. 31.37 for a dollar but as this policy adds to forex reserves the rate of monetary growth is allowed to rise with no let or hindrance.

It is not possible to do away with the entire stock of short-term capital which, by and large, is volatile in character. Ordinarily, the volatile capital is subject to shifts in response to interest rate differentials. If the interest rate offered on short term capital is reduced, India does not attract short-term capital inflows and to this extent the volatility of capital is reduced. In the second place before the capital flows in the Government should made it clear to the owners of this capital that any shift of capital outside the country before a fixed date would be subject to a tax to say between 0.5-1.0 percent of the capital so shifted. This is akin to what is called the "Tobin Tax" after James Tobin who proposed such a tax as early as 1978. This tax serves as a disincentive to any shift outside the country. This may be interpreted as an interference with the market mechanism but when the market mechanism disturbs macro-economic stability, this step is necessary. The Government could also consider a policy of dual interest rates a lower rate on the incoming capital meant to reduce the inflow and a higher rate on the capital which, having come in, is eager to move out. This policy will reduce the inflow of volatile capital and, at the same time, it will prevent the capital which having come in, is eager to move out. This policy will reduce the inflow of volatile capital and, at the same time, it will prevent the capital which having come in will be shifted outside the country. In this way the monetary system can be insulated from the disturbances caused by volatility of capital flows. A hefty short-term capital gains tax will discourage both inflows and outflows of hot money. This is good both ways. The extreme step would be to ban all volatile capital from flowing into the country unless a firm commitment is given by the owners of this capital that they would not move this capital outside the country during the pendency of this commitment under any circumstances. These are ways of removing the volatility from this capital and to introduce an element of stability into their holdings.

# 12

## Whither Macroeconomic Stability?

The fiscal balance of the Government of India is threatening to transgress into the area of imbalance. In the Union Budget for 1993-94 the Finance Minister made valiant efforts to achieve fiscal balance. He reduced the customs and excise duties; in the revenue account he showed a concession of Rs. 4,500 crore; he raised the Central plan expenditure by 32 percent. In compliance with the conditionality prescriptions of the IMF and the World Bank he agreed to reduce the budget deficit gradually. The IMF conditionality prescribed the reduction of fiscal deficit to 6.5 percent of GDP in 1991-92, to 5 percent in 1992-93 and to 4 percent in 1993-94. Accordingly this target of fiscal deficit reduction was realised in 1991-92. In 1992-93 the Finance Minister found it difficult to reduce the fiscal deficit to 5 percent of GDP. In fact, it was 5.7 percent in that year. But the IMF did not take this non-compliance seriously. In the year 1993-94 the Finance Minister assured in his budget speech that he would be able to reduce the fiscal deficit to 4.7 percent to GDP if not to 4.0 percent. The IMF was also satisfied that the fiscal deficit was being gradually reduced. It was the impression of the IMF that the Government of India was acting in compliance with the conditionality prescriptions. It was happy that the record of India in the matter of fiscal deficit reduction was far better than that of other countries which had borrowed massively from the IMF.

It was agreed that every three months the Government of India would review its fiscal performance and would stabilise the fiscal deficit. It was a condition that the fiscal deficit should not exceed the limit specified in the budget statement. But this condition has been relaxed from the current year. It is the present policy of the IMF that the Government of India should not be tied down to the rigid figure of fiscal deficit reduction but should be encouraged to tread the path laid down by it. It is this relaxation that seems to be at the base of the growing fiscal deficit. An examination of the figures relating to the fiscal deficit up till July 9, 1993 is bound to cause alarm. During this period the Central Government has borrowed Rs. 18,900 crore from the Reserve Bank of India. In the same period in 1992-93 the amount borrowed from the Reserve Bank of India was Rs. 9,193 crore. It is obvious from these figures that the Government is living beyond its means. Government expenditure is rising by leaps and bounds but the Government is unable to mobilise resources to match the burgeoning expenditure. The effect of this expenditure is the creation of money which generates excess liquidity in the economy. If the rate of monetary growth exceeds the rate of growth of output inflation is the consequence with all its destabilising effects on the economy.

The reason for this state of affairs is an open secret. The Government had planned to sell a part of the shares of the public sector undertakings. Certainly it sold the shares but it did not realise the expected amount. It was estimated in the budget that it would realise Rs. 27,727 crore and Rs. 33,751 crore respectively from customs and excise. It is apprehended that it may not realise this sum. The shortfall might be of the order of Rs. 5,000 crore. The Government is not in a position to reduce its expenditure. Subsidies are an important item of Government expenditure. Its calculations regarding the reduction of fertilisers subsidy are hopelessly upset. The Government has announced several subsidies to agriculture in the attempt to pacify the irate feelings of farmers. The budget indicated a food subsidy of Rs. 3,000 crore. The procurement prices of wheat and rice have been enhanced but the prices of food grains supplied through the public distribution system are not likely to be raised in the same proportion. The expenditure on this count is bound to exceed the limit imposed in the budget. Furthermore, the interest burden of public debt is consistently rising.

The Hon'ble Prime Minister announced several plans of social amelioration in his speech of August 15, 1993: assurance of employment to the unemployed; subsidy of Rs. 75 on the bank deposits of adult women; subsidy on loans to new enterprises in the small scale industrial sector. These concessions/subsidies are likely to increase the fiscal deficit by Rs. 8,000 crore. The assurance that the fiscal deficit would be brought down to 4.7 percent of GDP has gone with the wind. This is likely to rise by 1 percent to 5.7 percent. This means that it would be an achievement if the fiscal deficit in 1993-94 is equal to that in 1992-93. As a result of the incidents of December 6, 1993 and the subsequent developments like Bombay and Calcuta blasts the rate of growth of output has declined. In the first three months of 1992-93 the rate of growth of output was 6.2 percent higher than that in the comparable period of 1991-92. But in 1993-94 it has declined by 1.7 percent. The realisation of tax revenue has fallen. As a result of the economic crisis in 1992-93 the Government had to tighten its belt. This year the Government which is conscious of the reduction of the rate of inflation to 6.2 percent is not serious about tightening its belt. As a result the growth of expenditure is burgeoning.

The Government finds itself unable to root out certain tendencies which have set deep roots in the economic system. The revenue deficit in the budget is continuing year after year. There is excessive capital expenditure. The money realised from the sale of shares of public sector undertakings and from borrowing is being used to finance the revenue deficit. This is a dangerous trend. Asset creation has come to a standstill, the progress of plan programmes are slow and sluggish. The Central Government liabilities exceed its assets. In 1984-85 this was only 8 percent; it has now risen to 29 percent. A situation has arisen in which the Government has to pay interest without there being any income earned. The finances of the Government are on the brink of disaster.

It needs no emphasis that the Government is on the path of economic reforms; the controls over trade are relaxed; there is unshackling of the industrial system from the bureaucratic controls and licensing procedures. The licence-permit raj has become a thing of the past. But the winds of change have not yet reached the areas at public undertaking, labour policy, agriculture etc. The rate of growth of exports does not match the rate of growth of imports.

Even so, the IMF has got the impression that the Government of India is proceeding along right lines. It seems to have thought that it does not matter even if certain targets are not realised. It is even prepared for negotiations for a further loan to bridge the balance of payments gap. But this should not make India relax its efforts to regain macroeconomic stability.

The Finance Minister has engaged himself in a delicate fiscal exercise. The decision to reduce the excise duties was prompted by a desire to reduce the prices of goods so as to stimulate demand which would ward off recession in the industrial sector. At the same time, the decision to reduce the lending rates was also prompted by the same desire. The Government directed the industrial units to pass on the excise tax concessions to the consumers in the form of lower market prices and also threatened to withdraw the concessions unless they are passed on in full to the consumers. The industrial units are facing recession of demand and unless the demand for their products is stimulated the recession will persist rendering these units sick. It would be in their own interests to pass on the excise tax concessions in the form of lower market prices to the consumers in order to stimulate demand.

The reduction of excise taxes has the effect of reducing the Government revenue and increasing the fiscal deficit as a proportion of GDP. This has an inflationary effect. At the same time, the reduction of market prices of goods consequent on the reduction of excise taxes has the effect of reducing the inflation rate. The object of policy is to see that the reduction of the rate of inflation consequent on the reduction of the market prices of goods is greater than the rise in the rate of inflation following the rise in the fiscal deficit due to excise tax reduction i.e., that there is a net reduction in the rate of inflation. The rate of inflation which was 5.8 percent in the middle of August 1993 has risen to 6.2 percent in the last week of August. This may not necessarily be due to the inadequate fall in the market prices of goods. In other words, this may not necessarily be due to the excise tax concessions not being passed on to consumers. But the present indications are that the excise tax concessions are not fully passed on to consumers in the form of lower market prices. This means that the inflationary effect of a larger fiscal deficit has swamped the disinflationary effect of the excise tax concessions. If this analysis is correct, the industrial units would be foolhardy in not passing on the excise tax concessions in full to the consumers. It is not yet too late. It would be in their interests to pass the excise tax concessions to the consumers in the form of lower market prices of goods. This would help to hold down the rate of inflation despite a rise in the fiscal deficit, to revive demand for goods, remove the recessionary trends and the accompanying sickness of the industrial sector.

It must be reiterated that there is casual connection between the fiscal deficit and the balance of payments deficit. The rate of growth of exports is far short of the rate of growth of imports. This has caused a balance of payment gap. The remedy for it is obvious: the reduction of the fiscal deficit. As the fiscal deficit in 1993-94 which was estimated to be 4.7 percent of GDP is likely to be equal to that in 1992-93 i.e., 5.7 percent there is every likelihood of the inflation rate rising to a level close to the double digit rate than upsetting all the calculations of the Finance Ministry. Thus fiscal inbalance breads balance of payments imbalance. But there is a silver lining to the balance of payments. An estimated $ 400 million has come into the stock market in the form of portfolio investment by foreign institutional investors thus administering a shot in the arm to the balance of payments situation. The foreign exchange position is being considerably strengthened by the increased activity of the foreign institutional investors. As a consequence, the exceptional financing requirement of the Government and reliance on quick-disbursing loans from multilateral institutions may come down significantly. While the foreign investors are adding to the country's strength, they pass a problem if there is sudden repatriation of funds out of India. But if the foreign investors do so, it would be at a short-term capital gains tax of 30 percent which, although a concessional rate, will be a dampner on repatriation. It must be admitted that the foreign investors are strengthening the balance of payments position. Foreign direct investment in projects cleared by the Prime Minister's Office is also strengthening the balance of payments. Since the present Government took charge in June 1991 projects with around $ 3.4 billion worth of investment have been cleared. Although approvals do not necessarily mean an immediate inflow of funds, the medium term implications are important. It is hoped by the authorities that by the end of the current financial year the approvals would be much more than $ 4 billion. These inflows are strengthening the capital account of the balance of payments and consequently reducing the exceptional financing requirements of the Government. The Government is already going slow on the negotiations for an extended fund facility (EFF) arrangement with the International Monetary Fund. The current boom in foreign portfolio and direct investment will add to the strength. Meanwhile, the foreign currency non-resident (FCNR) deposits, the reliance on which led to the balance of payments crisis of 1991, have come down from $ 4 billion to $ 1 billion indicating a healthy switch in the balance of payments portfolio of the Government. While this is the position on the capital account the current account shows a yawning gap indicating the persistence of a macroeconomic imbalance.

The revised interest rate structure announced by the Reserve Bank of India on September 1, 1993 is intended to remedy the on-going recession but it has got other effects also. The cut in the floor-lending rate by one percentage point is intended to provide the much-needed boost to industry, which is facing a serious demand recession. It may not be correct to argue that the cut in interest rates will ease credit. The tight credit situation is as much the result of stricter lending norms followed by the banks in the aftermath of the securities scam as of high interest rates. This is unlikely to change if banks follow commercial practise strictly. It is held, quite rightly, in certain quarters that the on-going recession is more a consequence of the sharp reduction in investment spending by the Government than the result of a general decline in demand in the economy. If this analysis is correct then the cut in interest rates is unlikely to have an immediate impact on demand. It will take several months before investment demand picks up sufficiently to make a difference. The alternative is an immediate injection of investment spending. However, with the foreign investment still sluggish, it is for the Government to decide to what extent it can help industry. The reduction in lending rate will help to boost corporate profits by reducing the interest burden on companies. The industrial sector has been asking for lower interest rates but the result of the interest rate cut will be felt only after a lag of considerable duration.

For the banks the cut in interest rates is a mixed blessing. The banks are faced with excess funds which they can lend to borrowers. The lower interest rates will increase the demand for funds considering the fact that the demand for funds is elastic. At the same time they are bound to feel the pinch of lower interest rates which have the effect of reducing the profitability of banks. If the bank loans increase considerably the interest income they earn on loans may swamp the reduced profitability caused by the interest rate cut. The targets for priority sector credit have not been fulfilled in the current financial years and these targets have to be fulfilled before lending to the other sectors can be undertaken. It is to be seen how far the new interest rate policy is able to satisfy the credit needs of all the productive sectors of the economy.

The deposit rate has been reduced by 1 percent in order to maintain the profitability of banks. Since there is every likelihood of further reduction in lending rates by 1 percent in October 1993 at the time of the busy season credit policy there are apprehensions that interest rates on deposits will also be lowered by 1 percent to maintain the profitability of banks. If this happens there is the danger of a part of the deposits flying out of the banking system.

The banks have been asked to reduce the deposit rates by 1 percent to 10 percent. This move is going to affect the middle class who put their savings in long-term deposits. In fact about 70 percent of deposits come from this segment. Empirical research has shown that savings respond positively to real interest rates. A reduction in the money rate coupled with a rise in the inflation rate will reduce the real rate of interest and this will reduce the volume of savings or divert savings to other segments of the money market where the savers earn a higher interest rate. To the extent that savings fall, consumption rises causing a rise in the rate of inflation. To the extent that the deposits are diverted to the other segments of the economy, the deposit mobilisation effort of the banks will not be much of a success. Further, as there is the likelihood of the deposits on maturity being not renewed but being withdrawn from investment elsewhere at a higher rate of return the volume of deposits falls reducing the laudable resources of the banking system and making lending tight. In this situation, a cut in the lending rate will not be of much use in remedying the recession.

The possibility of the fiscal deficit rising to 5.7 percent of GDP in 1993-94 sets the stage for a resurgence of the inflationary pressure. The cut in lending rates which increases the volume of borrowing for investment purposes by the industrial sector will also generate inflation. In this way both fiscal and monetary policies will work in unison to unleash inflation.

There is urgent need to practise austerity in the matter of Government expenditure. The National Development Expenditure. The National Development Council strongly pleaded for austerity but austerity has remained only a theoretical proposition. It needs to be activated. The Government has taken a firm stand against implementing the recommendations of the Fourth Pay Commission, but it is dithering in the matter of wage freeze and DA freeze. Unless they are freezed their payment adds fuel to the fires of inflation not only directly but also through enlarging the fiscal deficit. If the Central Government takes the initiative the State Governments will follow suit and this results in considerable budgetary savings and helps to reduce the rate of inflation. The supply of money should not be allowed to be governed by the mechanism of wage escalation. The working class may resent this move but they are to be told that it would be in their interests to accept wage and DA freezes. Otherwise, India is bound to go on the labour standard as Professor J.R. Hicks calls it.

There are three items of non-plan expenditure: subsidies defence and interest payment on public debt. Admittedly India is on the road to a market economy. In a market economy subsidies have no place. This may strengthen the case for reducing subsidies of all kinds. India is not yet a full-flaged market economy and so subsidies are to remain for some more time. It is true that subsidies enlarge the size of the fiscal deficit and become a cause of inflation. But the abolition of subsidies is also inflationary. The abolition of fertiliser subsidy causes a rise in fertiliser prices. If the demand for fertilisers being elastic falls in consequence, the input of fertilisers falls causing a reduction in farm yield which has the effect of raising prices. If the demand for fertilisers is inelastic, the farm output will not fall. As the farmers pass on the higher fertiliser prices to the consumers of farm products in the form of higher prices, the rate of inflation rises. In a similar manner the abolition of food subsidy causes a rise in food prices. The engenders demands for higher wages. If higher wages are granted, they generate both cost-push and demand-pull inflations. Thus the payment of subsidies, by causing a rise in the fiscal deficit, causes a rise in the fiscal deficit, causes a rise in prices. The abolition of subsidies also causes a rise in prices. But the rise in prices caused by the fiscal deficit is not as harmful as the rise in prices caused by the abolition of subsidies. This means that subsidies are to be retained for the present and they are to be reduced in stages and finally abolished. But at present they are an item of non-plan expenditure which does not admit of reduction or abolition.

Defence expenditure does not admit of reduction. If anything there is a case for raising it. India is within a ring of fire with the major countries in the neighbourhood nursing hostile intentions against India. In this security context, India cannot afford to relax its defense preparedness exercise. There is imperative need for modernising the defense forces—army, navy and air-force. India is assured of the supply of Cryogenic rocket engines by Russia. Activating them involves considerable expenditure. In view of this the case for stepping up defense expenditure is very strong indeed.

Interest payments on public debt cannot also be reduced. But there are several ways in which the interest burden can be mitigated. The lenders could be paid 50 percent of the interest due to them on their bond holdings and the payment of the balance of 50 percent can be deferred to a future date. This is one way of reducing non-plan expenditure. Furthermore, there is the case for manipulating the maturity structure of public debt. If the Government converts short term debt into long term debt, the interest burden rises but this reduces the liquidity of the economy and as, in recent monetary theory, expenditure depends on liquidity, a reduction in liquidity causes a reduction in expenditure and, to this extent, it is disinflationary. If, on the other hand, the Government issues short-term debt the interest burden falls as the short term debt carries a lower rate of interest and this has the effect of reducing the fiscal deficit. But short-term debt increases liquidity in the economy and causes a rise in expenditure which is inflationary. Thus both the short-term debt and the long-term debt are inflationary in their own way. But issuing long-term debt is preferable to issuing short term debt as a method of inflation control.

There is another option open to the Government. There are two methods of financing the fiscal deficit: debt financing and monetary financing. Debt financing involves interest payment which increases the fiscal deficit which in turn exacerbates inflation. But monetary financing is also inflationary due to the direct spending of created money. It is held by fiscal theorists that monetary financing of the deficit is less inflationary than debt financing. Therefore, it appears advisable for the Government to report to monetary financing of the deficit instead of debt financing of it as far as possible. There is thus considerable scope for trade-off between alternative courses of action and the Government which aims at reducing the rate of inflation has to choose that course of action that is least inflationary.

The official sources argue that the Reserve Bank credit rises every year in the first quarter and comes down in the second half. But admittedly the growth of Reserve Bank credit has broken past records. The Government may, of course, bring down the budgetary deficit by increasing market borrowings. In fact, in the first quarter of fiscal 1993-94 itself the budgetary target of mobilising Rs. 3,700 crore through market borrowings has been exceeded already. But this only means storing up problems for the future as interest liability would increase further causing an increase in the fiscal deficit with all its inflationary consequences. Is this not a case for resorting to monetary financing of the deficit instead of the debt financing of it in the light of the relative inflationary consequences of debt financing and monetary financing of the fiscal deficits?

The supply of money is, by all counts, excessive causing a rise in liquidity in the economy. This calls for the introduction of monetary targeting. I proposed for the introduction of monetary targeting in India and suggested that the rate of monetary growth should not be a fixed rate but should move within a band of 3-5 percent depending on the behaviour of income velocity of money, the exchange value of the rupee and the rate of growth of output. The Finance Minister was pleased to reply to me stating that in the context of the on-going recession in the industrial sector the suggested band of 3-5 percent of monetary growth was too restrictive. My suggestion of the targeted rate of monetary growth of 3-5 percent was made only for illustrative purposes. But if monetary targeting is accepted in principle, the actual rate of monetary growth could be 4-6 percent or 5-8 percent as the case may be depending on the monetary requirements of the economy in recession. Whatever the permitted rate of monetary growth, monetary targeting is the fiscal course to follow to control inflation in the economy.

The Government finds itself in a dilemma. If it reduced expenditure in the second half of 1993-94 to control inflation industrial growth which was minus 1 percent in April 1993 would be further adversely affected. Alternatively, if industrial growth is of the order of 3-4 percent prices will rise rendering India's exports uncompetitive. The present stability of the Indian rupee will also be seriously threatened. The correct policy appears to be to opt for a low rate of inflation and low rate of growth. This would mean imposing a blanket ban on the largesse announced by the Government. But the Finance Minister finds himself facing a difficult choice. In fact, he is caught in a bind. However, the moderate inflation so far during the current financial year and the rising foreign exchange reserves seem to have bred a sense of complacency among the top echelons of the Government and of the Finance Ministry in particular about the need for controlling Government expenditure. As averred already, the IMF and the World

Bank have relaxed their vigil as no loan is in the pipeline. The Extended Fund Facility loan of $ 5 to $ 6 billion is to be finalised by this year-end and the Government will have to adhere to the fiscal and monetary targets only from next year.

The lower rate of inflation should not be a cause for exhilaration. The budgetary deficit which is touching a record of Rs. 20,750 crore during the first four months of the fiscal 1993-94 (i.e., till 22-7-1999) has enabled the inflationary potential to build up again. This deficit is more than double the amount in the same period of 1992-93. This indicates that the policy of macroeconomic stabilisation launched in July 1991 is showing signs of running out of steam. Although the set increase in Reserve Bank credit to the Central Government is a couple of thousand crore of rupees less than the budgetary deficit due to the introduction of short term treasury bills, the increase in Reserve Bank credit another name for just printing of notes has been phenomenal. This has already fueled 50 percent increase in the growth of reserve money due to the magnetisation of the deficit.

The prices have not started rising by a big margin as yet as the growth in money supply is moderate due to the sharp fall in bank credit to the commercial sector to Rs. 3,586 crore (March 19, 1993 to July 9, 1993) from Rs. 9,911 crore during the same period in the previous year. Of this non-food credit was only Rs. 579 crore as against Rs. 9,643 crore in March-July of 1992-93. But the situation may change drastically if industrial production starts picking up after the Kharif harvest and the demand for credit goes up. The pressure may be softened somewhat during the winter months due to seasonal factors but prices may start galloping from January 1994. There is said to be a time lag of 5-6 months between the increase in money supply and its impact on the price level. Unless immediate corrective measures are taken the current inflation rate of 6.2 percent may turn out to be purely temporary and the rate of inflation may escalate beyond all expectations to the neighbourhood of a double digit figure. This is bound to widen the current account of the balance of payments gap necessitating a larger inflow of foreign investment or, in the alternative, recourse to the IMF and the World Bank for loans.

The real corrective to this instability would be controlling the Government revenue expenditure. But it is easier said than done. Kashmir and Punjab constitute a drain on resources and the Government is too cautious about hunting the vote banks in view of the coming state elections. But, there are other areas where control over expenditure is possible. The Government has expressed its inability to implement the recommendations of the Fourth Pay Commission for Central Government employees. The Government also has not conceded the demand for merger of 51 percent of DA with basic pay as it would mean an extra expenditure of Rs. 800 crore per annum for the Central Government. The expenditure of the State Governments would be still higher around Rs. 1,600 crore. The decision of the Government to remain firm and unyielding on this issue is to be appreciated in the context of the grave economic crisis facing the country.

There should be a constitutional limit on both domestic borrowing and external borrowing. This would stabilise interest payments. Monetary financing of the deficit should take the place of debt financing as far as possible. This would reduce the burden of interest payments and help to reduce the fiscal deficit. The maturity composition of the public debt should be changed so that the debt includes more long term debt and less short-term debt. This would reduce the liquidity of the economy, the quantum of spending and the rate of inflation. It is true that the interest cost of long term debt rises but this would be more than offset by the reduced burden of inflation. The Government should go in for monetary targeting fixing the monetary targets at levels which are not restrictive of economic growth. In these ways the rate of inflation can be brought down and the volume of Government expenditure can also be brought down.

The formulation and pursuit of economic policy is bedeviled by the existence of stagflation in the Indian economy a combination of recession and inflation. Industrial output which had risen by 7 percent between April 1991 and April 1992 had declined by 1 percent in April1993 over April 1992. The most recent evidence of recession is the anticipated shortfall in Government revenues. The rise in Reserve Bank credit to the Government between April and July was double of what it had been during the same period in 1992. A part of this can be attributed to the disruption of production caused by the political turmoil in the post-Ayodhya incidents. But another large part reflects the slow growth of Government's revenues. It is the direct consequence of the stagnation of industry which has kept domestic production stagnant and therefore reduced the yield of customs and excise duties. The trade deficit is no more than $ 1.5 billion which is far below the anticipated inflow of foreign exchange on the invisible i.e., mainly services amount. The foreign exchange reserves have risen to $ 7 billion and there is a strengthening inflow of foreign currency deposits by NRIs.

The on-going stagflation can be remedied by three courses of action: (1) reflationary financing which pushes up incomes and demand. This would reduce the volume of exports; (2) bringing down interest rates on bank advances so that the cost of investment and production comes down; (b) reducing the customs duties further in order to bring down the cost of new investment and therefore the need to raise prices and tariffs. On all these fronts, the Government has to act cautiously and expeditiously in order to save the Indian economy from an impending crisis.

It is burgeoning public expenditure that is the villain of the piece. This expenditure is to be rationalised and streamlined so as to cut those items of expenditure which are not necessary and which can be postponed. What items are to be cut and what items are to be postponed should not be subject to arbitrary bureaucratic decisions. Certain norms are to be prescribed in the light of the objectives to be achieved. When the objectives are laid down the prescriptions of the norms for reduction or postponement of expenditure is easy. This task is to be assigned to an authoritative expert body. This body is none other than the Expenditure Commission. The Finance Ministry should take the initiative in setting up an Expenditure Commission giving it clearly specified terms of reference and its considered recommendations should be implemented in order to regain macroeconomic stability which is the need of the hour.

# 13

## Strategy of Inflation Control

The Finance Minister, in an interview to the PTI on Sunday 11-7-1993 asserted the obvious when he said that there could be no solution to the country's problems without reducing the fiscal deficit. The fiscal deficit as a proportion of GDP was 8.5 percent in 1990-91; it was brought down to 5.6 percent in 1992-93. It is planned to bring it down to 4.7 percent in 1993-94 and to 3 percent in the next three years. This, of course, is heartening.

The fiscal deficit has imposed a heavy debt burden on the Government and the debt burden is of the order of one-third of Government expenditure. This can be brought down by reducing borrowing to finance the Government deficit. In my speech on the 1993-94 Union Budget in the Lok Sabha I stressed the need to impose constitutional limits on internal borrowing and external borrowing. Unless this limit is imposed the Government is prone to borrow without limit and to impose a heavy burden on the posterity.

There are two ways of financing the Government deficit : debt financing and monetary financing. It is held in recent fiscal theory that debt financing is more inflationary than monetary financing. This is due to the fact that debt financing necessitates interest payment on the debt and interest payment is part of Government expenditure. When debt increases, interest payments also increase adding to Government expenditure and widening the Government deficit. But monetary financing which does not involve any interest payment does not involve a rise in Government expenditure and therefore it does not add to the Government deficit though it is inflationary it is not as inflationary as debt financing. Therefore, the need to impose a constitutional limit on borrowing is a categorical imperative if it is intended to reduce the burden of debt, reduce the Government deficit and to reduce the rate of inflation.

The rate of inflation has been brought down from 17 percent in 1990-91 to 5.8 percent in July 1993. This is no mean achievement. But more needs to be done. It is not enough to reduce the fiscal deficit of the Union Government. Other measures are necessary in order to bring down the rate of inflation.

The Government is at present focusing on the fiscal deficit of the Centre as if reducing it by itself will bring down the rate of inflation. In a tri-fiscal system deficit of the State and Local Governments are as much inflationary as deficits of the Union Government. Till recently the State Governments had to resort to overdraft facilities at the Reserve Bank of India but of late there has been reduced recourse to overdraft facilities. Even so, the deficits of the State Budgets persist and they contribute to inflation. Even if the Union Budget is in balance, the deficits of the State Government cause inflation. Therefore, the Union Government should not rest content with reducing its fiscal deficit. The deficits of the State Governments should also be brought down. Therefore, the Government should take into account the deficits of the State and Local Governments also in computing the fiscal deficit as a proportion of GDP. This gives a complete picture of the fiscal deficit and enables better control over the rate of inflation. The fiscal deficit of the Union Government is a partial picture.

At the same time, there is need to control the rate of monetary expansion. It was 18 percent formerly and it is claimed that it is now brought down to 11 percent. Even this rate of monetary expansion is excessive and is contributing in no small measure to inflationary pressures in the economy. This calls for adopting monetary targeting making money supply growth move not at a constant rate of 3 percent as advocated by Professor Milton Friedman but at a rate, which moves within a band of 3-5 percent. In the years when the income velocity of money rises, productivity falls and the exchange rate depreciates the rate of monetary growth can move towards 3 percent. Conversely, in the years when the income velocity of money falls, productivity rises and the exchange rate appreciates the rate of monetary growth can move towards 5 percent. Of course, marginal adjustments can be made in either direction depending on circumstances. Thus:

- the inclusion of the deficits of the State and Local Governments in the computation of the fiscal deficit,
- adoption of monetary targeting.
- Imposing constitutional limits on Government borrowing and
- Reducing Government expenditureare—necessary ingredients of a strategy of inflation control.

# 14

## Capital Adequacy : Norm for Banks

Many Commercial Banks are unviable and sick as their profitability has been eroded because of loan melas, waiver of farmers' loans and concessional lending to priority sectors which get 40 percent of the bank resources. They have not been able to satisfy the capital adequacy norm prescribed by the Basle Committee. The Finance Minister provided for Rs. 5700 crore in the Union Budget for 1993-94 and a further provision of Rs. 5600 crore in the Union Budget for 1994-95 to help the banks to meet the capital adequacy norm. These provisions are in the form of Government bonds on which there will be no immediate cash outgo. The idea behind these provisions was to help the banks to make necessary financial provisions against bad and doubtful debts and to meet the new capital adequacy norm.

Many nationalised banks have planned to enter the capital market to raise finance for the purpose. Thus in December 1993 and January 1994 the State Bank of India raised over Rs. 2200 crore from the public through the issue of equity and another Rs. 1000 crore through bond issues. In 1994 other nationalised banks are likely to enter the capital market to raise funds. The legislative provisions contained in the Banking Regulation (Amendment) Act passed by the Parliament on 16-3-1994 will help many of these banks to mobilise resources to meet the capital adequacy norm. A few private banks are also expected to enter the capital market in 1994 to mobilise funds for commencing their operations.

But it may not be easy for many nationalised banks to mobilise funds from the public. However, now that the Banking Regulation (Amendment) Act has been passed by the Parliament, they have no difficulty in starting the process. But they have to be careful in preparing the balance sheets for 1993-94 and beyond. They should scrupulously desist from sounding euphoric about the prospects of their banks as it is likely to be counter productive.

The Banking Regulation (Amendment) Act has removed a major obstacle in the way of the entry of private banks into the banking sector. The Act has made many sweeping changes like raising the ceiling for share holders' voting rights from the earlier level of 1 percent to 10 percent, restricting the number of directors to three with over 20 percent voting rights and permitting the appointment of part-time Chair persons. The removal of 1 percent voting rights has removed the major obstacle to raising capital from the market. This Act also helps the State Bank of India to make its public issue of equity and bonds successful.

In the light of the Banking Regulation (Amendment) Act the nationalised banks have to compete with the private sector banks in mobilising capital from the market. There are many weak nationalised banks and their problems have become a source of worry for the Finance Ministry and the Reserve Bank of India. There are proposals for merging the weak banks with the strong banks without any thought for the possibility of the strong banks themselves becoming weak after the merger. An alternative can be thought of a separate institution can be set up under the Companies Act. The capital of this institution can be subscribed by the strong banks and financial institutions. This institution can then be authorised to buy the bad debts of the weak banks at a discounted price. The idea should be to get rid of the non-performing assets (NPA) of weak banks and to make their balance sheets look healthy. In this connection the experience of Japan can be scrutinised and the appropriate action can be taken to restructure the banking sector. The weak banks are to be allowed to sell their debt to third parties at a discount and become healthy in consequence. The weak banks can also sell their real estate in prime localities in metropolitan centres where they can fetch a good price and relocate their offices or branches in localities where the price of prime land is much lower. In future these banks can concentrate in the regions where they have developed good clientele through the years and where their banking culture can be accepted easily. This is a device to strengthen the balance sheets of banks. While mobilising funds from the capital market the banks should see to it that they have to be sure that their earning per share does not decline substantially after such capital issues. If this is done the public response to the issues will be reasonably good. Revaluation of assets can also be tried as it raises the book value of the assets and makes the banks look healthier.

The Government is found to be pumping capital into the nationalised banks in order to enable them to meet the capital adequacy norms. But this decision appears to have been taken on political rather than on purely economic considerations. The Asset Reconstruction Fund (ARF) has to be created expeditiously and this has to be augmented partly from the revenue realisation from tax on profits of banks and other financial institutions. In 1993 the Special Recovery Tribunals were set up and were given statutory status but they are yet to be operationalised endowing them with sufficient powers to enable the banks to recover long-overdue debts. The present cumbersome and lengthy legal processes should yield place to quick process of recovery. The banks will then be able to lead a healthy existence. At the same time, the banks should be advised to desist from investing their resources in risky and speculative assets as such investment is likely to generate a scam of the type which shook the Indian financial sector in 1992-93. For this purpose there is need for a Board to monitor the investment activities of banks. Care also should be taken to see that the funds borrowed by the borrowers are used for legitimate purposes and are not allowed to seep through an osmotic process into unproductive areas. There should be a cell to monitor the utilisation of borrowed funds. The banks may resent this arrangement but they should be convinced that these changes are in their own interest.

The foregoing procedure will render unnecessary the financial provision being made in the budgets for enabling the banks to meet the capital adequacy norms. This will reduce the interest burden of the debt on the fiscal deficit, on inflation and other variables. While restructuring the banking sector the foregoing points need to be considered for adoption.

# 15

# Deferring Capital Account Convertibility: A Wise Decision

While presenting the 1994-95 Union Budget in the Parliament, the Finance Minister sounded euphoric about the unexpected spurt in India's foreign exchange reserves from $ 1.1 billion in July 1991 to $ 13 billion at the end of February, 1994. The Finance Minister is obviously under an embarrassment of riches. Others feel that the time is propitious for ordering full capital account convertibility of the rupee. This requires a close examination of the forex reserve profile.

The forex reserves are composed of export earnings, borrowings from the International Monetary Fund, the World Bank and other multinational financial agencies, portfolio investment by foreign institutional investors, direct financial investment invisibles in the form of remittances and corporate funds raised abroad through flotation of issues. The Reserve Bank of India has been buying dollars in the market in order to maintain the exchange rate stable which means preventing an appreciation of the rupee which would render the exports uncompetitive and reduce the rate of export growth.

The question of whether the present foreign exchange reserve position can be regarded as comfortable can be answered after an analysis of the outflows during the next four years.

Starting from 1995 and ending with 1998 the annual debt repayments will be of the order of $ 8 billion per annum. Though the import demand is slack because of sluggish industrial growth at 1.8 percent, import demand may surge not only because of the projected industrial growth rate of 4 percent but also because of the reduction of customs duties in the 1994-95 budget. This calls for an estimate of the import demand and the foreign exchange reserves necessary to meet this demand. This analysis is necessary in the light of the fact that the foreign exchange crisis of 1991 was brought about by the bunching of debt repayments and spurt in imports under the liberalized import regime.

Of the $ 13 billion forex reserves 70 percent is made up of foreign funds which are volatile, speculative and are recallable within 24 hours and the balance of 30 percent is made up of export earnings. Given the expected outflow the reserves they will not be sufficient to meet the surging import demand. The current account deficit in balance of payments in 1993-94 is said to be 0.5 percent of CDP compared with 3 percent in 1990-91 and 2 percent in 1992-93. This is the cause for cheer. But the cheer is bounded to be transitory.

The Reserve Bank's action in buying dollars is to prevent the rupee from appreciating. There is a general perception that the currency of a developing country under a fixed or nearly fixed exchange rate system is always over-valued. The Reserve Bank's action in buying dollars has the effect of preserving an under-valued rupee. It is expected that as soon as the Reserve Bank stops purchasing dollars, the rupee will appreciate with adverse consequences on the balance of payments.

India's exports have been rising since 1991 under the favourable impact of successive devaluations of the rupee. Indian firms have raised money from abroad through the sale of equities. Bank schemes have also raised over $ 11.5 billion. Foreign financial institutions have been pouring in dollars for the stock market. An extra $ 5 billion is expected to flow in the middle of 1994. Convertibility of the rupee in the trade account and the bullish upsurge in the stock market coupled with low import growth strengthened the case for full convertibility on current account. The Finance Minister is right in announcing full convertibility of the rupee on current account and in assuring that India fulfills the conditions prescribed by the IMF thereto.

But there is no equally strong case for full convertibility of the rupee on capital account. The money that is being brought in by the foreign financial institutions is not money which is migratory in character. As soon as they find that the returns elsewhere are more attractive or when they find that the Indian Stock market turns doubtful, that money will flow out. Furthermore, import growth is bound to surge up at present in order to enable output growth. This boosts the demand for foreign exchange. The huge debt burden and the likely increase in debt servicing obligation in the near future will call for higher inflow than the amount anticipated. For the time being, therefore, the Finance Minister is right in deferring the capital account convertibility of the rupee. But generally speaking there does not seem to be any concern about the increasing reserves. Obviously people have underestimated the volatility of foreign funds which are a major component of forex reserves.

The London Economist has warned against resorting to capital account convertibility at the present stage of India's microeconomy. Admittedly full convertibility of the rupee constitutes a crucial component of the liberalization programme. But the EXIM Bank in its recently published study "Rupee convertibility issues and implications" has warned that full convertibility will not succeed unless both macroeconomic stability and microeconomic preconditions are satisfied. But in the present Indian context they are not satisfied. Macroeconomic stability in year a far cry. The rate of inflation at present is 8.5 percent. With the pre-Budget hikes in administered prices of LPG cylinders, sugar, rice and wheat, hikes in railway fares and freight rates with their cascading effect on the price level and the fiscal deficit of 6 percent of GDP India is to go to the zone of double-digit inflation. This will make Indian exports uncompetitive in world markets. The EXIM Bank Study points out that the microeconomic benefits of protection cannot be brushed aside altogether in the opening up process and "the withdrawal of protection must be gradual and pre-announced". In the opinion of the Bank this is important because the efficiency of the industrial sector cannot be improved in the short run nor is resource reallocation possible due to low resource mobility because of structural and institutional rigidities. If, on opening up, large sectors of domestic industry become uncompetitive the loss of industries output and employment would occur. The study reminds all concerned that the newly industrializing countries introduced convertibility long after they achieved export-led growth: South Korea in 1988, Taiwan in 1980, Indonesia in 1988 and Thailand in 1990. It is further noted that the costs of imports have gone up substantially even after the tariff reductions in the 1993-94 budget. This is due to substantial nominal depreciation of the rupee during 1986-92.

At present the rupee has remained solid and stable. Forward premia on the dollar purchases have been moving down and at present they have moved down to all time lows. In the foreseeable future, the rupee is expected to be caught in a narrow band against all major currencies. A major threat to this rosy outlook is the prospect of an inflationary special arising from the recent hikes in administered prices, hikes in railway fares and freight rates and petrol and diesel. More analysts fear the resurgence of a double-digit inflation fueled by the fiscal deficit of 7.3 percent of GDP. Another factor is the volatility of foreign capital which has contributed to the so-called "comfortable" forex reserve position. The situation needs to be constantly watched.

# 16

# Ensuring Self-sufficiency in Edible Oil

For a very long time India has been experiencing deficit in the supply of edible oil. But thanks to the technological changes the Government introduced in the edible oil sector the production of oil seeds has increased significantly. In 1970-71 India produced 96 lakh tonnes of oil seeds. In 1980-81 it was much the same at 94 lakh tonnes. By 1989-89 it increased to 180 lakh tonnes and by 1992-93 it reached the staggering height of 202.7 lakh tonnes. But this year (1994-95) there is a slight decline. Though there is unlikely to be a noticeable decline in oil seeds production there is bound to be some decline because of excessive rainfall which damaged oil seed crops. Even the area under oil seeds cultivation has been reduced. It is the farmers who decide on which crop to grow. Their decision depends on several factors. The statistics regarding the area under cultivation under each crop and the yield of each crop is imperfect as a guide to policy.

In 1950-51 the area under oil seeds cultivation was 107 lakh hectares. By 1970-71 it rose to 166 lakh hectares. At present it is about 250 lakh hectares. Though the oil seeds yield has increased perceptible because of technological innovations the yield of oil seeds in India is far lower than in other countries. At a time when India has adopted the policy of liberalization and globalisation India has to be dependent on foreign countries unless it is competitive India has to continue to import oil to meet domestic demand. In India which accounts for the largest production of groundnuts the farmers grow 953 kg. per hectare. In contrast in Malaysia the average yields 3000 kg. per hectare. In view of this, how can India boast of completing with the foreign countries in world markets? In the decade of the 1980s India had to spend considerable foreign exchange to be able to import edible oil. The year 1987-88 was the peak year in this respect. In that year Indian imported 18 lakh tonnes of edible oil at a cost of Rs. 969 crore of foreign exchange. Though the import of edible oils has declined perceptibly since then it is still there constituting a drain on foreign exchange. In the year 1994-95 India may have to import 5-6 lakh tonnes of edible oil. Efforts are to be made as a warfooting to increase the per-hectare yield of oil seeds. It is also imperative to make efforts at modernization and technological upgradation of the oil industry. About three-fourths of the oil producing units are out of date causing a rise in the unit cost of production. Their technology is old and traditional and the cost of production is very high. There is considerable loss of oil during the process of production. There is no uniformity of legislation applicable to the oil producing units in the private sector. Co-operative sector and the public sector. As the public sector units store oil and oil seeds in considerable quantity it causes a sport in oil prices. There is no thoughtful programme of action in this sector.

Oil is an essential commodity occupying an important place in the consumers' budget. The people of the country irrespective of their socio-economic status use this commodity as a food item. Some poor families which cannot afford electricity for lighting use groundnut oil along with kerosene for lighting purposes also. If the price of edible oil rises it exacerbates inflation which raises the cost of living and generates demands for higher wages which unleash demand-pull and cost-push inflations. If oil is subsidised it adds to the fiscal deficit which is also inflationary. For this reason there is need to hold down the price of edible oil. This can be done by ensuring adequate supply of edible oils. Import of oil will increase the supply of edible oil and this helps to hold down the price of oil. But this constitutes a drain on India's forex reserves. At a time when India has a large stock of forest reserves the import bill can be paid without any difficulty. But in the years of shortage of forex reserves this generates a problem. Therefore, there is need to ensure adequate supply of edible oil domestically in order to hold down the rate of inflation and also to reduce the foreign exchange outflow. If necessary the supply of oil can be increased to a level where India can be a net exporter of oil. How can this be done?

- By increasing the area under cultivation of oil seeds.
- By increasing the yield of oil seeds to a level achieved by Malaysia.
- By modernization and technological up-gradation of the oil producing industrial units so that the yield of oil per unit of oil seeds input may increase.
- By reducing the wastage of oil at the stage of production, packing, storing and transportation.
- By scientific assessment of the supply and demand for oil and by making good the deficit by means of imports, if need be, well in time before the prices start shooting up.
- By providing incentives to farmers to produce more and more oil seeds by extensive cultivation or incentive cultivation of oil seeds.
- By discouraging the use of edible oil for lighting purposes by substituting kerosene.
- By means of harmonious working of the Ministry of Food and the Ministry of Civil Supplies.

In all these ways the production and supply of edible oil can be increased and India can be made self-sufficient in oil. This will not occasion any rise in price on this score and a loss of foreign exchange also.

# 17

## Is the Wheat Policy Good for the Country?

The decision to import wheat to strengthen the sagging wheat stock has generated an acrimonious debate in the Parliament and outside. At the beginning of this year the wheat stocks were uncomfortably low causing a rise in the price of wheat, engendering speculative accumulation of stocks and providing an upward thrust to the inflation rate. In order to hold down the rate of inflation the Government decided to import 1.0 million tonnes of wheat by the end of March 1992 on an emergency basis. However, because of the strident opposition mounted in the Parliament against importing unsubsidized from the United States of America, the decision to import wheat was not implemented. Consequently, the stocks of wheat have declined to uncomfortably low levels while uncertainty shrouds the success of the procurement drive. The international bids offered to sell wheat to India at CIF prices ranging from $ 163 to $ 205 per tonne. At the lower perch the landed cost of wheat works out to Rs. 424 per quintal against the Rs. 225 per quintal offered to the Indian wheat growers by the wheat procurement authorities. This disconcertingly wide differential made the authorities to decide against importing US wheat. Furthermore, the United States also refused to supply even unsubsidized wheat to India on the ground that India was committed to exporting rice to Cuba. In the light of these developments the Cabinet Committee on Prices (CCP) rejected all the bid offers thus dropping the emergency wheat import decision.

The sagging wheat stock and the decision to reject all the bid offers sent the price of wheat skyrocketing. The ruling price of wheat has thus reached Rs.480 per quintal. This made the authorities reconsider their decision not to import wheat. At present the authorities are found to be favouring high priced wheat imports to improve supply, narrow the differential between the market and procurement prices and thus weaken the retention of surplus grain by the farmers and hoarding by the traders. But this strategy will constrain the authorities to import more than a couple of million tonnes of wheat before stocks are released to the market and offerings increased from the current harvest to the procurement authorities. However, though the Reserve Bank authorities claim to have Rs.15,000 crore of foreign exchange it cannot be used to bring import pressure on prices. The best that can be done under these circumstances is to procure surplus grain under a levy. But the philosophy of liberalization governing Indian economic policy at present, rules out the use of any non-market instrument. Consistent with this philosophy the effective procurement price of wheat has been raised at the instance of the Agriculture Ministry by 10 percent.

In the fervid attempt to replenish the sagging wheat stock the Government on 7-4-1992 announced a bonus of Rs.25 per quintal of wheat over and above the revision of the procurement price by an equal amount to Rs.250 per quintal. The bonus will be paid to the farmers from 1-4-1992 to 31-5-1992. With the announcement of this bonus the total price to be paid to the farmers will be Rs.275 per quintal. This announcement is a sequel to the demand from the Chief Minister of Haryana for a further revision of the minimum support price in view of the higher cost of production of wheat. He felt that in view of the rising input costs even this Rs.25 bonus is inadequate. However, according to Mr. Tarun Gogoi, Minister of Food, this bonus was prompted by a desire to maximize the procurement of wheat and at the same time to extend additional benefit to wheat farmers. The Government hoped that the bonus would act as an incentive and help in achieving adequate level of procurement of wheat to meet the requirements of the Public Distribution System and provide food security to the country.

During the rabi marketing season the procurement of wheat was dismal; there was also increased off-take from the Public Distribution System. Against 11 million tonnes of wheat procured during rabi 1990, only 7.7 million tonnes were purchased by the

Food Corporation of India and the Government agencies. Four million tonnes of extra wheat was disbursed last year (1991) as compared to that in 1990.

The poor procurement, coupled with the hardened market situation with higher procurement prices resulting in the private traders mopping up the food grains, had resulted in a steep increase in the price of wheat. Consequently, the Government decided to go in for import of one million tonne of wheat with an additional one million if the need arose to contain the spiraling prices.

The rise in procurement price by 10 percent and the bonus of Rs. 25 per quintal together increase the procurement price by 22 percent over that in 1991-92. However, since this barely reduces the difference between procurement and market prices a surge in price-induced procurement is unlikely. Confronted with sagging stocks of wheat, the government will have to steeply increase the price of wheat sold through ration shops to check demand and thus to reduce wheat consumption. The Government's thinking is that if as a consequence of higher prices the consumption of and demand for wheat falls, to this extent the quantum of food subsidy falls and this helps to reduce the budget deficit and through it the rate of inflation in the country.

This argument draws strength from the assumption that with a rise in the price of wheat the demand for wheat falls. The Minister seems to forget that food habits die hard and, therefore, they are resistant to sudden changes because of a temporary rise in wheat prices. In areas where wheat is the staple food a rise in wheat prices does not cause a fall in the demand for and consumption of wheat. The demand for wheat in these areas is price-inelastic. In the areas where people consume both wheat and other food articles like rice or jawar or bajra, a sustained rise in the price of wheat beyond the margin of tolerance may cause a reduction in the demand for and consumption of wheat as there might be a substitution of rice or jawar or bajra for wheat on the assumption that the price of rice or jawar or bajra is lower than the price of wheat. But the price of rice is far higher than the price of wheat so that there is no possibility of substituting rice for wheat. Even here the demand for wheat does not fall as even with a higher price of wheat it is cheaper than rice. A continuous and sustained rise in the price of rice at a greater rate than the price of wheat may lead to a substitution of wheat for rice in both the wheat-consuming and rice-consuming areas. This, coupled with sagging wheat stocks, is bound to cause a rise in the price of wheat necessitating food subsidy. Even, assuming that there will be a fall in the demand for wheat and a rise in the demand for its substitutes, the prices of these substitutes will rise necessitating subsidy on these food articles. Thus, the subsidy saved on wheat will be offset by the subsidy enhanced on its substitutes so that there will be no relief to the budget from the side of food subsidy and no relief to the masses from any inflation emanating on this score.

Whether food subsidy is retained or not there will be no let up in the rate of inflation. If the food subsidy is reduced by the government suo moto or is reduced because of a reduction in the demand for the consumption of wheat consequent on the rise in the price of wheat, there will be a reduction of expenditure on food subsidy, a reduction in the budget deficit and thus a reduction in the rate of inflation. Good enough. But the rise in food prices following the reduction of food subsidy causes a rise in the cost-of-living index. The labourers and salaried employees demand higher wages to compensate for higher prices. If they are granted and they have got to be granted they will generate both cost-push and demand-pull inflation which get entwined and become difficult to disentangle. If the food subsidies are retained the Government's non-development expenditure rises, widens the budget deficit which causes inflation. Thus whether subsidies are withdrawn or retained inflation is inescapable. But inflation emanating from retaining food subsidies is preferable to inflation resulting from their abolition as the impact is not felt by the poor sections of society.

Remunerative prices of food grains including wheat to farmers are necessary to induce them to increase food production. But the Minister of Agriculture in his reply to the demand for grants to his ministry on 9-4-1992 expressed certain reservations about the offer of remunerative prices to farmers. It must be realised that remunerative prices are necessary for the success of the procurement drive. The behaviour of the Indian farmer is rational. It is responsive to price incentives. Empirical research has shown that the cropping pattern is responsive to price. If higher food prices are offered to the farmers they switch from commercial crops to food crops which causes a rise in food production; in the opposite case they switch from food crops to commercial crops which causes a fall in food production. This causes not only a fall in food availability but also a fall in the amount of procurement. This in turn causes a rise in food prices. The Minister for Agriculture while expressing reservations about the offer of remunerative prices to farmers argued that the government has to take care not only of the interests of farmers but also the interests of others in society. What he meant was that if remunerative prices are offered to farmers the food prices rise and while this may benefit the farmers this hurts the other sections of society who have to pay higher prices for food and bear the burden of higher remunerative prices. While trying to protect the interests of the other sections of society he, in fact, is trying to harm their interests. If remunerative prices are not offered to farmers and if, on consequence, food production falls, food prices have to rise and those sections of society which he wants to protect are in fact exposed to higher prices. Therefore, remunerative prices are necessary to protect the interests of farmers and the rest of the community. The Minister for Agriculture has failed to display an integrated perception of the entire gamut of complicated ramifications of each of the policy alternatives. An integrated perception is necessary to arrive at rational conclusions about the consequences of alternative policy proposals.

Imported wheat is unsubsidised. The price of this wheat plus the cost of transport will be more than the present procurement price offered to wheat growers by over 80 percent. If the Government wants to hold down food prices it has to heavily subsidize imported wheat. This involves budgetary support to imported wheat. This widens the budget deficit and generates fresh inflationary pressures. At the same time imported wheat imposes a strain on the foreign exchange reserves. If there is a choice between importing unsubsidised wheat and offering remunerative prices to wheat growers both of them causing a rise in food prices, offering remunerative prices to wheat growers is preferable to importing unsubsidised wheat for a while the former does not involve a drain of scarce foreign exchange reserves, the latter does involve it. The availability of imported wheat in the Indian market dulls the incentives to Indian wheat growers and reduces wheat production in the country and compels further wheat imports with all their inflationary and balance of payments consequences harmful to the economy.

While India is short of food supply to feed its population at satisfactory nutritional standards, it passes one's comprehension why India should export its inexpensive food to other needy countries and import expensive food from abroad. This may be a good policy from the point of view of strengthening international relations but it is decidedly bad economics.

It behoves the Government to revise its wheat procurement policy and wheat import-export policy in the larger interests of wheat growers, wheat consumers and macro-economic stabilisation efforts under way in the country.

# 18

# Should Banks be Brought under Parliamentary Control?

At last, the recommendations of the Narasimham Committee on Financial Reforms are being considered seriously for implementation. The Union Finance Minister initiated the proposal in the Finance Bill, 1993; in addition, the Joint Parliamentary Committee (JPC) enquiring into the multi-crore stocks scam has offered this advice.

The move to reduce to Statutory Liquidity Ratio (SLR) from 36 percent to 25 percent in the next three years is in the offing. Similarly the move to reduce the Cash Revenue Ratio (CRR) which at present is hampering the profitability of the banking system considering the fact a large sum of cash is impounded in the reserve is also being contemplated. A Board called the Board for Financial Supervision is also on the agenda with powers to oversee the banking system, the financial institutions and non-banking financial companies. This Board is to function under the aegis of the Reserve Bank of India and in co-operation with the banking frauds cell in the Central Bureau of Investigation. This Board will have an independent status with an advisory council to assist it.

At present the financial institution like Unit Trust of India and others formed under the Acts of Parliament are beyond the pale of official supervision. They argue that as they have a special status they should be free from inspection and supervision. But with the constitution of the Board for Financial Supervision these Companies have to come under the jurisdiction of the Board. It is held by the Chief of the Securities and Exchange Board of India (SEBI) that all institutions particularly the Unit Trust of India holding over Rs.30,000 crore investible funds need to be subject to periodic supervision and inspection.

The Study Group of the JPC has held the view that the multi-crore securities scam is the product of "running a rickety, over-regulated and undergoverned system. The solution lies in granting a greater degree of autonomy to RBI and also vesting it with more powers after the rapid strides that have been made in the financial sector". A number of JPC Study Group experts have proposed that the banks should be brought under the umbrella of the democratic system and should be made accountable to the Parliament. The banks are different from public sector units as they are simply intermediaries between savers and borrowers and do not take entrepreneurial decisions on their own. The JPC members believe that all banks—public sector banks, private and foreign banks—need to be made accountable to the Parliament. They argue that the banks are the custodians of national savings and that even foreign banks are scheduled banks in a sense. The JPC study group has drawn inspiration from the report of the committee on Public Undertaking which holds that the banks should also be made accountable to the Parliament.

As the Government has decided to implement the recommendations of the Narasimham Committee report, the foreign banks will be allowed to enter the Indian financial sector. These banks are the branches of their respective parent banks located in the foreign countries. These banks are not subject to Parliamentary control nor are they accountable to the Parliament in their countries. When this is so, they will not be prepared to make their branches in India accountable to the Indian Parliament. If the Government of India insists on these banks being made accountable to the Parliament they may be disinclined to enter the Indian financial sector. The condition of accountability to the Parliament has to be done away with in respect of foreign banks. If this is done, the domestic banks accuse the Government of discrimination if they are made accountable to the Parliament. There cannot be two sets of norms—one set for the domestic banks and the other set for the foreign banks.

The securities scam obviously made the JPC think of a device like this. But scams do not occur every year. They are a phenomenon which occurs once in a way. If the authorities fear that they will recur, there are other devices to forestall them in future. The proposed Board of Financial Supervision is there to monitor the operators of all the banks and their investment activities. This Board will function under the aegis of the Reserve Bank of India and in co-operation with the banking frauds cell. If they are found to be inadequate the remedy lies in vesting the Reserve Bank with more powers. Accountability to the Parliament is not the only alternative.

The business of banking is a complicated affair. The Parliament has neither the time nor the patience to scrutinize the operations of all the banks in great detail and to come to any definitive conclusions about them. Furthermore, to make the banks accountable to the Parliament is to politicalise the banking operations and politisation is not a desirable thing to do. Even under a scheme of accountability to the Parliament scams can occur when people like Harshad Mehta go gay with their activities.

# 19

## Industry Status to Agriculture?

In economics agriculture is regarded as the primary industry while manufacturing is regarded as a secondary industry. Though it is called an 'industry' it is yet to get the status of manufacturing industry. Demands are being voiced from time to time by the farming community to treat agriculture as an industry but these demands have remained, by and large, muted. The authorities did not take these demands with due seriousness for the simple reason that they regarded agriculture as an occupation depending on rainfall which is uncertain and that agriculture was considered by the farmers not as a business but as a way of life. When the demand of the farming community to accord industry status to agriculture became strong and insistent the government at the Centre appointed a committee under the chairmanship of Shri Bhanu Pratap Singh in 1990 to examine the possibility of according industry status to agriculture and its allied activities. This Committee stated in its report that the exact duplication of rules and regulations governing the manufacturing industry for the farming sector was neither necessary nor possible, because of the differences between industry and agriculture in the nature of production and these differences are too important to be overlooked. It was felt that so long as agriculture was accorded the same facilities as industry it was immaterial whether any formal status was given to agriculture or not. The report opined that agriculture could be given the status of industry.

Apart from the enthusiastic political initiative the Government is prepared to take, there are several other factors which weigh in favour of treating agriculture as an industry. During the decade of the 1980s public investment in agriculture and related activities declined adversely affecting the rate of agricultural growth. As public investment in agriculture is necessary to act as a catalyst to private investment in it and as public investment declined it caused a decline in private investment also.

The financial institutions lending finance to agriculture framed several stringent rules and regulations to govern the allocation of credit to agriculture. The enforcement of these rules and regulations on credit allocation caused a severe decline in the volume of funds flowing to the agricultural sector. It is necessary to mention here that the National Bank for Agriculture and Rural Development (NABARD) which had in its kitty as much as Rs. 5000 crore could not disburse it as the conditions governing its disbursement were extraordinarily onerous. How onerous they were can be gauged from the fact that the collateral demanded from farmers was stiffer than that demanded from industrial borrowers. An industrial borrower can get a loan if he puts 10 percent of the project cost. But an agricultural borrower had to put in nearly 75 percent of the project value in the form of collateral. Thus the decline in public investment in agriculture and the stiffer terms of lending to the private sector in agriculture meant that the financial institutions had to accumulate funds, which could not be lent to agriculture.

As a consequence, the contribution of agriculture to national income declined over the years though as a source of employment generation it has maintained its level. Though 16 percent of bank credit was allocated to agriculture, it contributed 70 percent to employment. In contrast to this though industrial sector got 35 percent of total bank credit its contribution to employment remained as low as 10 percent. But this can be explained in part by the fact that in manufacturing labour-capital ratio is low while in agriculture it is high.

This is not all. The rules applicable to agricultural exports were far different from those applicable to industrial exports. While there were no restrictions on the export of industrial products, the exports of agricultural products were canalized or were not permitted. Thus, while the profits accruing from industrial exports went to the entrepreneurs directly, his profits from agricultural exports went to the middlemen. Furthermore, while there were no restrictions on the movement of industrial goods the movement of agricultural products was subject to zonal restrictions causing a fall in their prices in the surplus zones.

Those who were behind the AICC resolution felt that unless agriculture was given the status of industry, it would not be possible to increase food supply of the quantity sufficient to provide food security especially in the years of floods and droughts. It must be realized that if the country did not produce food enough to feed the growing population at satisfactory nutritional standards food prices rise and they give a boost to the rate of inflation. This can be prevented by importing food but food imports impose a severe strain on the precarious level of foreign exchange reserves. The Indian tax payer paid $ 170 for a single tonne of wheat imported from the United States while he paid only $ 100 per tonne of wheat to the local farmer. This points to the fact that the terms of trade have turned against agriculture and are providing detrimental to agricultural growth. This calls for paying remunerative prices to farmers.

While the above considerations point to the imperative need to accord to agriculture the status of industry certain conditions which agriculture should fulfill to qualify for that status must be mentioned. In India agriculture is regarded as a way of life rather than as a business. This is particularly so in the case of small and marginal farmers. Labour input is not paid for at the going market rate of wages as in industry as it is the family that contributes labour power. Except in large farms and plantations where labour is employed on a contractual basis at the statutory wage rates, outside labour employed on small and marginal farms during harvesting and sowing seasons are paid wages in cash at rates arbitrarily determined by the farmer or in kind which is also arbitrarily determined. As there are no labour unions in agriculture in the same way as there are in industry, the farm labourers are unable to enforce the conditions of work and wages. The conditions of production are under the control of the industrial entrepreneurs while the farmer has no such control over production. Farming is mainly traditional going by the rule of thumb and is hardly scientific.

Except in the case of large farms and plantations the cost accounting techniques are not employed to determine the unit costs and unit prices. When the rains are adequate farm production accrues as expected but when there are droughts or floods farm production sharply falls. But in industry floods or droughts do not affect production. It is for this reason that though there is a strong case for taxing agricultural income the lack of farm accounts militates against the imposition of this tax on agricultural income. The cost of production in agriculture is not uniform for the same crop throughout the country. The cost of production depends on the nature of the soil, the mode of transport, wage rates paid to labourers, etc. which are not the same in different parts of the country. For this reason there are inter-state or inter-regional disparities in costs of production and prices of the same goods. This is not the case in respect of industry.

It is not just the removal of the onerous restrictions on the allocation of finance to agriculture that is necessary to enable its placement on par with industry, important though it is. The differences that exist between the two sectors in the matter of production, conditions of work and wages, cost estimation and price determination etc. should be minimized before agriculture could be given the status of industry. If these differences are allowed to persist it would be a futile exercise to place agriculture on par with industry.

# 20

## Economic Contents of the Letter of Intent

The IMF was keen that the government should reduce the fiscal deficit from 8.5 percent of GDP to 6.5 percent of GDP. The Finance Minister sought to achieve it though he could not make the grade on account of circumstances beyond his control. Now the IMF wants the fiscal deficit brought down to 5 percent of GDP. It needs hardly be said that the remedy for inflation is the reduction of the budget deficit even below 5 percent. Even this is inflationary but the rate of inflation will be considerably lower with a deficit of 5 percent of GDP than with a deficit of 6.5 percent of GDP. It is established in recent fiscal theory that in a full employment situation even a balanced budget is inflationary under certain assumptions. The Indian situation can be said to approximate the full employment situation for all practical purposes. If this is so, even a balanced budget can be expected to be inflationary. In view of this the reduction of the fiscal deficit to 5 percent of GDP is a welcome move whether the move is made by the Government of India on its own or under the advice from the IMF World Bank Combine. It is in this context that the Letter of Intent given by the Government of India to the IMF has to be viewed. The viewing has to be objective as far as possible. The reduction of the fiscal deficit *per se* has the effect of reducing the inflationary pressure on the economy not only by reducing the quantum of domestic borrowing which entailing a lower interest payment reduces the size of the fiscal deficit. But certain proposals contained in the Letter of Intent regarding the mode of reducing the size of the fiscal deficit have potently inflationary effects on the economy they are bound to raise the inflation rate. Thus, while the reduction of the fiscal deficit *per se* helps to reduce the rate of inflation, the measures adopted to reduce the fiscal deficit raise the rate of inflation. One of the measures has to be implemented in 1991-92 and others have to be implemented in 1992-93. Obviously these will have to be incorporated in the Union Budget for 1992-93.

The measure to be implemented in 1991-92 is raising of the price of diesel by 10 percent. This is expected to result in an increase in revenue by 1,200 crore in 1992-93. It must be admitted that diesel is an important source of power especially in the transport sector and the manufacturing sector. The rise in the diesel price by 10 percent will raise the cost of transporting goods and this, though the cascading effect, raise the final prices of products; furthermore, it will increase the cost of production of goods in the manufacturing sector using diesel. Both these influences operate on the prices of goods in the market and after inflation.

Increasing fertilizer prices in 1992-93 is expected to yield Rs.1,800 crore to the government and this is expected to close the fiscal deficit to that extent and is said to reduce the rate of inflation. At the same time, a rise in fertilizer prices is inflationary in its effect. The mechanism of the process has to be elucidated.

The demand for fertilizers may be elastic or inelastic with respect to price. If it is elastic, a rise in fertilizer prices causes a fall in demand for fertilizers, fall in the input of fertilizers in agricultural operations, a fall in the agricultural productivity and agricultural production. Unless the demand for food and other agricultural products falls in the same proportion as a fall in agricultural production, there will be a rise in the prices of these product. A rise in the price of food in India where food prices govern the general price index and, therefore, the rate of inflation, generates fresh inflationary forces. The government may consider raising the procurement prices in order to dissuade the farmers from reducing the input of fertilizers. But the Government should realize that higher procurement prices mean higher prices of food grains in the market and they result in a rise in the rate of inflation. If there is a fall in the output of agricultural raw materials there will be fall in the exports of these materials and this aggravates the on-going foreign exchange crisis forcing India to reduce the import of essential raw materials and capital goods or to resort to loans from international financial institutions on staff conditionality prescriptions.

If the demand for fertilizers is inelastic, there will be no reduction in the input of fertilizers, no reduction in the output of food and other agricultural products. But as the higher price of fertilizers will be passed on to the Consumers in the form of higher food prices, the general price level rises reflecting a rise in the rate of inflation. If the prices of agricultural products to be exported rise, the foreign demand for them will fall unless the demand for them is inelastic and this again causes a fall in foreign exchange earnings and aggravates the foreign exchange crisis compelling recourse to external loans with all the consequences they imply.

Freezing of Central D.A., is expected to yield nearly Rs. 1,000 crore. While the idea is good, its practicability is in doubt. This for several reasons. Freezing of Central D.A. without, at the same time, curtailing similar allowances in the case of State Government and public sector employees would go against the recommendations of the Fourth Pay Commission. As it is, the dearness allowances are paid on the basis of the cost of living index. And D.A. is paid for every 8 point rise in the index. At the same time, there is revision of pay at frequent intervals for both the Central Government and State government employees. These enhanced pay scales and dearness allowances are feeding fuel to the flames of inflation. At the same time, inflation generates demands for higher wages and salaries and dearness allowances. There is thus a two way causation a vicious circle. Indian currency can, therefore, be said to be on what professor J.R. Hicks calls the "Labour Standard".

Freezing of only dearness allowances will not be of much help. If possible there should be a wage freeze also. These freezes sound attractive in theory. But their practicability is in doubt. Introducing wage and D.A. freeze in the entire economy is possible only if the government declares an economic emergency. But this step is fraught with enormous difficulties. Already, the labour unions are sore with the New Industrial Policy (NIP) and the Exit and privatization provision of it and they are sure to indulge in strikes and demonstrations. If the wage and D.A. freezes are imposed they are bound to intensify their work stoppage activities to the detriment of industrial growth. It is true that the frequent payment of D.A. and their payment with retrospective effect has inflationary consequences and these consequences warrant a freeze but in the Indian work conditions unlike the Japanese work conditions these freezes are bound to become an anathema, to disturb industrial peace and to adversely affect industrial productivity and production with all their unsavory inflationary and balance of payments consequences.

Excluding the better-off sections of the population in the country from the benefit of the Public Distribution System has both inflationary consequences and political complications. If they are to be excluded at all, the question of identifying who are to be excluded is fraught with formidable practical difficulties. A policy paper on liberalization was prepared by the experts in the Finance Minister Office. This policy paper suggested an exclusion criterion for PDS- all the Government and Public sector employees earning more than Rs. 2,000 per month and all the income tax assesses should be excluded.

This exclusion criterion can be, if at all, applied to salaried employees earning more than Rs. 2,000 per month. Under the present scheme of income tax exemption of Rs. 22,000 per year all those who earn a monthly income of Rs. 2,000 automatically become excludable from the benefits of the PDS. If this is so, only those employees earning a monthly income of PDS. It must be understood that in an inflationary situation obtaining in India with rising prices of food, clothing and shelter even an income of Rs. 2,500 a month is not enough to make both ends meet. In this situation excluding these sections of society from the benefits of the PDS would be unfair and this measure would be resisted. If they are excluded from the benefits of PDS, they will have to purchase food articles in the open market by paying the higher prices charged there. This necessarily causes a rise in the cost-of-living index and engenders demands for higher D.A. If, as suggested in the Letter of Intent, the D.A. payment is freezed, those who are excluded from the benefit of D.A. demand upward revision of wages and salaries. But as wages and salaries are not to be frozen, they have to be raised upwards generating wage inflation. Thus, what the government hopes to gain from freezing D.A., it loses by enhancing wages and salaries.

This leads to inequity in society. Those whose income is more than Rs. 2,000 per month but whose income is not ascertainable will be eligible for the benefits of PDS. But the exclusion of others whose income is ascertainable would be unfair. Again, this kind of exclusion criterion generates political complications with adverse consequences on the stability of the Government especially when the labour unions are waiting for an opportunity to strike at the Government which they allege is in its pursuit of the New Industrial Policy, bound to generate unemployment. The Government has to bear these complications in mind before committing itself to pursuing the policy of excluding certain sections of the population from the benefits of PDS.

Limiting the 1992-93 plan expenditure increase to 6% in nominal terms is expected to yield Rs. 2,000 crore. The VIII Five Year Pan is scheduled to start in April, 1992. the aggregate plan outlay is of the order of Rs. 79,20,000 crore. This outlay has a built-in inflationary bias. Unless it is reduced drastically this country is in for a heavy dose of inflation. What matters for economic growth is not so much the size of the financial outlay as its efficient utilization. Thus, limiting the plan expenditure increase to 6% (6% of what is not known) will reduce the inflation rate somewhat without adversely affecting the real rate of economic growth. This is a highly desirable step. In fact, the reduction could have been greater.

Limiting the defense expenditure increase in the 1992-93 budget to 7% in nominal terms would yield Rs. 500 crore.

This step is not desirable in the context of the hostile neighbourhood. The IMF demands a cut in defense expenditure as a condition precedent to the sanction of the loan. India should persuade the IMF not to insist on this condition being satisfied. China is spending 10% and Pakistan is spending 7.8% of GDP on defense while India is spending only 3.8% of GDP on defense.

Pakistan has stated that its commitment to nuclear programme is irrevocable. It must be admitted that India is within a circle of fire and in this context the case for a step up in defense expenditure is strong indeed. Therefore, it appears that the proposal to limit the rise in defense expenditure is unwise though it may result a saving of Rs. 500 crore. National Security should be given precedence over all other demands.

Additional net revenue mobilization by the Union Government is expected to yield Rs. 1,500 crore. It is not known how and in what manner this revenue is to be mobilised.

There is at present a heavy reliance on indirect taxes. About 92% of the tax revenue is from indirect taxation. The long term Fiscal policy of December, 1985 aimed at shifting towards direct taxation. But this shift did not take place. The proportion of tax revenue yielded by indirect taxation is on the increase. This has got inflationary consequences considering the fact that these taxes are shifted forward to consumers and there is no corrective effect coming from the money supply front. A continuous expansion of the money supply accommodates this rise in prices caused by indirect taxes.

There is, therefore, a need to shift in favour of direct taxes. Taxation in India has not been very high as complained by income tax payers and by industry and trade if the extent of other various exemptions and allowances is taken into account. Taxes are levied only after the exemptions are granted. During the past three decades the poor had become poorer and the rich had become richer. The paid up capital of monopoly houses had gone up from Rs. 2,486 crore in 1985 to Rs. 4,855 crore in 1989. The legislations enacted all these years had not corrected the situation. The raising of the income tax exemption limit to Rs. 48,000 will provide the much needed relief to the income tax payers at the lower slabs. The rate on income above this level could be made progressive. In addition, gift and wealth taxes at steeply progressive rates can be levied as a method of securing equity in taxation, and of reducing the incidence of black money as gifts are made, for a great part, from out of black money accumulation. The move to set up courts to try income tax evaders is perfectly justified but the punishment to those found guilty of tax evasion should be deterrent enough to serve as a warning to others. Taxes on luxury articles, domestic or imported, should be steeply raised but taxes on essential article should be reduced to mitigate their severity on the poor. The Laffer Curve enthusiasts advocate a reduction in tax rates on the ground that lower taxes yield larger revenue as they induce greater tax compliance. In India tax yields are rising. This is due more to a rise in income leading to bracket creep than to greater tax compliance. Tax yields have not risen to the extent expected and furthermore there is the accumulation of tax arrears of the order of Rs. 6,000. Bearing these factors in mind, it should be considered necessary to make the tax rates mildly progressive in order not to affect the incentive to earn, save and invest. Fiscal restructuring should aim at this outcome.

The Finance Ministry Officials admit that there are serious problems involved in additional resources mobilization through disinvestments of enquity in the public sector. For the year 1992-93 the Finance Ministry has made provision for Rs. 2,500 crore of additional revenue from disinvestments of public sector equity. This is over and above the same amount expected to be generated through disinvestments in the current fiscal year 1991-92. This step will, besides disturbing industrial peace, go against the accepted path of economic advance as the selling of capital assets to fund current consumption will erode the capital base of the industrial structure.

The Letter of Intent also gives an assurance to the IMF that India will reduce the "overall public sector deficit". Now at 12 percent to 7 percent by the mid-1990s. The overall public sector deficit includes the deficits of the State governments, and therefore, committing the State Governments to this exercise is an unprecedented move. This has to be discussed and a decision taken at the meeting of the National Development Council. The implications of this for the backward States are drastic as they have to drastically cut down their essential expenditures also. Already, some states are demanding fiscal autonomy and any decision to reduce public sector deficits will make this demand more strident. The Government has to be careful about this outcome.

The Letter of Intent gives a commitment to the IMF that India will have a national exit policy in respect of industries. The New Industrial Policy has not laid down any guidelines in the matter of exit of unviable and sick industries.

The labour unions have the apprehension that in the event of exit of these industries the labourers will be thrown out of employment. They have, therefore, threatened to go on a nationwide strike and to observe 'Jail Bharo'. This is bound to disturb industries peace and affect industrial productivity and growth. But the government can allay these apprehensions by announcing a labour policy making provision for re-training and rehabilitation of the workers, unemployed under the exit policy. Not to allow the sick units to make an exit out of the industries would be to impose a burden on the community. Exit policy is necessary but it should provide safeguards to labourers. Furthermore, the institution of the National Renewal Fund proposed by the Finance Minister in his Budget Speech on 24-7-1991 and reiterated in Bombay on 16-11-1991 till help to revive the unviable units back to normal health. But the chronically sick units have to be closed down alternative, employment opportunity being provided to labourers unemployed as a result of closure.

The policy measures to which India is committed in Letter of Intent do not seem to have made any reference to the monetary assumptions. At present the supply of money is growing at the rate of 15 percent per annum. This includes credit supply also. The CRP and SLR constitute 52 percent. The IMF and the Narasimham Committee have both recommended a slashing down of this ratio. If this measure is undertaken, then supply of credit will increase exacerbating inflation. The reduction of the fiscal deficit may reduce the rate of inflation emanating from the budget but the slashing down of the reserve ration of banks will increase credit supply and engender inflation from this source. It is the money market which, in the last resort, releases and absorbs cash and which, in this sense, is a source of instability. Therefore it is suggested that the reserve ratio be retained at the present level of 52 percent. To slash it down would be to unleash money inflation which offsets any anti-inflationary effects of reducing fiscal deficits.

*Total yield*

| *Items* | *Rs. in Crore* |
|---|---|
| Rise in Diesel prices | 1,200.00 |
| Increase in Fertilizer prices | 1,800.00 |
| Freezing of Central D.A. | 1,000.00 |
| Excluding the better-offs from the P.D.S. | 400.00 |
| Limiting plan Expenditure | |
| Increase in 1992-93 to 6 percent | 2,000.00 |
| Limiting Defence expenditure increase | 500.00 |
| Additional net revenue mobilization by the Centre | 1,500.00 |
| Total | 8,400.00 |

If the exercise is successful, the total resources yield will be of the order of Rs. 8,400 crore. The important questions are: Will the exercise be successful? If it is successful, will it reduce the rate of inflation? The answer to these questions depends on several imponderables.

Total Assistance obtainable:

| **Agency Amount (in millions)** | **Disbursement Date** | **Disbursement Period** |
|---|---|---|
| World Bank $ 1,000 | Nov. 1991 | Instalments up to Nov. 1992 |
| IDA $ 1,500 | Nov., Dec. 1991 | Instalments up to June 1993 |
| IMF $ 1,030 | Sept. 1991 | Instalments up to April 1993 |
| $ 2,318 | Oct. 1991 | |
| $ 6,000 to $ 7,000 | Jan 1992 Up to Jan. 1995 | |

The projected "fiscal correction" cannot succeed unless there is strict control over the supply of money. Control over money supply can be exercised through monetary targeting. The supply of money can be made to move within a range of 3-5 percent per annum. In the event of a rise in income velocity of money, a fall in productivity and a depreciation of the exchange rate, the money supply target can move towards 3 percent, in the event of a fall in income velocity of money, a rise in productivity and an appreciation of the exchange rate, the money supply target can move towards 5 percent. This requires the adoption of the bond proposal regarding the exchange rate, the money supply target can move towards 5 percent. This requires the adoption of the bond proposal regarding the exchange rate movements. It must be mentioned that India is at present not mature enough for the adoption of a fully flexible exchange rate system. It passes one's comprehension why the Government of India which is keen on controlling inflation has not thought it necessary to adopt monetary targeting and the bond proposal. It also passes one's comprehensions why the IMF which insists on reducing the fiscal deficit obviously with intent to held down the rate of inflation, has not thought it necessary to advise the Government of India to adopt monetary targeting and the band proposal.

The package of measures to which India is committed in the Letter of Intent represents a scheme good in theory but difficult, if not impossible, to adopt in practice. Some of the measures though intended to check the inflation rate, actually exacerbate it. In this sense, what is actually achieved is the opposite of what is intended. Some others are mutually contradictory and their reconciliation bristles with formidable difficulties. In particular, the proposed exit policy is bound to encounter opposition from the Labour Unions unless a labour policy is announced assuring labourers that they would not be allowed to remain jobless in the event of the closure of the chronically sick industrial units. The proposed National Renewal Fund is intended to help unviable units. But this success depends on the size of the Fund and the mode of its administration. The proposed reduction of the public sector deficits depends on the co-operation of the State governments and their co-operation cannot be taken for granted especially when the poor and backward states are demanding fiscal autonomy. All these and other complications are there and the Finance Minister, his good intentions notwithstanding, had an unenviable task before him.

# 21

# Fears of India Catching the Mexican Disease Overplayed

India is half way through its economic reforms programme. Despite the reservations voiced by the anti-reform brigade, many foreign experts and investors have expressed happiness over the success of the reform programme. Foreign investors have expressed confidence in the economic reforms and the Government's assurance that the reform programme is irreversible.

The economic system of Mexico is indisputably in doldrums. Mexico is in the same economic status as India. It is a developing nation. It has also initiated economic reforms of the type which India has undertaken. Earlier it was held out as a model for the other developing countries to follow. It had removed the control regime and had introduced a regime of economic liberalization. The West had exhorted the other developing nations to emulate the fine example of Mexico in restructuring their economics.

At present things are not as rosy as they were before. The Mexican economy has made the foreign investors express apprehensions about the solvency of the economy. Even countries like India which are on the path of progress have begun to wonder whether they will face the same fate as Mexico. After the introduction of the liberalisation programme in Mexico, its foreign exchange position improved considerably. But all of a sudden, the foreign exchange position has deteriorated. The foreign investors have lost faith in the viability of the Mexican economy. The Mexican currency, Peso, has lost its strength and has become a weak currency. It has undergone a process of continuous depreciation. The foreign investors have begun to withdraw their investments. In the middle of December 1994 Peso was devalued and this devaluation has made the foreign investors lose faith in the currency. The Mexican share market has become a victim of bear speculators. Fearing that what has happened to Mexico may happen to the other developing countries, the foreign investors have started withdrawing their investments from them. This has affected the countries like Argentina, Brazil, Philippines, Thailand, Sweden, Spain and others. When these countries are affected by the "Mexican Syndrome" the question whether India can be free from it has been raised in international financial circles. In ten developing countries foreigners had invested as much as $ 225 billion. This was more than what the IMF and the World Bank could invest. But owing to the fear of the "Mexican Disease", it is feared that foreign investment might decline by half of this amount. The American money has begun to flow back to America. The American investors have begun to feel that their investments in America would yield higher returns than in Mexico. It is apprehended that this might affect India also sooner or later. It is further feared that this might adversely affect the programme of Indian companies raising capital in the European market by issuing Euro bonds and using it for investment in India.

Dr. C. Rangarajan, Governor of the Reserve Bank of India, has allayed apprehensions of India going the Mexican way. He has expressed confidence that what happened in Mexico will not happen in India. Though India has initiated the economic reform programme in the same way as Mexico, there are basic differences between the two in the matter of implementation of the reform programme. The Mexican Government did not manage the external sector with any degree of discretion. When foreign capital flowed into Mexico, it should have taken care not to allow it to flow out. It should have tried to match the outflow with inflow. But the Mexican Government failed to do it. The Mexican current account deficit was of the order of $ 30 billion. The foreign funds were used to meet this deficit. This was an act of indiscretion. Care should have been taken to use the foreign capital for investment in productive enterprises. But India has not committed this act of indiscretion. The current account deficit of India is not as formidable as that of India. If Mexican current account deficit is of the order of $ 30 billion. India's deficit is about $ 1.0 billion. For this reason, the fear that India would go the way of Mexico is unfounded.

It is a fact that the Mexican economic system is like that of India in several respects. But the Mexican Government is managing its finances more competently than the Government of India. It has also brought the inflation rate under control, albeit temporarily. There is extensive privatisation in several sectors. Industrial peace has been achieved. Despite these achievements the current account deficit has exceeded all limits of prudence. As the foreign investors started withdrawing their funds, the demand for Peso declined drastically and this led to its depreciation. In order to stabilise the Peso, the Mexican Government began to use its foreign exchange reserves to meet the capital outflow. The foreign balances were virtually exhausted. Another reason why the foreign investors started withdrawing their capital was the political instability in the country. The Government did not take any action to strengthen the forces of stability. After its foreign exchange reserves were exhausted the Government had per force to devalue the Peso. This generated a fear psychosis in the foreign investors.

The forex reserves of India during the past three years have improved considerably. These reserves which were $ 1.0 billion in 1991 have swelled to $ 20 billion at present and are poised to swell to $ 25 billion by April 1995. The foreign investors have begun to pour their capital into several sectors in the Indian economy. In the case of Mexico the inflow of foreign exchange between 1988 and 1993 was $ 18.00 billion. Of this as much as $ 16.00 billion was in the form of direct investment. This cannot flow out. Even so, the foreign capital has flowed out. The Indian case is more unstable than this. During the past eighteen months, of the $ 750 crore of foreign capital, the amount of direct investment is very small. The amount invested in shares is a major part of foreign investment. This is on the look out for more profitable avenues outside India. In the aftermath of the Mexican economic distress the share prices in the Indian stock exchanges have begun to fall. This is a source of anxiety.

But the Mexican experience is unlikely to be repeated in India. Of the total inflow of foreign capital about half was originally in India. In the context of instability it had flowed out and has now flowed back into the country. The investors have brought back their capital in the full awareness of the incipient instability and the prospects of losses. Therefore, they are unlikely to shift this capital outside the country. Even if some of them shift their capital outside India there are others who are prepared to invest in India. If they are sure of political stability they will keep their capital in India. At present there is no danger to economic stability in India. This is indeed a confidence building force.

Mexico adopted the structural adjustment programme in 1980. The Fund-Bank duo held up Mexico as a miracle of the structural adjustment programme. But due to fiscal profligacy and mismanagement things turned out to be different. The 90 million people of Mexico bore the burden of the programme, the Peso was devalued over and over again, prices rose by leaps and bounds, wages lagged behind prices and unemployment rose to heights. The different few on the top of the income scale were happy and comfortable. The advent of the North Atlantic Free Trade Agreement and the consequent lowering of the import duties by the Mexican Government meant a bonanza for US traders and speculators. Foreign institutional investors went to Mexico flocking. But the slashing of import duties led to a widening of the trade gap. The forex reserves were depleted when panic appeared foreign investors started to send their money back. Mexico lost $ 24 billion of foreign exchange in barely seven weeks during November-December 1994. These developments brought on several new measures: a devaluation of the Peso by 40 percent, an across the board increase in the prices of all essential commodities and a general wage out of the severest proportions. But Mexico is being bailed out by a $ 40 billion credit line arranged for by President Clinton. But Mexico has to hypothecate indefinitely her earnings from oil exports before the credit would start flowing in. This is the unhappy story of hapless Mexico. The anti-reform activists especially of the Left make the gloomy prognosis that India will meet the same fate as Mexico. But they are wrong. See the Indian situation in contrast.

The balance of payments is on a strong wicket. The transformation of the balance of payments situation from near-bankruptcy in 1991 has been dramatic. The forex reserves (excluding gold and SDR) which were $ 1.124 billion in June 1991 have increased successively. They grew to $ 5.631 billion by March 1992 and to $ 6.434 by March 1993. From January 1994 when they crossed the $ 10 billion mark, forex reserves have not looked back. By November 1994 they had reached the $ 20.00 billion mark and they are expected to reach $ 25.00 billion by the end of April 1995. This improvement in the balance of payments is not just a matter of forex reserves through the improvement of invisibles and exports. It was a combination of import compression and the opening up of the investment and financial sector that changed the situation.

The initial impact of liberalisation was the steep decline in the current account deficit from $ 9.67 billion in 1990-91 (largely due to the escalation of oil prices under the impact of the Gulf crisis) to $ 2.13 billion in 1991-92. Impact compression and the deterrent of high rupee costs of imports caused by devaluation of the rupee were responsible for the decline in current account deficit. In 1992-93 imports showed a modest rise by 10 percent in dollar terms. If the current account deficit hovers around $ 3.6 billion it is evidence of a transition with exports geared for expansion despite the elimination of export subsidies.

In 1993-94 the opening up of the economy had placed the external account in a formidable position. A significant buoyancy of exports had made a vital difference. From $ 18.90 billion export value surged to $ 22.7 billion. Imports, on the other hand rose modestly from $ 23.00 billion to $ 23.98 billion. The current account deficit was a meagre $ 300 million.

It was on the capital account that the new economic policy had its impact. Foreign portfolio funds of $ 1.66 billion entered the secondary capital market. GDR and Euro-bond issues resulted in a capital inflow of $ 2.4 billion. A net increase in forex reserves of $ 8.6 billion was an unprecedented development but it had pressures on monetary management. In the first half of 1994-95 the current account deficit was estimated at $ 400 million and for the whole year till the end of March 1995 it is expected to be $ 1.0 billion.

Until a year ago, exceptional balance of payments financing seemed indispensable. But thanks to the improvement in the prospects of direct foreign investment flowing into the country of the order of $ 2-3 billion in the next two years, the situation has considerably improved. Even in the flow of portfolio investment abates because of the expected rise in interest rates in the industrial countries and the opening up of capital markets in the other developing countries, the outlook for the balance of payments appears favourable. Due to the expansion and diversification of exports the prospects of the balance of payments improving on both the current and capital accounts is quite promising even without reckoning the possibility of invisibles contributing a large share of forex earnings. India's balance of payments position cannot be compared to Mexican balance of payments.

But there is one thing, which is a source of anxiety for India. It is the danger of a debt trap. The World Bank has cautioned India that though it is not in a debt trap now it could go into one if it does not ensure that its economic fundamentals were taken care of and did not rely on short-term funds to bail it out. The World Bank team has, of course, assured India that it is not in the middle of the debt trap. However, the lesson for India from the Mexican plight is the IMF lesson that could apply to half a dozen other countries that have recently increased their access to private capital flows, particularly relying on the shorter term fund of private capital flows.

India's debt profile reduces the possibility of the country facing a crisis. A bulk of its debt, $ 83.25 billion of the total $ 9.78 billion is a long-term debt of which $ 80.98 billion is from private non-guaranteed sources. India's short-term debt is only $ 3.6 billion, which is a risky element and is considered a factor fueling a currency crisis as in Mexico. India is the third largest debtor after Brazil and Mexico. But the undisbursed amount has been higher than that of most other countries. In 1993, the undisbursed debt was $ 18.566 billion though this was an improvement compared to the previous five years when the figures ranged between $ 19.195 billion and

$ 23.778 billion. But India's sovereign foreign currency debt ($ 91.781 billion in 1993) was below investment grade as of mid-September 1994 according to the rating by two US credit rating agencies.

The collapse of the Mexican Peso in the wake of the pronounced outflow of short-term capital has sent shock waves to other countries like Brazil, Thailand, Indonesia, Hong Kong and Malaysia. In view of the recovery in the industrial countries capital flows to developing countries surging during the past three years are likely to be reversed. But the Finance Minister and Dr. C. Rangarajan have dismissed the possibility of an assault on the rupee by speculative forces leading to abrupt withdrawal of funds by the foreign investors. The performance of the Indian economy being robust, there is attraction for large scale inflow of capital especially in the form of direct foreign investment. The current account deficit of less than 1 percent of the GDP has made the Indian situation very different from the Mexican crisis where capital inflows were resorted to in order to tide over large scale current account deficits. India's debt was $ 91.78 billion in 1993 next only to Brazil ($ 132.75 billion) and Mexico ($ 718.03 billion). But after the economic reform programme was launched in 1991 there has been a slowing down of the growth of external debt. From $ 87.95 billion in 1991 it increased to $ 90.93 billion in 1992 but thereafter only moderately to $ 91.78 billion in 1993. In terms of the ratio of debt to GDP, though the ratio erupted from 24.3 percent in March 1991 to 34.2 percent in 1992 there was a slight decline of 32.4 percent in 1993. The debt-service ratio based on export earnings has been hovering around 28 percent in recent times as compared to 30.6 percent in 1992. This certainly in a ground for optimism. What is important for exchange rate stability is the composition of external debt and particularly the element of volatile short-term funds in the form of foreign portfolio funds. This does not warrant any anxiety or tension though portfolio funds at present dominate in the overall capital movements. But for a short rise from $ 5.49 billion in 1990 to $ 6.00 billion in 1991 short-term debt has been on the decline to $ 4.45 billion in 1993. Therefore, the debt profile of India does not point to the danger of the onset of the Mexican Disease.

With the declining trend in debt servicing obligations and the expectation of a pronounced growth in GDP, it is estimated that the ratio of outstanding debt to GDP will tend to decline and the growth in absolute terms also may not be pronounced. It may even decline at particular stages on the basis of the projections of the World Bank. It can be expected that the current account deficit will not be uncomfortable in the coming years as the oil bill may not be rising inconveniently and non-oil imports too can be regulated with exceptional imports also being eliminated. The Union Finance Ministry is keen on avoiding an undue increase in borrowing in foreign currencies. Instead the mobilisation of foreign exchange resources through GDRs or convertible bonds is being encouraged. Foreign investment should take place only in the desired areas with a large equity component and a small proportion of loans. This is an encouraging development, which allays apprehensions of the onset of the "Mexican Disease".

The stock market travails also are said to be a cause of concern. The Bombay Stock Exchange's sensitive index of 30 largely traded scrips (BSE Index) fell to a 12 month low of 3411 on Tuesday (24-1-1995). Though it recovered soon after, the future course of the reform programme and the direction of the economy itself would come under a microscope. There are many players in the stock market including the NRI investors and mutual funds of both domestic and foreign origin. They have high stakes in the Indian capital market. Their decisions to buy or to sell or even to stay away are bound to have a profound impact on the way the share prices move. But they do not, by themselves, help in passing judgements on the efficacy of economic policies in the context of such stock market movements. Neither the present 12 month low of the BSE index as well as its all-time high of 4650 reached in September 1994 need be interpreted in contexts larger than what they actually are. They are pointers for the well-being of the capital market but not evidence enough to effect a change in the core economic policies of the country.

In August-September 1994 a few brokers took the index to artificially high levels by foul means. The Government and the Reserve Bank of India sought to determine the source of funds flowing into the market. As a result large Indian corporations were allowed to issue commercial paper at a comparatively steep floor rate. While the economy has been comfortable up to a point with foreign lending institutions, large equity participation and investment in Indian industry is a recent phenomenon. Given the unfortunate experience of Mexico it is possible to generalise and impute the unsustainable motives to the behaviour of foreign capital. It is necessary to arrive at a better understanding of the motivations of such institutions foreign or domestic so that policy makers can anticipate and respond to their actions within the broad contours laid down by policy. All this goes to show that passing judgements on the macro processes based on the movements of share prices is premature. What is urgently required is a policy of strengthening and reforming the stock market so as to increase the number of participants. This would reduce dependence on every source and increase the efficiency of the mechanism. This is a concern of the SEBI rather than that of the Finance Ministry. The burden of this song is that on the basis of the movements of stock prices no firm conclusions can be drawn about the future course of economic reforms and further to conclude that they are a pointer to the danger of India catching the "Mexican Disease".

The fears of India catching the "Mexican Disease" are unfounded at present but they cannot be dismissed altogether. The World Bank has warned India that recourse to short-term commercial borrowing cannot be a substitute for growth in exports to pay for India's increasing imports. Reckless short-term commercial borrowing to finance imports had caused India's balance of payments crisis in 1991. This was also the major reason for Mexico's present problems. A related development is the large scale selling of stocks by some foreign institutional investors (FIIs) setting off a slide in the Indian stock exchanges. Obviously, the reason for this is that the FIIs need funds to make up their losses in Mexico. The stock exchanges have reacted in panic fearing large-scale outflow of capital. The markets will, of course, stabilise soon but this development throws up lessons, which should not be ignored.

There is an increasing current account deficit caused by luxury consumer goods imports and this is added to by the slow down in the inflow of foreign investments. But the Mexican Peso was devalued raising doubts whether the Government would be able to meet its foreign payments commitments. In contrast, the Indian rupee is strong and the Reserve Bank has to buy dollars to keep the rupee from appreciating against the dollar. Though India's foreign debt has increased substantially, according to the World Bank statistics, as a percentage of India's GDP and the volume of exports the situation is far from a possible debt trap. Nevertheless, certain policy corrections are necessary. The role of FIIs in adding to the volatility of Indian stock markets, the tendency to resort to short-term borrowings, as the World Bank has warned, all need to be reviewed to ensure that events do not overtake India's economic reforms.

Given the precautionary measures to be adopted by the Government of India the risk of India going the Mexican way can be said to be remote. In this situation the capital account convertibility of the rupee may not prove to be feasible. If, per chance, political stability is threatened and the foreign investors shift their capital outside India in a regime of capital account convertibility, there is the danger of the rupee facing a crisis. For this reason prudence demands that the Finance Minister should keep in abeyance his proposal to introduce capital account convertibility of the rupee. The advice of Mr. Norman Lamont, former Chancellor of the Exchequer of the UK that capital account convertibility would boost investor confidence in India and it is a necessary step towards globalisation is patently premature at present. All said and done, the risk of India going the Mexican way can be said to be remote. There is need for abundant caution and not for undue panic. However, any complacency on the macro situation would be unacceptable. If inflation is not reduced to 7-8 percent or if the macro-economic management leads to populist give away gimmicks or if export growth falls short of the target of 15 percent external debt might pose a serious problem even if the Mexican ordeal is considered to be of little relevance to the Indian reform process.

# 22

# The Banking System is Buoyant under Economic Reforms

The economic reform programme initiated by the Narasimha Rao Government in July 1991 is in progress despite certain hurdles in the way. The Narasimham Committee Report on Financial Sector Reform is implemented in part though the other part needs to be implemented in order to serve as a catalyst for the economic reforms in general. However, it needs to be stated that it is the banking sector reform that has received the greatest attention and quite rightly too. The reform of the banking sector has started to yield fruits albeit slowly. This is evident from the distinct and discernible improvement in the areas of bank management. It must be said to the credit of the reform package that there is a decelerating trend of losses. Under the reform package there was a deregulation of lending rates of the scheduled banks for loans of over Rs. 2 lakh with effect from 16-10-1994. In April 1993 the six-tier lending rate structure was replaced by a three-tier structure. Previously the banks were free to fix interest rates on term deposits subject to a minimum of 11 percent. In April 1995 this minimum was raised to 12 percent. In 1993 the cash Reserve Ratio was reduced from 15 percent to 14 percent but in August it was raised to 15 percent. At the same time the rate of interest applicable to NRI deposits was reduced to a level lower than the international rate since November 1994. This measure was meant to reduce the cost of holding NRI deposits. In 1994-95 the Statutory Liquidity Ratio (SLR) was reduced in a phased manner to 34.25 percent and then to 33.75 percent. The objective was to increase the availability of funds to the banks for lending. This increased the income of the banks and the availability of funds for industry and business. In keeping with the philosophy of privatization the Reserve Bank of India allowed the establishment of six private sector banks. But many banks suffered losses due to unrealised loan funds. In order to enable the quick recovery of debts four special debt recovery tribunals were set up. The Banking Companies Act was amended to enable the public sector banks to have access to the capital market through the sale of equity shares. Prudential and capital adequacy norms including income recognition guidelines were introduced in the banking sector. They are all intended to enhance the efficiency of the functioning of the banking system and to enable the banks to have closer vigil over risky credit venture. In conformity with the Basic Committee recommendations a new capital framework was introduced for the scheduled commercial banks.

The ongoing reform measures have begun to yield fruits slowly but surely. This can be seen from the reduction of net losses of nationalised banks from Rs. 5078 crore in 1993-94 to about Rs.718 crore in 1994-95. This is a remarkable achievement. The accounts published by the 27 public sector banks show a dramatic increase in net profits from Rs. 730 crore in 1993-94 to Rs. 1599 crore in 1994-95. The programme of prudential norms relating to income recognition, provisioning and capital adequacy began in 1992-93. At the end of the three years period the score card looks impressive. But it must be mentioned that there are some public sector banks which are making losses. The heaviest loss maker is the United Bank of India which is saddled with both operating losses and net losses. Five banks, namely, the Central Bank of India, Bank of Maharashtra, Andhra Bank, Punjab and Sindh Bank and the United Commercial Bank have successfully arrested operating losses but still they show net losses. The Syndicate Bank and the Allahabad Bank have begun to earn operating profits but they are making net losses. The remaining 19 public sector banks are expected to register both operative profits and net profits. In subsequence, the ratio of non-performing assets is expected to decline to 20 percent. In 1993-94 the total value of the non-performing assets was estimated to be Rs. 39,000 crore. This indeed is a higher figure by any standard but it is still an improvement. In 1994-95 the Reserve Bank of India changed the depreciation of non-performing assets from three-quarters interest over dues to two-quarters overdues. This led to the quantum of non-performing assets of several banks going up and compelled them to pursue the recovery process vigorously in order to bring down the ratio. This indeed, is an impressive achievement.

The report of the Reserve Bank of India covering the period from July 1993 to June 1994 highlights the progress achieved in the area of financial sector reform with particular reference to banks. The report also underlines the fact that these public sector banks continued to operate at a net loss in 1992-1993. This is attributed to the insufficiency of the spread of interest rate to cover operating expenses. This means that the differential between the deposit rate and the lending rate was too narrow to enable the banks to cover the operating expenses and to earn a reasonable profit. But reports indicate that the banks have registered marked improvements in the results in terms of operating and net profit of public sector banks in 1994-95. Operating profits are calculated before provisions and contingencies are made and for this reason they are not as meaningful as net profits. In the absence of adequate statistical details, it is difficult to assess the extent of improvement in the net profits except saying that much of it may be due to reduced provisions and the Reserve Bank's relatively strict approach on accounting for Government securities. The Report, therefore, needs greater details for proper analysis of the performance of the banking system. It should reveal details of bank's capital structure, return on assets, spread of interest, the quantum of overdue assets. It behoves the Reserve Bank of India to come out with these details in the next report in order to enable a scientific assessment of the performance of the banking sector and to throw flight on the areas where improvement is needed.

Debt recovery procedures need to be streamlined and effective recovery mechanisms need to be defined. At present the work of the tribunals is slow and halting. This has to be speeded up. It is alleged that while the recovery of small dues is going well the recovery of big debts from industrialists and businessmen owing crore of rupees to the banks is slack. This may, in part, be due to the political clout being enjoyed by them. In matters of debt recovery objectivity and impersonality should guide the recovery process. Political interference needs to be disregarded.

The speed between the deposit rate and the lending rate determines the profitability by banking operations. At present the speed is narrow. The speed can be increased by raising the lending rate or by reducing the deposit rate or by doing both simultaneously. But each of these techniques has other effects which may affect the macro-economic fundamentals. At present the rate of inflation is poised to go down; it stands at 7.7 percent. In this context, a case is advanced for lowering the lending rate as a higher rate is not necessary to serve as an anti-inflationary device. In this event if the deposit rate is left untouched the spread gets very narrow and this reduces the profitability of the banking operations. If, on the other hand, the deposit rate is reduced to maintain the spread as it is, it will adversely affect deposit mobilisation. Empirical evidence shows that the rate of savings responds positively to real interest rate. A reduction in the deposit rate, unless the rate of inflation comes down further, causes a fall in the real interest rate and this reduces savings and the accretion of deposits. What should normally go for savings is devoted to consumption and this helps to raise the rate of inflation. A rise in the lending rate the deposit rate being held constant will, of course, increase the speed, but this involves the danger of a decline in private investment as it is elastic to interest rate changes. This will adversely affect the rate of economic growth. Furthermore, a higher lending rate will increase the interest cost of public debt and complicate the Government's borrowing programme though this may increase the profit of banks. In order to avoid these complications the Reserve Bank of India has kept the lending rate constant. The case of a reduction in the lending rate in the context of a decline in the rate of inflation has failed to carry conviction with the Reserve Bank of India. If the deposit rate is left untouched the spread gets narrowed and this adversely affects the profitability of the banking operations. If, to maintain the spread, the deposit rate is reduced, savings fall and consumption rises giving an upward push to the inflation rate. Thus the manipulation of the interest rate structure is unlikely to be of much help.

Action, therefore, needs to be taken to reduce the volume of non-performing assets by acceleration of the process of recovery of previous loans and for the banks to be extra-cautious in their future loan operations. There is also need for the banks to be cautious in their branch expansion programme so that there is no duplication and overlapping of banks. This will reduce the operating expenses of the banks and the operating loss. It can be said that on balance the banks in India have started to look up under the ongoing economic reform programme. Those who point an accusing finger at the economic reform programme need to note this.

# 23

## Options Before the Government in The Matter of Forex Reserves

Two major factors accounting for the present high rate of inflation are the fiscal deficit and excessive monetary growth. The fiscal deficit was 7.3 percent of GDP in 1993-94. The Finance Minister expects it to be brought down to 6 percent of GDP. The cause for this optimism is founded on the expected rise in revenues, consequent on buoyant economic growth. With favourable monsoons and high rate of agricultural growth the food supply is bound to reach the projected target. Furthermore, with adequate food stocks held by the Food Corporation of India the stage is set for the inflation rate to come below its present level. The Government is confident of bringing down the inflation rate to single digit by September 1994 through tighter control over fiscal deficit and reduction in money supply. The other factor contributing to inflation is the uncontrolled growth of foreign exchange reserves. At present foreign exchange reserves are of the order of $ 17 billion. This is double the absolute minimum level required for the country. An additional $ 2-3 billion could be absorbed without much difficulty but anything beyond this can be a problem for the country's balance of payments. In fact, it is expected that by the end of fiscal 1994-95 the forex reserves would rise to $ 25 billion. If this materialises the supply of money will be excessive exacerbating inflation. Inflation affects the balance of payment by reducing exports and increasing imports.

The official view is that an accretion of reserves of another $ 2 to 3 billion will cause serious problems. With reserves increasing by about $ 500 million every month this situation will be reached before long. The rapid build up of reserves over the past year has already contributed to double-digit inflation and put pressure on the exchange rate. The Reserve Bank has been making substantial purchases of dollars in order to prevent the rupee from appreciating against the dollars. But there is a limit beyond which the Reserve Bank cannot intervene for, if it does, it adds to money supply which puts upward pressure on inflation. To reduce the growth of money supply from last year's high level of 18 percent the Reserve Bank in its slack season credit policy increased reserve requirements. However, the Reserve Bank's capacity to take out of circulation a large part of the rupee equivalent of the increase in foreign exchange reserves faces constraints. The best strategy is to reduce the fiscal deficit as, in addition to controlling inflation, it will help the Reserve Bank to cope with the increase in reserves. Fortunately, the record therefore in fiscal 1994-95 points to a contraction of the budget deficit and greater adherence by the Government to the fiscal deficit targeted for 1994-95. But it is too early to be optimistic about it as the experience of 1993-94 showed that the fiscal deficit can quickly widen due to unanticipated increase in government expenditure. It is therefore necessary to consider other options.

The Reserve Bank of India has, in the main, three options which it could exercise to contain the inflationary effects of growing foreign exchange reserves: (a) allowing a larger inflow of imports; (b) appreciating the exchange rate; (c) raising the domestic interest rate.

The Finance Minister has made out a case for liberalising imports by easing import regulations. His case rests on several assumptions. Those who advocate a more liberal import regime as a major step towards speedier implementation of economic reforms have been quite articulate in recent weeks because of the large accumulation of hand currency reserves by the Reserve Bank of India. In addition to the $ 17 billion foreign exchange reserves in the vaults of the Reserve Bank of India. There is the improvement in the current account of the balance of payments, thanks to the 15 percent increase in exports during 1993-1994. In consequence, the country's trade-service ratio i.e., the annual repayment liabilities as a proportion of its total export earnings has declined from the danger level of 31 percent to 25 percent. The Finance Minister's view is that in these circumstances India can afford to be somewhat more liberal about imports. This will not only help that section of industry which needs to import capital goods and some critical intermediates to modernise and to compete in world markets and also to reduce the smuggling of a variety of consumer goods which would help to reduce the rate of inflation.

But there is a hitch in this assumption. For one thing a large part of these foreign exchange reserves consists of NRI deposits the utility of which has been questioned in the light of its volatility. These deposits are highly interest-sensitive and are bound to move away in search of higher returns the moment interest rates are reduced in India. The country's monetary policy is geared to maintaining domestic stability rather than keeping the NRI deposits stable in India. When the interest rates are reduced in order to meet domestic requirements the NRI deposits take flight. The NRI deposits are short-term deposits at best which India hardly needs for the moment. Even if one were to discount this category of foreign exchange reserves as being of questionable stability, it would still be hasty to presume that the other kind of foreign exchange deposits like investments by Foreign Institutional Investors (FIIs), corporation houses abroad and even loans raised abroad by Indian companies would maintain their present strong flows if India's exports, per chance, stagnate. Reports suggest that the rate of growth of exports has declined during April-May 1994 to 9 percent compared to the corresponding period in 1993. The need is for more substantial measures which are more likely to stand the test of time. In this connection other options need to be considered viz., the appreciation of the rupee against the dollar without the Reserve Bank of India intervening to prop up the value of the dollar and the reduction of the domestic interest rate to discourage the inflow of foreign deposits. The Government has to consider the merits of those proposals before committing itself to a measure which would later cause embarrassment which might force its withdrawal in the 1994-95 budget.

The main reason for the Reserve Bank of India intervening in the foreign exchange market to prop up the value of the dollar is to prevent the rupee from appreciating considering the fact that an appreciated rupee would adversely affect exports and encourage imports. The Government therefore was not in favour of allowing the rupee to appreciate. The Reserve Bank of India had allowed the foreign exchange reserves to increase rather than allowing the exchange rate to appreciate. The Government feels that with industrial production picking up in the coming months, imports are expected to go up and this would help to contain the reserves. At the same time the purchase of dollars by the Reserve Bank of India to prevent the rupee from appreciating is proving to be a disincentive to exporters. The inflationary impact of such operations by the Reserve Bank is causing concern to all. However, one fact which merits attention is that if the rupee is allowed to find its own level and appreciates against the dollar there might be a hastening of the reverse flow of dollars which would reduce the stock of foreign exchange reserves. As averred already, much of the capital inflow is in the form of portfolio investment by the FIIs and NRIs and investments through the Foreign Direct Investment route. The proposal for non-intervention by the Reserve Bank may result in a depletion of foreign exchange reserves. It is further argued that appreciation of the rupee is not an unmixed evil. It may adversely affect export growth by raising the prices of exports. At the same time, it can be argued that an appreciated rupee by making the imports of capital goods, raw materials and intermediates cheaper will make import intensive exports cheaper too and thus help to enhance the international competitiveness of India's exports. The balance of advantage is to be assessed before the Government decides to exercise this option.

Another option is the reduction in interest rates. This is an area where the impact of liberalisation and globalisation is yet to be felt. In the developed countries the interest rates vary from 3 percent to 9 percent per annum. In India despite the reduction in interest rates to remedy the recession in the industrial sector we are yet to see reduction below 15 percent. High interest rates may help to curb demand inflation though it may aggravate the on-going recession. At the same time, high interest rates have a cost-push inflationary effect. In view of this, a reduction in interest rates will help to remedy the recession though it may have a demand-pull inflationary effect. At the same time, a low interest rate helps to curb inflation by helping qualitatively the objective of selection sterilisation of forex inflow.

Of these three options, the option of liberalising consumer goods imports has to be examined in great detail as it is a pet proposal advocated by the Finance Minister. There is need to rationalise consumer goods imports on two fronts: (a) liberalisation of consumer goods imports *per se* and (b) further compression and rationalisation of the tariff structure. Admittedly the cause for liberalising imports of consumer goods is controversial but it is impeccable on the same. The Reserve Bank intervention in the foreign exchange market to prop up the dollar has led to the accumulation of forex reserves which are inflationary; any appreciation of the rupee by a policy of non-intervention in the foreign exchange market will lead to an appreciation of the rupee with adverse consequences on the competitiveness of exports though it may lower the import prices of capital goods, raw materials and intermediate goods. A liberalisation of imports will prop up private demand for dollars and reduce the pressure on the Reserve Bank of India to buy them in exchange for rupees.

The reason for liberalisation is founded on efficiency considerations. In the attempt to curb luxury consumptions, the Government has penalised the consumer, has protected the domestic producers of sub-standard goods. The availability of imported consumer goods will force domestic producers to produce goods of better quality.

The opponents of import liberalisation argue that it would enable the affluent consumers to divert their resources from investment to consumption. This argument sounds plausible but an in depth examination reveals several flaws in it. Restrictions on imports have the effect not of reducing consumption but of changing its composition. If the luxury imports are restricted the consumers use their resources to build mansions to display their affluence. They also spend their resources on non-tradable goods and locally made tradable goods. They also obtain foreign goods through illegal channels. A large part of consumer goods are today not luxury goods at all; they are used by several sections of society. Even if it is intended to curb the consumption of luxury goods the ideal instrument is an excise duty which does not discriminate between domestic and foreign sources of supply.

Those who oppose liberalisation do so on the ground that it would hurt the domestic consumer foods industries. Liberalisation might change the composition of consumer goods industries but it will not wipe them out. In the pre-reform period India devoted a larger proportion of its resources to capital goods production than China, Indonesia and South Korea. As India has a comparative advantage in the production of labour-intensive products, the resource will move into this sector and the manufacturers of this sector will export the domestic varieties of exports against the import of foreign varieties.

Though the process of liberalisation of imports is underway, it is not enough to meet the challenge of accumulated forex reserves. Baggage rules have been liberalised so as to enable the passengers coming from abroad to import many consumer goods on payment of 100 percent duty. Furthermore, beginning from October 1992 the Government has been giving Special Import Licences (SILs) to large exporters, the value of the SIL varying from 3 to 10 percent of the total export earnings. These licences are tradable and entitle the holder to import several consumer goods included in the positive list. But this degree of liberalisation is to be extended to cover many varieties of consumer goods. This calls for abolishing licensing on consumer goods imports and for subjecting them to the current top tariff of 65 percent and using a non-discriminatory excise tax to curb the consumption of luxury goods. The Government has accepted the recommendation of the tax reforms committee that there should be four tariff rates a maximum rate of 40 to 50 percent for consumer goods, 30 percent for intermediate inputs, 20 percent for capital goods and a minimum rate of 5 to 10 percent. This structure of tariff is a vast improvement over the existing structure. Even so it is not entirely satisfactory. The top rate of 40 to 50 percent provides a high degree of effective protection for consumer goods. Furthermore, the multiplicity of tariff rates across the commodities is not desirable. In a democracy any firm can lobby for a reduction of the tariff rate of 50 percent though its produce is remotely a consumer good and enjoy a high level of protection at the cost of the consumer. This calls for a smaller number of tariff rates existing within a narrow band. This calls for a review of the recommendation of the tax reforms committee. However, the burden of this song is that the import of consumer goods should be liberalised to absorb the embarrassingly large accumulation of forex reserves.

An important factor which should govern the choice of the option to cope with the surging forex reserves is the degree of volatility of these foreign funds. In 1993-94, the most stable component of forex reserves was direct foreign investment accounting for less than 15 percent of capital inflow. Foreign institutional investment and overseas issues by Indian companies, both of which potentially volatile, were the largest sources of external capital receipts. There is, of course, no immediate likelihood of these funds pulling out but the risk is always there. It is argued that if liberalisation is used as an option to reduce the reserves, any withdrawal of portfolio funds later could force the Government to tighten import controls, which are an antithesis of import liberalisation. But this danger is remote.

There is thus no serious risk of any heavy outgo of funds. The FIIs may not be inclined to increase their purchases of listed securities i.e., invest in blocks of equity shares offered by established companies on a preferential basis if there was no significant appreciation in the value of their holdings and it was not possible to ensure a return on their funds which would be higher than they could secure in other developed and developing countries. Their purchases may continue to be stable as there is no risk of depreciation in the value of the rupee which might result in a loss if funds have to be repatriated. In this situation the FIIs may be inclined to deploy larger funds especially if the performance of the economy in 1994-95 turns out to be more encouraging which is likely. There are indications that direct foreign investments may be on a large scale with the US interests being more keen on implementing power projects through joint ventures with Indian partners. Other major projects will also be coming up in the petrochemical and petroleum refining sectors while it has been pointed out by Government spokesmen that approvals for many Euro issues by established enterprises have been given and efforts may be made to launch these issues in the coming months.

The three options analysed above have both in-built advantages and disadvantages. None of them is an unmixed blessing or an unmixed evil. Liberalisation of imports of consumer goods will help to check inflation by increasing the supply availability and by promoting efficiency of domestic consumer goods industries. Liberalisation of imports of capital goods, raw materials and intermediate goods will help to reduce the price of inputs in exports and make them competitive in world markets. Import of consumer goods will help to reduce the rate of inflation; at the same time it reduces the stock of foreign exchange reserves. But when these reserves take flight the Government will be put to an embarrassment, as the reserves cannot be made good. The import of capital goods, raw materials and intermediates will promote import-intensive exports. Though they result in a reduction of forex reserves initially, they help to replenish them by increasing export earnings. Appreciation of the rupee will make exports costlier and affect export growth but by making imports of capital goods, raw materials and intermediates cheaper will increase the volume of import-intensive exports. Appreciation, by making the rupee costlier may reduce the inflow of dollars. Reduction of interest rates has the effect of remedying the recession but, at the same time, it generates demand-pull inflation, it also reduces the cost-inflation emanating from high interest rates. It also reduces the inflow of reserves which are sensitive to interest rates. In addition to this, it also causes an outflow of volatile capital. In these ways every option has several points in its favour and several points against. The authorities have to assess the balance of advantage and choose that option or that combination of options which prove to be beneficial to the country.

On balance, it is possible to hazard the opinion that liberalisation of imports and reduction of interest rates could be adopted with favourable effects on macro-economic stability.

The debate generated by the economic reforms has not transcended economic concerns of a short-term perspective. This is disconcerting although not surprising as all the interested groups joining issues are busy jockeying from one short-term advantage to another to focus on long-term concerns. But this dedication to short-term is a matter for concern, as a series of short-term optimals do not add to a long-term strategy. On the contrary short-term interests often militate against long-term goals. Seen in this perspective, our concern in implementing economic reforms should be long-term macro-economic stability even though it may militate against short-term interests which will be only for a brief period. The concern for the long-term makes the adoption of import liberalisation and reduction of interest rates highly desirable.

# 24

## Deregulated Interest Rates

The present economic reform programme with its ingredients of globalisation and liberalisation has exposed the financial sector to the bracing winds of competition blowing from the world abroad. The banking system, like the industrial sector, is glaring up to meet the new challenges in the competitive environment. The banks have begun to talk of the need to create a level playing field vis-à-vis the foreign and new private sector banks. In this case banks have begun to argue for more functional autonomy from the Government to decide on commercial matters. The announcement on 17-10-1994 of the new credit policy by the Reserve Bank of India resulted in a sharp fall in the prices of shares of both banks and financial institutions. This was for good reasons. With the interest having fallen bank profits were squeezed and this accounts for a sharp fall in share prices as is shown below:

**Share Prices**

| Agency Amount (in millions) | Before Policy (Oct, 14) | After Policy (Oct, 21) |
|---|---|---|
| SBI | 205 | 186.25 |
| Bank of Madurai | 560 | 540 |
| ICICI | 1580 | 1475 |
| SCICI | 123.75 | 111.25 |
| HDFC | 3060 | 2980 |

As the Reserve Bank of India removed the minimum level of interest rates on loans over Rs. 2 lakh and leaving banks completely free to charge whatever interest rate they wish to interest rates fell by an average of 1 percent to 1.5 percent. The minimum interest rate has declined to 13.5 percent and many banks have fixed their lending rates near this level. As the new credit policy has abolished the credit exposure limits that governed bank lending to individual companies, the competition for FIs has also increased. This means that banks can now extend long-term loans to the corporate sector in addition to financing its needs for working capital as in past. Reacting to this the FIs also revised their lending rates. Both the IDBI and the ICICI lowered the prime rate to 13.5 percent. The war of interest rates has begun.

This war will mean a definite squeeze on profit margins. The rates on deposits are still fixed at the same level. But with lending rates declining the spread between the two rates, which is what determines profit margin, will fall. The Indian Banks Association has come to the conclusion that commercial banks would suffer a net loss of about Rs. 1100 crore on the abolition of the minimum lending rate (MLR) on advances over Rs. 2 lakh and the stipulation of a CRR of 7.5 percent on FCNR deposits. There is a case for lowering the interest rate on advances considering the fact that the cost of domestic working capital cannot be significantly higher than prevailing abroad. Admittedly, total parity with the global situation cannot be considered even as a distant goal but still the Government has to proceed strongly in that direction.

Normally, if there is a corresponding cut in deposit rates the gains emerging from these cuts should neutralise the losses. The spread between the two rates has to be reduced to international standards. This is a legitimate demand of liberalisation. All the world over the banks operate with a minimal spread. But the ground realities in India are different. Indian banks have to work within far with too many constraints, which are partly self-imposed. Periodic hikes in SLR and CRR forced the banks into a situation where they had only half of the deposits mobilised by them to be made available for purposes of lending. Their viability was further reduced by the requirement that 40 percent of gross bank credit should be lent to the priority sector as embodied in the Bank Nationalisation Act of 1969. This condition still stands though the Government has moved towards a reduction of the SLR in line with the recommendations of the Narasimham committee on financial sector reform.

The foreign banks will also experience a decline in profits. They have been required to maintain a cash reserve ratio on deposits received under the foreign currency non-resident accounts scheme. This impounds Rs. 550 crore of the funds of the foreign banks. This will not be available for the foreign banks for lending. The banks will only receive a nominal interest from the Reserve bank of India on this account.

In order to minimise the impact of the narrow spread on the profitability of the banks the Reserve Bank of India has taken several steps such as cutting down the SLR from 33.75 percent to 31.5 percent. This will free Rs. 2800 crore for the banking sector to lend to industry. Higher rate of industrial growth will help in better deployment of funds. The banks have also been allowed to advance loans to State level financial and industrial corporations who in turn will lend it to the small-scale industrial sector. This will be counted as part of the banks' priority lending obligations but it saves them from many administrative problems.

The abolition of the ceiling on term loans and the exposure limit of banks towards project finance will increase profitability. The amount which the banks can lend for any profit has been raised from Rs. 200 crore to Rs. 500 crore. At the same time the ceiling of Rs.50 crore for individual bank lending has been abolished. The object of this measure is to enable the banks to participate in the financing of mega projects which were so far a prerogative of the FIs.

The impact of the reduction of lending rates on the corporate sector is, of course, beneficial. At present interest cost accounts for between 6 and 7 percent of total cost of production for well-managed companies. While the impact of a 1-1.5 percent cut in lending rate may be very marginal in terms of overall savings, as a proportion of profits it is fairly significant. During the past few years lower debt costs have been a major factor in increased profitability. In the past three years the Reserve Bank of India has reduced the minimum lending rate from over 20 percent to 15 percent. In 1993 lower interest rates and more public issues which reduced the quantum of debt for the corporate sector ensured that interest costs increased by just 5 percent as against the earlier average of 30 percent. It is estimated that at least a third of last year's 80 percent increase in operating profits was due to the lowering of interest rates.

At present there is a further reduction in the interest rate of between 1 percent and 1.5 percent the profitability of the companies has increased. In this new situation the companies are likely to go in for credit rating on the periodic basis. Any up-gradation of credit rating will enable the companies to negotiate loans at around 12.5 percent. Interest rates on consumer finance are also likely to fall by 0.5 percent to 1 percent.

The current deregulation of interest rates is an important step in the Government's attempt to make the banking sector more efficient. During the past three years controls on the banking sector have been reduced progressively and interest rate flexibility has also been allowed in keeping with the recommendations of the Narasimham Committee. While this part of the implementation of the Narasimham Committee recommendation is welcome the Government has not done much to reduce the burden of priority sector lending on banks at concessional interest rates. Even now interest rates on borrowings below Rs. 2 lakh continue to be regulated. As the banks by and large are not making profits from such lending the burden will be passed on to the middle and large sized corporate sector.

While deregulation of interest rates is necessary to improve the efficiency of the banking sector the spread between the lending rate and the deposit rate in the Indian banking sector is too inadequate to ensure sufficient profitability. There is need to tackle the other problems plugging the banking sector. The banking system is burdened by far too many non-performing assets. At the same time it has to bear the burden of maintaining far too many non-performing managers and inefficient staff. The banks have to shed this fat and render efficient service assisted by fewer personnel. The bank unions must co-operate with the bank managements in the task of reducing the number of inefficient employees. It is also important that there should be greater transparency. The banks should also shed the practice of window dressing. During the past several years the performance of the banking sector has been slow. The massive securities scam has exposed these ways of the banking system to public gaze. But for the scam nobody would have thought of capital adequacy and prudential norms. The Narasimham Committee recommendations would have been pushed beneath the carpet but for the agonising intervention of the securities scam. The banks are on the tight leash with the demand for transparency. The leash will be tighter as the foreign banks and private banks enter the field. The deposit growth in 1994-95 shows that depositors were not greatly discouraged by cuts in the deposit rates but if the alternative avenues open themselves up the situation might change for the worse for the banking system. While loans and advances provide the sustenance for the banks, the base is provided by the growth of deposits. If they dry up the banks will be in trouble.

The banking system at present is not in perfect health. It has accumulated non-performing assets. The Finance Minister has come to the assistance of the banking sector by providing considerable finance. But a lot more needs to be done. The loans advanced by the banking system are not returned to them by the borrowers. The money borrowed by them for productive purposes seeped into unproductive purposes through an osmotic process and these loans have become unrecoverable. Again, under the Loan Mela scheme initiated by the Minister of Finance a large sum of money was lent to the so-called poverty-stricken masses to enable them to engage themselves in self-employment schemes. Even these loans have become unrecoverable. These constitute non-performing assets, which have reduced the profitability of the banking system. The Parliament passed the Bill providing for Loan Recovery Tribunals but these Tribunals have become non-starters. Unless these loans are recovered in full and unless loans are made for genuine productive purposes and unless the expenditure of these loans is monitored the banking system is bound to continue with reduced profitability.

The banking sector is in a dilemma. If the lending rates are not reduced the industrial revival and industrial growth will be slow and sluggish. If the lending rates are reduced the profitability of the banking system will be eroded. If the deposit rates are reduced along with the lending rates, the spread will be maintained and this spread will ensure adequate profitability. But the reduction of deposit rates will weaken the deposit mobilisation efforts. The depositors will divert their savings into other areas like real estate and gold which appreciate in value as the time passes. While the spread between the lending rate and the deposit rate at present is to be maintained it reduces the profitability of the banking system. But profitability of the banking system can be assured not by raising the deposit rate but by reducing the magnitude of non-performing assets and by the banks lending in future for genuine productive purposes. Furthermore, the populist measure of waiver of farmers' loans should be given up. Loan waiver is valid only when the borrowers invest the borrowed funds in genuine agricultural operations but come to grief on account of natural calamities like floods and droughts but not in other cases. By making the banks conduct their operations strictly on commercial lines the banks can become viable financial institutions. It is true that the banks have to face the loss of Rs. 1100 crore because of the reduction in lending rates of between 1 percent and 1.5 percent. This loss can be made good by adopting policies detailed above and not by raising the lending rates or by lowering the deposit rates. Deregulation of interest rates is the right step and it should be followed to its logical end.

# 25

# Imports of Edible Oil are Unnecessary to Stabilise Prices

The object of the on-going economic reforms in India is to reduce the rate of inflation and thus to save the people from its rigours. The rate of inflation at the end of June 1993 was 5.8 percent according to official calculations and the intention of the Government is to bring it down further. It is obvious that in India it is the food prices that govern the general price index and thus the rate of inflation. In the years when there is plentiful food supply food prices fall causing a fall in the rate of inflation even under conditions of burgeoning deficit financing. In the years when there is inadequate food supply the food prices rise causing a rise in the rate of inflation even if the budget is in balance or in surplus. This means that the food prices hold the key to the inflation rate in India. Quite apart from this, when prices are rising the money income of the people being constant the real income falls pushing more and more people below the poverty line. Thus reduction of the inflation rate and poverty alleviation depend crucially on the behaviour of food prices. Seen in this perspective, holding down food prices assumes importance in the strategy of inflation control.

The Public Distribution System and the revamped Public Distribution System and the present controversy about keeping the creamy layer of society off the benefits of the public distribution system are intended to hold the price line and also to help the poor to obtain food supplies at fair prices through the fair price depots. To what extent these fair price deposits are really fair is a moot point. But the system is there in operation and its avowed objective is to make available food articles to the poor and the needy at fair prices.

There are different food articles consumed in different parts of the country: wheat, rice, jowar etc. The consumption of these food articles is area specific. Thus wheat is the staple food in the north while rice is the staple food in the south and jowar is consumed in some parts of south India. But there is an article of consumption which is used throughout the country. This is the edible oil. The price of edible oil is subject to violent gyration the prices falling in the years of excess supply and rising in the years of excess demand and its price is unpredictable. The supply of oil depends crucially on the area under oil seed cultivation and the farm productivity. The latter depends on the farm inputs used in production and this depends on the prices of these inputs. It also depends on rainfall. Even assuming that the rainfall is normal, the supply of oil seeds depends on the price of edible oil. Empirical research has shown that the area of cultivation of any crop depends on the price the farmers obtain for their farm output. If the prices are not remunerative enough, they switch over to other crops which yield higher income. Thus, the farmers are responsible to the price mechanism. Seen in this perspective, the price of edible oil is crucial to the supply of oil seeds and the supply of edible oil. The recent gift-import of edible oil under PL-480 from the United States of America has to be examined from this perspective.

In 1992-93 under the PL-480 agreement India imported 40,000 tonnes of soyabean oil from the United States. In 1993 the Government of India entered into an agreement with the United States for the gift-import of 44,000 tonnes of soyabean oil worth $ 23 million (Rs. 72 crore) under a commodity grant assistance agreement (PL-480). The co-operative sector in India is totally against the recent agreement for the import of soyabean oil. This sector avers that such a development would be in "violent contradiction" of the Government's integrated oil seeds policy. Such an import is compared to the mythical Trojan horse of the Greeks as it would stifle domestic oil seeds production and harm the interests of the oil seeds farmers who, in that event, would not get remunerative prices. This would also compromise the cherished goal of achieving self-sufficiency in the edible oil sector.

These apprehensions of the co-operative sector are unfounded according to the Minister of Civil Supplies who was stoutly defended the free-of-cost import of this commodity. He holds the view that this is part of the Government's avowed strategy to provide price stability and food security to the people. The official sources have asserted that free-gift imports are not the same as direct imports since the grants imply additional income for the country and help to raise the standard of living of the people, which means that there is nothing wrong in accepting the gift of edible oil.

The Minister justifies free imports of oil on the ground that the per capita consumption of edible oil in India is much below the international average of 6.5 kg. And the free import of edible oil will enable the people to consume more oil to maintain their nutritional standards. Besides, the Government would not release imported oil to the market immediately but would retain it as a buffer stock to be used to offset the price rise because of excess demand at a future date. At present the Government has a stock of 40,000 tonnes of edible oil. The gift-import of 44,000 tonnes of edible oil from the United States would raise the buffer stock to 84,000 tonne.

These arguments of the Minister have been contested by the co-operative sector. It is held that the value and significance of the donated oil is marginal. India's domestic consumption of vegetable oil is 64 lakh tonnes. Therefore, the donated oil of the order of 44,000 tonnes represents just 0.8 percent of the requirement. This is inspite of the stipulation of commercial imports of 2.5 lakh tonnes of edible oil, which is tied to the free gift. However, given the fluctuations in edible oil prices in the world market the total quantity of gifted oil is likely to be revised downwards in the event of adverse price fluctuations. Furthermore, the commercial import is to be made only from the United States. This is the string attached to gift-import of oil. There is also the condition of export production limitation by way of open auction. This means that India can export oil only through auction and not directly. The price India gets in the auction is anybody's guess.

This issue has raised a storm of controversy and the controversy needs to be examined in depth.

India has to make commercial import of 2.5 lakh tonnes of edible oil if it is to enjoy the benefit of the gift of 40,000 tonnes of oil. At a time when there is no excess demand for edible oil in the domestic market the commercial import of 2.5 lakh tonnes of oil is bound to depress the domestic oil price much to the disadvantage of the domestic farmer. The market prices are bound to be unremunerative causing a shift of land from oil seed cultivation to other crops. This causes a fall in the domestic production of oil seeds and oil as well. Given an unchanged demand this causes an excess demand, which normally causes a rise in price. But the import of gift oil causes a fall in the price of oil and, in consequence, the farmer will have no incentive to switch back to oil seeds cultivation. In order to steady the price of oil the Government may have to increase the commercial import of oil at considerable expenditure of scarce foreign exchange. In this event the argument that gift import of oil will lead to a saving in foreign exchange loses its validity. Furthermore, the international prices of oil are subject to violent gyrations. If they rise, the Government has to increase its commercial imports at a higher price and, in consequence, there will be a larger outflow of foreign exchange. There is no assurance that the quantity of donated oil will increase or will be held constant at 40,000 tonnes. This quantity will be reduced in the event of a rise in the international price of oil. As a result, the country has to increase its commercial imports of oil at the enhanced price. This will again constitute a further drain on the country's foreign exchange reserves. If the country is free to import oil from the country where it is available at a lower price there is something to be said for gift imports but the country, under the agreement, has to make commercial imports only from the United States. This stipulation works to the disadvantages of India.

The Government of India is committed to pursuing an integrated oil seeds policy. The market intervention operation is an important component of this policy. The Government had, infact, established the market intervention operation (MIO) in edible oil because the free and open market was rife with distortions which were detrimental to the short-run and long-run interest of both consumers are producers. Therefore, the free and open competitive auction is a serious infringement of the Government's prerogative to operate its integrated policy. At a time when there is a drastic fall in the international price of oil the free and open auction entails the sale of oil at the prevailing low price. In this event, the Government cannot, under the agreement, intervene in the market as a buyer in order to prevent the auction price from falling. The farmers, under this scheme, get a low auction price while the domestic consumers because of the auction sale have to put up with reduced domestic supply of oil which will be available at a higher price. Thus, both the producers and the consumers of oil will be adversely affected.

During the past three years there has been a dramatic improvement in the domestic supply of oil seeds and oil. If the Government imports, as it should, under the agreement, 40,000 tonnes of donated oil and 2.5 lakh tonnes of commercial imports, the aggregate imported oil will be nearly 3 lakh tonnes which will be 5.5 percent of total domestic consumption. But India may not need such a large quantity of imported oil in 1993. This is bound to depress the domestic price of oil to the disadvantage of the oil seeds producers. In consequence, there will be a shift of land from oil seeds cultivation to other crops causing a drastic fall in domestic oil supply and making India depend perpetually on imported oil at great expenses of foreign exchange. Furthermore, in the year of a rise in the import price of oil, the domestic price of oil will also rise besides entailing a large outflow of foreign exchange.

The Government holds the view that the imported oil will not be released to the market immediately but would be held as buffer stock to be released only when the market price of oil rises in order to stabilise the oil price. If due to favourable supply conditions the buffer stock remains intact, the Government has to reckon with the cost of storage and the deterioration in the quality of oil. If held in the buffer stock for a long time, the oil may deteriorate in quality and may become unfit for human consumption and if consumed will be injurious to health. If this oil is released in the market in order to avoid the loss due to deterioration in quality, the market price will slump to the disadvantage of the farmers. It is a fair presumption that the buffer stock of oil cannot be held for to long and a time comes when it has to be released on the market even under conditions of satisfactory supply in the domestic market. This will harm the interests of the domestic farmers who, guided as they are by the price mechanism, will switch over to other crops creating conditions of excess demand in the oil market which has to be met by oil imports at higher international prices and by incurring large foreign exchange expenditure.

While the avowed objective of holding the price line is laudable it must be conceded that the price of oil in the consumers budget is only marginal. It is the prices of cereals and pulses that for the most part determine the general price level and the rate of inflation. One can understand the desirability of holding their prices in the attempt to reduce the rate of inflation. But the consumption of edible oil by the poorest among those below the poverty line is insignificant and its price does not contribute significantly to the consumer price index. It is the rich sections of society that use edible oil to prepare delicacies for consumption. In their case also the influence of the prices of edible oil is not much. Therefore, the argument that import of edible oil donated or commercial is necessary to stabilise prices does not carry much weight. Considering the present favourable supply position in the oil market, the import of oil seems to be unnecessary. If anything, these imports will depress the domestic oil prices and involve expenditure of foreign exchange, which is, of course, avoidable. Furthermore, oil imports militate against the Government's integrated oil seeds policy.

As averred earlier, it is the prices of cereals and pulses that are important determinants of the general price level and the rate of inflation. In view of this, it is necessary to stabilise these prices. This can be done by holding buffer stocks of wheat and rice which can be released on the market in the event of excess demand conditions emerging in these markets. But the Government has thought it wise to export wheat on the ground that wheat supplies have increased. The decision to *export* wheat and the simultaneous decision to *import* edible oil gives evidence of *topsy-turvy* economics. Incentives can be given to the farmers to increase the supply of oil seeds and oil. This will obviate the necessity of oil imports donated or commercial and, in fact, enlarge the exportable surplus in the oil sector. It is, therefore, suggested that the agreement to import oil should not be renewed when the present agreement ends. It must be averred that the oil import policy will harm both the consumers and the producers of oil. This delayed critique of oil import policy recommends itself.

# 26

## Technology Parks: A Boon to India

In his 1995-96 budget the Finance Minister advanced the new strategy called the "two-track strategy" that would promote growth with social welfare. The two tracks are not parallel tracks which do not meet but the two tracks interact like the multiplier-accelerate mechanisms. One of the tracks is concerned with investment, production and productivity and the other track is concerned with raising the standard of living of the poor people in the country. The rise in the consumption standards raises the value of the Keynesian multiplier and this, in turn, raises the level of investment through the acceleration mechanism. The interaction between the multiplier and accelerator mechanisms raises the rate of growth of income.

The first track has to do with the poor people who live in the rural sector. Unless their lot is improved, the talk of poverty alleviation sounds hollow. How to improve the lot of the rural poor? The Union Budget for 1995-96 has a whole lot of measures meant to improve their lot. One of them is the establishment of the rural technology parks. Technology and infrastructure have a crucial role to play in developing human resources and raising the standard of living of the people. These ingredients have not so far reached two-thirds of the population living in the rural sector. As part of the strategy to carry forward economic reforms with a "human face", the Prime Minister who is also looking after industry has been laying special emphasis on ensuring that the rural poor have the benefit of science and technology to engage themselves in gainful productive activities contributing to nation building efforts. In the western countries which are small in size and are free from excessive numbers, technology is used as replacement for human labour and to improve the living standards of the people. In countries like India technology can be effectively used to harness the human resources. Views in this context, the Industry Minister's plan to set up about 1000 rural technology parks is an innovative approach to build up village infrastructure to prevent the rural people from migrating to urban centres.

The Nurkse-Lewis model of economic growth envisages the transfer of surplus agricultural labour to the urban centres as a method of capital formation. The assumption here is that the marginal product of labour on the farm is far lower than the wages paid to labour and the transfer of surplus labour from agriculture to urban centres will raise marginal productivity of labour in agriculture. The surplus labour so transferred can be used to foment capital formation and to accelerate growth. This model is good enough but it ignores several problems connected with transfer of surplus labour from agriculture. It has long been realized that the migration of rural people to urban areas in search of employment has led to over congestion and other problems in the urban centres. The Ministry's new plan can go a long way in tackling this problem. The aim of the rural technology park concept is to provide all the necessary infrastructural facilities in the villages. The parks will provide to farmers and to rural craftsmen all the necessary infrastructural facilities in the villages. The parks will provide to farmers and craftsmen facilities like credit, courses for technological upgradation, inputs and tractors under one roof. It is proposed to tap the Rs. 2000 crore sanctioned to the National Bank for Agriculture and Rural Development in the Budget for 1995-96. The scheme will also be financed through the Ministry's own resources and funds from multilateral institutions. Initially, it is decided to develop a few villages on a large scale as specialized pockets. It will be useful to have a product specific approach on turning out products for which inputs are locally available. Among the industries identified for development are leather, bee keeping, hand-made paper, food processing, biotechnology, floriculture and coir.

If these industries are developed on proper lines they can become captive sources for private sector companies and multinational corporations. Big industrial units need to supplement governmental efforts by promoting ancillary industries in rural areas in order to facilitate speedy spread of technology to the grass roots level. These ancillary units can produce goods to meet the needs of the domestic market as well as for exports. It is also time to have a second look at the system of technical education in the country to make it relevant to domestic needs so that proper technical training is available to develop motivated and skilled labour force to build a sound local and national industrial structure. Given proper training and encouragement the rural people who are hard working and intelligent could make a valuable contribution to the growth of the Indian economy through employment generation and poverty alleviation.

The scheme will wean away surplus rural labour from agriculture to the other agro-industrial sectors in the rural area and not to the urban centres as in the Nurkse-Lewis thesis. This will generate employment in the rural sector and raise rural incomes. This, in turn, will have an acceleration effect on investment. The interaction between the multiplier and the accelerator will raise national income and take the economy to the high growth path. The Government wants the rate of economic growth to 10 percent. The rural technology exercise will make the attainment of this goal easy. This will also improve the quality of life in the urban settlements by eradicating slums and squatter settlements which are generating all kinds of diseases by causing environmental degradation. The rural scene will be humming with activity. The interaction between the rural sector and the urban sector will be conducive to a life of elation and prosperity. Seen in this perspective the technology parks in the rural sector will be a boon to the Indian economy. At the same time adequate financial assistance should be provided to these parks.

# 27

## Full Convertibility can Wait

After the Indian rupee was made partially convertible in March 1992, it was made convertible on Trade Account in March 1993. It is now sought to make the rupee fully convertible. The IMF wants the reform process speeded up and it hopes that the Union Budget for 1994-95 will do it in right earnest. The IMF representatives who met the Indian Government officials recently made it clear that the IMF wanted the pace of on-going economic reforms stepped up. The discussions that took place at this meeting will be contained in the Report on India to be submitted to the IMF Board. The report will contain certain prescriptions, for instance the full convertibility of the rupee in conformity with Article 8 of the IMF charter. The IMF informs on all the Member to graduate towards Article 8 statutes. The economic intelligence unit of *The Economist* has stated categorically that full convertibility must come about if not in this year then at least in the next 18 months.

India's foreign exchange reserves at present are $ 11.1 billion. For this reason the Government is confident of making the more towards full convertibility. But before making a "dash to full convertibility" certain ground realities must be considered.

It is held that three conditions are necessary for the success of the full convertibility experiment.

- The minimum balance of foreign exchange reserves must be $ 25 billion.
- Export income should comprise at least 80% of the foreign exchange earnings.
- The rate of inflation must be not more than 6%.

But more of these conditions are fulfilled at present. A large part of the foreign exchange reserves of $ 11.1 billion are the foreign investors funds invested in the equities of Indian companies. These funds are subject to recall by the honour. There are also direct foreign investment funds and stakes of multinational firms in their Indian subsidiaries. It is only the export earnings that can provide strength and stability to the foreign exchange position. Unless exports earnings picked up and their components in the foreign exchange reserves improves significantly it would be unsafe to resort to full convertibility.

At present India's external debt is $ 85 billion. Besides defence imports and imports of essential goods and capital equipment have to be financed. There is also need for the Reserve Bank of India to ensure the stability of the rupee as against the US dollar. But at present the Reserve Bank is bringing dollars to keep the value of the rupee stable. It should therefore be in a position to pump in $ 5 billion at one go to check violent fluctuations. This means that the Reserve Bank of India will be able to manage the fully convertible rupee if it is in possession of $ 20 - $ 25 billion.

Quite apart from this the financial sector reforms must be undertaken before the rupee is made fully convertible. At present interest rates are administered by the Reserve Bank of India. But interest rates should be allowed to be market-determined as a precondition to the full convertibility experiment. In the countries of the West deregulation of the interest rate structure preceded full convertibility. Furthermore, there is also need to ensure the efficient use of credit and to eliminate bad debts in the Banking sector.

At present the rate of inflation in India is 8.5% and this is higher than that in most countries. The in-flow of foreign funds has added to domestic liquidity which is fueling the price rise. If the rate of inflation is not brought down Indian exports will be uncompetitive in world markets and they will be priced out, with a further inflow of foreign funds the rupee will become strong and a strong rupee adversely affected export promotion efforts. There is no guarantee that the rate of inflation will remain at 8.5%. The recent hikes in the price of sugar, wheat, rice, LPG cylinders and the expected hike in the passenger and freight rates which will have a cascading effects, on the price level and likely to take the rate of inflation to the double digit zone. This will adversely affect the India's export prospects. These adverse circumstances must be taken into account before embarking on the full convertibility experiment.

If per chance the Finance Minister ventures to make the rupee fully convertible several issues relating to the IMF will arise. They are:

- Bilateral arrangements not based on the market rate of exchange such as those with Russia;
- Payment of discriminatory rates of interest on NRI deposits.

Discriminatory interest rates paid to NRIs are indefensible. If they are able to be paid at all they must be paid to the other depositors also. Further the IMF is critical of India's bilateral relations with the former Soviet Union. It would like to know how India is going to pay back their exchange for projects that have been agreed on already. In the financial market payments are always made in terms of the market rates of exchange. If this is done it is Russia that owes money to India and not the other way about. But India can argue that India's bilateral and diplomatic relations would operate in the case of Heavy Engineering Corporation (HEC) in Ranchi paid for by Russia.

In view of the foregoing there is need to exercise caution and circumspection in the matter of rendering the rupee fully convertible right now. At present fiscal deficit and the rate of inflation are high. In 1985 India's foreign exchange reserves where $ 10 billion is real terms they were higher than the present $ 11.1 billion. The fiscal deficit then was 5.8% of GDP lower than at present. The improvement in the trade balance in the fiscal 1993-94 is due to a decline in imports reflecting recession in the industrial sector and to low price of petroleum in world market.

In view of the foregoing it is the task of economic statesmanship not to be in a hurry to make the rupee fully convertible unless the essential pre-requisites for the success of the full convertibility experience are established it should not be attempted in a spirit of our confidence.

# 28

## The Busy Season Credit Policy

Recessionary conditions have been in existence in the Indian industry for several years. Despite remedial measures adopted by the Government of India recession has remained impervious. In the attempt to remedy this situation the Reserve Bank of India has adopted a new credit policy. How deep is the recession and how far the new credit policy will be successful in remedying it?

It was earlier expected that 1993-94 would witness a revival of industrial growth. But now this expectation appears to be impossible of realization. According to the latest projection made by the Reserve Bank of India in its Annual Report for 1992-93 is that industrial output would grow at about 4 percent during the second half of the financial year 1993-94. Even if the forecast turns out to be correct it will mean very little in real terms at the end of the period. Industrial output declined in 1991-92 and in 1992-93 it registered a small increase. But industrial output at the end of 1993-94 will not be able to catch up with that in 1991-92. In fact, the performance of the industrial sector during June-September 1992 is a cause for concern according to a study by the National Council of Applied Economic Research. This directive in industrial output cannot be attributed to inadequate infrastructural support. The output in the coal and power sectors is better than it was in 1992-93. Even so, the steel and fertilizer industries have not been able to reach their targets. Even a good monsoon has not been able to help the Railways to increase its revenue earning freight traffic. Therefore, it must be concluded that the slow response of the industrial sector is due not so much to supply constraints as to inadequate demand. The steep decline in Government's investment expenditure is believed to be one of the reasons for this. Sensing this the Reserve Bank of India in its Annual Report which suggests that public investment needs to be stepped up to stimulate demand. Though good harvests are assumed to increase the purchasing power in the hands of the farmers who spend it to finance their new demand for industrial output. But good harvests are not enough to stimulate demand to the required degree. Despite a succession of good harvests during the past 6 years there prevails a critical gap between the aggregate demand of the farm sector and what the industrial sector needs to keep its wheels going. In fact, the farm sector itself is in a state of recession with surpluses accumulating because of the inadequate rise in the incomes of the other sectors which are the consumers of farm products. The warehouses of the Government are holding unsold stocks. The Government stock holding of food grains in September 1993 was more by 9 million tonnes than the 25 million tonnes it held in September 1992. There is talk of stepping up farm exports but the increase in exports is in respect of processed foods and marine products and, in consequence, large surpluses are likely to remain in consequence of inadequate demand.

The Union Budget for 1993-94 gave several incentives to industry. Even so, the recession in this sector is deepening. The rate of industrial growth is low even when compared with that in 1992-93. The Reserve Bank of India made major announcements in the interest rate front a few weeks ago; the industrial sector looked for further reductions in interest rates and further concessions from the banking sector as it saw cheap credit as a way to come out of the industrial recession. However, the banking circles were of the view that further reductions in interest rates would not be possible as the rate of inflation had shown an upward trend. As the Reserve Bank had announced that SLR and CRR would be reduced to 25 percent and 10 percent respectively within a period of three years, the banking industry expected further reductions in these two ratios.

The uncertainty that surrounded the credit policy environment was directly linked to the financial sector reforms currently underway. Despite the banks being flush with funds as a result of the gradual reduction in the SLR and CRR, the credit-deposit ratio of several banks has declined in the recent period. Banks attribute this trend to the drastic erosion of profitability due to the new provisioning norms and the severe strain on the capital base as a result of the new norms about capital adequacy. The new provisioning norms which require the banks to classify the assets into performing and non-performing have resulted in greater transparency in the balance sheets. It is true that the Government announced a capital contribution to the banks of the order of Rs.5700 crore by July 1993 in order to strengthen their capital base. But the promised transfer of funds is yet to take place. In this situation the banks could go to the capital market to borrow in order to strengthen their capital base, but they are faced with legislative hurdles. The Government has to amend the Banking Regulations Act to allow the banks to enter the capital market. But there are several stumbling blocks and the Government is yet to take a decision in the matter. Even the bank debt recovery tribunals are yet to be set up. These factors have made the banks very cautious over their lending practices. But the banks say that there is no restriction of credit. The banks are meeting the credit targets of the export sector and the priority sectors and they are not going in search of new clients. It is alleged that the demand for credit is slow to pick up due to recession. The banks prefer to invest their funds in risk free ventures. They, therefore, have begun to invest their funds in Government treasury bills. The completion of the banks has changed from lending banks to investment banks. The banking circles hold the view that this is only a temporary phase. As soon as industry emerges from the recession and the capital base of the banks is strengthened, a more clear-cut policy will emerge. The period of recovery is put at 4-5 months. As it is, the banks are faced with uncertainty and as soon as this uncertain environment is cleared, banks will resume their credit policy to help the industrial sector. At the same time the rate of inflation which had fallen to 5.4 percent has, in the middle of October 1993, risen to 7.4 percent and is likely to resume its upward trend. This is a case of stagflation.

Recognizing the need to put industry on a higher growth path through liberal credit policy, holding the rein on the rate of inflation at the same time, the Governor, Reserve Bank of India announced the busy season credit policy reducing the SLR by 2.5% thus releasing around Rs. 4150 crore for the banking sector as lending resources. As in the recent past the credit-deposit ratio of several banks had declined this is a welcome initiative as far as industry is concerned. Two aspects of this development are worth considering: (a) bankers have pointed out that the slow down in credit supply is related to several issues like the financial sector reform, industry's dependence on the capital market and even the demand for credit. These issues were highlighted by the governor of the Reserve Bank of India; (b) the second aspect relates to the assumption underlying credit policy: that a higher volume of credit will lead to industrial recovery. While the industrial sector's need for credit cannot be denied, its poor performance cannot be attributed to the slow down in credit supply. There are those who dismiss the banking sector's argument that it was the poor demand for credit from the industrial sector that led to the slow down in bank credit extension. This may be dubbed as an one sided view. Even so, it can still be maintained that industry's dependence on resources outside the banking sector was increasing during this period. This means that the slow down in credit supply was not due to poor demand for credit from the industrial sector. What is forgotten in this controversy is the demand squeeze. Ever since 1990, there has been a steady increase in the prices of essential commodities especially after the economic reforms were initiated in July 1991. The drastic erosion of purchasing power especially in the rural sector as a result of the price rise is a critical factor affecting industrial growth. Another factor is the phenomenon of exchange rate fluctuations in recent years which led to an increase in the prices of imported raw materials and equipment and generated recessionary trends.

On Monday October 11, 1993 the Reserve Bank of India announced the busy season credit policy and, as part of this policy, it released an additional Rs. 3050 crore as lendable resources in a bid spur investment and industrial production. It slashed the Statutory Liquidity Ratio (SLR) by two percentage points to 34.75. This is in addition to the Rs. 1100 crore released by the Reserve Bank of India in the month of April 1993. While the Reserve Bank reduced the SLR on net demand and time liabilities (excluding external liabilities) from 36.75 percent to 34.75 percent, the incremental SLR has been slashed from 30 percent to 25 percent with effect from October 16. This reduction of SLR is part of the financial sector reforms as recommended by the Narasimham Committee on financial sector reform. This measure is expected to improve the liquidity and profitability of commercial banks. The Reserve Bank also announced changes in consortium lending arrangements, commercial paper and lending norms to give greater autonomy to banks and increased access to borrowing apart from introduction of new pre-shipment export credit facility in foreign currencies and changes in the composition of priority sector lending. The threshold limit for obligatory consortium arrangement has been raised from Rs. 5 crore to Rs. 50 crore bringing down large borrowal accounts from 934 to 76. "Borrowers will be free to induct new banks into a consortium. The banks will also have the freedom to leave the consortium after a minimum period of two years from the date of the bank joining a consortium" said Shri C. Rangarajan, Governor of the Reserve Bank of India.

The Reserve Bank introduced a new pre-shipment export credit in foreign currencies which would be available to exporters for financing domestic inputs of goods exported. This scheme would provide credit to Indian exporters at internationally competitive rates of interest. The base year for the existing two-tier export credit (rupee) refinance formula would be brought forward by one year. Under the refinance facility against post-shipment credit denominated in US dollars, banks would be eligible for export credit refinance limits equivalent to 90 percent of such outstanding export credit provided by banks as against the earlier 100 percent. As a result of certain changes in the export credit refinance, the rupee export refinance limits of banks would be reduced by Rs. 1970 crore and the dollar denominated limits by Rs. 500 crore. The Reserve Bank Governor added: "..... The change in the dollar-denominated refinance facility will encourage the new scheme of rediscounting export bills abroad and the overall credit available to the export sector will increase."

The Governor of the Reserve Bank also announced changes in the composition of priority sector lending. Under the overall stipulation of priority sector lending of 40 percent of the net bank credit and 18 percent sub-target for agriculture, direct and indirect categories for advances to agriculture have been clubbed.

As the Government has redefined small-scale industry with the investment in plant and machinery up to Rs. 60 lakh (Rs. 75 lakh in the case of ancillary units and EOUs), the Reserve Bank has decided that all advances granted by the banks to the SSIs as per the revised definition of the Government would be treated as priority sector advances. It is also decided that 40 percent of the total credit to SSIs by each bank should be to the cottage industries, Khadi. and village industries, artisans and tiny industries with investment in plant and machinery up to Rs. 5 lakh and other units availing credit limits upto Rs. 5 lakh.

In order to support the rabi operations, the Reserve Bank has raised the general line of credit to the National Bank for Agriculture and Rural Development (NABARD) by Rs. 400 crore to Rs. 3700 crore. Bank advances against wheat, cotton/Kapas to all borrowers have been exempted from selective credit controls. The Reserve Bank also raised the ceiling for investment by banks in bonds/ debentures of PSUs from 1.5 percent to 5 percent of incremental deposits. Companies would be allowed to issue commercial papers for maturities between three months and less than a year. The bank-wise limits for issue of certificate of deposits (CDS) have also been withdrawn. The Governor of the Reserve Bank said:

"While observing prudential norms, a slow down of lending by banks would be inappropriate. Banks should meet the genuine and feet requirements of borrowers and the hesitancy of banks in taking credit decisions in the aftermath of the securities irregularities needs to be overcome".

The Reserve Bank Governor who was concerned about the slow-down of credit supply he said that normally of operations was long over due and asked the banks to ensure that the delegated credit sanctioning powers were duly exercised. He also asked the banks to process the pending proposals for new loans as also renewals within three months. In doing so the Reserve Bank Governor has greatly helped the Government to maintain macroeconomic stability. The Finance Minister aims at achieving fiscal consolidation meant to reduce the rate of inflation. The Reserve Bank Governor aims at remedying industrial recession, which has impeded the rate of economic growth. The two instruments of policy are meant to promote non-inflationary growth.

The industrial sector has by and large, hailed the new credit policy though it is unhappy about the decision not to reduce the interest rate structure. While some industrial organizations have hailed it as "pragmatic and flexible", others seem to be disappointed that the lending rates are not reduced by 2-3 percent so as to enable them to cut the production costs to help face stiff international competition. Some others feel that the reduction of the SLR by 2.5 percent is inadequate. They feel that the primary liquidity ratio needed to be reduced further for a level playing field. Thus the new credit policy has generated mixed reactions.

The Reserve Bank's policy gives a clear signal to the bankers to take appropriate decisions to meet the genuine needs of industry, especially agriculture, small scale industrial sector and the export sector. This is evidently a continuation, with certain marginal modifications, of the objectives of bank nationalization. The bank nationalization scheme envisaged priority sector lending at concessional interest rates. The above three sectors constituted the priority sector. The banks were asked to earmark 40 percent of their resources to this sector. The banks continued to lend to the priority sector. Agriculture is the backbone of the Indian economy. It supplies food for the growing population, raw materials for industry and for export. Of these, food supply is important. In India it is the food prices that govern the general price index and the rate of inflation. In years of plentiful food supply, the food prices fall and with them the rate of inflation fails. If food supply falls, the food prices rise exacerbating inflation. In order to contain it, the country has to import food to make up the domestic shortfall and spend its scarce foreign exchange reserves or else to borrow from the multilateral financing agencies. This adds to the debt burden.

In order to avoid these complications the policy should aim at ensuring adequate food supply. Furthermore, the present trade policy aims at increasing agricultural exports. These are possible if agriculture is prosperous. In order to ensure this supply of credit to agriculture at a concessional interest rate is necessary.

The small scale industrial sector has been making significant contributions to exports and to employment generation. In fact the small scale industries are an important foreign exchange earner. Furthermore, it contributes to employment generation and mitigates the problem of unemployment to a great extent. The small scale industries can be set up in the rural sector especially to undertake production by making use of the locally available raw materials and locally available manpower. Considering the great export potential and employment potential of the small scale industrial sector, the scheme of making more funds available to this sector is well conceived.

In the context of the continuing balance of payments deficits which have necessitated resort to external borrowing stimulation of exports is inevitable. Despite devaluation of the rupee in July 1991, partial convertibility of the rupee in 1992 and full convertibility of the rupee in 1993 rendering exports cheaper, exports are not picking up to the expected degree. Under the policy of trade liberalization imports flow in unimpeded. Thus while imports flow in large quantity, exports do not rise to the requisite degree. As import liberalization is a policy matter, imports cannot be reduced. In fact due to the cuts in customs duties in the Union Budget for 1993-94 imports have begun to flow in beyond all expectations. In this situation the stimulation of exports is the only solution to the balance of payments problem. Making adequate finance available to the exporters to increase exports was well conceived. The introduction of the new pre-shipment export credit facility in foreign currencies incorporated in the new credit policy, is a step in the right direction. The new credit policy has to be assessed in the context of the important attached to the development of the priority sectors.

The busy season credit policy is a reflection of the concern of the Government about the stagnation in industrial growth. The consortium lending norms are less restrictive than before. This, coupled with the increase in the threshold limit for obligatory consortium arrangement from Rs. 5 crore to Rs. 50 crore will allow greater flexibility to banks in working out lines of credit for the industrial sector. Furthermore, the greater degree of freedom allowed to banks on working capital and inventory requirement will enable the banks to sort out many of the major procedural problems faced by them in financing industries. The industry is understandable appreciative of the new measure. However, an undercurrent of dissatisfaction is evident from the fact that the policy falls short of some of the measures that were expected. In particular the industrial sector is not happy about the maintenance of the interest rate structure as it is. Interest rates were reduced a little while ago and a further reduction was considered unnecessary and improper given the inflationary situation prevailing in the economy. The Reserve Bank Governor has made it clear that he has several problems to keep his eye on. The Reserve Bank credit to the Government is on the increase creating a condition of excess liquidity generating inflation. Though the net increase in Reserve Bank Credit to the Government is a couple of thousand crore less than the budgetary deficit due to the introduction of short-term treasury hills, the increase in Reserve Bank credit—another name for just printing of notes—has been phenomenal. This has already fuelled 50 percent increase in the growth of reserve money due to the monetisation of the deficit. There is normally a time-lag of five to six months between the increase in money supply and its impact on prices. Unless immediate action was taken the inflation rate of 7.4 percent might turn out to be purely temporary and there was the danger of the inflation rate reaching the double-digit figure before long. It is obvious that increased Government borrowing is an important reason for the high growth in money supply during the year of 2 percent more than the targeted money supply of 12 percent. This scenario prevented the Reserve Bank of India from being more liberal in its credit policy which would have had the effect of increasing the liquidity in the banking system as it would hold out the threat of fuelling the fires of inflation. Faced with this threat of an upsurge in the rate of inflation the Reserve Bank of India had to confine itself to a few administrative measures to increase the availability of credit. Despite the reduction of the SLR from 37.25 percent to 34.75 percent which is expected to release Rs. 4150 crore of commercial bank funds the Reserve Bank's projection that the rate of industrial growth will increase by about 4 percent during the second half of 1993-94 is a cause for concern. In the wake of the securities scam the banks became excessively cautious in their lending policy. But the Reserve Bank which has asked the bank managements to ensure that their sanctioning powers are duly exercised has sought to change the atmosphere of excessive caution in the matter of sanctioning loans to industry. The banks have also been directed to clear all pending applications for loans and renewals within three months. The banking operations are even now hidden from public view. The new credit policy has to do something to end this atmosphere of secrecy and to introduce some degree of transparency into the banking operations.

At present, there is imbalance between the high growth of agriculture as evidenced by the large accumulation of food grains stocks generated by bumper crop and low growth of industry. To tackle this imbalance the Government has resorted to deficit financing to make up the lagging of import duties behind target and the stagnation in excise duty collections. The monetary demand boost to industrial production cannot be pursued for long. After the completion of elections, deficit financing will have to be cut down. The Government is committed to meeting the IMF target of fiscal correction for 1993-94 as close as possible. But rolling back deficit financing is not a simple matter of squeezing public investment. If this is done, it is bound to recoil on the Government in the shape of stagnating tax revenues. Therefore, a substantial part of the massive credit the Government has tapped from the Reserve Bank of India will have to be converted into dated securities which are already in excess supply. People are not prepared to buy them unless the return exceeds the prevailing 13.5 percent. If coupon rates on Government loans are hiked, banks will demand correspondingly higher rates of interest on lending to the commercial sector. Therefore, it cannot be assumed that reform means cheap credit to the private sector. As there are limits to raising the coupon rates, not all the Reserve Bank credit to Government will be converted into dated securities. The non-convertible deficit will add to money supply and raise prices in the short run. In this event nominal interests will rise but if these rates are discounted for inflation, they will be lower in real terms.

As it is, the inflation rate is rising. In the middle of October 1993 it stood at 7.4 percent. But once the current harvests are in and the deficit spending is rolled back in the last quarter of the current fiscal year, inflation will be subdued and, therefore, too much should not be made of the creeping rise in the annualized rate of inflation of the present 7.4 percent. In this situation fiscal deficit reduction is necessary to control and hold down the rate of inflation. Monetary policy should be used to remedy recession and not add to inflation.

A segment of the industrial sector demands a reduction of the interest rate to cut the production costs and to help industry to face stiff international competition. It must be remembered that Production costs are not a matter of interest cost alone. They are a matter of labour and capital productivity, managerial efficiency and economy in other items of expenditure. A reduction in the rates of interest in the context of low productivity of factors, managerial inefficiency and rising non-interest rate costs will not help to cut production costs and to promote competitive efficiency.

Interest rate has two effects: cost effect and liquidity effect. In a situation where the demand for loanable funds is interest-inelastic a reduction of interest rate will not stimulate borrowing and spending. In this situation a low interest may not be a remedy for recession. In accordance with the Roose Effect, a fall in interest rate will have a liquidity effect. It raises the prices of securities and, in the absence of elastic expectations of interest rate decline, gives an incentive to bond holders to sell their bonds for cash which can be used for spending on consumption and investment activity in general. The liquidity effect is exercised by the reduction in the SLR by 2.5 percent despite the constancy of interest rates. The reduction of SLR releases Rs. 4,150 crore of funds to the banks for purposes of lending. The liquidity effect to be generated by the reduction in interest rate is generated by the reduction in SLR. At a time when the need of the hour is to reduce the rate of inflation, the reduction of interest rate will generate a liquidity effect. If this liquidity effect is added on to the liquidity effect of a cut in SLR the two jointly may exacerbate inflation while their combined effect on recession may over reach the mark. The reduction of SLR will help to remedy recession without exacerbating inflation. It is held in certain quarters in the industrial sector that the present cut in SLR would not bring in sufficient funds to meet the needs of hungry borrowers. If the Reserve Bank is convinced of the veracity of this argument, it can reduce the SLR by another 1.0 percent or so. This is different from asking for a cut in the interest rates. A cut in lending rates necessitates a cut in the deposit rates. But this exercise causes a fall in bank deposits and this adversely affects bank lending. It is apprehended that while the cut in SLR releases Rs. 4,150 crore to the banks, the funds may not reach the needy, medium and small borrowers if its distribution is not spread equitably over all the sectors. This apprehension can be allayed by taking special measures to allocate the funds equitably. It can, therefore, be said that the new credit policy in the context of ongoing inflation is well conceived.

The Reserve Bank Governor on October 23, 1993 ruled out a further cut in the lending rate of commercial banks as it would have an adverse effect on deposits. He stated that if the lending rates are reduced the deposit rates would have to be reduced and this is impossible. He observed that the interest rate structure had been simplified to enable the banks to reflect a true account in their balance sheets by introducing recognition norms. He said that non-performing assets and accruing assets were not to be included for this purpose with the result the banking operations had been rendered more transparent. As the banks clamour for a further increase in lendable resources, the efforts would be made to increase lendable resources and therefore the cash Reserve Ratio would be reduced by one percent to enable the banks to lend a larger amount of credit to the commercial sector. This weakens the case for a reduction in interest rates further.

The credit policy aims at remedying recession without stocking the fires of inflation. While announcing the credit policy the Reserve Bank Governor made it clear that "While observing prudential norms, a slowdown of lending by banks would be inappropriate. Asking the banks to process the proposals without delay he stated that all genuine demands of borrowers must be met. In line with this statement, the banking sources rule out the possibility of a drastic change in the pattern of credit in the immediate future. Banks would continue to look for safe investment channels and in this context, the raising of the ceiling on investment in Public Sector bonds assumes significance. These bonds and treasury bills will, of course, continue to be attractive for some more time. On the other hand the larger volume of loanable funds and the larger volume of consortium lending that is now allowed will benefit the industrial sector in the long run, that is when the banking sector finalises its lending strategy. Anybody who takes an integrated perception of the Indian macroeconomic scene has a word of praise, even admiration, for the ingenuity displayed by the Governor of the Reserve Bank of India. Monetary and credit policy is an important segment of macroeconomic policy. Given the need for maintaining macroeconomic stability the present credit policy is commendable. It satisfies the norms of the "Policy mix".

# 29

# Moody's Upgradation of India's Credit Rating

There are several credit rating agencies: Moody's Standard and Poor's and Japanese Bond Research Institute are important among them. They rate the creditworthiness of borrowing countries and enable the financial institutions to decide on investment in these countries. If the credit rating is downgraded the lending institutions, concerned as they are about the safety and security of their investment are either reluctant to lend or hesitate to lend or decide not to lend. Even when they lend the amount so lent will be modest and the interest they charge is low. If, on the other hand, the credit rating is upgraded the lending institutions are more than willing to lend, and they lend large sums at low interest rate. In this manner, they are of great assistance to the lending institutions and agencies. Several factors are taken into account in rating the creditworthiness of the borrowing countries: their solvency, the fiscal deficit, balance of payments situation, repaying capacity of the borrowing countries and their previous record of repayment. In the Indian case the Moody's and JBRI have taken all these factors into account in upgrading India. In what follows these variables are assessed.

## THE STATE OF FISCAL DEFICIT

The fiscal deficit which was 8.5 percent of GDP in 1990-91 has been brought down in the following two years. But in the third year it slipped badly. As against the target of 4.7 percent of GDP it rose to 7.3 percent in 1993-94. For the year 1994-95 the Finance Minister set a target of 6 percent of GDP. The fiscal deficit appears to elude the grasp of the Finance Minister again. There has been a considerable increase in subsidies. According to sources in the Finance Ministry subsidies on account of sugar imports and fertilizers would be considerable in 1994-95. Added to this is the high interest burden on the carry forward stocks of food grains. The GDP for 1994-95 is estimated to be Rs. 9,00,000 crore. With annual inflation rate of around 10 percent against 8.4 percent last year the GDP at current prices should be up by Rs. 15,000 crore. The larger GDP in money terms makes the task of limiting fiscal deficit to the targeted level easier.

Because of inflation the revenue receipts will be larger. Excise duty and sales tax are collected ad valorem. This accounts partly for revenue buoyancy this year. The total revenue collections from customs and central excise during April-October 1994 have been placed at Rs. 34,024 crore. This is 17.96 increase over the revenue collections during the corresponding period of 1993. Further more, the rising import demand has boosted customs revenue during this period to Rs. 13,882-26 crore. This is up by 16.91 percent from the collections during April-October 1993. Since May 1994 industrial production has been on the rise. The rise is of the order of 8-9 percent. This generates higher excise revenue. Central excise collections during April-October 1994 stood at Rs. 20,141 crore registering a 18.68 percent increase.

The Government's efforts to rationalize the tax system and rely more on voluntary compliance *a 1a* Laffer Curve Analysis have paid off in the form of a 50 percent increase in direct tax collections in the first half of the 1994-95 fiscal year. According to figures available up to September 22, 1994 fiscal year. According to figures available up to September 22, 1994 from April of this year total tax collections amounted to Rs. 8394.50 crore compared to Rs. 5605.29 crore in the corresponding period of the fiscal 1993-94 year. A particularly noteworthy feature was that corporation tax registered a quantum jump of 78 percent during the period to touch Rs. 4524.41 crore compared to Rs. 2535.95 crore in the corresponding period of April 1 to September 22, 1993. This also reflects the fact that recessionary forces in the industrial sector have slackened. It is quite likely that with further instalments of advance tax flowing in collections on the direct tax front would pick up. The chances are that the ambitious target of Rs. 26,090 crore of tax collection through direct taxes this year might well be achieved if not exceeded. These developments on the revenue front hold out the hope that the fiscal deficit will not exceed the target.

In the year 1993-94 there was a slippage in the gross fiscal deficit. Even so, there has been an important development in that the monetisation of the Budget deficit has been moderated. In 1994-95 there has been a fundamental reform was announced in the Budget under which the automatic monetisation of the Budget deficit through the issue of *adhoc* Treasury Bills will be phased out over a period of three years and from 1997-98 this instrument would be totally abolished. For 1994-95 the creation of adhoc Treasury bills is scheduled to be restricted to Rs. 6,000 crore by the end of the year and it is stated that it will not be allowed to exceed Rs. 9,000 crore for more than ten consecutive days. Against this self-imposed constraint in the current fiscal year up to September 9, 1994 there was an absolute decline in adhocs by Rs. 7,379 crore against the large increase of Rs. 13,865 crore during the corresponding period in 1993-94. Further more, during the first 24 weeks of 1994-95 there was an increase in adhocs over the March 31, 1994 level in only six weeks and in most of these weeks the increase was only nominal. Thus, the sharp reduction in adhocs upto September 9, 1994 is reflective of an enduring trend during 1994-95. Furthermore, even if one takes into account the large above-the-line market borrowing in the current year the overall financing has been significantly smaller. While it might appear to early to draw any definite conclusions what is redeeming is the formal acceptance of the commitment by the government that the phenomenon of automatic monetisation of the Budget deficit would soon be a thing of the past. But fiscal deficit still continues to be a problem but given the buoyancy of revenues, there is no problem in containing the fiscal deficit to the targeted limited.

## THE STATE OF BALANCE OF PAYMENTS

Even on the balance of payments front there is no cause for concern. There is satisfaction over the 12 percent growth in exports during the first six months of 1994-95 while the target for the year is set at 15 percent growth. Imports, on the other hand, recorded a growth of 19.1 percent signifying a pick up in industrial activity at present and there is a distinct possibility of further acceleration of imports. The commerce Minister is confident that the trade deficit during the current financial year will be contained to the level of about \$ 2.5 billion notwithstanding the sharp rise in imports.

Resurgence of industrial activity needs more imports and the build up of foreign exchange reserves in the country would help to meet the growing import demand. During the first six months of the current financial year, the country's exports were placed at about 11.62 billion while imports registered a faster growth rate to touch \$ 12.85 billion leaving a trade gap of \$ 1.23 billion. Imports had recorded a depressed growth of 6.1 percent during 1993-94 in sharp contrast to the 19.6 percent growth of exports which brought down the trade gap to \$ 1.4 billion from the level of \$ 3.3 billion in 1993-94. Imports of petroleum, oil and lubricants during the first six months of 1994-95 came down to \$ 26 billion from \$ 3.04 billion in the corresponding period of 1993-94 reflecting relatively sharp crude prices abroad though domestic consumption of energy remained strong.

As a result of the measures taken since 1991 India's exports registered a modest increase of 3.8 percent in dollar terms during 1992-93 as against negative growth in the preceding year. During 1993-94 export-growth was consolidated and exports reached a level of about \$ 22.2 billion recording a growth of 20.4 percent over 1992-93 performance and exceeded the target. This was achieved despite the fall in exports to the former Soviet Union from \$ 1.6 billion during 1991-92 to \$ 0.7 billion during 1993-94.

The trade deficit is not a cause of any serious concern at least in the short-run. With foreign exchange reserves touching \$ 20 billion and expected to touch \$ 25 billion at the end of the fiscal 1994-95 year and with the latter's implications for money supply and inflation, greater imports are certainly welcome. But the difference between the import and export growth rates is leading to a widening trade deficit. The Commerce Ministry is not altogether happy about this situation. They are perhaps reminded of the second half of the 1980s when similarly widening trade deficit led eventually to a balance of payments crisis. With debt-servicing likely to peak in 1996, with a significant portion of the foreign exchange reserves composed of volatile portfolio investments, and with FDI not picking up adequately, the Commerce Minister appears to be worried that unless exports increase commensurately with imports, India would be in trouble again. There is some legitimacy in this concern. The Commerce Ministry has suggested a number of measures whereby exports can be increased much further.

The economic reforms initiated in July 1991 brought about fundamental changes in the functioning of the foreign trade sector. The changes in the trade, industrial and foreign investment policies combined with the reform of the exchange rate system eased the balance of payments constraint on the economy. The two-step devaluation in July 1991, the move to a dual exchange rate system in March 1992, the unification of the exchange rate in March 1993 and the steps towards current account convertibility in 1994 and completed in August 1994 all brought about an appropriate pricing of foreign exchange while the trade policy reforms reversed the earlier policy which had an implicit bias against exports. All these have established and reinforced the credibility of economic reforms. With changes in policies relating to capital flows, inflows through foreign institutional investors and Euro-issues have become substantial improvements in exports under the impact of new policy measures it would not be surprising if there is a significant improvement in the balance of payments in 1994-95.

## THE STATE OF EXTERNAL DEBT

All is not well with India's foreign debt profile. In its Annual Report accompanying the 1992-93 World Debt Tables (WDT), the World Bank acknowledged the existence of a debt crisis in India even though India had become a problem debtor country much earlier in terms of the criteria set by the Bank to identify problem-debtors. The debt crisis was, however, put in perspective by the

Government of India itself in its Status Report on External debt published in 1991. After a large increase in 1990-91, the rate of growth of external debt decreased in 1991-92 and in 1992-93 also. But the magnitude of the debt was still large. At the end of 1990 the debt stock was $ 69 billion. This went up to $ 71.5 billion in 1991 and by 1992 end it increased to $ 77 billion. At the end of 1993-94 it had swelled to $ 90 billion. These figures indicate that India has been accumulating foreign debt since the launching of the structural adjustment programme at a rate faster than even that recorded by the South Asian region as a whole. At present India is the third largest debtor among developing countries. Unlike some other large debtors India's debt service has remained at a level which has not been difficult for it to manage. The liquidity crisis of 1991 was actually over blown. The composition of India's external debt has been favourable. At the end of 1991 over 90 percent of India's debt was a long-term debt and concessional loans still constitute more than 40 percent of the total debt stock. India reached the threshold of crisis in 1991 and it was forced to seek IMF support to prevent the lines of credit flows totally drying up. India's debt servicing ratios have become worse after the initiation of the economic reforms in July 1991. In 1994 the debt service ratio was well over 31 percent, and the total debt-stock to export ratio was over 300 percent. The debt-GDP ratio also increased considerably over the 1991 level.

This gives rise to the fear that the debt crisis would get accentuated in the coming years. Of the external debt more than a third or about $ 25 billion is due to be repaid in the next four years. This would put severe pressure on the country. As per the RBI estimates the total repayment of principal and interest in 1995-96 will be as high as $ 10 billion. The rising debt still poses a problem.

## INFLATION CAN BE MANAGED SOON

The rate of inflation in July 1991 when the economic reforms were initiated by the Narasimha Rao Government was 17.5 percent. This was, of course, unduly excessive. Thanks to the competent macroeconomic management by the Finance Minister it came down successively to 7 percent. But of late it has begun to rise and at present it stands a 9.69 percent. It must be admitted that the inflation rate is rising erratically, then falling and rising again. The Finance Minister has assured the nation that before the start of the fiscal year 1995-96 it will come down to 7 percent or even below. The present rate of inflation is purely due to political factors and it has no relation to the economic reforms programme. However it can safely be predicted that better days are ahead.

## CREDIT RATING BY MOODY'S AND JBRI

There are several credit rating agencies in the United States and in Japan. Keeping in view the nature of the macroeconomic management of the economy and the ability of the countries to avoid or to face the Liquidity crisis they rate the countries, which want to borrow in the international financial markets. In 1990 standard and Poor's and Moody's announced their decision to downgrade India. The one important reason for them to do so was their perception of the "political risk" at the time. The rating agencies were convinced that the fluidity of Indian politics at the time and the gathering storm of communal and caste conflict would leave the Government battered and incapable of taking the decisions required to manage a liquidity crisis. Even now Standard and Poor's has withheld an upgradation on the grounds that the fiscal health of the Government and the structure of the balance of payments do not as yet warrant an upgradation.

However Moody's and the Japanese Bond Research Institute have favoured upgradation of India's credit rating without bothering to know how the results of the Assembly elections in South India will affect economic policy in the country. There is the emergence of a gradual consensus on the policy of economic liberalization underway in India. However, on fiscal consolidation there is, as yet no consensus. It is true that political pressure in favour of increased public expenditure both on subsidies and investment is growing and is irresistible. The Government cannot afford to ignore these pressures and will have to turn to larger resource mobilization to meet these demands. Having faith in India's ability to mobilize resources adequately the credit rating agencies have upgraded India even before the results of the State Assembly elections were announced.

In the winter of 1990 these rating agencies had placed the Indian debtors on the "credit watch" and in 1991 downgraded the sovereign credit rating to below "Investment grade" and placed India in the "speculative grade". This triggered off, in part, the balance of payments crisis. The process of fiscal stabilization and structural adjustment launched in July 1991, after the Government came to power has finally restored India's credit rating with Moody's and Japanese Bond Research Institutes. With this only one credit rating agency, standard and Poor's still remains unconvinced about the turn-around in India's risk rating.

The Moody's credit rating agency has pushed up India rating from Ba2 (having speculative element) to Baa3 (medium term obligation). Admittedly, the managers of the Indian economy have gone euphoric over this upgradation. This takes India to the investment grade. It must be remembered that India even now is well below the rating it had in 1988 and Moody's latest pronouncement is only a grudging acknowledgement of the country's changing economic status.

The Indian economy at present seems to be slightly better placed than it was in 1988 when Moody's rated the country AaZ (bonds which are rated Aa are judged to be of high quality by all standards). In 1987-88 gross fiscal deficit as a percentage of GDP at prevailing market prices was 8.13 percent with net being 5.54 percent according to the Reserve Bank of India. The gross primary deficit was 6.48 percent, monetised deficit was 1.97 percent and revenue deficit was 2.75 percent. In 1993-94 (R.E.) the gross fiscal deficit was lower at 7.29 percent while the net fiscal deficit was marginally higher at 5.57 percent. The gross primary deficit was 2.62 percent, the net primary deficit was 2.72 percent, monetised deficit was 0.03 percent and conventional deficit was 1.13 percent only revenue deficit was sharply higher at 4.24 percent indicating a slackening of control over current expenditure. As averred already the Union Finance Ministry has not much of a say in the matter of expenditure control with non-plan expenditures like subsidies, interest payments and defence expenditure goffling up funds. But this trend cannot and should not be held against the country as the government has held out the promise that it would cap its expenditure. This, of course, is a Herculean task.

S.S. Tarapore, Deputy Governor of the Reserve Bank of India has developed a new measure to estimate India's solvency. He has elaborated the concept called "Net Foreign Exchange Assets (NFA) to currency ratio". According to him "this ratio has moved up from the little less than 32 percent in March 1993 to 60 percent in March 1994 and further to 71 percent in November 1994. A sharply rising NFA-currency ratio during the period of the inflow (of foreign funds) given an element of comfort to the foreign investor as it indicates that domestic currency expansion has been moderated and when the outflow starts there will be sufficient foreign assets to meet the currency contraction". Elaborating Tarapore said: "A rising NFA-currency ratio is an assurance that when currency contracts, as a result of the operation of the foreign trade multiplier and / or a loss of confidence resulting in a reversal of the capital flow, the foreign currency assets will be large enough to sustain as currency contraction to the pre-inflow period". Moody's may have a quarrel with the NFA-currency ratio but it cannot dismiss the point made by Tarapore that "with the substantial improvement in exports, it would not be surprising if it were to see the clear emergence of a current account surplus in 1994-95 in the balance of payments. In September 1994 the foreign currency assets of the Reserve Bank of India amounted to \$ 18 billion and with a little over \$ 4 billion of gold the foreign exchange reserves are now close to a year's imports". In March 1991 when Moody's downgraded India's Baa3 the Government has just about \$ 500 million in the vaults.

The decisions of the rating agencies will reduce the interest rates charged on India's debt. But the fact is that global lenders have been willing to lend to India even without a formal upgradation by the agencies. In view of this the Moody's and JBRI's decision to upgrade India is not as historic as their decision in 1991. When the downgrading had the effect of choking off funds. Now it will have the effect of reducing the cost of funds since there is already an easing of access to capital markets abroad. It is significant that in the assessment of Moody's India is seen as not only, capable of "facing a liquidity crisis" but also of being able to "avoid any such crisis". This faith in macroeconomic management is a credit and a compliment to the Government of India.

Despite the upgradation of India's credit rating the Moody's is not fully impressed. This is because in its opinion the liberalization process has to regain its lost pace. There are many areas like telecom, aviation, agriculture, insurance where liberalization is yet to make headway. The Finance Minister's message has not yet seeped to his counterparts manning other ministries and also State governments. This calls for speeding up the process of liberalization.

The decision of Moody's Investor Service to upgrade India's sovereign foreign currency debt rating after almost four years is a shot in the arm for the Indian Government and for Indian business. As a result of this upgradation Indian can get finance from foreign creditors at low interest rates. Moody's is aware of the slow pace of economic liberalization process in India but it is understanding and appreciative of the reasons accounting for the slow pace. However, it has immense faith in the potentialities of the Indian economy and the seriousness of purpose of the government, which wants foreign capital to finance the economic development of the country. This is indeed creditable.

During the growth process India has been a victim of the tyranny of twin deficits: the fiscal deficits and the balance of payments deficits. Fiscal deficits are there, of course, but attempts are being made to reduce them to the targeted level. With increasing buoyancy of tax revenues the revenues have been rising. This buoyancy can be attributed in part, to the rationalization of the tax structure. It is the expenditure of the Government that is apparently irreducible because mounting non-plan expenditure-subsidies, interest payments and defence outlay: They cannot be reduced noticeably in the short-run but, given time, they can be reduced considerably. The possibility of this holds out the hope of reducing the fiscal deficit.

Even the balance of payments deficit is not of much serious concern. The recently released trade figures for the first seven months of 1994-95 suggest a development which may be of long-term consequence to the Indian economy. There is a resilence of exports and a quantum jump in the long term growth rate. This is borne out by the 26.9 percent increase in exports in a month which may be worked by the plague scare that resulted in the imposition of import restrictions by some countries. The seven-month average export growth rate of 13.9 percent is above the 7-8 percent average that the country saw in the pre-reform period. This figure has been rising since August and there is reason to believe that the average for the year may be higher still. Together with the 20 percent export growth rate achieved in 1993-94 this is definite evidence that India has made some advance on the reform's objective of a major step-up in exports. Imports during the first seven months of 1994-95 increased by 19.8 percent, non-oil imports by as much as 30.6 percent. These are no doubt feeding industrial recovery and there can be little cause for complaint at least in the short-run. In view of the accumulation of $ 20 billion of foreign exchange reserves the financing of these imports creates no problem. The Commerce Ministry has proposed several measures to promote exports much further. Some imports serve as inputs to exports and they help in promoting export growth. In view of this the balance of payments deficit creates no problem at all. This also underlines the solvency of the Indian economy. It is true that external debt at $ 91 billion is very heavy but if the foreign exchange reserves are used to repay high cost external debt, the burden of debt and its servicing will fail. The rate of inflation which was 17.5 percent in July 1991 was brought down to 7 percent in March 1994 but since then it has been rising and at present it is 9.69 percent close to the double digit. The Finance Minister is confident that it will be around 7 percent by the end of 1994-95. It can be said with confidence that he is not overoptimistic.

Having taken into account all these factors the Moody's and JBRI have decided to upgrade India in the matter of credit rating. Standard and Poor's is hesitant about upgrading India for reasons best known to itself. Now that its associated agencies have upgraded India it cannot be hesitant any longer about upgrading India.

# 30

# Will Liberalisation of Consumer Goods Imports Jeopardise Small Scale Industries?

Addressing the Economic Editors' Conference in Delhi on 21-9-1994, the Union Minister of Commerce and Deputy Chairman of the Planning Commission expressed himself against allowing consumer goods imports under the Open General Licence, saying that any such move would remove the only incentive available to exporters. Market development assistance and export promotion incentives in the form of subsidies had come down drastically from 8 percent in 1990-91 to just 1 percent. Their share as a proportion of GDP had declined from 2 percent to 0.03 percent. In the absence of this subsidy to exporters the only available fillip was the Special Import Licence for import of consumer goods for offloading in the domestic market at a premium. He explained that a large number of small-scale industries would be jeopardized as they are manufacturing consumer goods. Besides this would also endanger employment in the organized sector.

At present the forex reserves in the vaults of the Reserve Bank of India are about $ 13 billion and they are expected to reach $ 25 billion towards the end of the fiscal 1994-95. It needs to be underlined that they are inflationary as they raise the rate of monetary growth and generate excess liquidity in the economy. If the inflationary effects are to be toned down it is necessary to increase the import of consumer goods. These imports by increasing the availability of goods in the economy absorb excess liquidity and help to bring down the rate of inflation. There is no danger of the trade gap widening to create a balance of payments crisis. The trade gap at present is of the order of Rs. 700 crore. The imports can be financed by drawing down the vast amount of forex reserves. For this reason, there is no fear of a balance of payments crisis.

The fear that the imports of consumer goods would jeopardize the small scale industries producing consumer goods in the country is overly exaggerated. In India there is social dualism and cultural dualism. The vast majority of the people are in the lower middle class and poverty groups. The upper and upper middle class people are hardly one-third of the population. They are socially and culturally advanced and have a strong economic base too. Their lifestyles are different from those of the lower middle class and poverty groups who account for two-thirds of the population. The upper class consumers always go in for sophisticated goods and gadgetry and are averse to the goods produced by the domestic consumer goods industries. They feel that the goods produced by the small scale industries do not come up to the standards of sophistication of the imported consumer goods which have a high degree of "snob" value. They always prefer imported consumer goods to the domestically produced goods as the former are believed to confer on them an elevated social status. The consumer goods produced by the small scale industries are, for the most part consumed by the lower middle class and poverty groups. These goods are cheaper than the imported consumer goods which these groups can afford; untouched as they still are by the cultural invasion of the west, they are satisfied with the domestic goods. The small scale industries provide employment, they are less capital and technology intensive and they cater to the local markets. The impact of the imported consumer goods on these industries is marginal, if at all. They may buy imported consumer goods in the same way as the upper and upper middle class groups may also buy domestic consumer goods. Consequently, the net impact of liberalization of consumer goods imports is not big enough to jeopardize the small scale industries or their potential for employment generation. The dualistic nature of Indian society allow the imported consumer goods to jeopardize the domestic small scale industries. In fact it may energize them. Facing foreign competition they may concentrate on modernization and technological up-gradation of their production techniques in order to reach the standards of sophistication reached by the foreign consumer goods industries.

In this event, other things being equal, the demand for domestic consumer goods increases. The domestic goods become prefect substitutes for imported consumer goods and in a regime of price parity the domestic industries conquer the market despite import liberalization.

The Commence Minister's fear is that due to the reduction of export subsidies, the exports will fall. This fear is true to some extent. India is on the road to a market economy and subsidies of all hues are an anathema in a market economy. What is necessary for export growth is not subsidies but price and quality competitiveness of exports. There is great demand for Indian exports of consumer goods in the developing countries mostly and to some extent in the developed world. These markets have to be conquered and expanded. The only way to do it is to increase the price and quality competitiveness of Indian exports of consumer goods. If this is done, the domestic small-scale industries do not have to fear loss of markets and loss of employment potential. Therefore, there is no harm in allowing consumer goods imports under OCL.

# 31

# Computerisation and Automation of Operations of Nationalised Banks

The Indian banking sector has three major segments: nationalised banks, foreign banks and indigenous private banks. These banks are in intense competition with each other for deposits and loan operations. Since 1969 when 14 banks were nationalised foreign banks were not allowed to be set up in India. In like manner, even the domestic private sector was not allowed to set up banks. But after the economic reform programme was initiated in July 1991the Government opened the banking sector to foreign banks and to the domestic private banks. In the beginning the foreign banks were allowed to set up their branches in India. This exposed the domestic banking industry to the bracing winds of foreign competition and enhanced its operative efficiency. With liberalization of the Indian economy the Reserve Bank of India decided to permit the private sector to open up banks. The Reserve Bank of India observed:

"There is an increasing recognition of the need to introduce greater competition which can lead to higher productivity and efficiency of the banking system".

This was part of the guidelines announced by the Reserve Bank on the entry of new private banks in January 1993. The objective of the Reserve Bank behind allowing private banks is being broadly realized. There are six private banks and they have all announced encouraging results in 1994-95. Their aggregate deposits during the year were of the order of Rs. 2400 crore while the total advances were of the order of Rs. 1700 crore. In contrast, the aggregate of advances and deposits of nationalised banks is over three lakh crore rupees. Thus, the figures furnished by the private banks look insignificant. However, it must be noted that the private banks within so short a time as just over two years have made a good beginning.

While the nationalised commercial banks are given to "mass" banking, the private banks are given to "class" banking. The former accept even small deposits. But the private banks have virtually left out the small depositors. The minimum deposit required for opening an account in a private bank is Rs. 10,000 which is beyond the capacity of the small depositors. There is ample justification for this high deposit requirement. The cost of servicing of private banks is very high. The operations of these banks are highly computerized and automated and, for this reason, acceptance of lower deposits would not be viable. Furthermore, the interior of these banks is tastefully decorated and highly sophisticated. The idea is to attract big depositors. As they are in intense competition with each other they are in a bid to be one up over the other in establishing posh offices. There are applications from others for permission to start banks. But the Reserve Bank of India is yet to take a decision about them so far.

In the year 1995-06 the private banks are facing a tough time. The interest rates have gone up and liquidity has become tight. During 1994-95 all the six private banks did well, as the fund position was easy and the cost was low. Some of these private banks were able to raise short term funds at 9 percent. But during 1995-96 the funds have become dearer and the foreign banks and nationalised banks are determined to tone up their performance. In view of this, the private banks will find it difficult to repeat the performance of 1994-95.

While this is the fact of the private banks things are not easy for the nationalised commercial banks which are faced with the rising cost of operations and declining productivity. The possibility of the deposits moving from nationalised banks to private banks is real. The quality of customer service in the nationalised commercial banks is very poor. As the operations are manual there is considerable delay in the operations. Due to frequent enhancement of wages and salaries in the banking sector, the cost of service has gone up. These two factors induce the big depositors in the nationalised banks to move their deposits to the private banks. While this eases the liquidity position of the private banks it tightens the liquidity position of the nationalised banks. With the Government entering the market as a major borrower, the deposit mobilization of the nationalised commercial banks is bound to be slowed down.

This calls for the nationalised banks computerizing their operations. The cost may appear to be high but the increasing productivity following computerization and automation is bound to reduce the unit cost of operation. The bank employees are likely to oppose this move as it is feared that the computers displaced labour but computerisation is necessary if the nationalised banks are to survive in business. The Government can think of an exit policy of the type envisaged for the industrial sector and introduce the "safety net" to help the employees who face retrenchment. A fund to administer the exit policy has to be built up soon. If the operations of the nationalised banks are allowed to continue as they are, the banks will have to come to grief. These banks are already saddled with considerable non-performing assets and their burden has to be reduced. In view of this computerisation and automation of the operations of the nationalised commercial banks is a categorical imperative.

# 32

# Is the Debt Crisis Imminent?

According to the World Debt Tables released by the World Bank in the middle of January 1995, India's external debt had reached the magnitude of $ 91.78 billion in 1993. India is the third biggest debtor among the developing countries next only to Brazil ($ 132.75 billion) and Mexico ($ 118.03 billion). This vast accumulation of external debt threatening to open the doors of the debt trap for India's entry was mainly due to earlier trade gaps. They led to large external borrowing which was occasioned by huge recurring trade deficits. There was heavy borrowing especially in the form of short-term loans. This led to the rise in outstanding debt from $ 20.61 billion in 1980-81 to $ 83.96 billion in 1990-91. This big rise was mainly due to current account transactions as there were no large investments in the public or private sectors in ongoing or new projects involving heavy expenditure of foreign exchange. The interest rates on these loans were also high and in consequence, the burden of debt repayments and interest changes proved onerous. The debt servicing obligations accounted for 31.9 percent of export earnings in 1990-91 against only 11 percent in 1980-81. In 1991-92 it rose to 31.2 percent but declined to 30.8 percent in 1992-93 and further to 25.1 percent in 1993-94. This was due to the surge in exports and to a growth in Gross National Product.

The outstanding debt increased from $ 85.30 billion in 1991-92 to $ 89.99 billion in 1992-93. This was due to large borrowings from the International Monetary Fund for meeting the difficult balance of payments position and improving India's credit-worthiness in world markets. The balance of payments crisis of 1991-92 was largely due to mounting external debt and declining foreign exchange reserves. Against the current account deficit of only $ 300 million in 1993-94 it was as high as $ 8.0 billion in

1988-89, $ 4.87 billion in 1985-86 and $ 2.80 billion in 1980-81. Even in 1989-90 the deficit was $ 6.84 billion and in 1990-91 it was as much as 9.68 billion. The big deficits were due to huge trade gaps which were $ 1.04 billion in 1993-94, $ 5.53 billion in 1988-89, $ 7.16 billion in 1985-86, $ 7.38 billion in 1980-81, $ 4.61 billion in 1989-90 and $ 5.93 billion in 1990-91. In the light of the emerging debt scenario it was felt that there should be strict control over short-term borrowings and current account deficits. The measures adopted in 1991-92 and a smart rise in exports in 1992-93 prevented the emergence of sizeable trade deficits. In 1993-94 there was an improvement in exports and a reduction in the trade gap to $ 1.04 billion. But the trade gap was of the order of $ 300 million because of larger invisible receipts.

On account of the repayments of short-term obligations and determined efforts to prevent an increase in short-term deposits in external accounts, the composition of external debt has been changed for the better. In consequence, the debt servicing obligations are unlikely to give rise to serious problems. It can be hoped that the current account deficit will not be uncomfortable in the years ahead as the oil bill will not rise and non-oil imports can be effectively regulated. The Union Finance Ministry is keen on avoiding undue increase in borrowing in foreign currencies. Instead, recourse is being taken to mobilize foreign exchange resources through GDRs or convertible bonds. Foreign investments will take place only in the desired areas with a large equity content and a small proportion of loans.

While the aggregate external debt is enormous, the rate of accretion to the debt is on the decline since the inauguration of the economic reforms programme. From $ 87.95 billion in 1991 it increased to $ 90.93 billion in 1992. After this it increased moderately to $ 91.78 billion in 1993. In terms of the ratio of debt to GDP it is found that even though the ratio swelled from 24.3 percent in March 1991 to 34.2 percent in 1992, there was a slight decline to 32.4 percent in 1993. The debt-service ratio based on export earnings has been hovering around 28 percent in recent months as compared to 30.6 percent in 1992. This, indeed, is a ground for optimism on the external debt front. There is another factor, which removes the risk of loss of control over exchange rate stability. This is the changed composition of external debt involving the element of volatile short-term funds in the form of foreign portfolio funds. The situation is not a source of panic though portfolio funds currently dominate the overall capital movements. Except for a sharp rise from $ 5.49 billion in 1990 to $ 6.0 billion in 1991, short-term debt is on the decline to $ 4.45 billion in 1993.

The year 1993-94 provided evidence that the opening up of the economy had placed the country's external accounts in a formidable position. Exports surged from $ 18.90 billion to $ 22.7 billion. But imports rose moderately from $ 23.0 billion to $ 23.98 billion giving a current account deficit of only $ 300 million. The impact of the economic reforms programme on the capital account was more tangible. Apart from the $ 1.66 billion of foreign portfolio funds entering the secondary capital market, GDRs and Euro-bond issues led to a capital inflow of $ 2.4 billion. There was a net increase in the forex reserves of $ 8.6 billion. But this had the inevitable consequence of inducing monetary expansion with inflationary consequences. In the first half of 1994-95 the current account deficit is estimated to be $ 400 million and for the whole year it is expected to be $ 1.0 billion. This should not be a cause for concern.

Given the improving prospectus of direct foreign investment of the order of $ 2.3 billion in the next two years, the country seems to have moved out of the situation where exceptional balance of payments financing seemed indispensable a year ago. Even on the assumption that the flow of portfolio funds would abate in view of the likelihood of interest rates rising in the industralised world and also of the opening up of capital markets in other developing countries attracting foreign capital, the outlook for the balance of payments appears favourable.

In the context of the current accounts deficit and the heavy burden of external debt, exports are the critical variable. There is at present scope for diversification and expansion of exports. If this materializes the chances of the balance of payments improving on both the current and capital accounts are bright even without the invisibles contributing a larger share of forex earnings. Considering the liberalization of consumer goods imports meant to hold the price line Herculean efforts are needed to stimulate exports to the requisite degree. Any complacency on the macro situation is untenable. The rate of inflation in India is around 10 percent and despite euphoric pronouncements from the Finance Ministry it is unlikely to come down in the near future. The rate of inflation in the western world is between 2 and 3 percent. While the rate of inflation in India is 10 percent. This inflation rate differential makes India's exports uncompetitive in world markets. Unless the rate of inflation is brought down to 7-8 percent the export growth rate may fall short of even the reduced target of 15 percent. In this event the external debt may pose a serious problem for the country despite the recent reduction in its magnitude.

The collapse of the Mexican Peso in the wake of the massive outward flow of short-term capital funds from that country has sent shock waves through other emerging economics like Brazil, Thailand, Indonesia, Malaysia, Hong-Kong and other countries. In the context of economic recovery in the industralised world there are speculations that capital flows to developing countries which have been surging during the past three years will be reversed. If this happens even to a limited extent, the apprehensions of serious economic destabilization in some of the emerging countries cannot be dismissed as over-reaction to the Mexican economic crisis.

The currency crisis in Mexico involving the devaluation of the Peso by 40 percent against the dollar sent ripples to the Indian share market. Foreign investors with huge holdings of Mexican stocks suffered heavy losses. To balance their losses in Mexico they sold heavily in India sending Indian share prices crashing. Operators in the India are watching the American interest rate movements. The American interest rate is expected to be raised by half a percent and this will again have a bearing on Indian share prices. The prospect of a rise in the American interest rate has promoted FIIs to move their investments away from markets like India. Against this background the Indian share prices have taken a beating in the last few weeks. But this is temporary. The Indian stock market still remains buoyant if not overly bullish.

The Finance Minister and Dr. C. Rangarajan have lost no time in allaying the apprehensions of a possible assault on the rupee by speculative forces leading to abrupt withdrawal of funds by foreign investors. There is no cause for alarm on this count considering the robust performance of the Indian economy and other factors which continue to provide the attractions for large scale capital flows into the country especially in the form of direct foreign investments. It has to be borne in mind that the current account deficit of less than one percent of GDP in India makes the Indian situation very different from the Mexico-like crisis where capital inflows were resorted to in order to tide over large-scale current account deficits.

The Government has taken care to repay short-term debt and to reduce its magnitude. This has made the composition of debt look healthy. The outstanding debt of over $ 90 billion in 1993-94 consisted of bilateral debt and debt owed to multilateral institutions both of which have a large amount of concessionality to the tune of 48 percent. The share of external commercial borrowings in different forms was 18 percent, the liabilities to IMF around 5 percent, long term component of NRI deposits at 13.9 percent and rupee debt owing to the Soviet Union and other countries 11.1 percent.

Due to the decline in debt-servicing obligations and the expectations of a pronounced growth in GDP the ratio of outstanding debt to GDP will tend to decline and the growth of debt in absolute terms may not be pronounced. On the basis of the projections of the World Bank it may be forecast that it will decline at particular stages. It is, however, expected that there will be a significant increase in external indebtedness on non-Government account as the new projects in public and private sectors may involve heavy capital outlays particularly in the power and telecommunications sectors which will have a heavy foreign exchange component mainly in the form of loans. The Government has taken a decision that additional commercial borrowings on non-Government account should not exceed $ 3.5 billion annually and that borrowings by public sector enterprises, banks and industrial units in the private sector should be within affordable limits keeping in view the future foreign exchange earnings through exports and services. It is not clear how payments will be made against loans taken for new large projects along with interest changes. The country may experience difficulties if there cannot be substitution of imports or increased exchange earnings. It is expected that an improvement in the availability of power will lead to a reduction in the consumption of petroleum and will reduce the oil import bill or an increase in the output of manufactured goods which can replace related imports and also push up exports.

Due to the boom in exports and sluggishness of imports the current account deficit will be less than anticipated and reserves more plentiful. These developments are the result of the earlier action on trade policy. Faster exports and slower imports imply a smaller current account deficit. In turn this means lower borrowings from the rest of the world. These favourable developments on the balance of payments front provide the broad context to view the status of India's external debt profile.

The foregoing account of the external debt situation and the current account deficit lends evidence to the belief that the Mexican Disease will not affect India whose current account deficit and debt profile are not weak. The Indian rupee is strong and stable and the threat to its stability is not there on the horizon. The debt crisis is not imminent.

# 33

# A Case for Financial Emergency

It is reported that the bank employees throughout the country numbering seven lakh have threatened to go on a day's strike on August 31, 1995 and would call for two more strikes in September if their demands are not met. Their main demand is reconstruction of pay scales of subordinate staff and clerks with 120 percent and 175 percent neutralization to maintain relativity with the lowest category of officers in banks (scale 1) who have been given 115 percent neutralization at the same level of index. The representatives of the bank employees who met the Indian Banks' Association representatives for a two hour talk on August 5, 1995 stated that their attempts at a negotiated settlement had been 'frustrated' by the management as the Indian Banks' Association representatives rejected their demands.

The rate of inflation which had reached 17.5 percent in 1991 has gradually declined to 7.65 percent and it is expected to decline further if the process of fiscal consolidation goes apace. It has been difficult for the Finance Minister to reduce the fiscal deficit to the targeted level of 6 percent. With the announcement of the new welfare package of over Rs. 3,000 crore by the Prime Minister the fiscal deficit which shows distinct signs of a decline gets an upward thrust pushing the rate of inflation higher. With the announcement of the procurement prices by the Minister for Agriculture the food prices in the market are bound to rise. This will further give a fillip to the price level. With the implementation of the Fifth Pay Commission recommendations the fiscal deficit is bound to become bigger. All these are harbingers of a high rate of inflation. If the employees in the Government service demand compensatory adjustments in the salary scales, the employees in the private sector demand the same treatment. All these factors collectively have to be accommodated by monetary expansion which in turn pushes up the rate of inflation. There will thus be a vicious circle of prices and salaries/wages chasing one another without end. This is a dangerous situation indeed.

The bank employees are a pampered lot. They get far higher scales of pay than their counterparts in the other sectors possessing comparable qualifications and doing less strenuous jobs. They are found to be staging strikes and demonstrations at frequent intervals holding the public to ransom and causing inconvenience to them. If their demands are met the banks have to find resources to meet their enhanced wage bill. They will have to find resources by raising the service charges which inevitably fall on the banking public. In the alternative they have to raise the lending rates with adverse consequences on investment activity or again they will have to reduce the deposit rate which will adversely affect deposit mobilization efforts. A lower deposit rate means lower savings considering the fact that savings respond positively to real interest rates. A reduction in savings widens the savings investment gap which is inflationary. All these complications which are not evident at first sight make themselves felt with disaster consequences on economic stability.

A higher price level needs to be accommodated by monetary expansion. Under the traditional gold standard, as Professor D.H. Robertson argued, money supply wound be expanded only if there was an inflow of gold and not otherwise. Therefore, unless gold flowed in, there would be no monetary expansion and there would be no money to pay the higher wage bill. But when the monetary system is permissible, monetary system is permissive, monetary expansion does take place in order to enable the authorities to foot the higher wage bill. This is a situation where the supply of money is conditioned by what Professor J.R. Hicks calls the "Labour Standard". When the Labour Standard takes over as the determinant of monetary growth the stage is set for a runaway inflation causing harassment to the very beneficiaries of higher wages for what Normal Angell called the "Unseen Assassin" inflation cuts into the purchasing power of money leaving their real status no better than before. At a time when the need of the hour is a steady reduction of the inflation rate, monetary permissiveness induced by wage escalation has to be restrained. This can be restrained if the wage escalation is restrained. But such a restraint induces militancy on the part of the wage earners and this renders any restraint fruitless.

In its *Review of the Indian Economy* (January-March 1995), the National Council of Applied Economic Research (NCAER) says that there is the possibility of a rise in the inflation rate. Broad money in India registered an increase of 21.2 percent as on March 1, 1995 as against an increase of 18.4 percent in the previous year. The increase in the quarter under review at 6.4 percent was also higher than 5.5 percent in the same quarter of the preceding year. The monetary expansion has accommodated the higher price level. While the inflation rate is presently under control the Government is recourse to RBI credit at a relatively high level signals the possibility of a rise in the inflation rate. The fiscal deficit which has occasioned a rise in the inflation rate causes a further rise in the current account deficit in addition to the rise in the oil bill and the rise in non-oil imports. This has to be financed by capital inflows or drawing down of surging forex reserves. In fact, in the context of a rise in prices liberalization of consumer goods imports has been recommended as an anti-inflationary measures. This will further worsen the current account deficit. The reduction of forex reserves does not lead to a reduction in monetary growth. These are the complications associated with fiscal deficits and monetary growth.

This situation calls for the imposition of financial emergency for a couple of years during which the economy will have a chance to recover. Under financial emergency:

- The prices in all the sectors primary, secondary and tertiary should be held constant. This is necessary to hold down the rate of inflation.
- The implementation of the Fifth Pay Commission recommendations should be held in abeyance as this would help to hold down the fiscal deficit.
- The accumulated income tax arrears need to be recovered in order to reduce the fiscal deficit.

- The manufacturers should be directed to pass on duty reduction to consumers in the form of lower prices.
- Apart of the accumulated stocks of foodgrains of the order of 37 million tonne should be released to the market to bring down the prices of food which govern the general price index or it should be exported in order to balance external accounts.
- The black assets accumulated by various people in the country should be confiscated and should be used for national development.
- Restrictions should be imposed on conspicuous consumption in the context of the influence of sophisticated consumerism which is holding away over the Indian masses. This will reduce the need for consumer goods imports and reduce the current account deficit.

The imposition of financial emergency in the election year is difficult for the Government but it is necessary to maintain economic stability.

# 34

# An Autonomous Sebi

The Government of India on 26-1-1995 promulgated an Ordinance to amend the Securities and Exchange Board (SEBI) of India Act of 1992 and the securities Contracts (Regulation) Act of 1956 to empower the Board with additional powers for ensuring the orderly development of the capital market. The major amendments include the empowering the SEBI with regulatory powers over corporates in the issuance of capital, the transfer of securities and other related matters. Thus for the SEBI did not have these powers. This impeded its ability to protect the interests of investors. Under the amendment the SEBI is empowered to impose monetary penalties on capital market intermediaries and other participants for major violations which have been listed. Previously the SEBI Act provided for the suspension and cancellation of registration and for the prosecution of intermediaries. Suspension and cancellation had the danger of stoppage of business. But the proposed monetary penalties constitute an alternative mechanism for dealing with capital market violations.

The ordinance arming the SEBI with greater powers fulfils a long standing need for without these powers the SEBI was restrained from paying an effective role. It needed clearance from the Finance Ministry for any and every measure it proposed to take. This curtailed the speed with which the SEBI could act. Furthermore, since information about future measures often leaked out to the markets, it generated pressure from vested interests even before the measures could be announced. The ordinance confers new powers on the SEBI to impose fines on the violators of rules and the inclusion of infringement of listing agreements by the companies liable to punishment under the SEBI Act. Though the SEBI has the power to suspend or disqualify any operator found to be violating the rules such punishment is considered to be too severe for relatively minor offences. Furthermore, suspension of business also caused inconvenience to innocent clients of guilty operators.

The ordinance raises the question whether the timing of this measure is opportune. The powers now conferred on the SEBI have been discussed for months. The issuance of the ordinance at a time when the stocks are experiencing a liquidity exists is indicative of the intention of the Government to attract fresh funds from the small investors rather than from the larger operators in the market. In the case of the larger operators, the withdrawal of the 25-year-old embargo on options trading is more relevant. This is bound to assure the small investors that their interests can be safeguarded by the SEBI which is empowered to punish anybody violating listing agreements in contrast to the stock exchange managements which have been hesitant to act against defaulters under pressure from powerful brokers. But the ordinance is yet to define the relationship between the Department of Company Affairs and the SEBI and their respective areas of authority. This is bound to generate confusion. It is also quite likely that the differences of opinion between the Company and the SEBI when aired in public will defeat some of the measures to reform stock markets.

Under the amendment the Government can appoint Directors with expertise and experience of the capital market. This is necessary to prevent the appointment of all and sundry as Directors under political pressure. Under the amendment the SEBI has become an autonomous institution as it is empowered to file complaints in courts and to notify its regulations without the approval of the Union Government. These powers will enable the SEBI to respond speedily to changing market conditions.

These measures are intended to cope speedily with the complications to be created in the working of the stock exchanges and other capital market institutions in the context of the globalization of the Indian economy and the inflow and outflow of foreign investment funds. The foreign financial institutions are given to acting with speed and dispatch in coping with the problems that arise. The SEBI with its outmoded methods was unable to cope with the problems calling for urgent remedial actions. The amendment will take the SEBI closer to the foreign stock market regulating agencies in the matter of speed and efficiency in dealing with problems.

The Government has to be proactive rather than reactive in amending the powers of the SEBI in future years. It must anticipate the complications that might arise in the working of the capital market institutions and their coordination with the capital market institutions in the foreign countries. Unless the Indian capital market is efficient in handling the issues arising out of foreign capital flows the foreign capital flow will be slow and sluggish. This will harm the cause of industrial and infrastructural development in India. Prudence demands that the SEBI be made a purely autonomous institution with clear-cut measures of control and supervision over the operations of the Indian capital market. It is said that there is nothing more requisite in business than dispatch.

# 35

## Need to Grant Interim Relief to Pensioners

The Fifth Pay Commission is in session and has called for responses from knowledgeable persons in various sections of society to the thousands of questionnaires. The Pay Commission was appointed in order to assess the impact of inflation on the cost-of-living and living standards of the Government employees both working and retired drawing pension and to assess the extent of relief that needs to be granted to them in order to save them from the depredations of inflation which Norman Angell (a former Governor of the Bank of England) called the "Unseen Assassin". The Pay Commission has to scan the thousands of responses to the questionnaires to assess the extent of erosion of the purchasing power of the rupee and to award compensatory variation in the relief to the harried employees. This takes several months before the Commission submits its report. After the report is submitted, the Government takes its own time to consider the recommendations of the commission and to decide on the extent of compensatory relief to be granted keeping in view the financial crunch it is facing at present. After a decision is taken to provide the requisite relief, several months have to pass before the decision is implemented and the employees get the benefit. These procedural delays are time-consuming and the sufferings of the employees mount without any let or hindrance. In view of these inevitable delays, the Government has already sanctioned interim relief to the employees in service a year ago pending the final settlement of arrears due to them after the recommendations of the pay commission are implemented. This is good enough. But the pensioners are totally ignored. This, I think, is discriminatory.

The pensioners, after rendering dedicated service to the Government and through it to the nation, get pension which is at best one-fourth of the salary they drew when in service. When the employees in service drawing full salary considered to be groaning under the weight of the rising rate of inflation, the pensioners who get just one-fourth of their salary as pension are literally harried by the burden of rising prices and falling value of the rupee. If the claim of the employees in service for interim relief is considered legitimate, the claim of the pensioners for interim relief should be considered four times more legitimate. Therefore, the pensioners are entitled to greater consideration that the employees in service. The case of the pensioners for a similar interim relief is just and fair. For this reason the pensioners too need to be granted interim relief on par with the employees in service with retrospective effect. The present policy of the government discriminates against the pensioners and thus violates the principles of natural justice.

The pensioners are hard-hit by the on-going inflation. The burden of bringing up their children, maintaining the family and fulfilling their other commitments is heavier on them than on those still in service. They have to educate their sons, marry off their daughters and meet their loan commitments in addition to maintaining their large families. This with their paltry pensions which in real terms is rendered paltrier by the raging inflation merits more favourable consideration. It is their claims that should be the primary concern of the Government. When the interim relief if granted to those in service it stands to reason that interim relief should be granted to the pensioners also. In fact, interim relief granted to the pensioners should be at a higher rate than that granted to the employees in service who are drawing full salary. In ignoring the legitimate claims of the pensioners the Government has violated the principles of natural justice and parity of treatment.

In the memorandum on the Union Budget for 1995-96 I suggested the introduction of the "Deferred Payment Scheme" in order to reduce the flow of spendable income in the economy and through it to cap and inflation rate. If this scheme is introduced it should be applicable to all kinds of employees in all the sectors of the economy including the pensioners. But when those in service are paid new emoluments at the rates recommended by the Pay

Commission, the principle of parity of treatment demands that the pensioners should also be paid new pensions along with the arrears the amount depending on the date from which the new scales of pay or pensions become operative. In a similar manner, when the employees in service are paid interim relief, the same principle of parity of treatment demands that the pensioners should be paid interim relief from the same date. I can go a step further and say that the pensioners should be paid interim relief from the same date. I can go a step further and say that the pensioners should be paid interim relief at a higher rate than the employees in service considering the paltry pension to which they are entitled and which they are getting.

It is hoped that the Government of India will view the plight of the pensioners with sympathy and understanding and grant interim relief to them in the same way as is done in the case of employees in service. It would be ideal to grant interim relief to the pensioners at a higher rate in view of their growing financial commitments and reduced income by way of pensions. The Finance Minister may be having a headache in capping the fiscal deficit but he should not seek relief from withholding the interim relief from the poor pensioners.

# 36

## The New Euro-issue Guidelines

The monetary impact of the inflow of forex reserves has occasioned unpredictable shifts in the policy to regulate such inflows. Between April 1994 and November 1994 the foreign exchange reserves excluding gold and SDRs increased by around 30 percent from $ 15.073 billion to $ 19.496 billion. But during the subsequent four months the reserves increased by only around 2.3 percent to $ 20.945 billion. Though the rate of accretion of forex reserves has fallen the reserves in absolute terms have risen. In April 1995 the forex reserves including gold and SDRs were of the order of $ 25.15 billion.

The Government allowed Indian companies to raise capital in the European capital markets and to repatriate it to India. These Global Deposit Receipts (GDRs) swelled the forex reserves with their impact on the rate of monetary growth. In order to mitigate the inflationary impact of the GDR inflow guidelines for Euro Issues were announced by the Government on May 11, 1994 followed by certain amendments on October 28, 1994. In terms of the guidelines dated October 28, 1994 issuing Indian companies were required mandatorily to retain the Euro Issue Proceeds abroad to be repatriated as and when expenditure for the approved end uses including up to a maximum of 15 percent of funds earmarked for general corporate restructuring uses were incurred.

On may 24, 1995 the Government modified the earlier Euro Issue guidelines regarding the retention of funds abroad and permitted the issuing companies to also retain the Euro Issue proceeds as foreign currency deposits with banks and public financial institutions in India. These Euro Issue proceeds could be converted into Indian rupees only as and when expenditure for the approved end uses (including up to a maximum of 15 percent of funds earmarked for general corporate restructuring uses) are incurred. The interim development of funds retained abroad or as foreign currency deposits with banks and public financial institutions in India should conform to the manner of deployment that will be indicated by the Reserve Bank of India in their letter of approval.

The Ministry of Finance took this step in order to give a book to its sagging forex reserves. This is a step towards repealing the earlier guidelines of October 28, 1994 prohibiting companies from repatriating their Euro Issue Proceeds back to India provided the rate of inflation remained under control at around 8 percent for some more time The Finance Ministry feels that this measure would be required to give a boost to the stock market. The market has remained continuously at the bottom level due to the liquidity crunch and this is feared to affect the rate of industrial growth this year. In the light of this scenario, it is argued that if the repatriation of the Euro Issue proceeds could help in ameliorating the situations the Government must permit repatriation of Euro Issue proceeds to India. The Government's earlier decision to prohibit the repatriation of the Euro Issue proceeds triggered a chain reaction for a downslide of the market. In fact, in the weeks after October 28, 1994 when the Government announced its guidelines prohibiting the repatriation the market started crashing. Full repatriation of the proceeds along with their conversion into Indian currency would of course, cause an expansion of money supply. But if inflation came down to less than 8 percent and remained there for four consecutive weeks the Government would allow the repatriation along with the conversion into Indian currency.

The new guidelines would boost the forex reserves of the Reserve Bank of India at a time when they had started dwindling because of the reduced capital inflow after November 1994. This had started putting pressure on the rupee dollar exchange rate. The rate of accretion of reserves had been declining. Between April and November 1994 they accrued at the rate of 30 percent. But between November 1994 and March 1995 they increased by 3 percent. During the current financial year the reserves had taken a dip. On April 21, 1995 the reserves had depleted by around $ 460 million. This situation put preserve on the dollar exchange rate. In April 1995 the rupee had depreciated to the average rate of Rs. 31.60 per US dollar as against the earlier rate of Rs. 31.37 per US dollar. At present the trade deficit is widening due to a higher rate of imports. If this situation continues the rupee is bound to depreciate further. Inspite of this the Government was unwilling to permit the repatriation of Euro Issue proceeds as it was feared that it would cause money supply to increase and exacerbate inflation. The latest decision of the Government would help the companies raising capital abroad as they would get a higher interest rate of 8 percent on their foreign currency deposits in India as against the prevailing rate of 6 percent abroad.

The accumulation of forex reserves of the order of $ 20 billion is the result of the opening up of the Indian economy to foreign financial flows. Many have expressed the opinion that a large part of these forex reserves are hot money liable to shift outside the country either because of higher interest rate abroad or because of the expectation of political instability in the country. They cite the case of Mexico whose forex reserves declined from $ 27 billion to $ 7 billion within a short span of two weeks due to the sudden shift of short-term capital outside the country. They do not seem to realize that the macro-economic fundamentals of India are vastly different from those of Mexico. Inflation was reaping in Mexico and the current account deficit was 8 percent of GDP. The rate of inflation in India is 8.5 percent and the current account deficit is 0.5 percent of GDP. The rupee is strong and stable unlike the Mexican Peso which was depreciating at a rapid rate making the foreign investors lose faith in its stability. There was a massive capital outflow forcing the authorities to devalue the Peso.

Even so, the forex reserves held by the Reserve Bank of India are far too excessive and they are a major factor in the inflationary process. The rate of monetary growth is 20 percent against the targeted rate of 16 percent. It is this which made the authorities to issue guidelines regarding the Euro Issues and to direct that the capital raised by the Indian companies in the European capital markets should be held by these companies abroad until they are actually required in India for expenditure. The intention was to mitigate the monetary impact of the forex reserves. This was, of course, a sound decision. But the present guidelines are intended to make good the dip in forex reserves caused by the reduced rate of inflow. The new guidelines permit the issuing companies to retain the Euro Issue proceeds as foreign currency deposits with banks and financial institutions. The Euro Issue proceeds can be converted into Indian rupees when the expenditures for the approved end uses are incurred. This means that the inflow of Euro Issue proceeds will not cause monetary expansion unless they are converted into Indian rupees and they will not be so converted to Indian rupees unless the need for expenditure arises. This means that the inflow of Euro Issue proceeds will be sterilized until and unless they are converted into rupees at the time of expenditure. In this sense the new guidelines are a factor of monetary stability. The hot money component of the forex reserves is a source of danger. The sooner this component is got rid of, the better it is for the country. Only long term capital or capital that will be held for an agreed period of time will ensure monetary stability.

The London based Economist Intelligence Unit (EIU) in its quarterly report predicts a slow growth in consumer demand as a result of higher interest rates, disruption to production caused by the 1996 elections and devaluation. The EIU warns that the rupee may reach an incredible level of Rs. 42 to the US dollar. The warning about devaluation may not materialize as there have been denials by the Commerce Minister of such a prospect. Apart from giving a temporary boost to exports, devaluation at this juncture is bound to create problems for the economy as imports will become more expensive and foreign investors will find the returns to their investment dwindle in terms of dollars. But the possibility of current account deficit increasing due to a deluge of imports cannot be ruled out and a large outflow of funds can also take place if the current political instability lasts. It is inflation that is putting pressure on the rupee. Therefore, the control of inflation will be a better solution than devaluation.

# 37

# The Indo-Dollar Market Proposal Modified

During the past three years inflation surged generating apprehensions that it might reach the 1991 level. Apart from various factors which go towards creation of inflationary pressures within the economy the prime cause identified in 1994 was the massive inflow of foreign exchange into the economy. The flow most visibly through foreign institutional investments into the Indian capital markets and aided by the successful raising of capital abroad by the Indian corporate sector started in late 1993 and continued unabated till September 1994 supplied the monetary base. This inflow of foreign capital had the tendency of pushing up the value of the rupee since there was no accompanying demand from the import side consequently the Reserve Bank of India intervened repeatedly in the forex market to buy up the dollars in order to maintain the rupee-dollar rate at a stable Rs. 37.37 per US Dollar.

The resultant expansion of the money supply was identified as the prime cause for continuing high inflation in the economy. In mid-October 1994, as part of the busy season credit policy announcement the Reserve Bank of India Governor stated that the source of reserve money expansion in 1994-95 till September had been through the increase in net foreign assets of the RBI which showed an increase of Rs. 15596 crore as against a rise of Rs. 3933 crore in the same period of the previous year. Consequently steps were taken by the Reserve Bank in terms of making a policy announcement that money raised abroad by the Indian Corporate sector should be parked abroad till the actual requirement within the country. This eased the pressure on the RBI to buy up dollars. For reasons not anticipated then, the inflow through the foreign institutional investor route also dried up dramatically, dipping from over $ 230 million during September to a paltry $ 10.1 million in

November 1994. The inflow continues through at a drastically reduced rate.

The problem of foreign exchange surges into economics going in for liberalization has cropped up in many parts of the world, particularly in Mexico and China as in India. While the Mexican experience is now familiar China too is said to be facing massive problems with inflation. While the official rate of inflation is said to be somewhere in the region of 28 percent, unofficial figures put the rate at over 40 percent. Fortunately, India has not yet reached that league because the inflow of foreign exchange has not been of the magnitude witnessed in China and Mexico. Unfortunately, for the newly liberalizing economics the IMF has not designed a proper response mechanism to the problem.

It is argued by a section of Indian economists that the Finance Ministry made haste in going in for full scale liberalization without first completing the task of fiscal consolidation. In other words they feel that when the Government decided to open up the Indian capital markets to foreign institutional investors, the efforts to contain the fiscal deficit were on especially so in 1993 when the fiscal restraints became extremely lax and the deficit ended up at a substantial 7.3 percent of GDP. In fact, the fiscal consolidation process had been halted by liberalizing the subsidy scheme and the Government found it difficult to profitably disinvest public sector equity to mobilize resources. Thus when enough potential for the creation of inflationary pressures remained within the economy small liquidity was invited from abroad, particularly through portfolio investments, adding to the problem. Foreign direct investment which is coming in small doses may not have posed problems of such dimensions, though that too might do so in future.

Various proposals have been made from time to time in the context of the forex reserves/inflation connection. They include the liberalization of capital outflow and further liberalization of consumer goods imports which would reduce excess demand which is pushing up the price level. Other proposals include the premature repayment of more burdensome external debts and judicious discouragement of financial inflows. These may be necessary but are not sufficient to deal with the problem.

In this context a proposal has been made and this proposal concerns the establishment of an "Indo-dollar market". Under this proposal the Reserve Bank of India should sell at least $ 5.0 billion worth of foreign currency from the official reserves of $ 20.0 billion to Indian nationals. It is estimated that this will absorb more than Rs. 15000 crore used to buy up dollars at the current rate of exchange. In this way, the supply of money can be reduced by 10 percent. Ceteris Paribus the price level can be brought down by 8-10 percent. These are the main features of the proposal. But the condition is that the authorities (the RBI) should not ask the buyers of dollars about the source of money used to buy up dollars.

Admittedly India's foreign exchange reserves of $ 20.0 billion are far in excess of requirements. The maintenance of these forex reserves entails the maintenance costs. These reserves of dollars and other currencies were acquired in exchange for rupees and these rupees were poured into the market, which had the effect of increasing liquidity. This increased the money supply in the country and raised the level of prices. The question to be answered is : why did India buy up dollars in the first place? Could India not have remained neutral leaving the market to settle things? If this was done the rupee would have appreciated and this would have reduced India's exports by reducing their international competitiveness and would have increased imports by making them cheaper and thus would have caused a big current account deficit. This situation was considered undesirable. If, for instance, the dollar was worth only Rs. 25 instead of Rs. 31.37 the rupee earnings of dollar would have greatly declined. If the dollar was allowed to fall or if the rupee was allowed to rise the inflow of dollars would have abated. For this reason the incoming dollars were purchased and this led to the vast accumulation of reserves which had their inevitable inflationary impact.

If the dollars are sold to Indian nationals at the exchange of Rs.31.37 per dollar there will be no adverse exchange rate impact on the trade balance. But when the dollars are sold to the Indian nationals there will be an excess supply of dollars and this causes a fall in the exchange value of the dollar. This means that the rupee appreciates and this will exercise an adverse effect on the current account. This can be avoided if, along with an increased supply of dollars, an increase in the demand for dollars is also engineered. If this is done, the rupee-dollar exchange rate remains unaltered. In this event the Indian nationals who held rupees earlier would now hold dollars instead. Since dollar is not a national currency it cannot be used in domestic transactions and so the possession of dollars does not generate demand in the same way as the possession of rupees. But if the buyers of dollars which is now in excess supply demand a fall in the exchange rate of the dollar will make Indian exports uncompetitive and keep Indian exports unhappy.

There are several other questions to be answered before putting this scheme into operation. How long could they hold the dollars? Are the holders of dollars free to demand conversion of their dollar holdings into rupees again? In a free market the dollar exchange rate falls when the Reserve Bank of India sells dollars for rupees; again, when the Indian nations seek conversion of dollars into rupees the dollar falls again unless the Reserve Bank of India stands ready to buy the dollars offered by the Indian nationals. The circuitous route adopted by the Reserve Bank of India does not leave us any better. Rupees which flow into the values of the Reserve Bank flow back into the hands of the original owners to generate inflationary pressures. The stock of rupees which fell will rise to its old level leaving us no better than we were before the scheme was put into operation.

This scheme results in a laundering of black money and legitimizing it. According to a recent estimate the stocky black money in the country is of the order of Rs. 1.75 lakh crore. If $ 5.0 billion of foreign exchange reserves are sold to Indian nationals the Reserve Bank temporarily absorbs Rs. 15500 crore of black money. This is only 1/12 of the existing black money. The balance of the black money hoarder remains intact defeating the effectiveness of any anti-inflationary monetary-fiscal policies. Those who purchase dollars with the help of black money will, after a while, sell the dollars for rupees which will now be white money and masquerade as such generating demand for goods and services and exacerbating inflation. The following modification is proposed to the proposal.

- In order to check the entry of black money into the scheme, those who purchase dollars in exchange for rupees should be asked to disclose the source of the rupees they offer in exchange for dollars. This will prevent the laundering of black money into white.
- The purchase of dollars should be at a fixed exchange rate. This will prevent the appreciation of the rupee or depreciation of the dollar with adverse consequences on the balance of payments.
- Those who purchase dollars should hold them for a period of 5 years. During this period the rupees surrendered to the Reserve Bank of India by the buyers of dollars will not enter into circulation. The rate of inflation which comes down in its wake has no chance of rising again.
- Those who seek conversion of their dollar holdings into rupees need to be told that the conversion would be allowed at a discount the rate of discount varying directly with the period that has to lapse between the date of conversion and the final date of settlement. This is similar to but more effective than the Tobin Tax. This will discourage the holders of dollars from seeking conversion of dollars into rupees before the expiry of the period of five years. If dollars are so converted despite the discount mechanism an equivalent amount of dollars should be sold.
- The exchange rate at the time of conversion of dollars into rupees should be the same as the exchange rate that prevailed at the time of purchase of dollars for rupees.
- If there is the danger that the rupees obtained in exchange for dollars on the expiry of the five year period will aggravate inflation the holders of dollars should be given the option to renew their dollar holdings for a further period of five years or if they insist on being paid rupees they should be given not rupees but rupee bonds which will be convertible into rupees at the end of the maturity period. This will make them renew their dollar holdings.

- Those holding dollars should be free to invest them in the government bonds outside India. This will mitigate the pressure on the rupee. When the foreign bonds mature the investors will get dollars, which will have to be converted into rupees as per the prescribed rules.
- Individuals holding dollars but needing rupees can sell their dollar holdings to other individuals directly at the prescribed exchange rate. Rupees in the possession of the buyers of dollars will come into the hands of sellers of dollars with no net increase in rupees.

The modified scheme has the following advantages:

- This will sterilize rupees and thus help to mitigate the inflationary pressures.
- This will prevent the rupee from appreciating with its adverse effects on the trade balance.
- This ensures freedom of concession of dollars into rupees before the expiry of the five year period but at a discount.

The modified Into-Dollar market proposal can be got examined by a team of experts who could refine it wherever such refinement is considered necessary. The scheme is worth trying. If successful the other countries facing a similar problem can adopt it to suit their macroeconomic fundamentals.

The modified Indo-Dollar Market Scheme has the effect of reducing the supply of rupees in the economy and of holding down the rate of inflation so necessary to ensure price competitiveness of India's accounts. This will also help to avoid wage escalation which in turn will help to reduce the fiscal deficit of the Centre and of the states. This scheme supported by fiscal consolidation at all levels of government will eliminate the danger of inflation in the Indian economy and will be a source of solace to the people harried by rising prices. This is a delicate and beautiful scheme and this can be tried with advantage.

# 38

## A Year of Slow Reform Process: Priorities Need to be Reordered in 1994

The on going economic reforms were initiated by the Government in July 1991. After two and a half years of structural adjustment programme several worrying trends are persist. The rate of industrial growth has slowed down because of recession, interest payments on the public debt are soaring widening the fiscal deficit and inflation as on 12-3-1994 has reached the 9.4 percent figure holding out the threat of reaching the double digit figure before long. But there is a silver lining. In July 1991 the foreign exchange reserves were $ 1.1 billion. At present they have reached the $ 14 billion figure though a large part of it is the money borrowed from the IMF, the World Bank and other financial agencies. After three years of reforms in the areas of trade, industry and banking it is still the agricultural sector that is imparting strength and resilience to the economy. The growth rate of agriculture sector has been put down at 4.5 percent in 1993-94. In September 1993 food stocks were 22.6 million tonnes. They were higher by a staggering 117.42 percent when compared with their level in September 1992. Furthermore, on account of lesser off-take by the Public Distribution System the pressure on the existing stock has declined.

But what is worrying is the rise in food prices despite the comfortable level of food stocks. The rise in food prices is accentuated by the hikes in the procurement prices of wheat, rice, sugar, coffee and other essential articles of consumption. Though there is a rise in the rate of inflation to 9.4 percent, the rising prices of food articles are particularly worrying because of their regressive impact on the living standards of the poor. If the food prices are to be brought down, the Government has to release the food stocks to the market as it did in the case of sugar. The fiscal deficit of

7.3 percent of GDP in 1993-94, the sharp rise in the Net Reserve Bank credit to the Government with its impact on the money supply are also factors which have contributed to inflation which at present remains a problem area for the policy maker. The increase in Net Reserve Bank credit to the Government was due to poor revenue collection caused by the reduction in customs duties and excise duties and rising expenditure. This made the Government spokesmen say that the fiscal deficit target of 5.7 percent for 1993-94 could not be met. In fact, it has not been met. It is actually 7.3 percent of GDP. The fiscal deficit target for 1994-95 is put at 6 percent of GDP.

On the expenditure side the Government was able to reduce its expenditure by reducing the subsidies further; on the revenue side collections dropped because of recessionary trends in the industrial sector and the reductions in customs and excise duties which together brought down revenue by Rs. 8000 crore. The recession caused a further fall in revenue collections. Imports also fell causing a fall in customs collections. The general index of industrial production grew by 1.2 percent but the fall in bank credit to the commercial sector points to the persistence of recession. The banks which were flush with funds were investing in safe investment channels like Government securities. But the large procurement of food articles led to a massive increase in food credit. But the year 1993-94 saw an uncertain credit environment as stipulation on capital adequacy and the new provisioning norms have led banks to restrict credit as the year 1994-95 is expected to usher in more reforms in the banking sector. But the reduction in the lending rate by one percent from 15 percent to 15 percent is expected to prove to be anti-recessionary.

Exports picked up dramatically. They rose from 5.4 percent in April to September 1992 to 20.1 percent in the same period in 1993. The main reason for the sudden burst of exports is the bunching of export orders after a lull in the wake of the Bombay riots in December 1992 and January 1993. At the same time a sustained rise in exports is the categorical imperative to enable the country to pay the interest and repay the capital. The net aid receipts declined precipitously pointing to the increased repayment commitments. Payment of interest is also high consuming 30 percent of export proceeds. In 1994-95 the repayment is expected to increase further. This will exert pressure on the forex reserves In this situation export earning is the only answer to the rising repayment commitments though the Government claims that the short term debts have been coming down.

The negotiations for an Extended Fund Facility (EFF) loan were postponed because of the comfortable foreign exchange reserve position. At the same time it must be borne in mind that the strai jacket conditionalities associated with the loan would have put the political will of the policy makers to severe test. On the other hand, after the full convertibility of the rupee on trade account, the exchange rate of the rupee remained stable throughout the year though this stability is to be attributed to the Reserve Bank purchases of dollars as otherwise the rupee would have appreciated against the dollar and other hand currencies to the detriment of international competitiveness of India's exports. The reform process is in line and its pace is accelerating. The Union Budget for 1994-95 is a pointer to the speed of the reform process and its ultimate success. While addressing the World Economic Forum at Davos in Switzerland on 31-1-1994 the Prime Minister underlined the commitment of his government to the success of the reform process.

The success of the reform process is dependent on the understanding of the macroeconomic linkages. A weak link in the Chain will make the entire chain weak. In a system of mutual interdependence where the performance of every link depends on the performance of every other link in the chain all the links should be given due attention. Neglect of any chain under political compulsions will slow down the reform process and, in consequence, the process will not yield the expected results.

A major advance has to be made in the area of poverty alleviation. The 1990 World Development report has estimated that there are 420 million poor in India and 250 million of them are extremely poor. These estimates reflect on the very limited impact of the several poverty alleviation programmes pursued during the era of planning and beams strong signals to politicians, policy makers and development experts to take a fresh look at the basic philosophy which guides the current poverty alleviation programmes. They also highlight the need to design more appropriate programmes to accelerate the process of poverty alleviation. This is all the more relevant today when the new economic reforms are unfolding, albeit slowly and the general impression is that the new policy is not poor-friendly. The poor themselves are suffering from "dependency syndrome" and have resigned to their fate. The future under these circumstances does not hold much promise to the poor in India unless, of course, they come out of their stupor and struggle to break the "low level trap" in which they are caught for long.

In the era of reforms a sea-change has occurred in the economic thinking and policy prescriptions of the Government Liberalisation or no Liberalisation, no economic reform package would have any meaning whatsoever unless it is primarily designed to build safety nets for the poor. Standing on the threshold of the 21st Century, if starvation deaths stare us in the face this may negate the very idea of civilized existence. The current situation warrants a reordering of the priorities in the economic reform package. Food, including supply of drinking water, shelter and health are the only three imaginable pillars on which the edifice of any reform programme should be built.

Poverty alleviation programmes are closely allied to employment generation. A fully employed family is not poor as it commands all the necessities of life. Unemployment is the cause of poverty. Therefore poverty alleviation programmes have to tackle the problem of unemployment first in the sequential order. It is therefore necessary that in 1994 the focus of the reform process should be shifted to the programmes of employment generation and poverty alleviation. These programmes have to be associated with the programmes of reducing the rate of growth of population. The transition to the new era is not painless. The Government has so far fought shy of taking unpleasant decisions. It cannot avoid doing so any longer. For the economy, the current year (1994) would be crucial.

# 39

# Notification of The 60-40 Formula in Partial Convertibility

The Finance Minister, while presenting the Union Budget for 1992-93 on 29-2-1992, announced that the rupee would be partially convertible and that the exporters and NRIs making remittances of foreign exchange can so remit 40 percent of it to the Reserve Bank of India at the official rate and the balance of 60 percent could be sold by them at the market rate. This decision would have inflationary consequences on the Indian economy as the market rate at which the importers buy foreign exchange to pay for imports is higher than the official rate and at the higher price of foreign exchange the importers are sure to raise the prices of final products which use imported goods as inputs. This 40-60 formula was made applicable to NRIs and Indian workers abroad also. This formula had the effect of stimulating Havala transactions where black money is used to purchase foreign exchange.

In order to circumvent this the Reserve Bank of India is contemplating a proposal enabling the migrant workers and other NRIs to exchange their entire remittances at the market rate as against the 40-60 formula.

The Reserve Bank of India authorities feel that the Government can afford to keep the remittances part of the forex inflow out of the 40-60 formula since, according to the official estimates, they have already covered the exchange needed for essential imports made by the Government already.

The Philosophy behind this move is to seal the second most major Havala route (after bullion and silver smuggling) in the country. It is obvious that a number of workers and NRIs prefer to remit money through the alternative channel to profit from the difference in the official and unofficial dollar-rupee rates.

Many Indians working abroad are given the privilege of dual salary: one part of the salary which is recorded is paid to them as white money and the other part which is unrecorded is remitted to their families through the Havala traders. Over 1,75,000 Indian workers are based in the Persian Gulf area. These workers and NRIs remit $ 2.0 billion. The decision of the Reserve Bank of India to allow these people to remit their money at the market rate is expected to curb Havala operations and to bring in consistency in the floating stock in the market available for importers. This is also expected to have a favourable impact on the sentiments in the forex market. The Reserve Bank authorities feel that this move will encourage workers and NRIs to make remittances through the official channel and cut down the scope for generating black money. The Indian workers and NRI remitting foreign exchange to India have good cause for cheer as they are able to sell their foreign exchange at the market rate which is higher than the official rate.

But the Reserve Bank authorities seem to have underplayed the inflationary consequences of this move. The Indian importers who need foreign exchange will have to bid for the foreign exchange remitted by the NRIs and Indian workers in the market. This cause a rise in the market price of dollars and, at the same time, it causes a depreciation of the rupee. The importers who pay the market price for foreign exchange have to pay for imports whose prices rise and they have to raise the prices of the final output embodying the imported inputs. This provides a boost to the rate of inflation domestically and, to the extent that these goods are exported, it retards the export promotion efforts. For this reason, those who remit foreign exchange have to be asked to do so to the Reserve bank of India at the official rate. This should be made applicable to all remittances whether the salary is recorded or unrecorded. This will block the Havala trade and will free the Indian economy from the inflationary consequences of allowing Indian workers and NRIs to remit their foreign exchange earnings to India and sell them at the market rate.

At present every Indian, including infants, returning to India can bring in 5 kgs. of gold and he is free to sell it to others in India at its appreciated value. Those who buy it are, by and large, black money barons who do not mind paying a high price in the attempt to launder their black money into white money. The Reserve Bank now desires that those who bring in gold do not have to carry it in their bags. Instead, having bought the gold they can deposit it with the travel authorities in exchange for a certificate of gold deposit which on arrival in India can be recognized. This will eliminate the risk factor for those who bring in gold but will also enable the authorities to maintain a record of gold arrivals. This is not enough, for those who bring gold to India can surrender the gold certificate on arrival in India, get the gold back and sell it to the black money barons in exchange for black money at the appreciated value. The gold arrivals will go on record but gold will not flow into the vaults of the Reserve Bank. For this reason, the Reserve Bank of India can keep the gold and pay for it in Indian currency at a premium. This will not only increase the stock of gold with the Reserve Bank but will also prevent the laundering of black money into white money.

The above modifications are in the best interests of the country and I hope they will be given due consideration. Mere doctrinaire approach to these intricate problems will not do. It should be given a practical touch in keeping with market realities.

# 40

# Monetary Financing and Debt Financing of the Fiscal Deficit

The fiscal deficit for 1994-95 does not take into account the loss of revenue caused by many tax concessions, however desirable they may be in a recessionary situation. Further the Finance Minister provided for Rs. 5700 crore in the 1993-94 budget and Rs. 5600 crore in the 1994-95 budget to help the banks to meet the capital adequacy norms prescribed by the Basle Committee. These provisions do not enter the budget figures. They are proposed to be in the form of Government bonds and therefore will not involve an immediate cash outgo. But interest payments and amortization will be a charge on the future budgets. Though the Finance Minister has condemned the waiver of loans to farmers he has not hesitated to cover the bad debts of urban commercial interests and of the industrial sector. The public sector under-takings and nationalized banks are required to raise equity and bonds, which will have to be serviced outside the budgetary provisions. It is also proposed to sell equity of public sector undertakings to raise as much as Rs. 4000 crore next year to cover the revenue expenditure of the Government. In consequence the revenue, budget and fiscal deficits next year will therefore be larger than shown in the budget estimates. Side by side the burden of interest payments on the budget is proposed to swell next year and in the years following. The interest payment as a non-plan expenditure of the Government will increase compared to that in 1993-94 by as much as Rs. 8000 crore in 1994-95.

The deficits uncovered in the budget for 1994-95 are claimed not to fuel inflation. This is because the Finance Minister has agreed with the Reserve Bank of India that the net issue of adhoc Treasury Bills during the year should not exceed the estimated Rs. 6000 crore-budget deficit. This is contingent on recouping the loss on account of tax concessions from higher realizations of revenue at reduced rates of taxation by widening the tax base. It must be admitted that covering of revenue deficit by resort to the issue of adhoc Treasury Bills is inflationary as the created money to cover the revenue expenditure of the Government swells demand without generating matching supplies to meet the demand. But it is decided to phase out the issue of adhoc Treasury Bills over a three year period. Besides the decision to restrict the issue of adhoc Treasury Bills to one and half times the budget deficit for not more than ten continuous working days at any time during the year is welcome. This will reduce resort to the Reserve Bank for money.

This, by itself, is insufficient in wiping out the revenue deficit, which is already as much as 40 percent of the revenue expenditure. This is due to the interest payments on the accumulated interest bearing debt of the Government. Borrowing from the market for covering the revenue deficit and even the fiscal deficit when such borrowing is used to meet revenue expenditure or even if productively spent does not result in revenue yield higher than the rate of interest on borrowing may not pump created money into the economy and therefore cannot have a direct and immediate impact on inflation as the Quantity Theory of Money makes us believe. But it is inflationary all the same for two reasons; (a) such borrowing forecloses available resources for the Government to be used for non-productive and non-profitable purposes and adds to interest burden on the budget. This makes it difficult to balance the revenue budget and generate surpluses for productive investment in economic development. (b) it is held in recent fiscal theory that while money financing and debt financing of the deficit are both inflationary, debt financing is more inflationary than money financing. While money financing raises the price level once, debt financing raises it year after year. Debt financing results in interest payments which are an item of non-plan expenditure. This widens the deficit and is inflationary. As the interest burden is to be borne so long as the debts remain un-repaid it adds to the deficit every year and raises the price level every year during the pendency of the loan.

The Government has been borrowing from the market in the form of interest bearing dated securities, 364 days Treasury Bills and so on to cover the revenue and fiscal deficits. This merely postpones the day of reckoning and is unhelpful in keeping the inflationary forces under effective control which is the ostensible purpose of phasing out recourse to adhoc Treasury Bills. The recourse to borrowing imposes a severe burden on the future generations besides exacerbating inflationary pressures in the economy.

The Finance Minister's proposal to put a cap on Government borrowing from the Reserve Bank of India is welcome for two reasons: (a) if there is a limit on Government borrowing from the Reserve Bank of India, the Government will be compelled to manage its finances better; (a) indiscriminate borrowing from the Reserve Bank hampers efficient conduct of monetary policy since such borrowing leads to the creation of high-powered money which fuels inflationary fires in the economy. Therefore, the limit and subsequent phasing out of Government's recourse to the Revenue Bank will instill much needed fiscal discipline in Government expenditure and enable the Reserve Bank to frame its monetary policy over a longer time period. However, if the imposition of a limit on Government borrowing from the Reserve Bank causes a shift in the source of borrowing from the Reserve Bank to the public without tackling the problem of mounting fiscal deficit, the proposals, from the point of view of inflation control is not of much use.

The idea of imposing a limit on Government borrowing from the Reserve Bank is not new. In fact, it has been a long-standing demand of the Reserve Bank of India. The Finance Minister has conceded the merit of this demand and has placed a limit of Rs. 9000 crore on the net issue of Treasury Bills at any point of time. The arrangement is that if this limit is exceeded for more than 10 continuous working days the Reserve Bank will automatically sell Treasury Bills in the market to bring down the level of outstanding adhocs. Over the subsequent three years, recourse to the Reserve Bank is to be progressively reduced. By 1997-98 direct recourse to the Reserve Bank is to cease altogether and in subsequent years the entire Government requirement is to be met through Government borrowing from the market.

The impact of this proposal has to be gauged when viewed in the context of the sheer volume that will have to be mobilized from the market if the fiscal deficit continues unchecked. Currently, the deficit is financed partly by borrowing and the balance is automatically covered by the issue of adhoc Treasury Bills. The issue of adhoc Treasury Bills which began as a temporary arrangement in the mid-1950s to enable the Government to tide over short-term mismatches in its funds flow has, over the years, degenerated into something quite different into a routine recourse to adhocs. This arrangement had its effect on the management of the Government finances. The budgetary deficit rose from Rs. 6858 crore in 1991-92 to Rs. 12,312 crore in 1992-93, and though it declined to Rs. 9060 crore in the revised budget estimates for 1993-94 the figure was much higher during the greater part of the year.

Correspondingly, there has been a phenomenal increase in the total outstanding Treasury Bills. Until 1955 the outstanding was well below Rs. 500 crore. Subsequently it rose to Rs. 2518 crore by March 1971 and further to Rs. 12851 crore by March 1981. The profligacy of the Government in the 1980s saw the figure rise to Rs. 19,266 crore a decade later. In fact, but for the funding of Treasury Bills to the tune of Rs. 71,000 crore during the 1980s the actual outstanding as at the end of March 1993 would have been Rs. 90,266 crore. A large part of these Treasury Bills was held by the Reserve Bank of India resulting in the monetisation of the budget deficit. Thus the outstanding reserve money created by the reserve Bank as at the end of March 1993 stood at Rs. 1,10,943 crore. Of this the Reserve Bank credit to the Government accounted for 87 percent. In such a situation a ceiling on Government borrowing from the Reserve Bank marks the beginning in controlling a situation that was threatening to go out of control.

With the gradual closure of an easy route to financing the fiscal deficit market borrowing will have to fund an increasingly larger part of the fiscal deficit. This entails a greater danger than monetary financing.

However, in the past market borrowing posed no problem as the banks were compelled to hold Government debt through the imposition of the Statutory Liquidity Ratio (SLR) which ensured a captive market for Government securities at low rates of interest. As long as the SLR could be raised funding an ever increasing volume of Government borrowing was not difficult as any short fall could be bridged by the issue of adhoc Treasury Bills. But such fund raising had a price attached to it. A high SLR reduced bank profitability. After a while SLR borrowing were bound to plateau. This has happened at present. At present any attempt to improve bank profitability is linked to a reduction in the SLR. This reduces the extent of the captive market for Government debt. Thus the success of such a borrowing programme depends on the pricing of such debt.

The average rate of interest on internal liabilities rose from 8.2 percent in 1990-91 to 9.1 percent in 1992-93. For 1993-94 it is well in excess of 10 percent. According to the budget documents interest payments for the coming year are estimated at Rs. 46,000 crore or 53.4 percent of revenue receipts. With newer loans raised at higher interest rates, interest payments will account for an overwhelmingly large share of the total revenue receipts. Ideally the higher interest cost should restrain Government borrowing in order to bring down the fiscal deficit by restraining the Government expenditure / raising its revenue receipts. But the impact of costly borrowing will be felt only after a lapse of time. As a result the willingness to reduce such borrowing is weak in a democracy. In this situation the burden of future servicing of the debt may assume astronomical proportions. This is bound to reduce the availability of funds for financing developmental expenditure.

As averred about there are two methods of financing the deficit; (a) monetary financing and (b) debt financing. Monetary financing is inflationary in the short run but it does not impose any burden of debt on future generations. Debt financing of the deficit is inflationary in the medium and long run as it involves payment of interest, which widens the fiscal deficit. The Government has chosen to reduce its dependence on monetary financing and to increase its dependence on debt financing. It must be borne in mind that the market is no longer captive to lend to the Government at a reduced rate of interest. The reduction of interest rate involves a raising of the SLR which involves the erosion of profitability of the banking system. Restoration of profitability of the banks and their observance of the capital adequacy norms involves a reduction of the SLR and a raising of the rate of interest on market borrowings. This imposes a burden on future generations besides enlarging the fiscal deficit which would have inflationary consequences greater than those involved in monetary financing of the deficit. Both types of financing are to be brought down. The imposition of a cap on adhocs Treasury Bills has the effect of reducing monetary financing. At a time when the rate of monetary growth has jumped from 11.5 percent to 14.5 percent, this is a welcome step. But this has to be followed by a ceiling market borrowing involved in debt financing of the deficit. In my earlier memoranda on the subject I have proposed the imposition of a constitutional limit on Government borrowing relaxable only by parliamentary approval. If, at any time, borrowing becomes inevitable to meet the budget deficit, monetary financing, subject to a ceiling, should be resorted to, as it does not involve an accentuation of the fiscal deficit or a burden on the taxpayers.

# 41

## Restructuring of Regional Rural Banks

Regional Rural Banks are urgently in need of restructuring in order to involve them in rural renaissance. They were conceived as alternatives to the nationalized commercial banks which had virtually neglected the credit needs of the rural sector. The nationalized banks were to reserve 40 percent of their resources for lending to the priority sector at concessional rates of interest. The rural sector was denied access to these banks for credit let alone at concessional rates of interest.

The Narasimham Committee on Financial Sector Reform recommended for reaching changes in the structure, organization and policy of the nationalized banks. According to the Committee 40 percent of the resources reserved for the priority sector had to be phased out in order to improve the profitability of these banks and to make them satisfy the capital adequacy norms. Their operations since they were nationalized in 1969 have landed them in losses. They have relegated to the background the regional rural banks which they themselves sponsored in order to meet the credit needs of the rural sector.

Is there any justification for the regional rural banks to maintain a separate identity? The root of the problem is that the present differential credit system does not seem to have worked well. The Narasimham Committee has come to the conclusion that this is one of the several practices responsible for the low profitability of the nationalized banks. There were other resources besides like large over-dues often encouraged by political leaders, inefficient management and large administrative expenses. The Narasimham Committee held that unless the rates of interest were such as to ensure sufficient margin for the banks they would not be able to generate adequate returns on the capital employed by them. In view of this Committee recommended that the concessional lending to the priority sector should be phased out. But the Committee made an exception in the case of setting aside atleast 10 percent of the credit for the weaker sections of society and the areas otherwise considered necessary.

In the light of these recommendations the whole question of the continuance of the regional rural banks has been called into question. The RRBs were conceived as the low cost alternative to the nationalized banks to meet the credit needs of the rural sector. The licensing policy required that a certain number of rural branches had to be opened before the banks could open a branch in the more profitable metropolitan areas. The philosophy behind this condition was that the banks have a social function to perform in conformity with the objectives of nationalization. The banks took heed of this condition and opened many branches in the rural areas. Even these branches could not fully meet the credit needs of the rural sector. This can be explained by the inability of the co-operative credit structure to expand to the extent required. It was then realized that the commercial banks were unable to provide rural credit at low interest rates on account of the high and rising overhead costs. This perception made the Government structure the RRBs as low cost and often single person branches, the recruitment of personnel being made mostly within the area of operation of these banks. These employees were paid low salaries lower than the salaries paid to the employees of the commercial banks. The plea of the employees of the RRBs that their salary should be on par with the salary of the employees of the commercial banks was upheld by the Tribunal as legally valid. With this the rationale for the separate existence of the RRBs has ceased to exist as they have failed to satisfy the original intention of the sponsorers of these RRBs. The employees of the RRBs draw the same salary as the employees of the nationalized banks; the Government emphasizes that all banks should follow the rules of Commercial operations in order to ensure adequate profitability. In view of this, the RRBs are not in a position to supply cheap credit to the rural sector.

The detractors of the RRBs seem to have made much of the failure of banks to ensure lower over dues in agriculture. This is quite understandable. But the problem of overdues in large and medium industries is as serious as that in agriculture. But not many talk about these overdues. Even if the talks take place it is at best hush-hush. This is blatantly discriminating.

There are at present 196 loss-making branches of the RRBs. The Finance Minister in his budget for 1994-95 has provided for undertaking comprehensive restructuring of the 50 RRBs which are making losses. The restructuring process includes cleaning up of their balance sheets and infusion of fresh capital. The Finance Minister has stated that the experience of these 50 RRBs would guide the Government in its future approach to the remaining Regional Rural Banks.

The mode of restructuring of the RRBs has to be elucidated.

- The RRBs are to supply credit to the rural sector at a cheaper rate of interest. The overheads are not as heavy for a rural branch as for a branch in the metropolitan areas. From this reason the RRBs can make loans at cheaper interest rates without any erosion of their profitability;
- In the rural areas there is the possibility of the loans obtained ostensibly for agricultural purposes seeping into non-agricultural purposes especially social purposes through an osmotic process. This makes the recovery of loans very difficult and the banks are sure to be overloaded with non-performing assets. Therefore, a machinery to monitor the use of the borrowed funds should be designed so that the borrowed funds are put to the uses for which they were borrowed. This will ensure prompt repayment of the principal and the payment of interest as per schedule;
- The RRBs have to satisfy the capital adequacy norms in the same way as the nationalized banks. The Government in the 1993-94 budget provided for Rs. 5,700 crore to the banks to enable them to satisfy the capital adequacy norms and in the 1994-95 budget it has provided for Rs. 5,600 crore for the purpose. In a similar manner the Government should make adequate provision for ensuring that the RRBs observe the capital adequacy norms;

- The recovery of the loans except in case of natural calamities like floods and drought should be ordered. Those who delay repayment on payment of interest should be asked to pay a penal interest rate on the amount outstanding;
- Computerization of the banking operations is on the cards. But, computerization of the operations of the RRBs are unnecessary at the present stage as the banks have to deal with unsophisticated rural folk. The employees who feel that their jobs are secure in the absence of computerization will have no cause for raising disputes with their employers;
- The loans should be advanced just before the agricultural operations start in order to avoid the misuse of borrowed funds involved in early sanction. The reason for this procedure should be explained to the farmers so that they may understand the rationale behind this scheme;
- Frequent transfers of the bank employees is to be avoided and if transfers are found to be inevitable the employees should be transferred to the other branches in the rural areas and not to the Bank branches in the metropolitan areas;
- Medium term loans should be extended for works associated with agricultural operations like digging irrigation wells, purchase of electric pump sets and other equipment necessary for farming operations;
- There will be demands for loan waivers for any and every reason. But the loan waiver should be resorted to only for genuine reasons after the receipt of satisfactory reports from the monitoring cell;
- The bank officials in a defined area should meet once a month to discuss their problems, to exchange ideas about loans and recoveries and matters connected with administration.
- Adequate funds must be placed at the disposal of these banks so that the genuine needs of borrowers do not suffer;
- A team of experts should be appointed to suggest the modalities of restructuring;

In these ways the RRBs can be made to play a vital role in agricultural growth and rural renaissance, remaining commercially viable at the same time.

# 42

## Exit of Industrial Sickness

The market-friendly economic reforms initiated by the Government of India in July 1991 are in progress. But the future of these reforms is dependent crucially on the attitude of organized labour. The major trade unions are united to demonstrate their solidarity over the major economic issues affecting them. Their attitude which was one of the gentle persuasions has transformed itself into one of militancy. The labour unions are apprehensive that in the event of the economic reforms being implemented in all their segments of the economy, especially in the industrial sector, they have to face the spectre of unemployment and the associated poverty and destitution. They are also resentful of their not being involved in the emerging economic structure.

The Indian economy is to undergo a process of globalisation. Its industrial structure is to be attuned to face the highly developed industrial structure the world over. Admittedly this is not an easy task. The old and ante-deluvian industrial structure hardly fits the new system. Consequently, if the industrial structure is to be able to face world competition, it has to be drastically refurbished. But refurbishing the industrial structure is not possible unless redundant and inadequately skilled labour is retrenched. The labour unions are not prepared to welcome this situation. They are also apprehensive of the invasion of industry by foreign capital and technology. The present economic reform process does not embody a strategy to employ the vast army of labourers in the new areas of employment that will emerge. It is assumed by the authorities that the labourers will find their footing in the new industrial environment on their own without any assistance from the Government. Both the Government and the labour unions have adopted rigid positions which could distort the reform process.

In recent months labour is adopting a militant posture. The labour unions have already drawn up schedules of strikes and demonstrations for September 1993. The employees of the banking sector, major public sector undertakings and the railways are to join the fray. This is to be expected considering the pitched opposition of labour to the on-going economic reforms.

In this context the exit policy announced by the Government in July 1991 has come in for a good deal of uninformed opposition as the labour unions see the exit policy as a threat to their employment prospects. The confederation of Indian Industry (CII) has made it clear that the exit policy need not be an essential part of economic reforms. It has sought to find a via media through the mechanism of voluntary retirement. This seems to be based on the assumption that a form of "golden handshake" could be evolved in a manner acceptable to labour and this scheme would solve the problem of surplus labour in the industrial sector. But the voluntary retirement scheme so far had not had the desired impact. Furthermore, this scheme is unlikely to reduce the employee strength to the degree necessary to free the industrial sector from the burden of redundant labour as the funds required to implement the scheme are not there to meet the needs of golden handshake. For instance, in the railways 20 percent of the total labour force employed or 4 lakh labourers are surplus. To implement the voluntary retirement scheme in this sector the Government needs thousands of crore of rupees. The implementation of the scheme in other sectors needs colossal sums of money which it is not easy to mobilize. The reason for this scenario is the static employment situation. The remedy for this situation appears to be not wholesale lay-off but the creation of alternative job opportunities.

As it is, the industrial sector is sick. This has been made abundantly clear in the report of the Goswami Committee on industrial sickness. This report has focused attention for the first time on industrial sickness. A dynamic economy forging ahead at globalization has to encounter a certain degree of industrial mortality as the neo-classical economic paradigm has made it so obvious. The primary task of the Government in the present phase of liberalization is to tackle the problem of industrial sickness on a priority basis. Though the Act on industrial sickness was passed eight years ago and though the economic reforms programme was implemented over two years ago, the approach of the Government to this problem is clouded and hazy. There have been a number of expert studies on the causes of industrial sickness but the Government has not paid any attention to the findings of these studies. It expounds the popular misconception that industrial sickness is largely due to technological progress and financial constraints. What is ignored is the fact that the quality of management and its integrity are the decisive factors. This approach can be checkmated by the interested lobbies which do not want a quick solution to the vexing issue. Industrial sickness does not necessarily mean that losses are incurred all-round. It is an open secret that corrupt managements which siphon off funds and even inventories of raw materials and spare parts from healthy units are a cause of the problem. Many sick industries which are propped up by unquestioned and almost continuous flow of funds from the banks have become lucrative hunting grounds for corrupt managers. These facts have to be duly recognized if an effective solution to the problem of industrial sickness is to be found. The Goswami Committee report has come in for a good deal of criticism. But it cannot be again said that it is the only official study which has so ably brought out quite candidly the scamier aspects of the problem of industrial sickness. The Government's refusal to face the truth fully all along has made the situation worse generating cynism among the labourers. They are suspicious of any move initiated by the Government to solve the problem of industrial sickness and they are prone to attack any idea that smells of rehabilitation of retrenched labourers. The first step that the Government should take is to restore the credibility of its intentions.

The exit policy was announced by the Finance Minister in his Budget speech in July 1991. Financial provision was made for this purpose. The provision is of the order of Rs. 2500 crore. Even the World Bank has made its contribution to it. This is called the Society Safety Net meant to help the retrenched labourers to get training in the new skills and to re-deploy them in the areas where their newly acquired skills are required.

The private sector industrial units are generating subsidiary employment opportunities. It is beyond one's comprehension why the public sector units have not been doing the same. It is necessary to emphasise that ancillary and small scale units are the most acceptable means of generating employment. They generate additional income and employment in the regions where they operate; they also serve as efficient vendoring system for the larger plants. The present policy in the matter of small scale units is hardly conducive to the development of these units though they are necessary to have a close relation of supply and purchase with large scale units which need their services. Some State Governments have developed industrial estates tailored to specific kinds of industrial needs. But this experiment needs to be tried out on a large scale throughout the country in view of its great employment potential.

The major trade unions have issued a call for the Bharath Bundh on September 9, in protest against the Government's new economic policy. This strike is likely to paralyse general life and have a wide impact on the country's economy. The trade union leaders say that several issues in the new economic policy like privatization, disinvestments of PSU shares, exit policy, closure of several sick units, retrenchment of workers etc., have forced the workers to totally oppose the policy. The joint statement issued by them said, that its charter of demands "constituted a defence of India's economic sovereignty and refusal to be dictated by the IMF and the World Bank" and solicited the support of all "democratic and patriotic forces".

There is admittedly a stalemate on the industrial front and this stalemate is not conducive to industrial growth or to the success of the economic reforms programme in general. This underlines the need to evolve a comprehensive policy on the industrial development which takes due notice of the needs of labour. Labour and capital are two important factors of production besides technology. Unless labour cooperates with capital and technology, abundance of capital and highly sophisticated technology will be of no avail. Exit policy is absolutely necessary to revitalize the industrial sector and, in the process of revitalization, certain unviable and chronically sick units have to be closed down. The labourers who are retrenched are to be retrained in the new skills and re-deployed in the units requiring their newly acquired skills. The industrial sector cannot be dynamic and vibrant if it encompasses sick units also for sickness being contagious the healthy units may also catch sickness. If this happens the industrial economy cannot be competitive and unless it is competitive it cannot face global competition. Hence, the urgent need for an exit policy. The labour unions apprehending unemployment are opposed to exit policy. But if they are assured, the assurance being made credible, that they need not fear the onset of unemployment as the social safety net is there to cushion the impact of any unemployment of a transitory nature; there is no reason why they should resist the exit policy. Of course adequate financial provision needs to be made for the social safety net. The Prime Minister, fearing the militancy of the labour unions has given the assurance that the exit policy will not be pursued. If this is the Government's policy the flow of foreign capital and technology is likely to be impeded to the detriment of vibrant industrial growth. The World Bank insists on the exit policy being implemented. The Government's delay in the matter has obviously made the World Bank unhappy. It lends a helping hand to India in times of acute financial distress. This goodwill has to be preserved and strengthened. The Government will do well to :

- Take measures to eradicate sickness in the industrial sector as recommended by the Goswami Committee, in particular, by eliminating corrupt managements and by increasing managerial efficiency.
- Pursue an exit policy arranging for retraining and re-deployment of retrenched labour.
- Seek the active cooperation of labour in order to ensure the success of exit policy.

The sooner this is done, the better it is for the industrial economy of India. It is only then that the philosophy of liberalization and globalization has any meaning. What should be allowed to make an exit, along with unviable units, are corruption, inefficiency and sickness in the industrial economy as a whole. The country is on the road to marketisation. The pangs of progress are inevitable and the country has got to put up with them. Mao Tse Tung of China once said that development does not mean participation in free lunch. He was quite right. What is necessary is a drastic restructuring of the economic system. Cosmetic exercises of the kind being attempted on the periphery at present are not the answer. Exit policy which entails the mortality of sick units is the right answer. It is high time that the Government revises its stand and implements the Exit policy with no loss of time. The labour unions cannot be allowed to hold the country to ransom.

# 43

# Financial Sector Reforms are an Urgent Necessity

The Narasimham Committee Report on Financial Sector Reforms submitted to the Government nearly two years ago was for the most part kept in cold storage. Fortunately it is about to be activated as it is a "crucial conditionality" prescribed by the World Bank in connection with its $500 million financial sector loan being negotiated at present. A high level four member team visited Bombay in the last week of July 1993 to hold discussions with the Reserve Bank of India authorities on this loan. The Financial Sector loan has been under negotiations for over a year. But it had to be shelved due to the break down of the negotiations in February 1992 over the issue of doing away with priority sector lending. If the present negotiations succeed and, in consequence, if the loan of $500 million is made to India, it will be used to recapitalise banks whose capital has been badly eroded after the recently announced clean-up of their balance sheets.

The World Bank team is reported to be insisting on a more comprehensive implementation of the Narasimham Committee recommendations. During the past year several recommendations made by the Narasimham Committee have been accepted. But there are several issues over which differences persist like the formation of an Asset Reconstruction Fund for bad and doubtful loans of banks and doing away with priority sector lending and behest lending. But this time the Government is likely to give in and to agree to these conditionalities also. The financial sector loan of $500 million may not be crucial to India at the present juncture, but the banking sector reforms are said to be part of the cross conditionalities for the structural adjustment loan which is crucial to India. The World Bank team held discussions with the leading nationalised banks such as the State Bank of India, Bank of Baroda and others in the matter of implementing the financial sector reforms. The World Bank team is likely to demand the stricter provisioning norms in respect of banks bad loan portfolio, further reduction in directed lending, restructuring of rural banking, giving more teeth to the Securities and Exchange Board of India (SEBI) and further de-regulation of non-banking finance companies, allowing nationalized banks a greater degree of financial, functional and operational autonomy and permitting the entry of foreign capital in the financial services sector. The Government is yet to announce a comprehensive policy regarding foreign equity holdings in financial services companies. But a priority list for reforms in the financial sector is said to have been prepared by the Government and in all likelihood they will be implemented by the end of November 1993. The November deadline assumes importance considering the fact that by the time India's ongoing negotiations with the IMF for a loan of $5 billion under extended fund facility will be reaching an advanced stage of completion. Added to this, are the negotiations for a $500 million World Bank loan for financial sector reform.

It is expected that by the end of November 1993 the Government would complete the task of recapitalisation of banks. At present the scheme for the allocation of Rs. 5,700 crore among the nationalised banks to meet a part of their additional capital requirement are being worked out. This money will be provided in the form of bonds. The interest income earned by the banks annually will increase their profitability. Furthermore, the bonds by virtue of their being treated as capital assets will help the banks to meet the capital adequacy norms. At the same time, a framework of performance norms is being worked out to evaluate the performance of the nationalized banks, the idea being to improve the quality of assets. The Asset Reconstruction Fund as suggested by the Narasimham Committee to take over bad and doubtful loans can allow the banks to begin their operations with a clean slate. Till the issue is sorted out, the new lending norms would check deterioration of the banks performing assets. It is suggested that the recapitalisation fund provided in the Budget should be allocated only to those nationalized banks which are reasonably viable. As on today, only seven nationalized banks have earned net profits in their operations in 1992-93, four have made net losses and nine have made operating losses. In view of the new accounting norms including provisioning for depreciation and bad debts, the number of banks which will be suffering net losses during 1993-94 is likely to increase further. As per the new accounting norms, including provisioning for depreciation and bad debts, the banks with huge losses should be closed. But as these banks are government owned it is impossible to close them. In this case they will have to be merged with bigger banks with a high degree of viability. It is held in official circles that once the merger is effected the culture of better banks will prevail. This is only a sweet conjecture and the possibility of the viable banks succumbing to the evil influence of the merged banks cannot be ruled out. There is bound to be friction between the employees of the viable banks and those of the merged banks. The staff of the merging banks will have to be done or two grades below their counterparts in the larger bank with better work culture. It is hoped that this arrangement would be accepted by the bank employees' unions and the Indian Bank Association as the chances of promotion are likely to improve for the employees of the merger banks once the merger is completed. The employees of the merged banks may take the stand that they are not responsible for the losses suffered by their banks and despite their best efforts at maintaining ideal bank culture the losses occurred and they are not to blame for these losses. They say that it would be to damage their self respect if they are placed one or two grades below the employees of the bigger banks. That there will be promotional opportunities in future is a poor consolation for them, for even after promotion they will have to remain one or two grades below the employees in the bigger banks considering the fact that the promotions will be given to employees of all grades and the employees of the bigger banks will move above the employees of the merged banks even after the promotions of the latter. This they consider to be *infra dig* for them. It would, therefore, be wrong to take the concurrence of the merged employees for granted. The proposed arrangement is bound to result in friction. Already, the bank employees are determined to go on the war path in the event of computerization of the banking operations. It would be too much to expect them to view with any degree of equanimity the proposed arrangement regarding the grades to be given to the employees of the merged banks. The question of delinking the functions from salary to reward the really talented staff is important. The bank employees are placed in different grades and they move from a lower to a higher grade with the salary scale attached to it and this salary must be paid to them. The idea of rewarding the really talented staff with higher emoluments is good but it is bound to smack of arbitrariness on the part of the benefactor. There is also the idea of the Chairman of the banks being given wide powers to select their respective teams without reference to seniority. There is a proposal to set up a search Committee headed by the Chairman of each bank to select the really talented among the existing staff. Promotion by seniority is the rule unless the officer who has been superseded suffers from infirmities in the course of his service. But normally if his record of service is good (though not very much talented) he has to be handpicked for jobs requiring talented performance. What the talent is, of course, is a subjective judgement and the person who is not selected despite his fine record of service is bound to feel aggrieved and to take the matter to the bank unions who are bound to fight out his case. These frictions are real and it would be hazardous to overlook them.

The issue of entry of foreign capital to the insurance sector is thorny. But there does not seem to be any clear thinking on this subject at the official level. But this is a major conditionality prescribed by the IMF and the World Bank and they do not seem to be prepared for any compromise on this issue at the time of granting the extended fund facility of $5 billion by the IMF and the financial sector loan of $500 million by the World Bank. However, the Finance Ministry has set up a committee to look into the matter. The Government has on its agenda the recapitalisation of the nationalized banks by tapping the capital market by November/ December 1993 by effecting the necessary legislative changes.

For nearly two years since the Narasimham Committee submitted its report no major recommendations have been touched upon either by the Government or by the Reserve Bank of India. The Government should realize that having introduced the liberlisation process in trade and industry and also some positive action on the fiscal front, there is an urgent need to take prompt action in the financial sector. The Reserve Bank has to initiate an action programme for the commercial banks for implementation. What is necessary is to allow the market forces to determine the interest rates and to remove the existing ceiling and flow rates of interest rates on bank deposits and lending rates and to arrange for restructuring of the commercial banks based on the four-tier system as suggested by the Narasimham Committee. The system should consist of (a)large banks international in character, (b) 8 to 10 national banks engaged in universal banking, (c) local banks confined to specific regions and (d) rural banks catering to the needs of agriculture and rural sector.

The present banking structure is unable to meet the challenges of global competition. The step to be taken in this regard is the freeing of the determination of the prices of various commodities in the real sector of the economy. Such market mechanism exists in the developed countries of the world and this can happen in the Indian economy provided the government takes bold action to liberalise the economy still more. Furthermore, all interest rates are to be left to be determined by the market forces. There should be no discrimination between the commercial banks and the cooperative banks. The rationalization of the interest rate structure by the Sukhamoy Chakravarty Committee to review the working of the monetary system examined this issue as far back as 1985 observes as under:

"Interest rates applicable to a substantial portion of bank asset portfolio are either lower than or barely above its cost of funds. This is not a healthy situation".

The Committee has also expressed the view that the growth in the real sector of the economy will depend on the entire restructuring of our financial system which has become inefficient and weak. According to the Committee, "As the financial system has an important role to perform in the growth and development of the economy it is essential that the system (a) functions at a high level of both allocational and operational efficiency (b) stable and (c) introduces instruments and financing techniques to meet the everchanging preferences of the savers and investors". Therefore, the need for restructuring and improving the financial system has been rightly conceived by the Narasimham Committee when it states in its report that "there is a need to improve the efficiency and effectiveness in order to improve the health of the present financial system".

According to the Narasimham Committee, the banking sector which is an important segment of the financial sector, is almost collapsing; its efficiency is at a low ebb and its profitability is almost eroded. The Committee recommended the restructuring of the banking sector so that it can face the emerging global challenges. According to the Committee the banking industry during the 1990s should imbibe the spirit of competition; it should become aggressive in its marketing strategy and for attaining and enhancing its profitability: the banking system should strengthen its international management system. In the realm of interest rate structure the Committee suggested reduction in the number of lending and deposit interest rates. The World Bank authorities who had examined the financial system earlier advocated, in their report on "India's Financial Sector", the strengthening of the financial system by gradual reduction of the Statutory Liquidity Ratio (SLR) and cash Reserve Ratio (CRR); rationalization of the interest rate structure, introduction of new prudential norms for income recognition; provision for bad debts and reclassification of health code systems, etc.

The financial sector plays an important part in the development process. The financial system during the past four decades has met the requirements of agriculture, industry, trade and commerce remarkably well. However, there was a deliberate attempt on the part of the government and the Reserve Bank of India to allocate credit. This measure ensured the distributional aspect of credit management industry-wise, sector-wise as well as region-wise satisfactorily.

Although India's achievements in the growth of the financial sector are outstanding and its spread has been broad-based, the World Bank is not satisfied with its progress. It feels that the financial sector has to be liberalized if the country has to register faster economic growth in the 1990s. In 1989 the World Bank Development Report observed that "In the past, government's efforts to promote economic development by controlling interest rates, directing credit, to priority sectors and securing expensive funding for their own activities, has undermined the financial development". In short, the World Bank feels that state intervention in the financial system has constrained its growth, and it can play a crucial role in the 1990s provided it is left to and develop through market forces which, in turn, will help accelerate economic development process in the country.

The structure of administered interest rates in the past hampered the efficiency of the financial system. In April 1985 following the recommendations of the Chakravarti Committee a beginning to rationalize the interest rates was made. The Reserve Bank of India announced that the number of prescribed maturity periods for fixed deposits was shortened from 9 to 5. Thereafter the Reserve Bank took a further step to fix a minimum lending rate for commercial banks. The call money rate which had remained pegged to 10 percent for a long time was freed in September 1989 keeping with the spirit of liberalization. A bold step was taken in September 1992 when all sector specific and programme specific interest rate structure was discontinued. In order to reduce the complexity in the administered interest rate structure, the Reserve Bank decided to link interest rates to size of loans with only a fixed floor rate of interest. In March 1993 the interest rate slabs were reduced from four in 1992 to three in March 1993. These are vital steps taken by the Reserve Bank of India to liberalise the process in the financial sector, and the Reserve Bank allowed the commercial banks to charge higher interest rates to borrowers as no ceiling was prescribed for them. These steps in the direction of gradual deregulation of interest rates were in the right direction since it wanted to establish a clear relation between the risk and the return on investment. The Reserve Bank has to deregulate the entire interest rate regime and should not intervene in fixing the interest rates on deposits as well as the lending rates in future.

What has been attempted in the area of financial sector reform so far are not of much consequence even though they are important. A lot more needs to be done. But the Government is dithering. It is therefore understandable that the World Bank has made the grant of a loan of $500 million conditional on financial sector reform. The Government is committed to complete the process by the end of November 1993. But caution is necessary in respect of one of them.

The Bank Nationalization Act directed the commercial banks to earmark 40 percent of their aggregate resources to be lent to the priority sectors at concessional interest rates. This is said to be one of the causes of low profitability of the banking system. The Narasimham Committee redefined the priority sector and fixed the target for this sector at 10 percent of aggregate bank credit. The World Bank insists on observing this target limit. This part of the reform needs to be negotiated making it necessary for the priority sector lending to fall to 10 percent in gradual stages and not at one go.

The plan for priority sector lending was evolved with a definite objective. There were three priority sectors eligible for concessional lending; agriculture, small scale industry and the export sector. Agriculture was to be a targeted sector of growth meant to increase food supply to feed the growing population and to increase the supply of agricultural raw materials for exports. Small scale industries were to receive the benefit of concessional lending as this sector, being labour intensive, would generate employment in the rural and urban sectors. The export sector had to receive the benefit of concessional lending in order to promote exports in the context of the growing balance of payments gap. The priority status of these sectors remains unaffected whatever be their new definition. Agriculture is on the threshold of globalisation and in the context of the Dunkel Draft Text the process of globalisation has to be accelerated; small scale industrial sector has to be made viable in the context of growing sickness and it should be made to increase its employment potential; the export sector has to be made vibrant in the context of the growing balance of payments gap. The justification for treating them as priority sectors is as valid now as it was in 1969. But in the light of experience care should be taken to see that the funds lent to these sectors are properly utilized. Experience has shown that funds borrowed for productive purposes seep into unproductive channels through an osmotic process. This should not be allowed to recur. A monitoring cell is necessary to ensure that the funds borrowed are used for the purpose for which they are borrowed. An ombudsman should be set up to direct the use of the borrowed funds for legitimate purposes. If the bank resources lent to these sectors are suddenly reduced to 10 percent of the banks credit these sectors are sure to labour under paucity of funds and to come to grief. Therefore, it is suggested that the priority sector lending should be reduced in gradual stages and not in one go. Admittedly priority sector lending at concessional interest rates is inconsistent with a market economy. But India is not yet a fully marketised economy though it is on the road to it. Therefore, the priority sector lending should be brought down from 40% to 30% to 20% and then to 10% wholesale liberalization at one go may do more harm than good. For this reason, this part of the conditionality should be negotiated with the World Bank which should be persuaded not to press this part of the conditionality for adoption.

Economic reform is not an isolated process. Only an integrated approach covering all the major sectors of the economy simultaneously can ensure the success of the steps taken in July 1991. However, in the entire process of reforms an important area like financial sector has not been as stressed upon as it ought to have been. The reforms in the financial sector are long overdue. The financial policy matters documented in the Narasimham Committee Report have created an environment for change in the financial sector of the Indian economy. The Government which is committed to the philosophy of market driven economy in contrast to the earlier centrally controlled economic planning must assume a greater role in implementing the recommendations of the Narasimham Committee to speed up the reform process. The delay in implementing the financial sector reform can affect the growth of the real sector of the economy. Furthermore, any inconsistent action without regard to the pace and sequencing in the financial sector reforms programme on the part of the Government or the Reserve Bank of India, can lead to disaster. But care must be taken to ensure that lending to priority sectors at concessional interest rates is not reduced with catastrophic suddenness. The World Bank which is making the loan should understand the special problems of the priority sectors and should not make the sudden reduction of lending to these sectors a crucial conditionality. The World Bank should realize that even the United States of of America which is a market- friendly economy is not fully market-friendly considering the fact that its agriculture is heavily subsidized and subsidies have no place in a market economy. Therefore, it would not be an undue dilution of financial sector reforms in India if the priority sector lending is reduced not at one go but in stages.

# 44

## The Case for an Emergency Relief Fund at the IMF

The foreign exchange crisis erupted in Mexico over two months ago necessitating the announcement in the first week of February 1995 of an emergency aid package of $50 billion by the United States. But the fact remains that Mexico is yet to tide over the immediate problems. The Mexican crisis has implications for the other developing countries, for the international financial system and for the International Monetary Fund as well. This has posed the issue to the developing countries of their ability to integrate themselves with the global economy, especially with respect to foreign capital flows at a time when the international financial markets are able to exercise far more powers over the macro fundamentals than the central banks and the governments. The Mexican crisis has amply demonstrated how loss of confidence by global financial companies can destabilize the otherwise stable economy and send shock waves all over.

The Mexican Government had announced its intention not to devalue its intention not to devalue the Peso. But the devaluation of the Peso under pressure of circumstances caused the eruption of the crisis. The foreign investors who had pumped in huge sums of capital suddenly found that the Mexican economy was no longer stable and that the Peso was over valued staged a run on the Mexican currency. This was only the final stage of the crisis which had been brewing for a long time. Large inflows of foreign capital into Mexico were used to finance the import of consumer goods as the Mexican rate of savings was hardly 15 percent of GDP. Mexico initially took advantage of the confidence of foreign investors in the viability of the economy. As soon as this confidence was undermined the economy was found to be unviable and unstable too. The investor confidence in Mexico did not have a strong basis and it can be said that the speculative attack on the Peso was also unwarranted. This means that the large inflow of foreign capital into the developing countries is not a positive development unless exports are growing rapidly and debt servicing is kept within manageable limits.

Many in India apprehend the outbreak of a crisis of the Mexican variety though a review of the macroeconomic fundamentals in India does not suggest a parallel between the Mexican and Indian cases. India's short-term external debt is not large as that of Mexico; its current account deficit is not massive, hardly $1.5 billion; low import tariffs on imports of consumer goods though the Finance Ministry is for liberalizing consumer goods imports in order to bring down the rate of inflation from the supply side and to sue the vast forex reserves to pay for these imports and thus to bring down the rate of monetary growth which is fuelling inflation; absence of capital account convertibility of the rupee though the Finance Minister has gone on record that he would announce capital account convertibility of the rupee shortly. All these factors were present in the Mexican economy and their cumulative effect was to cause the crisis. Indian non-oil imports are surging and in the event of liberalization of consumer goods imports these imports also rise enlarging the current account deficit. This is not a problem as India has $20 billion of forex reserves to meet the current account deficit and as India's exports are poised for an accelerated growth in the coming years. However, careful management of the economy is the need of the hour considering the fact that only 20 percent of foreign capital inflow during the past two years is invested in plant and machinery meant to increase production for the domestic market and for the world market portfolio fund investment in the stock markets and in Euro- Issues is "hot money" which is liable to move outside the country without giving notice. The accumulation of over $20 billion of forex reserves may enable the country to meet this outflow with not much difficulty but it will cause a strain on the economy all the same. For this reason there is imperative need to guard against the outflow of hot capital money and to make adequate provision to meet it in the event of its occurring.

The problem of foreign exchange surges into the economies which have initiated the process of liberalization has cropped up in many parts of the world in Mexico and China and to some extent in India. While the Mexican experience is now familiar China is also facing the massive problems with inflation. While the official rate of inflation is said to be in the region of 28 percent, unofficial figures put the rate at 40 percent. Fortunately, India has not yet reached that stage also because the inflow of foreign capital has not been of the magnitude witnessed in Mexico and China. But the IMF has not found a proper salvage mechanism for the newly liberalizing economies.

The US Government came to the aid of Mexico well in time by organizing an aid package of the order of $ 50 billion and the IMF announced a financial assistance of $ 7.8 billion. But such help is unlikely to be organized to help all the developing countries which face the crisis of the type and dimension of Mexican crisis. There is need to organize a massive fund to help the developing countries which face an outflow of volatile capital of massive dimensions. It is true that the IMF took strains to contribute to the Mexico rescue package. If the developing countries in their collectivity encounter the crisis of the Mexican variety, the IMF will not be able to help all of them out. Many developing countries have suggested the creation of a suitable funding facility but the international community has remained unresponsive so far. In 1994 there was a massive global capital movement of over $150 billion to the developing countries. But this does not render multinational economic cooperation unnecessary.

This calls for the institution of a fund (Emergency Relief Fund) to help the developing countries facing outflow of volatile capital. This capital may be contributed by increasing the quota of every member of the IMF. This fund should be used exclusively for meeting the crisis situations in the developing countries involving massive outflows of capital. At the same time the member countries, especially the developing countries should be asked to keep their houses in order by placing upper limits on the rate of inflation and the current account deficit. The management of their economies should be under international surveillance applying the brakes when the rate of inflation and the size of the current account deficit threaten to get out of control. The political parties in the opposition in these countries may complain that this constitutes the surrender of national sovereignty. If this is so, then why should they create conditions which necessitate the aid package from the emergency fund. If they need aid from the fund, they should be prepared to forego a part of their sovereignty; if on the other hand, they want to retain the sovereignty unimpaired, they must manage their economies with due sense of responsibility. They cannot have it both ways. Considering the massive amount of foreign capital held in the various developing countries the institution of a financial facility in the IMF is a basic necessity if the world is to be saved from the crisis of the type which shook Mexico. The international community will do well to organize the emergency fund and contribute liberally to it to help the developing countries in dire need.

When India obtained the loan from the IMF in July 1991, it undertook to abide by the conditionality prescriptions of the Fund and it did observe these prescriptions in the beginning in the matter of macroeconomic management of the economy. When the need for IMF assistance was not pressing the Government gave a go by to these prescriptions. The fiscal deficit which rules at 7-8 percent at present and the rate of inflation has reached the 11.55 figure. Though the buoyancy of tax revenue is likely to reduce the fiscal deficit somewhat there does not appear to be respite on the price front partly due to the monetary impact of the burgeoning forex reserves. A part of the forex reserves is used to prepay the IMF loan. A significant part of the foreign capital is of the short-term variety and it is, for this reason, highly volatile. In the event of a change in the investor sentiment this capital is likely to flow out. In this context resort to capital account convertibility is not desirable. This offers scope for the shifting of capital outside India and generates the danger of a financial crisis of a sort though not of the Mexican magnitude. This should make the Finance Minister to defer the capital account convertibility of the rupee. In the present context this, I think, is the right thing to do.

# 45

## Fertiliser Subsidy to Reduce the Inflation Rate

The Report of the Joint Parliamentary Committee on Fertiliser pricing and fertilizer subsidy has disturbed the hornet's nest throughout the country. The farmers are to be the worst hit. At a time when the New Agricultural Policy is to be enunciated by the Government the farmers are asking the question whether the new fertilizer pricing policy will enable the country to reach the production targets in the agricultural sector.

The Report of the Joint Parliamentary Committee envisages the enhancement of the prices of different varieties of fertilizer. The new prices are as under: The price of Chemical fertilizers per bag of 50 kg has risen from Rs. 60 to Rs.170. The price of DAP fertilizer has risen from Rs. 238 to Rs. 300 per bag of 50 kg. The price of 17:17:17 has risen from Rs. 172.30 to 220 per bag of 50 kg. The price of 15:15:15 has risen from Rs. 138.50 to Rs. 200 per bag of 50 kg. The price of 16:20 has risen from Rs. 153 to Rs. 200 per bag of 50 kg. The price of Potash has risen from Rs. 86.50 to Rs. 250 per bag of 50 kg.

The Government of India has gone by the conditionality prescription imposed by the IMF that the fiscal deficit should be brought down from 8.5 percent of GDP in 1991-92 to 6.5 percent of GDP in 1992-93 and to 5 percent of GDP in 1993-94. The best way to do this, according to the IMF, is to reduce the fertiliser subsidy. The IMF imposes the condition that the rate of inflation should be brought down to a single digit figure. But it has not realized that though the rate of inflation can be brought down by a reduction of subsidy, the rate of inflation will receive a boost by the rise in fertilizer prices following the reduction of fertilizer subsidy and the decontrol of fertilizer prices. It is yet to dawn on the IMF and the Government that subsidizing farm inputs is 8-10 times cheaper than subsidizing farm outputs.

When the price of fertilizers rises, the demand for them being elastic, the input of fertilizers falls causing a fall in farm productivity and farm production. The small and marginal farmers lose interest in farming and produce enough for their family consumption with no marketable surplus that can be sold. This causes a situation of excess demand which enhances the prices of farm products especially food prices. It is an empirically established fact that in India it is the food prices that govern the general price index and therefore the rate of inflation. When the food prices rise the rate of inflation rises and therefore the design of reducing the rate of inflation by reducing fertilizer subsidy will be frustrated. In order to avert this danger the Government has to increase food subsidy. Thus what is gained by reducing the fertilizer subsidy will be lost by enhancing the food subsidy. And the loss may be more than the gain thus causing a net loss to the Government while the rate of inflation remains unaltered.

It is an empirically established fact that the cropping pattern in India is conditioned by relative prices. If, owing to the reduction of fertilizer subsidy, the fertilizer prices rise the big farmers might shift from food crops which require a larger input of fertilizers to cash crops which require a smaller input. This may enhance their cash income from commercial crops but it reduces the output of food thus causing excess demand for food and a rise in food prices. This also generates a need for increasing food subsidy. This means that the reduction of fertilizer subsidy may reduce the fiscal deficit but the enhancement of food subsidy will increase the fiscal deficit. The increase in the fiscal deficit caused by the enhancement of food subsidy may be greater than the reduction of the fiscal deficit caused by the reduction of fertilizer subsidy. The consequence is a net rise in the fiscal deficit which runs counter to the design of the IMF and the Government of India.

Several alternative policy programmes can be envisaged to overcome the unwelcome consequences of a reduction of fertilizer subsidy. In the first place, the Government could permit the farmers to export their produce and, with the help of the foreign exchange so earned to import farm inputs including fertilizers which are cheaper than the domestic fertilizers. This, of course, requires a modification of the present Export-Import Policy. This could be done by maintaining a separate foreign exchange budget by which the import of fertilizers can be financed by the foreign exchange earned through the export of farm produce. This does not entail any utilisation of the foreign exchange earned through other sources. In this event the demand for the higher priced domestic fertilisers falls causing a fall in their prices and encouraging the use of domestic fertilizers if their prices fall below the prices of imported fertilizers. In this way, the movement of relative prices can adjust the supply and demand for fertilizers.

At present the Government is paying food subsidy which during the VII Plan period was of the order of Rs. 10,326 crore. During the VIII Plan period it is bound to be still more. This is the cost of distributing food through the Public Distribution System (PDS). This system benefits the poor as well as the rich and is therefore regressive. Instead, the Government could stop the distribution of food through the PDS and introduce a system of 'bread entitlement cards' as in Sri Lanka. This system makes the rich households desist from applying for these bread entitlement cards as they are considered to be infra dig so that the benefit of the PDS will be appropriated, for the most part, by the poor and the needy. This is a progressive measure and this could be tried in the interests of interpersonal equity.

The Government which raises the fertilizer prices should desist from the levy collection of food from the farmers as this scheme was introduced under a scheme of fertilizer subsidy. If this happens the farmers can sell their produce in the market at the going market price with no deleterious effects on farm output. Furthermore, under a system of zonal restrictions on the movement of food grains prices of food grains will be higher in the deficit zones and lower in the surplus zones. This causes interzonal disparity in food prices. While the farmers in the deficit zones gain the farmers in the surplus zones lose. Therefore, there is need for removing zonal restrictions on the movement of food grains. If this happens there will be free movement of food grains from the surplus to the deficit zones in response to relative price differentials and thus leads to the inter-zonal equalization of food prices.

It is true that the fertilizer subsidy has grown to gargantuan proportions. This is to be attributed to the economic policies being pursued by the Government. In July 1991 there was a two-step devaluation of the rupee in compliance with the IMF conditionality prescription. This led to a rise in fertilizer subsidy by Rs. 900 crore as the fertilizer prices rose due to the rise in the post-devaluation prices of imported fertilizer inputs. The Gulf surcharge of 15 percent on petroleum imports was another factor; the enhancement of the prices of petroleum products by 10 percent in the 1991-92 budget; the rise in the railway freight rate by 10 percent. These factors also enhanced the prices of fertilisers. These factors combined with the decontrol of fertilizer prices led to a rise in the price of potassium from Rs.1760 per tonne to Rs. 5000 per tonne; the SSP price rose from Rs. 1240 to Rs. 3000 per tonne; the DAP price rose from Rs. 4680 to Rs. 9000 per tonne. This is indeed a great burden on the farming sector.

The justification advanced by the Government for decontrol of fertilizer prices and the reduction of fertilizer subsidy is that the benefits of subsidy are appropriated by the big farmers who are able to pay the enhanced price. This may be true to some extent in the States where land reforms have been haphazard. But 70 percent of the landholdings in the country are less than one hectare each. Even though these landholders do not produce food for the market, they depend upon fertilizers for increasing food output for their family consumption. The enhancement of the prices of fertilizers will adversely affect food production on these small farms and will make them depend on the public distribution system or to purchase food in the market by paying the market price which cuts into their real income and reduces the demand for other products of the industrial sector causing recession there in the same way as happened in 1957-59 when the II Five Year Plan was through. Thus in a system of intersectoral interdependence the enhancement of the prices of fertilizers will affect not only the farm sector but other sectors as well.

What is necessary at present is the reduction in the rate of inflation. This can be realized not by reducing fertilizer subsidies but by enhancing food output by encouraging greater input of fertilizers which causes a rise in food output and thus causes a decline in food prices. If this happens, the rate of inflation will decline without there being a reduction in fertilizer subsidy. The IMF which has prescribed a reduction of fertilizer subsidy owes it to itself to examine the various ramifications of its prescription and to desist from being firm on the subsidy conditionality.

# 46

## Welcome to Multinationals

The New Industrial Policy (NIP) announced by the Government of India on 24.7.1991, intended to unshackle the Indian industrial system from bureaucratic controls and licensing procedures, allowed majority equity participation for foreign investors. This concession to foreign investment was imperative as the foreign investors would bring in capital, technology and managerial techniques. This policy is being pursued with unabated vigour. But it is too soon to expect spectacular results.

However, this policy has come under heavy fire from the opposition of the Left Front which alleges that it marks a sell out to foreign multinationals. This allegation, on closer examination, appears unfounded. Indian industry thus far flourished behind the protective wall. Being secure of protection it did not make any efforts to update its technology, managerial techniques or methods of production. In short, it did not think it necessary to improve competitive efficiency. For this very reason it did not make a mark in global trade. Indian exports which were 2.5 percent of world trade two decades ago have sunk to 0.5 percent at present. The newly industrializing countries like Taiwan and South Korea which are smaller than any small State in the Indian Union have become world class competitors to the countries of Europe and North America. Their exports are booming and they have been able to acquire vast foreign exchange resources. Taiwan has accumulated foreign exchange reserves of $80 billion while India's foreign exchange reserves are only $4.4 billion. Even they are borrowed funds. In this scenario, India cannot afford to live an insular existence. Her industries are to be exposed to foreign competition in order to make them improve their price and quality competitiveness. This is the message of the New Industrial Policy and this should be taken in the right spirit. The allegation that this marks a sell-out to foreign multinationals is without foundation. A small country like Singapore with a population of 2.5 million has got as many as 700 multinational companies within its jurisdiction. But these companies hardly interfere in the domestic politics of the country. When this is the case, how can they interfere in the politics of India which, with it 850 million people, is the biggest democracy in the world? Seen in this light, the multinational companies are economic entities with no political ambitions unlike the British East India Company. This is not a casual statement but has an authoritative support.

The study entitled "Towards Globalization - A Case for Foreign Investment" undertaken by the Economic and Scientific Foundation (ESRF) has come to the conclusion that the multinationals will not have any adverse effects on Indian companies and the latter will not collapse under pressure from the multinational entry. This study rightly recommends that instead of protecting the Indian companies from multinationals, steps should be taken to expose them to the MNCs which will essentially lead to an increased competition and therefore efficiency in the Indian companies. Competitive efficiency is the need of the hour for Indian companies to make their mark in the global markets.

It is admitted that the MNCs in India are not always good in redesigning products to suit Indian markets, in controlling prices or in best marketing strategies. For this reason, Indian companies are in a far better position in the Indian market. The accusation against the MNCs is that they do not update their technologies and that they use obsolete technology in India though in the tea and jute industries started by foreigners latest technology is used. While in the other countries the MNCs use the latest technology, they do not use similar technology in India because they find that the conditions in India are inhospitable and the terms unfavourable. In the other countries the MNCs keep 100 percent equity while in India they are allowed only 51 percent equity. Furthermore, while the effective rate of taxation in the other Asian countries is about 10 percent in India, after deductions, it works out to 40 percent. In addition, patent protection in India is less favourable than in other countries.

The MNCs in India are labouring under inadequate infrastructural facilities in the areas of telecommunications, port facilities and power supplies. These facilities should be increased to those foreign companies which are net exporters than giving them better facilities to meet the demands of the domestic market only. It is also necessary to improve the investment climate in India which the foreign investors find not so hospitable.

The multinationals have a great role to play in stabilizing India ... its industry and trade. India is labouring under acute shortage of foreign exchange which is why it has to approach the multinational financial agencies for loans at frequent intervals accepting often severe conditionality presumptions. In this situation export growth is a categorical imperative. It would not appear to be wise to delink MNCs from export growth. To keep MNCs out would be to hinder the growth of exports. In view of this, India must attract MNCs by offering them facilities and a favourable investment climate. In the alternative Indian companies should become multinational in the same way as Japanese and Korean companies are. Considering the financial and technological handicaps of Indian companies they can be multinational only in the long run. In the short run, the only way available to India is to attract foreign multinationals. The fear of political instability in India inhibits the entry of foreign investment on a large scale but when things settle down and political stability is assured, foreign investment will flow in on a large scale.

Foreign investment will flow into India when there is freedom for capital to flow in and flow out and this will help to augment exports. The building up of the export industry causes a trade gap initially and a current account deficit and the balance of payments shows an improvement later on. The Government must, therefore, accept the current account deficit in good grace and allow capital inflows to offset the current account deficit. The currency controls prevalent in India at present reflect capital flows to other countries. While the Government woos NRIs to invest in India, currency controls prevent the outflow of capital. Therefore, it is necessary to ensure an ideal investment climate in India a climate which allows funds to flow freely into and out of the country and permits investment to be made or liquidated easily. The foreign investors panic at the thought of being locked permanently into an investment by currency controls which allow the inflow but block the outflow of capital invested already. This strengthens the case for liberalizing capital flows into and out of the country. Currency controls are inconsistent with the philosophy of liberalization.

The burden of the song is that there is no need to be apprehensive about the entry of MNCs into India, that they should be attracted to India by offering infrastructural facilities and competitive tax concessions and that currency controls should be liberalized to allow two way flow of capital.

The Finance Ministry has asked four private firms in India to come out with proposals to raise funds in the overseas markets. These proposals are likely to hit the western financial markets between July and September 1992 to raise an aggregate amount of \$250 - \$300 million. These four companies will come out with Euro-equities to be sold to western institutional investors. The response to the four issues is expected to be good. Institutional investors in the USA and Europe are keenly interested in the emerging markets in Asia like India.

India, of course, has made rapid studies on the industrial front and has developed a strong infrastructural base though much more needs to be done. The Bombay Stock Exchange is one of the most modern stock exchanges in the world. The stock exchanges of the countries like South Korea, Taiwan, Thailand and Indonesia do not stand comparison with the Bombay Stock Exchange. Even so, India has remained a closed-door economy with severe restrictions, procedural delays and bureaucratic tounges. All these obstacles are going albeit at a slow pace. But the pace of their removal must be quickened. The New Industrial Policy aims at removing them. This is absolutely necessary for the free flow of direct foreign investment.

# 47

## The Securities Scam : Is the Reserve Bank of India Responsible?

The securities scam which convulsed the Indian financial system has all the ingredients of a tragicomic drama. Harshad Mehta and Bhupen Dalal are the super heros of this drama. Their supporting actors are scores of bank officials already booked by the Central Bureau of Investigation (CBI). They all played their respective roles with consummate histrionic talents. They all functioned in the James Bond style.

The securities scam became a subject of heated debate in the Parliament in the Monsoon Session. The House was divided on party ideological lines. The leading lights of the Opposition held the Finance Minister and the Governor of the Reserve Bank of India morally responsible for the scam and demanded the resignation of the former and the dismissal of the latter. This was part of the sordid political game. The leading lights of the ruling party were one with the Opposition that the actors in the high drama were responsible for the scam and they deserved the punishment permissible under the law of the land, but they differed from the Opposition holding that the Finance Minister and the Reserve Bank Governor were totally ignorant of the origin and the development of the drama and that the drama was enacted stealthily, the audience being the actors themselves. It was Shri Venkitaramanan who discovered the plot and unmasked the dramatis personae and exposed them to public gaze. This grand discovery must go to the credit of Shri S. Venkitaramanan who has rightly denied any moral responsibility for the scam. Unless the Reserve Bank Governor knew about the scam, how can he communicate to the Finance Minister that a scam is developing in full swing to convulse the banking and financial system? If a manager of a branch of a nationalized bank commits fraud, can it be demanded that the Managing Director of the banking network should run moral responsibility for the fraud and should resign or should allow himself to be dismissed? The trouble spot lies elsewhere and this trouble spot must be exposed and the trouble shooters should be brought to book. The demand that the Managing Director should resign or be dismissed is to miss the target and to go off the mark. This is most unfair. This was the line of argument I pursued and this line got instantaneous support from the main sections of the House. Harshad Mehta's clandestine operations, shocking though they were, did not attract the attention of the immediate authorities until the Reserve Bank Governor caught the thief successfully and exposed the scam root and branch and laid them bare to public view.

There are many who employ circuitous logic to argue that the Reserve Bank Governor is morally responsible for the scam as it was he, as Governor of the Reserve Bank, laid the base for the thief's operations. They employ premises which do not allow any one to deduce the inference that they have deduced. They allege that the scam is the consequence of the Reserve Bank's administered interest rates and deployment of funds; they also allege that the fiats issued by the Reserve Bank from time to time made it impossible for banks to pay interest to the depositors unless they cooperate with Harshad Mehta and his gang of operators.

Under the banking system the banks accept deposits from the depositors at an interest rate and lend the money to borrowers at a higher rate of interest. It is banks which decide where to invest, how much to invest and at what interest rate that gives them a margin of profit after paying the interest to the depositors.

It is alleged that the Reserve Bank distorted the normal functioning of this process by issuing fiats on investments and interest on deposits and loans. The Reserve Bank stipulated that the banks should invest 40 percent of their deposits in government securities and public sector bonds which, of course, yielded a lower rate of interest of 10-11 percent while they have to pay an interest of 12 percent to depositors on 46 day deposits. In a free market no bank will invest its funds in a government security which yields an interest of 10-11 percent while it has to pay interest of 12 percent to depositors. But the financial market is not a free market. The banks are, under the statute, required to buy these securities. They cannot violate the statute. Besides this, the Reserve Bank decreed that the banks should keep with it 15 percent as Cash Reserve Raio (CRR) and get a very low interest on the funds so deposited-9 percent. The new Reserve Bank fiat stipulates that the larger the magnitude of the funds so deposited, the lower the interest rate earned.

In the 1980s the Reserve Bank used to impound only 7 percent of the bank deposits. But in 1991 it issued a fiat requiring the banks to deposit 10 percent extra of any additional deposits accruing to the banks after a prescribed date. This means that out of every 100 rupees of deposits the bank gets it has to surrender 25 rupees to the Reserve Bank. This is in addition to the bank investing 40 percent of their deposits in government securities and public sector bonds. The banks are thus left with only 35 percent of the deposits which they can lend at interest rates enough to make both ends meet and to leave a margin of profit. But in fact the banks are not free to fix the interest rates on their loans and advances. The Reserve Bank fixes this interest rate also. If the banks charged any higher interest rate on loans they are accused of impeding the flow of funds to industry and engendering recession there. In fact, the Reserve Bank, lowered the lending rate to just 19 percent though the industry was prepared to pay a higher interest rate than this. This is not all. While the lending rate was reduced to 19 percent the Reserve Bank allowed freedom to the banks to raise the interest rates on short-term deposits. The interest rate went up from 11 percent to 13 percent on deposits of more than 46 days. But this was considered to be short sighted. Therefore, the cartle of the nationalized banks in the second week of August 1992 rolled back the interest rate to 12 percent on deposits upto six months and 12.5 percent on deposits from 6 months upto 12 months.

Under these circumstances the profitability of the banking system drastically declined. The banks wanted to raise cash to meet deposit withdrawals and to lend to borrowers. The banks began to trade in the government securities and the public sector funds among themselves. They began to issue banker receipts (BRs) promising to give the securities and the bonds within 90 days. The buying bank takes the BRs and pays money to the selling bank which needs money to meet deposit withdrawals and to lend to borrowers. It became important to service the borrowers like Harshad Mehta who were ready to pay fancy interest rates on short-term loans which they used to exploit the stock markets. Banks began to issue BRs to meet the demand of this class of borrowers and to make a gain in the form of hefty interest receipts.

Matters came to a head in April 1992 when some banks could not supply the securities and bonds against the BRs which matured in the meanwhile. Many had issued the BRs hoping to buy the actual securities and bonds from the money the broker-borrower returns. But the brokers' money was blocked in the stock exchanges. The BRs started bouncing and the banks were unable to reconcile the figures. And this was the origin of the securities scam.

It was generally accepted that the BRs were a normal banking practice designed to earn high interest rates on the government securities and the public sector bonds which the Reserve Bank forced the banks to buy. But the Reserve Bank did not do anything to stop this practice as it was considered to be a normal banking practice. But the allegation against the Reserve Bank Governor is that even after the scam was exposed, he clamped more restrictions on the banks' dealings in the securities. And this aggravated the problem.

The Reserve Bank Governor is held responsible for pushing the banks into this practice of issuing BRs. If everything had gone right, the Reserve Bank Governor would have been crowned with glory. Now that it went awry he is held to be morally responsible and for this reason he is held to deserve punishment.

Quite apart from the changing of interest rates both borrowing and lending rates and the prescription that the banks should invest 40 percent of their deposits in Government securities and public sector bonds yielding a low interest rate and the banks surrendering

25 percent of their deposits to the Reserve Bank. All of which had the effect of drastically reducing the profitability of the banking system. There were other factors which were equally responsible for the low profitability of banking business; they were the lending to the so called priority sectors at concessional interest rate, loan melas where colossal sums of money are lent to borrowers without any security and the farm loan waiver scheme which rendered the banks sick and the banks had to find a way out of their sickness. BRs proved to be a convenient escape route. The Reserve Bank of India and its Governor are, therefore, held to be morally responsible for the securities scam.

It must be remembered that the measures which the Reserve Bank adopted from time to time in the matter of lending and deposit rates, impounding of a certain percentage of the deposits of the banks in the form of Cash Reserve Ratio and the enforcement of the requirement that the banks should invest 40 percent of the deposits in government securities and public sector bonds were all part of the overall monetary policy of the Reserve Bank in which neither the Reserve Bank nor its Governor had any independent choice. These measures were adopted at the instance of the Finance Ministry which wanted them adopted as part of the monetary strategy. Neither the Reserve Bank nor its Governor can be said to be morally responsible for the scandal. The Reserve Bank is an employee of the Government and when the Government wants something done, he dare not refuse to do it even if he knew that it was not the right thing to do. The reason is that the Reserve Bank is a nationalized institution.

The Bank of England, before it was nationalized in 1946, was an independent monetary authority of the country. It could take decisions independent of the Government. It was so important that Professor D.H.Robertson of Cambridge remarked that in the golden days of the gold standard the tides would neither rise or fall without the permission of the Bank. But after it was nationalized it became a department of government and lost its independent status. In September 1949 sterling was devalued. The Chancellor of the Exchequer (Sir Strafford Cripps) held several parleys with the

Governor of the Bank of England (Sir Henry Cabbold) about devaluation. The Chancellor of the Exchequer wanted sterling to be devalued in the attempt to remedy the balance of payments deficit and he advanced several cogent arguments in support of devaluation. The Governor of the Bank of England who was opposed to devaluation advanced equally cogent arguments against it. Finally, in a mood of exasperation, the Chancellor said: "You are my creature; you have to agree to devalue". The Governor of the Bank of England said: "Yes Sir, I will carry out your orders but against my will". Sterling was devalued against the US dollar on 18.9.1949. This was the devaluation drama and the Governor of the Bank of England was an unwilling actor.

The policy measures adopted from time to time were those enforced on the Reserve Bank of India and neither the Reserve Bank nor its Governor had any choice in the matter. These measures might have reduced the profitability of the banks and rendered them sick. But who is to blame for it? Certainly not the Governor of the Reserve Bank who, as a dutiful servant of the Government, implemented the measures. The Government did not, of course, mean to reduce the profitability of the banks though its policy measures had this effect. If the detractors' logic is pursued to its logical end, it means that it is the Government that should be held morally responsible. To hold the Governor of the Reserve Bank of India morally responsible for the scam is to aim at an innocent (wrong) target. One should have the patience to wait for the report of the Joint Parliamentary Committee which is seized of the matter. In the meanwhile one should desist from injecting party politics into it.

The Finance Minister has gone on record asserting that the securities scam is due to the failure of the system. If the Reserve Bank of India had foreseen the possibilities of a scam of this kind and dimension, it would have tightened up the screws and would have issued directions to the banks warning them against the issue of BRs which bounced. It had not foreseen it and the blame for this cannot be laid at its doors. Furthermore, the detractors of the policy of liberalization adopted by the Government in July 1991 attribute the scam to the liberalization policy implying that it should be reversed. But they fail to see how the two are unrelated. It is heartening to note that the liberalization policy is declared to be irreversible. To connect liberalization policy is declared to be irreversible. To connect liberalization with the scam in a cause and effect sequence is illogical and even absurd. The Narasimham Committee Report on Financial Reform is for the most part kept in cold storage. It is high time that the Government implements all its recommendations barring, for the time being, those that impinge on social obligation.

# 48

# Managing Coffee Prices

The price of coffee has been rising steadily and at present it has reached the dizzy height of Rs. 140 per kg. In earlier years the rural population and those below the poverty line were not used to drinking coffee but with the spread of modernization of social values and their impact on life styles, coffee has become an essential beverage and is occupying an important place in the family budget of almost every household. Almost every family, whatever its socio-economic status, begins the day with a hot cup of coffee for, as the saying goes, "coffee cheers but does not inebriate". Drinking coffee has become a symbol of social status. A rise in the price of coffee compounded by the rise in the price of sugar has caused concern in the minds of almost every section of society. If the price of milk also rises their cup of misery will be full.

In earlier years, there was the system of compulsory pooling of coffee and the dual marketing system for 50 years. Under this system export and domestic markets were segregated and these markets were fed from the central pool separately. At present, there is the Free sale Quota system. Under this system the coffee board has allowed 50 percent free sale quota to the coffee growers for the 1993-94 season. The existing free sale quota has led to an integration of the domestic and international markets. This integration coincided with the boom in international prices of coffee and these prices have led to a rise in domestic prices of coffee. This has disturbed the coffee consumers and the coffee growers as well.

The main reason for the rise in the prices of coffee is the low price fixation and the reduced input of fertilizers which have jointly led to a fall in coffee production and per acre yield also. This situation is not peculiar to India. In fact, this is true of other coffee growing countries as well. In Brazil which is a leading coffee producer in the world there was a drastic fall in coffee output. Brazil was producing 28 million bags of coffee per year; but last year it produced only 15 million bags of coffee.

It must be noted that one of the main reasons for the decline in coffee output was the disinclination of the governments in the coffee growing countries to determine the remunerative price for coffee. The price of coffee in India is related to the price of coffee quoted in the New York and London terminal markets. When the prices in these markets rise, the domestic prices of coffee also rise immediately. In this situation, the task of bringing down the prices of coffee in the domestic market bristles with practical difficulties. One way of doing it is not to impose restrictions on the export of coffee as it goes against the philosophy of liberalization but to impose an export tax. This will have the effect of reducing the import of coffee from India and of increasing domestic availability of coffee with a salutary effect on coffee prices. At the same time, the domestic supply of coffee has to be increased. At present the coffee growers find the price of coffee too unremunerative for them to increase its supply. With the fixing of minimum support price for coffee, the coffee growers will find coffee production remunerative and increase its supply.

Apart from this, the per-acre yield of coffee has also to be increased. As is obvious, the yield depends on and varies directly with the various farm inputs the most important of which is fertilisers. As the price of fertilizers is high, the coffee growers are reluctant to use the appropriate quantum of fertiliser input. A subsidy on fertilizers will reduce the price of fertilizers and enable the coffee growers to increase its input. This will increase the per acre yield of coffee and increase its availability.

At present, there is the commission on agricultural costs and prices (CACP) for recommending remunerative prices for various agricultural commodities. The conditions governing the production of coffee are far different from those governing the production of agricultural commodities like wheat, rice, bajra etc. Coffee is a plantation crop which requires the employment of wage labour and wages are to be increased with every rise in the rate of inflation.

In a similar manner the prices of other inputs keep on rising. These factors raise the cost of production of coffee. Keeping these factors in view, the remunerative prices of coffee have to be determined. For their determination a separate commission on coffee costs and prices (CCCP), seems necessary. This commission should go into the entire gamut of costs of coffee production and recommend remunerative prices so that the coffee growers may have the incentive to produce more coffee.

Under the earlier dispensation there was the compulsory pooling of coffee and the supply of coffee from the pool was made separately for the domestic market and the export market. Whenever the domestic prices of coffee rose coffee would be diverted from the export market to the domestic market and this would help to bring down the price of coffee in the domestic market. Under the existing Free Sale Quota System, the coffee board has allowed 50 percent free sale quota to the coffee growers. This is insufficient to meet domestic demand and excess demand for coffee has contributed to a rise in coffee prices. The reduction in the supply of coffee in the major coffee growing countries like Brazil has led to a phenomenal rise in coffee prices in the world market. The domestic coffee growers who are allowed to sell 50 percent of the coffee production under the free sale quota system find ample justification from this for their raising the domestic prices of coffee. This makes one feel that the former system of dual marketing of coffee is desirable as under this system any rise in the domestic price of coffee would divert coffee from the export market to the domestic market and would help to steady the domestic prices of coffee. Furthermore, under the earlier system nobody but the coffee board could sell coffee seeds. But under the present dispensation where there is free sale quota, the workers in the coffee plantations can steal (and infact are stealing) coffee seeds and sell them to needy buyers. The present system has thus led to corruption and pilferage of coffee seeds.

For these reasons, the segregation of the domestic and international markets for coffee seems desirable. The production of coffee sufficient to meet domestic demand could be retained and the surplus can be exported. It is only when the domestic production falls short of domestic demand that imports sufficient to make good the domestic shortfall can be obtained.

What is necessary at the moment is to bring down the domestic price of coffee to the level that prevailed before the integration of markets and the introduction of the free sale quota system. This is possible if the Government takes recourse to compulsory pooling and the dual marketing system that prevailed earlier. At the same time, in order to provide an incentive to the coffee growers a system of remunerative prices as recommended by the commission on coffee costs and prices should be introduced. As the input of fertilizers varies inversely with the price of fertilizers, the supply of fertilizers should be made available at subsidized prices. These are the essential preconditions for reducing the price of coffee. If this is not done, the coffee prices remain high as at present and may rise even higher raising the cost of living and engendering demands for higher wages which generate cost push and demand-pull inflations.

It is also necessary to make coffee available to the poor at reduced price for this purpose, the sale of coffee under the public distribution system should be free from sales tax. It is necessary to underline the fact that coffee has become an essential beverage in every household rich or poor. Time was when coffee was an unaffordable luxury for the poor but now it has become a basic necessity, and it occupies an important place in the family budgets of all sections of society. The poor need to be assisted by means of supplying coffee at lower prices. Hence this suggestion.

# 49

## Banks Need to be Customer Oriented Rather Than Employee Oriented

The commercial banks in the country have two sets of obligations; one set towards the employees and the other set towards the customers. The employees need to be paid enough to maintain themselves and their dependants and they need to be compensated for the rising cost of living. This obligation the banks are fulfilling efficiently judging from the frequent hikes in their salaries and the dearness allowances. The employees in the other segments of the economy envy the lot of the bank employees for this and other reasons as well. The banks provide 1 percent extra interest on deposits made by the bank employees and by the former employees. This is not only iniquitous but is also often to misuse. The bank employees may also keep the money belonging to others as their own deposits and get 1 percent extra interest and keep this extra as their commission and pay the normal interest income to those whose money they have deposited. This malpractice on the part of the bank employees or former employees has been brought to light. Furthermore, the bank employees enjoy the facility of making demand drafts without having to pay bank charges. If this is allowed as it is being allowed, the employees of postal and telecom Departments and their former employees have a legitimate right to demand free postage and free telecom use (subject to a maximum, of course). Can the Government extend these facilities to the postal and telecom employees.

The burden of the frequent hikes in salaries and dearness allowances for bank employees and the 1 percent higher interest rate allowed on the deposits made by the bank employees and former employees falls squarely on the depositors and other customers.

This is evidence that the banks are employee welfare-oriented rather than customer welfare oriented.

As early as September 1990 the Reserve Bank of India appointed a committee under the Chairmanship of M.M.Goiporia to review the customer service in banks and to suggest measures to improve it. The committee had the representatives of bank management, employees' Union, Officers' Association, Industry, Bank Depositors and the Reserve Bank of India. This committee submitted its report to the Reserve Bank in 1991. The committee examined in detail the quality of customer service rendered by the banks and made as many as 97 recommendations. In respect of only three of them the employee representatives offered dissent. In respect of the other 94 recommendations there was unanimity and they were endorsed by the committee as a whole.

Following the submission of this report the Reserve Bank of India issued directives to banks on the following dates: 28.1.1992; 27.5.1992; 11.2.1993; 27.10.1993;

As per these directives repeatedly given to the banks they had to implement 70 recommendations in the first instance. They included special value dating facilities, penal interest on banks for delay in clearing cheques, staff attendance 15 minutes prior to the opening of banks. For instance, the Reserve Bank directive of 28.1.1992 states, inter alia.

"It has been decided that banks should speedily implement them to provide better banking service to the customers". It is therefore essential to especially impress upon the branches and the concerned staff that customer service would improve perceptibly only if the recommendations of the Talwar Committee as well as of this committee are wholeheartedly implemented with a missionary zeal, both in letter and spirit rather than only in form and content".

In the context of globalization of the Indian economy and liberalization banks have got necessarily to be customer oriented. This calls upon them to improve their operational efficiency. This is necessary when the banks are found to be increasing service charges and interest rates on loans. Higher service charges should mean better quality of customer service.

In the context of globalization foreign banks are allowed to operate in the Indian money market. Being of foreign origin they are capable of providing and, in fact, they are providing satisfactory customer service. In a similar manner, the private banks which are now allowed to operate in India are also providing satisfactory customer service, Unlike these banks the commercial banks in India are employer oriented rather than customer oriented. In this situation, given the competitive environment, customers are prone to move towards the foreign banks or the private banks. If this happens, the commercial banks will come to grief finding it difficult to attract deposits which are the wherewithal for their operations. If these banks are to face the competition of foreign banks and private banks it is imperative that they should improve their operational efficiency. The Employees' Union and the Officers' Association which have endorsed the recommendations of the Goiporia Committee should have no objection to the implementation of these recommendations. The case for early implementation of these recommendations is strong and unassailable.

At the same time, the extra 1 percent interest rate paid on the deposits made by the bank employees and the former employees has led to a myriad of malpractices like benami deposits. The employees can also make bank drafts without having to pay service charges. These two concessions are unfair and inequitous. If they are continued, the employees in the other service like the postal and telecom services will demand similar concessions to them and quite legitimately too. And their demand cannot be overlooked. If they are overlooked they will be provoked to stage demonstrations and to paralyse the economy. It is therefore suggested that the concessions given to bank employees be reviewed.

# 50

## Oil Crisis and Inflation: How to Overcome Them

India is facing a grave foreign exchange crisis which is forcing the Government to approach the International Monetary Fund for loans agreeing to its stiff conditionality prescriptions which have the effect of surrendering India's sovereignty to international financial institutions which see an opportunity in India's difficulties. The import bill has been displaying a consistently upward trend while the export earnings hardly match the import bill. The export-import gap is widening generating the foreign exchange crisis and compelling recourse to the IMF loans.

The rising import bill is in no small part due to the rising oil bill. The present oil requirement of the country is about 55 million tonnes per year. Of this India imports almost 40 percent of crude oil and products valued at Rs. 10,000 crore which is 30 percent of the total import bill.

According to an estimate by the turn of the present century, despite the country's own expected annual production of about 52 million tonnes the level of imports would be about 50 million tonnes. The total import bill at the present day prices would be between Rs.25,000 crore and Rs. 30,000 crore annually by the end of the century as the product demand exceeds crude supply and refining capacity. If, as is possible, the OPEC hikes the oil prices the oil bill would be larger still. Apart from this, the supply and demand gap for middle distillates largely used in transport and household fuels would further widen raising the import bill still higher. At this rate the foreign exchange scenario will be dismal making further IMF loans on stiff conditionality prescriptions inevitable. This has to be avoided.

The rise in oil prices has a decidedly inflationary impact on the economy and with rupee devaluation at successive stages on the advice of the IMF inflation is bound to be raging in the country adding to the inflationary forces generated by the growing budget deficits. If the supply of money is held constant the rise in prices triggered by the rise in oil prices will generate forces which make the general price level fall towards the original level. A rise in the price level generated by the rise in oil prices causes a rise in the transactions demand for cash. As the stock of money is held constant the transactors have to obtain cash by selling their bond holdings for cash. The sale of bonds generates excess supply of bonds which causes a fall in bond prices and a rise in the rate of interest which checks investment activity. Furthermore, a rise in prices, the stock of money being held constant causes a fall in real balances. To the extent that consumption demand depends on real balances, there will be a fall in consumption. Again, if the consuming units maintain their money expenditure constant when the prices are rising there will be the money illusion effect which also causes a fall in real consumption. Thus, with the stock of money being held constant, there will be a fall in aggregate demand which causes a fall in the price level. If, on the other hand, the supply of money is allowed to expand the contractive effects will not come into play and the price level having risen will remain at its new higher level. In this sense the rise in oil prices is inflationary.

In India money supply is accommodative of the higher prices generated by the rise in oil prices. The budget deficit is financed partly by domestic borrowing and partly by monetary expansion. The monetary financing of the budget deficit accommodates and sustains higher prices. The remedy is to reduce the rate of monetary expansion by adopting the technique of monetary targetry. If this is done the inflationary forces unleashed by higher oil prices can be held in check.

Quite apart from this there is need to exploit the natural gas resources however limited they may be. West Asia holds 30 percent of the known natural gas resources with the Soviet Union's share being 38 percent and that of the US and Canada being 6.5 percent and 10.4 percent respectively. But India's share is less than 1 percent for gas as well as for oil. There is need to develop technology for conversion of this gas into useable liquid fuels for transport.

The discovery of gas during the 1970s and large reserves during later years was a welcome development and transformed the technique of strategic planning protocol. But the record of its gainful utilization has not been satisfactory.

At present there is a daily flaring of 17.5 million cubic meters of gas signifying colossal wastage. This is happening at a time when the country is facing a grave foreign exchange crisis coupled with dismal energy scenario. The utilization of these resources can bridge the energy gaps in vital sectors like transport and communications.

Furthermore, extensive surveys should be undertaken to discover large natural gas reserves. This discovery could bridge the gaps in several sectors like transport, fuel additives, power generation, domestic fuels, petrochemicals and fertilizers. This would also reduce the pressure on foreign exchange reserves. What is urgently necessary at present is strategic planning and the avoidance of unbusiness like approach which is causing colossal waste of natural gas.

The energy scene in general and petro-product markets in particular have undergone significant cyclic turbulence since the beginning of the 1970s. For India, these fluctuations are a matter of serious concern because of dependence on imports for almost 40 percent of liquid fuel requirements. The country has passed through several oil shocks starting with the one in 1973 and the Gulf War of 1990 was a grim reminder of the fact that India was depending for almost 70 percent of its oil imports on the Gulf region.

Considering the persistently rising oil bill causing a serious drain on India's foreign exchange reserves and the possibility of a still further rise between 1992 and 1997 owing to the energy intensive production technologies to be adopted under the Eighth Five Year Plan there is urgent need to undertake extensive oil exploration programmes by enlisting the cooperation and involvement of the private sector and by rationing oil for the vehicle users. Rationing of oil is used successfully in Japan and there is no reason why it should not be used in India. The argument against rationing is that it leads to corrupt practices. But given effective enforcement machinery and stringent punishment to offenders, rationing of oil can be made a success. What is necessary is to bring home to the people the seriousness of the crisis the country is facing and to underline the need for inculcating a spirit of patriotism of the type the Britishers displayed during the Second World War in response to the persuasive eloquence of Sir Winston Churchill, the then British Prime Minister.

It is the Government consumption of oil more than private consumption that is persistently rising. The Government offices/ officers use the vehicles more to serve their private purposes than to facilitate official business. There is thus a gross misuse of Government vehicle cars, jeeps and vans. Private use of Government vehicles should be banned. Any officer however high or mighty violating the ban order should be subject to stringent punishment. In a situation of grave economic crisis any punishment to offenders, however draconian, is in order. Auditing of oil use should be introduced and strictly enforced and the users of Government vehicles should be made accountable for the oil they use any deviation from the prescribed oil use being made a punishable offence. In the private sector any vehicle owner using more than the rationed quantity of oil by obtaining it by subterfuge should be rendered liable to stringent punishment. A desperate situation should call forth drastic remedies. This will be an effective antidote to the foreign exchange crisis, domestic inflation generated by the oil bill and to the rising debt burden.

# 51

## India's Cotton Policy: A Long Term Strategy is Needed

The Government's cotton policy has generated a great controversy in India. During the past two months the price of cotton has risen phenomenally causing concern to the textile manufacturers and to the consumers of cotton textiles. In the past, it was usual for the price of cotton to rise even before the cotton crop arrived. But this year, the price has risen not only for this reason but for the reason that the cotton crop has not yet arrived. There is a tendency in certain interested quarters to raise the price for no reason whatsoever but when a reason is there, they feel fully justified in doing it to their advantage.

The fear that the cotton crop has suffered grievously in Punjab, Rajasthan and Haryana and in consequence the crop arrivals are far less than expected is said to be the cause of the rise in the price of cotton. But there is no conclusive evidence to substantiate this point. There is evidence to prove that during the past two months (Dec. 1993 and January 1994) the supply of cotton to the market from Punjab is more than what it was during the corresponding months last year. If, per chance, the cotton crop has suffered, it is estimated that the supply of cotton this year will not be far less than what it was last year. In 1992-93 the output of cotton was 135 lakh bales. But in 1993-94 it cannot fall by more than one lakh bales as per the estimate of the cotton advisory committee. Even if this year the output of cotton falls, the supply of cotton to the mills will not fall significantly. At the start of the cotton season, there was a stock of 30.74 lakh bales of cotton. Even assuming that the output of cotton this year will be 134 lakh bales the total stock will be around 164.74 lakh bales. If the import of 50 thousand bales of imported cotton is added the total stock of cotton available in the country will be 165 lakh bales. The country uses just 134 lakh bales of cotton. Of this, the cotton mills utilize 117 lakh bales; the small scale textile units use 3.5 lakh bales; exports account for 5.7 lakh bales; others take 8 lakh bales. After this there should be a balance of about 31 lakh bales at the end of the year. This will be more than the stock of cotton at the end of the previous year. In this situation there can be no question of either shortage of cotton or a rise in its price. Even so, the price of cotton has been rising. This rise is but artificial caused by the manipulative tactics of the interested persons and organizations. It is also possible that this is due to the accumulation of stocks of cotton in anticipation of a future rise in its price. The prices of cotton have risen by over 59 to 91 percent above the support prices fixed by the Government for several varieties of cotton. The cotton mills are also found to be accumulating stocks of cotton in anticipation of a future rise in prices. This has provided an upward thrust to the prices of cotton. The cotton growers union in Maharashtra and the Indian Cotton Corporation have assumed the role of profit making enterprises and in order to make profits they are raising the prices of cotton. They are being supported by certain vested interests. The state cooperative cotton growers union has the monopoly privilege of buying cotton. It has raised the prices of cotton several times on a single day. This is bound to adversely affect the textile units and the poor users of cotton textiles.

The cotton textile industry has extensive ramifications in India. The poor and the lower middle class people use cotton cloth even now. The non-cotton fabrics are beyond their reach. For this reason, any rise in the prices of cotton textiles would adversely affect the interests of the poor consumers. This will also adversely affect the cotton textile industry. In 1991-92 the cotton mills had used 103 lakh bales of cotton. In 1992-93 it rose to 116 lakh bales. It was estimated that in 1993-94 it would use more than 120 lakh bales of cotton. Any rise in the price of cotton will raise the prices of yarn and cotton cloth. The price of cotton will be 60-70 percent of the price of yarn and 40-50 percent of the price of cotton cloth. This is the prime factor in the cost of production of cloth. When the price of yarn rises, the handlooms and power looms cannot afford to manufacture and sell cotton cloth at higher prices. Those who cannot afford to pay the new higher prices will not purchase cotton cloth. The demand for it falls and the innumerable cotton weavers will get into trouble. In this manner the rise in the price of cotton has extensive ramifications throughout the economy. In order to avert this danger it is suggested that the cotton weavers could use 10 percent of viscose and produce viscose mixed cloth. But it is doubtful whether the demand for this cloth will rise enough. It is held that any rise in the demand for viscose will reduce the demand for cotton and cause a fall in its price. The right remedy for this syndrome is to keep a watch on those out to raise the price of cotton and to place an upper limit on cotton prices. It is dangerous to confer monopoly power on any cotton organization. Even if they happen to be cotton growers' organisations, the vested interests controlling them will misuse their power and raise the prices of cotton. It is therefore suggested that the cotton market should be made free and open in keeping with the general policy of liberalization.

The Government of India has adopted measures to reduce cotton export and to increase the stock of cotton in the country. It has restricted the balance of the export of the export quota for the current year 1993-94. But as the export of cotton from the Soviet Union has stopped, the possibility of India taking advantage of this has been negatived. This constitutes a danger. Action has been taken to reduce the stock of cotton and to make the cotton stockists to submit reports about the stock in their position. But action has to be taken to check corruption that will exempt as a result of the Government interference in the cotton trade. It appears necessary to create free market conditions and to see that no vested interests will raise the price of cotton by increasing the stocks of cotton held by them. If the prices of different varieties oif cotton cannot be brought down in these ways, it becomes necessary to import cotton from abroad, to reduce or remove the customs duty on cotton to create conditions where the weavers can get both cotton and cotton yarn at competitive prices. The Government is thinking of steps in this direction. The Government should desist from adopting adhoc patch work measures and should instead, adopt a long term plan of action in the matter of cotton supply and cotton trade.

The following plan of action is suggested for the consideration of the Government.

- An estimate of the requirements of cotton of all varieties by each of the manufacturing sector, small scale sector and the handloom sector has to be prepared for each year.
- Given the crop yield of each variety of cotton, the supply of cotton should be so regulated by determining the area under cultivation of each variety of cotton so as to avoid both excess supply and excess demand for cotton.
- If, for any reason, the excess supply of cotton emerges this should be purchased by the government and held in stock so as to prevent a decline in cotton prices. If, the stock held is found to be excessive, it must be exported to earn foreign exchange.
- If, for any reason, excess demand for cotton arises, threatening to cause a rise in the price of cotton, the cotton held in stock should be released in order to prevent the cotton prices from rising.
- If, for any reason, the stock of cotton is not enough to offset excess market demand, import of cotton free of customs duty should be allowed. In this manner release and accumulation of cotton stocks and the export and import of cotton to offset excess supply of cotton causing a fall in price or an excess demand for cotton causing a rise in price will help to stabilize the prices of cotton in the same way as the buffer stock operations help to stabilize the price of food.

It is necessary to underline the need for the payment of remunerative prices to the cotton growers so that there is no disincentive for them to reduce cotton supply.

At present an important focus area of exports is that of farm exports. It is necessary to explore the cotton markets abroad and to supply to each market that variety of cotton, which is in great demand there. It is also necessary to explore the markets where cotton cloth using different varieties of cotton is in great demand.

This will enable India to earn foreign exchange. This may necessitate a shift of land from food crops to cotton crops. It is apprehended that this might cause a reduction in food output. But this apprehension is unfounded. The use of hybrid seeds, fertilizers, insecticides and pesticides, provision of irrigation facilities and the advanced techniques of cultivation are sure to increase food output more than sufficient to offset any reduction of food output caused by the shift of land from food crops to cotton. In the extreme case of food supply falling short of demand, food can be imported footing the import bill out of the foreign exchange earnings made possible by the export of cotton/cotton cloth.

The majority of Indians, especially those subsisting below the poverty line, are underfed and underclothed. Next to food, it is clothing that is an important item in the family budgets of households below the poverty line. As the objective of planning is to improve the quality of life of the people instead of maximizing the rate of growth of GNP per se, it is necessary to increase the supply of cloth at reasonable prices to the destitute section of society. This section cannot afford sophisticated varieties of cloth especially non-cotton cloth. It is necessary to increase the supply of coarse and semi-refined varieties of cotton cloth to them. All these require a long range planning of cotton cultivation, cotton supply, cloth production, cotton trade and supply of cotton cloth at reasonable prices, so as to be within the reach of the poor people in India.

# 52

## Exit for the Exit Policy

Exit Policy has been on the cards since July 1991 when the New Industrial Policy (NIP) was announced. The NIP was intended to unshackle the industrial system from bureaucratic controls and licencing procedures. In fact it was intended to unchain the Indian Tiger to leap forward with courage, conviction and confidence. An important adjunct of the NIP is the Exit Policy which was considered necessary to enhance the international competitiveness of Indian Industry. Contributions to the National Renewal Fund (NRF) which was described as safety net were made by the World Bank, the Asian Development Bank and by the Government of India. The idea was to retire redundant labour force or the fine labourers out of the industries facing closure and to finance their retaining schemes and to pay them compensation during the period of retaining. The Finance Minister announced early on the institution of the National Renewal Fund that the industrial policy would have a "human face". It is not known whether he meant by it relaxation of the Exit Policy or relegation of it to the backyard under political compulsion. The Union Budget for 1994-95 has enhanced the provision for National Renewal Fund by Rs. 320 crore. This is all that the Finance Minister has done about an important part of the reform process.

It is a basic text of neo-classical theory of the firm that there should be freedom of entry and exit of firms into and out of industry. If the firms in the industry are making super normal profits, the entry being free, new firms enter the industry, their entry enhances supply which causes a fall in price and therefore a fall in profits to the normal level. Thus supernormality of profits is a sign of disequilibrium which can be corrected by the entry of new firms into the industry, conversely, if the existing firms in the industry are making subnormal profits exit being free they leave the industry. This causes a fall in supply, a rise in price and a rise in the profits to the normal level. Thus subnormality of profits is also a sign of disequilibrium which can be corrected by the exit of existing firms out of the industry. But the Indian industrial policy appears to violate this basic text of neo-classical economics.

The Government does not seem to have picked up courage to implement the exit policy. The Finance Minister in the course of his Budget Speech on 28.2.1994 emphasised : "Our policies are geared towards promoting a dynamic and internationally competitive industrial sector. I am confident that given our vast reservoir of skilled manpower and entrepreneurship, Indian industry has the capacity and the will to meet the challenge of global competition". This enlightened statement is not backed by firmness on the closure of sick units in the public and private sector. Global competitiveness cannot be had for the asking; it depends entirely on the closure of sick units. Even so, the Government is reluctant to act firmly with the issue. While addressing the World Economic Forum at Davos in Switzerland on 31.1.1994 the Prime Minister declared himself strongly against the policy of hire and fire. Such a policy stance is not in consonance with the scheme of industrial restructuring. The Prime Minister has also assured a trade union delegation recently that he was not for closure of any of the sick NTC Mills. Has the exit policy staged an exit? One feels inclined to ask.

During the past four decades the Government has been pursuing weak-kneed policies on industry making concessions after concessions to trade unions and their supporting political parties. The Government cultivated a protected market syndrome and encouraged the public sector to grow more sick. In July 1991 when the NIP was announced it was generally agreed that the Government would move strongly towards liquidation of sick units. The Goswami Committee on industrial restructuring reflected this perception. But the Government has surrendered weakly to the threats held out by the trade unions and the Left parties. A summary rejection of the New-classical postulate which is an essential corporate principle of hire and fire is the antithesis of a policy of liberalization and globalisation. But it is not known how the Indian economy can be made globally competitive with a populist policy bearing on the organized working class.

An early implementation of the exit policy is necessary to ensure international competitiveness of Indian industry and to unchain the Indian Tiger. The other Asian Tigers hold out lessons for India. The announcement of the Exit Policy was made nearly three years ago. India's export trade growth has to equal, if not to excel, the record of the Newly Developed countries of Asia Korea, Hong Kong, Singapore, Malaysia. This can be achieved by a ruthless implementation of the Exit policy with no loss of time. The burden of this song is: implement the Exit policy and operationalise the social safety net.

In May 1991 just before the initiation of the economic reform process and liberalization, the *Economist* published a detailed review of the Indian economy. It said:

"Nowhere else, not even in Communist China or the Soviet Union, the gap between what might have been achieved and what has actually been achieved is as great as in India. This is not the fault of former colonial masters or wicked western capitalists or the cruel hands of fate. It is largely India's own doing".

This provides food for thought.

The article further stated that an economic miracle is going to happen. India is a Tiger caged. Can we not uncage the Tiger and make it leap forward? We can. But, we must muster courage.

# 53

## The Economics of Education Cess

The meeting of the Chief Ministers of States in Delhi on 15.2.1994 was memorable for more reasons than one. It underlined the need for spreading literacy throughout the country and proposed a measure to raise resources to meet atleast a part of the educational expenditure. The Prime Minister, in his thought provoking address at the Conference, called for substituting "a virtuous circle" for the present "vicious circle" of illiteracy, ignorance and poverty. The virtuous circle involves literacy, enlightenment and economic well being. That this task is a categorical imperative was highlighted by the Prime Minister. When a person is illiterate and ignorant he is satisfied with a low and substandard of living. He becomes unaware of the opportunities that open up for him; even if he becomes aware of them he does not have the knowledge or expertise so necessary to make use of them. Thus, illiteracy, leads to ignorance and ignorance leads to poverty and poverty breeds illiteracy. This vicious circle is to be broken and the people of the country are to be placed in the virtuous circle of literacy, enlightenment and improved economic well being.

At present the Government is spending 3.7 percent of GDP on education. This is to be increased to 6 percent of national income. This would mean as five year plan allocation of Rs. 53,000 crore on education considering the enormity of illiteracy, this outlay is grossly inadequate. However, resources are to be mobilized to meet this outlay.

The Prime Minister has proposed the re-introduction of the educational cess. This cess is nothing new. It was there during the colonial rule. The farmers paying land revenue had to pay an education cess. The cess paid by all the farmers would flow into the Treasury and this would be used to meet the education outlay.

But this cess was abolished after Independence. There is now a strong case for re-introducing it in the changed circumstances.

The education cess was levied as a percentage of the land revenue paid by the farmers in the rural sector. This cess was moderate and would not constitute a heavy burden on the farmers paying land revenue. With the passage of time the land revenue has increased several fold. The education cess at a higher rate and on a larger land revenue payment would be able to procure a large amount. There might be some initial resistance to pay it on the part of the farmers. But by educating them on the need to pay it and the use to which it would be put it is possible to break the initial resistance.

Apart from the farmers paying land revenue there are non-farming artisans in the rural sector. Even their children are to be educated and they should be asked to make their contribution to the education outlay. As their income cannot be assessed in any precise manner, it would be humanly impossible to make them pay a certain percentage of their income towards education outlay. For this reason the non-farm families should be made to pay a certain fixed sum as education cess.

Those who pay income tax (and they live mainly in the urban centres) have to be made to pay a fixed percentage of their gross income towards education outlay. This should be apart from and in addition to their normal income tax payments determined in the Budget each year. Those who send their children to Navodaya Schools and schools meant for the children of the affluent sections of society may protest on the ground that their children are going to the privately managed schools inculcating the "mummy-daddy culture" and not to the State managed schools and, therefore, they do not have to pay the education cess. Their protest becomes irrelevant considering the fact that they are part of society subject to all the laws promulgated by the Government. Therefore, whether they send their children to the state-run schools or not they are under a social obligation to pay the education cess.

Apart from this there is need to encourage philanthropic individuals to make their contributions to the education outlay. In their case, the contributions they make should be exempt from income tax.

"Education for all" is the slogan at present, it should be amended to road as "compulsory education for all". If this is so the education cess should be made compulsory as well. Quite apart from the cess paid by every family, the schools should levy a fee on every student enrolled therein. As the focus is to be on female literacy. The rate of fee should be lower on the girl students than on the boy students. In these ways it is possible to meet the education outlay envisaged by the Prime Minister.

The Education Policy announced by the Government of India in 1986 is in a limbo. The operation Black Board envisaged therein is only a partial success. The student enrolment in the schools is not upto the mark and a large percentage of students joining the schools drop out after two years of schooling. The drop out rate is higher in the case of girls than in the case of boys. The present scheme envisaged by the Prime Minister assisted by the scheme of resource mobilization detailed above will go a long way in universalizing primary education to the betterment of society. The virtuous circle implicit in the scheme will make boys and girls better educated, better enlightened and will improve the quality of life of the people which is the objective of planning. Seen in this light the education cess and the other accompanying measures of resource mobilisation will be of immense value in furthering the cause of elementary education and in improving the quality of life of the people.

# 54

## Need to Reconstitute the Audit Committee of Public Sector Banks

It is common knowledge that the Reserve Bank of India, in consultation with the Ministry of Finance, has issued fresh guidelines to the banks in the matter of furnishing accounts to the Reserve Bank every six months. There is, in addition, the need for an Advisory Committee of the Board of Directors (ACB) which has to perform the duties mentioned herewith. The composition of the ACB and its functions are as under:

The ACB attached to every public sector bank has five members who are:

- Chairman and Managing Director
- Executive Director of the Bank (and in the case of State Bank of India a whole-time Director)
- Two Official Directors one of them being a nominee of the Government and the other being a nominee of the Reserve Bank of India).
- Two non-official, non-executive Directors, one of them being a Chartered Accountant.

The meetings of the ACB are to be chaired by any one of the non-executive Directors.

The Audit Committee has to perform the following functions: Providing directions to the Banks and overseeing the total audit function. Total audit function comprises organization, operationalisation and quality control of internal audit and inspection within the bank. This has to be followed by the statutory external audit of the bank and inspection by the Reserve Bank of India.

As regards the internal audit the ACB has to review the internal audit function including the quality and effectiveness of the audit. It has to review the inspection reports in respect of the specialized and large branches and of all branches with unsatisfactory ratings. In particular, it has to focus on the following functions:

- Inter-bank adjustment accounts,
- Unreconciled long standing entries in inter bank accounts,
- Arrears in the balancing of books in various branches and the frauds, if any,
- All other major areas of house keeping. The banks usually transfer the big account to loss-making branches in order to enable them to earn profits. The Reserve Bank of India has levelled serious objections against this practice.
- Obtaining and reviewing the half yearly reports from the banks as per the instructions of the Reserve Bank of India.
- As regards the statutory audit the ACB has to follow up the issues raised in the Long Form Audit Report (LFAR). It has to interact with the external auditors before finalizing the annual / semi annual financial accounts and reports.
- The ACB has to be concerned with all the issues raised in the inspection reports of the Reserve Bank of India.

The Audit Advisory Committee of any nationalized bank is an important committee constituted as per the Reserve Bank guidelines. This committee consists of the following members:

- Executive Director
- A Government nominee
- A Reserve Bank nominee
- A Chartered Accountant

It is suggested here that an advocate should be a part-time Director in order to enable the effective functioning of the Audit Committee. This suggestion gains relevance in the context of the large number of waivers of loans taken by both the genuine and bogus defaulters the latter being in large number.

In the year 1994-95 the waiver of the loans ran to a hefty Rs. 1000 crore as stated by Shri Talwar, Deputy Governor of the Reserve Bank of India. If this is shared by 20 nationalised banks the share of each bank on an average will be Rs. 50 crore. This is in addition to the non-performing assets of the order of Rs. 4000 crore.

The Reserve Bank introduced this scheme in order to clear up the balance sheets of the nationalised banks. However, the scheme was misused both by the bank officials and the borrowers acting in collusion. In consequence, the depositors' money was wrongfully appropriated by the willful defaulters in collusion with the complaint and corrupt bank officials. The benefits of write-offs have gone to willful defaulters rather than to genuine defaulters. If an advocate is made a member of the committee, as suggested above, he will exercise vigil over the inclusion of willful defaulters and take care to eliminate them from the benefit of write-off. Some may raise the objection that even the advocate member might get into collusion with the bank officials, willful defaulters and make a gain in the process. But this venture is risky for him for, in the event of an enquiry by the CBI or by any other agency he will be caught as his notings will be on record in the files. This risk deters him from getting into collusion with the bank officials and the willful defaulters. Therefore, the presence of an advocate whose opinion has to be obtained in all cases of write-offs is felt imperative as he serves as a watch dog keeping vigil on the write-off exercise.

The presence of an advocate on the committee will lend credibility to the bank operations. If the existing committee (without an advocate on it) is allowed to continue, the burden of write-off is likely to escalate into Rs. 2000 crore. The public is raising the question: Whose money is being written off. In order to avoid the wilful defaulters misusing the write-off provision the appointment of an advocate on the committee is a categorical imperative.

# 55

## NRI Investments in India

In June 1991, when the Government assumed office in Delhi, the policy of economic liberalisation was initiated in order to integrate the Indian economy with the world economy. The chief objective was to open the economy to the bracing winds of external competition to enhance the price and quality competitiveness of Indian goods in world markets, to unshackle the industrial sector from bureaucratic controls and licensing procedures, to accelerate the rate of economic growth, to offer incentives to foreign capital and to non-resident Indian investment which would increase the productivity of the industrial sector and help bridge the yawning balance of payments gap etc. One of the ingredients of this policy is the encouragement given to NRI investments in the Indian economy.

Ever since the adoption of the policy of economic liberalization, the Government has been offering various incentives to NRI investments tax concessions, 100 percent equity participation, facility to repatriate profits, opportunity to avail permission to the NRIs to start industrial units in new ventures and to purchase sick industrial units. These are some of the concessions offered to NRIs. Though these concessions were offered with intent to push through the economic reform measures, it is held in certain quarters that these concessions are harmful to domestic industries. It is held by them that this would damage the economy in the long run. In the short run it is unsafe to depend on NRI investments.

The Government has opened several sectors to the NRIs including the service sectors. For instance, in respect of hospitals, oil exploration, fisheries, shipping and others the NRIs are permitted to make 100 percent investment, they can also repatriate profits. Even in areas where the industrial units could be started only under licence the NRIs can operate with the above facilities. Even the sectors which till recently were reserved for the small scale industrial sector are now open to the NRIs. The domestic industries fear that this kind of a policy of economic liberalization which has discrimination built into it is harmful to them.

The NRIs are also given free entry into hotel and tourism with 100 percent investment. The word 'hotel' embraces restaurants, sea side tourist centres, food supplying units and lodging units. 'Tourism' embraces travel agencies, those who arrange for travel to tourist centres through vehicles and those that make arrangements for tourist traffic including air travel. The purchase of shares of companies and investment of funds in building and development sectors are also kept open to the NRIs.

It is obvious from the foregoing that the government is actuated by the thought that the flow of NRI investment to India will solve all the problems faced by it and will make India a land of flowing milk and honey. But a study of India's experience with NRI investment during the past two years shows how disappointing the reactions of the NRIs are. Despite all the concessions given to the NRIs, the number of NRIs who have invested in India is not much and the quantum of investment is a trickle. In 1991-90 the NRI investment was of the order of Rs. 123.37 crore; in 1991 it was Rs. 19.7 crore. Despite the various concessions offered to them at the beginning of 1992, the NRI investment in 1992 was only Rs. 439.16 crore. In the first three months of 1993 the NRI investment record is as under: January nil; February Rs. 55.49 crore; March Rs. 5.78 crore. This record is proof if proof is needed that the NRIs are interested in increasing their returns rather than in solvingly India's economic problems. It was disturbing to note that during 1991 when India was faced with an acute foreign exchange crisis, the NRIs were more concerned with their financial solvency than with the external solvency of the country. Instead of assisting India during the crisis, they withdrew their deposits and aggravated the crisis. In 1991-92 the amount they withdrew was $ 165.4 crore. In April, May and June of 1991 the amount they withdrew was respectively $ 39.1 crore # 24.9 and # 31.2 crore. These figures underline the danger of implicity trusting the NRIs.

Many knowledgeable persons hold the view that the various concessions so liberally offered to NRIs amount to discriminating against the indigenous investors. The corporation tax payable by the domestic corporations is 45 percent. This is higher than the tax payable by the NRI corporations. While the NRIs are free to transfer their capital to any country in the world, the Indian investors are not so free. The NRIs bring in investible funds and invest them by taking advantage of the concessions offered to them while the going is good. But they transfer their capital at the unfavourable turn of events. This attitude of the NRIs is damaging not just to the industrial sector but to the economy as well.

The discriminatory treatment accorded to NRIs vis-à-vis the foreign investors has come in for a good deal of criticism. The foreign investors can hold just 51 percent of equity shares. Furthermore, the foreign investors do not get permits as easily as the NRIs. The tax on foreign investors is 25-30 percent while the tax on NRIs is just 20 percent. This kind of discrimination is an impediment to the free flow of foreign investment to India. Despite the host of concessions offered to them, the NRIs are not satisfied. They are demanding citizenship rights in India. The Government of India is, as yet, undecided about it. It is asked, and rightly too, why the concessions offered to NRIs should not be offered to indigenous investors. The Government has obviously no answer.

The Government of India has adopted a policy of discrimination between foreign investors and NRIs on the one hand and between the domestic investors and NRIs on the other. India needs foreign capital not only to accelerate the rate of economic growth but also to bridge the balance of payments gap. But the discriminatory treatment between foreign investors and NRIs cannot be justified. The NRIs are volatile and they are prone to withdraw their investment at the first signs of an unfavourable turn of events thus generating and then accentuating the crisis and causing acute embarrassment to the Government. Both the foreign investors and the NRIs should be treated on par in the matter of concessions. At the same time the NRIs should be told that the concessions could be availed of by them only if they hold their investments for a fixed number of years and they should be asked to execute an agreement to this effect. They should not be allowed to adopt the "heads I win and tails you lose" philosophy. This is harmful to the economy. The agonizing feeling that the domestic investors are discriminated against should be assuaged by reducing, in stages, the discriminatory gap between them and the NRIs. The NRIs are Indians in origin and they should be asked to be actuated by a patriotic spirit instead of by purely pecuniary considerations.

It is agreed on all hands that the most effective way to avert the balance of payments crisis is to step up exports and to enhance their price and quality competitiveness. NRI investment has a vital role to play in the export sector. These investments and foreign investments should be allowed to flow into the export sector, of course, by making them execute the agreement that the investments made would not be withdrawn at their sweet will and pleasure. In this way the stability of the export sector could be ensured. The NRIs are Indians and appeals should be made to their patriotic sentiments in order to assist the mother country to grow and prosper.

# 56

## Aid by the Aid India Consortium and its Economic and Political Implications

The Aid India Consortium which met in Paris recently agreed to release the aid of $7.4 billion to India in 1993-94. It has been a convention for the donors to meet every year and to announce the quantum of aid each of them is prepared to make available to India. The Government of India can, on the basis of the promised aid, formulate its policy programme or to make adjustments in it in the light of this promise. Before these countries commit themselves to extend aid, the World Bank forwards to them a report on the economic situation in India and its prospects for the future. The World Bank also recommends the quantum of aid which the consortium should extend to India. The Government of India has to make out a case for the aid it asks for. In a sense, the consortium provides an occasion for an authoritative assessment of India's progress, capability, lapses and the path of progress it has to chart for itself. It also provides an idea of the economic picture for the international community to act upon.

Though it is called Aid India Consortium; the word "aid" has to be understood in the sense of "loan". This loan demands a commitment of the Government of India to repay it as per schedule along with the prescribed interest. Even so, the interest rate and the repayment schedule can be said to be liberalized. This loan is cheaper than the commercial loans which India contracts off and on. In recent years, the number of donors is diminishing and the number of donees is on the increase. The aid extended by the consortium is absolutely necessary but, at the same time, it increases the burden of debt. If the aid received by the country is invested in productive enterprises the problem of repayment can be easily solved. The consortium demands that the aid be productively invested in order to render the problem of repayment easy.

The Aid-India Consortium has pledged $7.4 billion for 1993-94. ($740 crore or Rs. 3300 crore). This will add to the existing external debt of Rs. 1,17,200 crore. This year's aid is Rs. 600 crore more than the aid given in 1992-93. This increase in aid is evidence of the deep appreciation of the donors of the progress India has made on the path of structural adjustment. The Government of India had made out a case for $7.2 billion (or $720 crore or Rs. 2,700 crore). Even the World Bank had recommended aid equal to the aid extended in 1992-93. But the donor countries on their own volition have agreed to extend $740 crore to India. This is evidence of the faith the donors have in the progress of reform measures. Despite the Ayodhya incident, the subsequent communal flare up, the Bombay blast and the political instability following them, the donors have stepped up the quantum of aid. They are convinced of the ability of India to repay the loan on schedule. It is true that the international credit rating agencies lowered India in the credit rating chart. Even so, the fact that the donors have agreed to step up the quantum of aid is a source of satisfaction.

Admittedly, India is on the road to economic reform. But the progress of the reform measures is slow and sluggish. Any delay or dithering is dangerous as they will add to the existing problems. Modernisation and technological upgradation of industry and the need to adopt follow up measures, reduction of the fiscal deficit, liberalization of import controls, encouragement to exports, the need to close the balance of payments deficit and other problems raise their heads and demand immediate attention. Even though India has achieved a comfortable foreign exchange reserve position, there is imperative need to stabilize and further strengthen it. For this reason, India has to borrow from the International Monetary Fund. In the attempt to push the economic reform measures to their logical conclusion several challenges crop up and these challenges have to be faced squarely. In order to deepen the process of economic reforms, there is need to re-examine the tax structure, Government expenditure should be pruned, the financial sector reforms should be adopted with no loss of time, agricultural sector reforms should be founded on scientific basis, the flow of capital to this sector should be encouraged. These are some of the conditionalities prescribed by the Aid India Consortium. All these require substantial aid. The fast disbursement aid is $220 crore according to the consortium. The World Bank had recommended just $ 180 crore. Of the aggregate aid of $740 crore, the World Bank, the IMF, Asian Development Bank the United Nations Aid Agencies have a share of $420 crore. The balance of $320 crore is the share of the members of the consortium. It appears that the aid promised by the IMF is included in the total aid. If this is so the total aid coming from the consortium is far less. A clarification of the position is needed.

The aid extended by the consortium has been increasing year after year. The following Table gives an idea of the aid India has received:

| Years | Aid in crore of dollars |
|---|---|
| 1986-87 | 440 |
| 1987-88 | 540 |
| 1988-89 | 630 |
| 1989-90 | 670 |
| 1990-91 | 650 |
| 1991-92 | 676 |
| 1992-93 | 720 |
| 1993-94 | 740 |

It will thus be seen that the aid increased from $440 crore in 1986-87 to $ 740 crore in 1993-94 or by 68 percent. Considering the depreciation of the rupee, the aid in terms of rupees has increased by much more than in terms of dollars.

Quite apart from borrowing from the external agencies, it is incumbent on the Government to take measures to repay the external loans and thus to reduce the burden of external debt. As it is, India's external debt is enormous. The per capita debt burden is Rs. 850. There is only one way to repay it. India's exports should be in excess of imports. This is possible only with modernization and technological upgradation of the industrial sector in order to step up its output, modernization of agriculture, the reduction of fiscal deficit as promised, to 4.7 percent of GDP and to 3 percent in the next three years; the reduction of the balance of payments deficit down to 1.8 percent of GDP this year, the raising of GDP to 5 percent. If these are achieved external solvency is possible. Otherwise, India, during the next two years, has to face a crisis on the external front.

While the quantum of aid commitment by the consortium is welcome, the other aspects of this commitment are to be considered to put the matter in the right perspective. The aid including the fast disbursing credit pledged by the consortium does not provide the resources required to accelerate India's socio-economic development programme. It is also meant to service the outstanding credits and to provide a financial "safety net" for the Government to pursue policies prescribed by the donors. But the conditionality prescriptions are made more stringent.

The foreign aid is meant to meet the exceptional financing needs of the Government rather than to augment the resources for development. For this reason, the aid enhances the scope for interference and surveillance by the foreign creditors. The guidelines laid down by the consortium for "further early and significant progress" in the policy directions and the political implications are made explicit. But the Government of India has to accept the guidelines. The aid givers are, no doubt, liberal in the grant of credit but in the past the aid givers have not only threatened but also held back some of the committed credits on the facile ground that the Government is delaying and dithering over the implementation of the conditionality prescriptions. The foreign creditors think that they have acquired formidable power which would enable them to make India accept their terms. The foreign aid is welcome but it should not be considered solely in terms of credits pledged and disbursed and even the efficacy of their utilization. It should be judged in terms of its wider political implications. Already the opposition parties in the Parliament are changing the Government with surrendering India's national sovereignty and selling out India to foreign creditors. In view of this, the Government should be careful not to compromise its national sovereignty. Certain conditionality prescriptions like reducing the fiscal deficit, reducing the rate of inflation, undertaking financial sector reform, modernization and technological upgradation of Indian industry and agriculture are welcome as they help to accelerate economic growth and to integrate India with the world economy. But the Government should take care to see that the country's national sovereignty is not sacrificed for any reason.

# 57

# The Euro-Issue Guidelines

On 28th October 1994, the Government of India issued new guidelines to govern the Euro-Issues by Indian companies and the transfer of proceeds to India. The new guidelines for the current financial year (1994-95) remove the earlier stipulation that Euro issue proceeds should be utilized for the approved end uses within a year of the date of issue. According to the modified guidelines, the issuing companies would instead be required to retain the Euro issue proceeds abroad to be repatriated as and when expenditure for the approved end uses including upto 15 percent earmarked for general corporate restructuring uses, are incurred. This will enable the companies to tap markets abroad for approved purposes while also avoiding monetary expansion as a consequence of Euro-issue inflows in advance of the need for funds. This requirement will be added to all final approvals given henceforth. Information regarding periodic repatriation of Euro issue proceeds into the country and the manner of their deployment for the approved end uses should be furnished in detail in the quarterly statements that the issuing companies are required to submit to the Government at the end of every calendar quarter duly vetted by the auditors. However, the relaxation of the approved end use criteria will be allowed to enable the selected all India financial institutions to have access to the Euro market considering the multiplier effect and generally beneficial impact for small and medium industries who are unable themselves to have access to the Euro market. According to the fresh guidelines for Euro issues (1994-95) companies will not be permitted to issue warrants along with their Euro issues.

Earlier, the guidelines for Euro issues (1994-95) were announced by the government on May 11, 1994. These guidelines had stipulated that Euro issues would be permitted only for certain specific end uses to be incurred within one year from the date of issue. The Government received several representations with a request to review the stipulation that the Euro issue proceeds should be used for the approved end uses within a period of one year from the date of issue on the plea that capital expenditure projects invariably have a long gestation period and that it would be difficult for companies to comply with the one year restriction. These representations were considered by the Government and the guidelines were modified to remove the stipulation that Euro issue proceeds should be utilized for the approved end uses within a period of one year from the date of issue.

When the guidelines were first issued in May 1994 it was indicated that the guidelines would be reviewed periodically. During the first half of the present financial year Indian companies mobilized over $ 1.0 billion through the issue of global depository receipts (GDRs) and Euro Convertible bonds. This indicates a healthy and sustained interest by overseas investors in India.

The revised guidelines are a distinct improvement. Earlier, as averred already, Euro issue proceeds had to be remitted immediately to India and utilized for specified end uses within one year. This made it difficult for companies to follow the sensible course of raising funds when opportune and investing them when the time was ripe. It also fuelled an inflow that swelled forex reserves necessitating sterilization by the Reserve Bank of India to check inflation. The Reserve Bank of India bought the forex, increasing the money supply and then mopped up excess liquidity by selling government securities. It had to forego a yield of 11 percent on securities while getting a return of only 4-5 percent on foreign gifts that it bought, a financial loss of around 6 percent of the amount sterilized (Rs. 9000 crore last year). Now by obliging the companies to park their Euro issue proceeds abroad till the use for approved end uses, the Government has in effect passed on the cost of sterlisation to the issuing companies. Earlier, they bought cheap funds into India and benefitted from the interest rate arbitrate or played the stock markets. As per the new guidelines, they have to keep funds abroad at lower yield rates prevailing there. Companies will typically keep their money in more high yielding instruments than the Reserve Bank of India can, so that the economy as a whole will be the gainer. Arbitrage is still possible by routing the money through foreign port-folio investment in India but such investment is subject to a 70:30 ratio of equity to debt. In view of this the new guidelines will curb the interest arbitrage more than stock market speculation.

Why is India not welcoming the inflow of scarce resources that will bring down capital costs and stimulate the economy? The answer seems to be that the Government has failed to stimulate a strong enough investment boom to absorb the dollar inflow. The guidelines amount to an admission that the reserves have an inflationary impact on the economy by forcing a greater increase in the domestic money supply than is prudent in terms of the rise in the level of domestic economic activity.

The new guidelines are intended to check the rise in the rate of inflation. In recent weeks the inflation rate as measured by the Wholesale Price Index has risen to 8.6 percent. The sharp decline witnessed in August and the first half of September 1994 has not been in evidence. This calls for a renewed emphasis on with the adverse effect of the accumulated foreign exchange reserves on the price level. The Government has attempted to tackle one of the factors contributing to the continuing increase in foreign exchange reserves which are estimated to be $20 billion and which are expected to rise to $25 billion by the end of the fiscal year 1994-95. This has been attempted by means of revising the guidelines on issue and use of capital raised abroad by Indian companies. The objective of the new measure is to phase out and delay the inflow of capital mobilized abroad so that the build up of foreign exchange reserves is slowed down. Finance raised through the issue of instruments like the Global Depository Receipts (GDRs) has been the largest single source of foreign capital in the past year and a half. In 1993-94 Euro issues fetched $2.5 billion. This accounted for more than half of the capital inflow of $4.7 billion into the country. (Direct foreign investment brought in $600 million and foreign institutional investment in the stock market was worth

$1.6 billion in the last financial year). In the current financial year there has been no noticeable decline in the amount raised abroad by the Indian companies. In the first six months of 1994-95 about $1.1 billion are estimated to have entered the country through the Euro issue route even as the Government is believed to have given its approval for proposals for the issue of an additional $ 5 billion of share capital in foreign markets.

The new Euro issue guidelines should help to reduce the inflow of foreign funds. But their effectiveness depends on the ability of the Government to monitor the situation. As per the new guidelines, the companies have to give quarterly reports on the amount retained abroad and the expected need for funds within the country. The temptation to incumbent the guidelines will be strong since interest rates abroad continue to be lower and far more can be realized in the interim in India from inter-corporate lending, deployment in the stock markets and investment in real estate. In view of this more needs to be done to either slow the buildup of forex reserves or neutralize the effect on the price level. At present, despite the adoption of many measures the rate of monetary growth has not slowed down. The fact that this has happened despite the efforts by the Finance Ministry and the Reserve Bank of India to contain the budget deficit for 1994-95 points to the massive inflow of foreign capital as the main culprit of money expansion.

In the busy season credit policy announced recently by the Reserve Bank of India, certain new measures to cope with the inflow of foreign capital have been proposed. They are, the imposition of cash reserve ratios on deposits into the foreign currency non-resident accounts and the lowering of interest rates on some kinds of bank deposits by NRIs. These measures along with the new Euro Issue guidelines are necessary to reduce the rate of monetary growth of broad money supply (M3) is averaging 18.5 percent on an annual basis. The trend of monetary growth in the first half of 1994-95 has forced the Reserve Bank of India to raise the target for monetary expansion in the entire year from 14-15 percent to a new one of 16 percent. Even this figure may not be achieved if the recent measures do not yield results. With the expected pick-up in industrial growth, a higher growth of M3 can be accommodated but a monetary expansion of 18 percent is bound to unleash inflationary forces.

The need to control the growth of forex reserves can be seen from the fact that while M3 expanded by under 8 percent between March 31 and September 16,1994 the net foreign exchange assets of the banking sector grew by more than 23 percent in the same period. The growth of forex reserves so far in the current financial year has accounted for 10 percent of the increase in reserves or high powered money because it directly leads to the increase in money supply.

The Reserve Bank credit to the government sector, which is one important component of reserve money, has declined sharply in the first half of 1994-95. The other component, bank lending to the commercial sector has increased to a smaller extent. But the growth of foreign exchange assets has set the pace for the expansion of reserve money. In this context the new Euro issue guidelines will make Indian companies to retain the proceeds of Euro issues outside the country until they need it for the execution of projects. This will help to slow down the rate of monetary growth.

The reduction of monetary growth is only a partial answer to the problems posed by the huge foreign exchange reserves which, at present, stand at $20 billion and are expected to reach the massive figure of $25 billion by the end of the fiscal 1994-95. Besides the question of inflation, the recent debate on this issue has also focused on the largely volatile nature of the forex reserves since they consist mostly of speculative funds which cannot be counted upon for long term foreign exchange planning. As a corollary to this debate, the question has also been raised whether the country has any use for hard currency reserves of this colossal magnitude. This poser would ordinarily be regarded as redundant anywhere else in the world because hard currency is precious and can be put to many uses but in the Indian context it has become necessary to ask to what use the reserves are being put.

The nature of the problem becomes clear when it is considered that of the $5 billion that have come into the country during the current financial year, Indian corporate funds amount to $1.0 billion only. Foreign direct investment (FDI) which is the funds brought into the country by foreign companies for direct investment in industry for this period has been less than $800 million. This means that the bulk of hard currency funds has been largely directed at the Indian stock market. Considering that even the Annual Report of the Reserve Bank of India has noted that the eventual capital formation in industry through the stock market is quite a small percentage of the funds employed, it is important there is a clear strategy for the utilization of these short-term funds flowing into the country. The Finance Minister is of the view is that the import of consumer's goods should be liberalized. Lately the Commerce Minister has suggested that the funds should be utilised to repay the country's short-term debts. This indeed is a subject of another debate. In the meanwhile, it is heartening to note that the need for a foreign exchange strategy has been recognized by the Government.

As averred above, India's foreign exchange reserves at present are estimated to be $20 billion and they are expected to reach the $25 billion level before the end of the fiscal 1994-95. Are these reserves too much for the Indian economy? This question is put by several experts and the answer is 'yes'. Other experts hold the view that they constitute no problem at all. In July 1991 they were $1.1 billion then worth Rs. 2300 crore. In the third week of October 1994 they were about $20 billion not including gold coins and bullion worth $4.08 billion. The rupee is riding high against the dollar and the Reserve Bank of India continues to buy dollars to prevent an appreciation of the rupee. In fact, the rupee is appreciated already by the difference between the rate of inflation in India and the rate of inflation in the US.

It is argued by many that there are countries which have accumulated larger forex reserves than India but they do not see any problem in it. Among the emerging economies Singapore's reserves are $55 billion (Rs. 1,70,500 crore), South Korea $25 billion (Rs.77,500 crore), Hong Kong, Brazil, China, Malaysia, Thailand and Mexico fall between the two with China's reserves placed at $35 billion (Rs. 1,08,500 crore). The reserves must be seen in relation to the volume of foreign trade. Normally, reserves are measured against import requirements and three months' reserve requirements are considered adequate. The Finance Minister considers it expedient to import more and to cut the forex reserves. In July 1991 the Government set a five year time table and promised to allow import of consumer goods at the end of the structural adjustment and stabilization programmes. The year 1996-97 remains as the year when quantitative restrictions on the import of consumer goods will be removed and their imports put on a tariff basis. But in the context of continuing inflow of forex reserves there would be no harm in advancing the time table for liberalizing the import of consumer goods. At the same time the reserves (non-volatile part of the reserves), can also be used to retire external debt carrying a higher rate of interest. This will reduce the external debt burden on the economy besides reducing the quantum of forex reserves.

The new Euro issue guidelines will reduce the inflow of foreign reserves into India unless they are required to finance the projects. This will slow down the rate of accumulation of forex reserves. To this extent, it will slow down the rate of monetary growth and the rate of inflation. At the same time, the reduction of the fiscal deficit is also necessary to reduce the rate of inflation. These two measures will contribute immeasurably to the maintenance of macro-economic stability.

# 58

# Need for Constitutional Limits on Government Borrowing

The balance of payments deficit as a percentage of GDP has been fluctuating generating a crisis sometimes and declining to a modest level at other times. This deficit is financed by external borrowing with attendant increase in the debt burden. This generates the balance of payments crisis which necessitates recourse to further external borrowing.

The Rangarajan Committee has gone into the genesis of the crisis that faced the country in 1991 and made far-reaching suggestions intended to stabilize the balance of payments position in the medium term. It ruled out the suggestion to swap debt for equity as it felt that such a course would send wrong signals by equating India with some of the debt ridden countries that had defaulted in honouring their debt obligations. It also ruled out debt refinance i.e., borrowing to specifically repay loans for similar reasons and for the reason that very small amounts could be subjected to refinance. Be that as it may, going into the background of the crisis the committee stated that there was a widening of the current account deficit during the Seventh Five Year Plan from 1.6 percent of GDP to 2.4 percent. As a result current account deficit was financed by external assistance, commercial borrowings and deposits by non-resident Indians thereby increasing the debt service ratio from 13.6 percent in the beginning to 21 percent by the end of the plan. The use of foreign currency reserves was minimized mainly on account of capital flows and partly due to recourse to short term debt to finance imports of canalized commodities. Exports achieved a high growth rate but, import intensity of manufactured exports rose sharply. Non-oil imports increased at an average annual rate of 12 percent but the total import bill did not rise because of the relatively lower oil prices though the volume of import of POL increased significantly. The invisible account which had given considerable support to the balance of payments in the past showed a sharp deterioration with stagnant earnings from tourism, a modest increase in private transfers and mounting interest burden. Thus, according to the committee the positive developments on the export front were overshadowed by structural problems in the external sector. With the onset of the Gulf crisis and political uncertainties that emerged towards the close of 1990 there developed a crisis of such a magnitude that economic policy making had to be devoted to the management of the balance of payments during 1991-92. The Gulf crisis had an immediate impact on India's oil import bill which could have been managed with appropriate restraints on imports. But the liquidity crisis caused by the rapid withdrawal of NRI deposits and denial of normal access to external commercial borrowings as a result of the downgrading of India's credit rating came in the way. The liquidity crisis manifested itself in harsh measures of import restriction, access to exceptional financing through the IMF, the World Bank, ADB, bilateral channels and temporary utilization of gold available with the Government and the reserve Bank for raising foreign currency resources to meet contractual commitments.

The experience of the past holds out important lessons for the future. They are: the current account deficit must be limited to a level that can be sustained by normal capital flows. While current account deficits caused by draught, or floods or volatility in POL prices are inevitable, persistent deficits financed by relatively expensive capital flows, are bound to affect the sustainability of the balance of payments.

The remedy for this situation has to be attempted on several fronts; expansion of exports, reduction of imports of POL products, fertilizers and defense equipment. A target level of reserves is to be determined. India's figures on debt service payments are an under estimate. They do not include repayments to the IMF on the loans taken after March, 31, 1991. Since the World Bank uses different estimates to calculate debt, its debt repayment figures are different from the Government's figures. If they are considered, total debt repayments would amount to $ 63.65 billion till the year 2001.

Those who are closely watching the external debt scenario find the situation a throw back to the balance of payments crisis of 1990-91 when the country came perilously close to defaulting on its debt worth $ 71 billion according to World Bank figures. It is likely that the chance of a recurrence of the crisis in the mid-nineties is almost certain due to the burden of debt servicing. This is held to be certain because of the following reasons:

- Total external debt as percentage of GNP in 1991 jumped to 29.2 percent from 25.0 percent in 1990.
- As a percentage of exports of goods and services total external debt rose to 303 percent in March 1992, 85 percent higher than the World Bank's acceptable level of 220 percent and much more than the 1990 level of 278.4 percent.
- High debt service payments have already resulted in declining net aid receipts on external assistance and net capital transfers on external commercial borrowings. Net aid receipts (gross aid minus repayment) stood at 6285 crore in 1992-93 lower than the 1991-92 figures of Rs. 7965 crore. Net aid inflow (gross receipts minus repayment minus interest) was even lower at Rs. 2339 crore for 1992-93 over the 1991-92 figure of Rs. 4959 crore. The figures available with the Finance Ministry for April-May 1993 show a worsening position. Debt aid receipts amounted to Rs.126 over the 1992 figure of Rs. 210 crore. Net aid inflow was Rs. 744 crore against Rs. 279 crore in April-May 1992.
- Net capital inflows and transfers on external commercial borrowings have become negative. From $1.01 billion in 1985-86, net capital inflow declined to 0.05 billion in April-December 1992 while the capital transfers dipped from $ 0.51 billion in 1985-86 to $ -0.46 billion in April-December 1992.

Another disturbing trend is the outflow of NRI funds from hard currency accounts. The monthly economic report for August 1993 released by the Finance Ministry shows that net outflow from NRI accounts in April-May and June 1993 was $ 212 million. While

1992-93 had also begun with sizeable outflows, the trend seemed to have been arrested over the period June 1992 to March 1993 when there was a net inflow of $ 9 million. In contrast, the first three months of 1993-94 witnessed steady outflows - $50 million in April, $46 million in May and $116 million in June. Thus, there were total outflows of $212 million in April-June 1993. This despite the fact that the figures do not include flows into and out of the non-resident external rupee (NRER) accounts for May and June which are not available. What is worrisome is that this outflow is taking place from the foreign currency non-resident (FCNR) accounts, which are denominated in hard currency unlike the NRER accounts held in rupee. While an outflow from NRER accounts means an outgo in rupees, an outflow from FCNR accounts implies a depletion of hard currency reserves. In 1992-93 FCNR accounts had declined in outflows over the first six months. This gave way to inflows of $411 million over the second half of the year. But in the first three months of 1993-94 there was an outflow of $212 million. It is obvious from the foregoing account that the mounting debt burden looms menacingly over the country's future growth prospects. In order to meet the impending crisis, the Government is banking on three factors. High export growth, improvement in invisible receipts and increased direct foreign investment. Is the task easy?

There is, of course, a slight uptrend in exports but the overall scenario is uncertain. The trade balance recorded a surplus of $40.47 million in April 1993, it became negative for April-May 1993 at around $6 million. The incentives provided to boost exports are, for the most part, financial. But there is no one-to-one relationship between financial incentives and export performance. It is true devaluation has benefitted India's exports. But at the same time it benefits India's competitors also. They have also devalued and have provided export incentives. The western world is hit by recession. All the developing countries are vying with each other to capture the export market and India appears to be a poor competitor. Whatever export gains there are, are nullified by the rise in imports. Imports recorded a 20 percent jump in 1992-93 over that of 1991-92. The deficit of $1.5 billion in 1991-92 jumped to $3.5 billion in

1992-93. The chances of a decline in imports are remote. The import duty cuts in the Union Budget for 1993-94 and the possibilities of further cuts in the year 1994-95 budget have the effect of stimulating imports. The new EXIM policy allowing unrestricted imports and the high import intensity of Indian industry and also high import intensity of India's exports will widen the payments gap despite a rise in exports. As the Government is publicly committed to an open import policy, it is unable to take action to restrict imports.

The coming three years till 1995-96 are crucial for India's balance of payments. In this period, India's repayment obligations are expected to reach $10 billion (including repayments to the IMF). In the years after this, there will be some relief. The World Bank estimates show repayments declining from around $9 billion in 1995-96 to around $4 billion by 2001. If exports grow at the rate of 15 percent per annum there will be some relief on the balance of payments front. The Commerce Ministry projects an export growth rate of 22 percent for 1993-94 but the Finance Ministry projects an annual growth rate of exports of 14 percent.

In the middle of October 1993 the foreign exchange reserves had risen to a record level of $8 billion providing cover for atleast five months of imports. With this the reserve position is fairly comfortable. A heartening fact is that they are rising by an average of $45 million a week and mainly because of higher export earnings and lower outgo on imports. This sudden spurt is also due to the foreign aid for Lattur earthquake victims. The rise on account of trade is in line with the Government's strategy that exports will rise rapidly in three years from the day the stabilization policy and structural adjustments were initiated in July 1991. They are expected to be sufficient not only to pay for the liberal imports but also as a cushion for the future. However, it is necessary to remember that the foreign exchange reserves are made up mainly of credits from the IMF and the World Bank from which fresh line of credit is being sought. These loans will have to be repaid and it is essential that exports rise sufficiently over the five year period during which no repayments are required. Another reason for the high level of reserves is that disbursements of bilateral aid has been made by several countries simultaneously. While this helps the foreign exchange reserves, they also add to the external debt burden which is rising. But the country's international credit rating which plunged during the balance of payments crisis of 1991, still remains unchanged and this could discourage direct foreign investment. Talks with the IMF for a line of credit from the Extended Structural Adjustment Facility are to start in November 1993. This is in addition to the $2.2 billion already disbursed by the IMF under the emergency stand-by arrangement. The exact size of the IMF credit under Extended structural adjustment facility is still to be determined though the estimates put it at $4.7 billion Some believe that such a large loan is unnecessary as the foreign exchange position is comfortable and the exports are rising. The Finance Ministry believes that the loan is necessary to serve as a cushion against needs that may arise in future.

The rise in exports is a part solution to the problem. A high rate of invisible receipts and foreign direct investment are required to fill the gap. Remittances from abroad have picked up since 1992 but tourist earnings are still low. The success in attracting foreign tourists depends on political stability, law and order and improved infrastructure. Unless they are there, tourist earnings continue to be low.

What about the prospects of foreign direct investment? Foreign investment approvals since July 1992 roughly add up to $2.5 billion against the historic amount of $300-400 million. This is a quantum jump in terms of approvals. But approvals are approvals. What matters is actual investment. Going from approval to actual investment is a critical step and it takes time to get actual investment of that magnitude. Mere announcement of the policy of liberalization and putting up welcome signs to foreign investors does not automatically mean that corporations with money will come rushing in. With a number of developing countries opening up their economies, the foreign investment regime has become an extremely competitive environment. Beyond policy pronouncements, there has to be a track record of implementation and provision of infrastructure to foreign investors. Approvals of

$2.5 billion of foreign direct are not enough. The Government should concentrate on translating the approvals into actual investment. Compared to China the figure is small but China has been at it for more than a decade and China too had to build up slowly. If about 100 companies come to India with about $50 million each and lay the base on which to build later. 10 years from now, if reforms continue China-type figures can be reached in India. India does not need very huge amounts of foreign investment but $10 billion per year in the next few years would be adequate. But the Government is not optimistic about foreign investment coming to its rescue in the short run leading upto 1995-96. There are too many imponderables like country-risk perception and political instability. Investors would like to be assured of the irreversibility of the reform process. Realistic assessment would not put the figure above $500 million a year. But this is far below China's record. This situation calls for an indepth study of the Chinese model of foreign direct investment and to emulate this model so as to accelerate the flow of foreign direct investment into India.

In the meanwhile apprehensions are expressed about the onset of a balance of payments crisis though such fears are exaggerated. India's case is not as hopeless as that of the Latin American countries though abundant precaution is necessary. Latin America fell into the debt trap due to three factors: indiscriminate borrowing; a world-wide rise in interest rates which added to the burden of debt servicing and a crash in the export market for traditional commodities of which Latin America was a major exporter. But these factors do not confront India at present. International interest rates have remained stable. From 1980 to 1989 there was just a one percent rise in the interest rates. India's export markets have also not collapsed though their intake of India's good is slow and sluggish despite devaluation of the rupee. The Indian balance of payments crisis was caused by indiscriminate borrowing to finance the growing public sector expenditure. Throughout the 1980s PSU expenditure was above 6 percent of GDP. At the same time public sector savings declined from 4.5 percent of GDP in 1981 to 1.7 percent in 1989. They had to be met through borrowing. Since then, the Government has moved fast. Fiscal deficit was reduced from 8.5 percent in 1990-91 to 5.7 percent in 1992-93 though there are doubts about the fiscal deficit being brought down to 4.7 percent in 1993-94 because of the fall in revenue caused by the cuts in customs and excise duties. Public Sector expenditure has been considerably reduced and commercial borrowings by the PSUs have been held constant temporarily though. But the near impossibility of reducing the fiscal deficit to 4.7 percent as planned in the 1993-94 Budget coupled with the enhancement of the procurement prices of wheat, rice, barley and other food articles and the pursuit of a liberal bank lending policy have helped the rate of inflation to rise. The price situation has deteriorated slightly in the first half of fiscal 1993-94 compared with the corresponding period in the preceding year. The rate of inflation which had declined to 5.4 percent in June 1993 rose to 6.8 percent in the first week of September 1993 and it stood at 7.4 percent at the end of September 1993. With the recent upward revision of the procurement prices of food articles, and liberalized credit policy for the busy season of 1993 the rate of inflation is expected to rise still higher. This means that India should not be lulled into believing that the problems were over. The task is as yet unfinished and there is imperative need to keep consolidation of macroeconomic strategies in the forefront of policy formulation. At the same time a consistently high export growth, improved invisible receipts and foreign direct investment are necessary to weather the coming crunch.

What role do the Multinational Corporation have to play?

As *The Economist* pointed out in its issue of march 27, 1993, "MNCs are the embodiment of modernity and the prospect of wealth; full of technology, rich in capital and replete with skilled jobs. Governments around the world, especially in developed countries, are queuing up to attract MNCs. The United Nations, which spent decades tut-tutting about these firms and drawing up codes of conduct to control them now spend much of its time advising countries on how best to seduce them".

The *Economist* revealed that at present there are 35,000 MNCs controlling some 70,000 foreign affiliates and that the largest MNCs, excluding those in banking and finance, accounted for $ 3.1 trillion of world-wide assets of which $1.2 trillion were outside from the respective home countries. In this background India is, of course, justified in encouraging MNCs to invest in India. But at the same time it should adopt a more selective policy. They should be discouraged from investing in consumer's goods industries like soft drinks, ice cream and processed foods. The Government should also take care to see that the MNCs do not pose a threat to the growth of the indigenous industries particularly those in the small scale industrial sector.

The Goswami Committee on industrial sickness and corporate restructuring has recommended that foreign investors should be encouraged to take over viable sick units. The Committee admits that this is a radical suggestion. But it holds the view that it attracts foreign capital. But it is to be examined whether such a procedure is really in the national interest. At the same time, whatever foreign capital comes into the country should not be allowed to be concentrated in a few states thereby aggravating regional disparities.

These measures are easier suggested than implemented. They are, of course, medium and long term measures which do not provide short term solutions. What is necessary is to reduce the burden of interest cost on external debt. In my speeches in the Lok Sabha on the Union Budgets and in my Memoranda to the Prime Minister and the Finance Minister, I have repeatedly argued for the imposition of constitutional limits on both domestic borrowing and external borrowing the former to hold down the rate of inflation and the latter to reduce the interest burden on the balance of payments and to enhance its solvency. Following this logic, the Finance Ministry is reported to have decided to impose a limit of Rs. 7,500 crore ($2.5 billion) a year on foreign commercial borrowings with intent to help the country to keep future external debt within prudent limits. This decision seems to have been taken in the light of the burgeoning quantum of external commercial borrowings. They soared to unmanageable heights in the last few years reaching a peak of an extraordinary Rs. 43,000 crore in 1991-92 when the foreign exchange crisis erupted and seriously eroded hard currency reserves. In the first half of fiscal 1993-94 commercial borrowings have been limited to roughly Rs. 4,806 crore, of which total disbursements are Rs. 1668 crore. The disbursements on account of commercial borrowings comprise loans, bonds and export credits and amounted to Rs. 4196 crore in 1989-90, Rs. 3053 crore in 1990-91 and Rs. 2744 crore in 1991-92.

Frequent resort to the IMF and the World Bank has generated adverse reactions in the country on the part of the opposition political parties in the country. They consider these borrowings as an attempt to surrender national sovereignty and a sell out to multilateral financial institutions. Furthermore, these institutions prescribe conditionalities which the Government is committed to implement in letter and spirit. This also involves sureveillance of the reform process by the lending agencies. For this reason resort to borrowing from them must be limited. Again, the repayment obligations and interest payments impose a burden on the balance of payments and generate a crisis to resolve which further borrowings become necessary. There is thus a vicious circle of foreign borrowing. Seen in this perspective limiting the quantum of foreign borrowing seems imperative. Commercial borrowing involves a higher rate of interest and this imposes a burden on the balance of payments. In view of this the limit imposed on commercial borrowing is well taken. While foreign borrowing is necessary, it must be limited to the minimum. If this is done, foreign direct investment is the only remedy and the object of policy should be to accelerate its flow into the Indian economy.

The Aid India Consortium which met in Paris on July 1-2 had been impressed by India's economic reforms. It was felt that the 4.5 percent growth that India had achieved, was a commendable effort for a country going through a major reform process. The pledges made at the consortium meeting exceeded both the figures for 1992-93 and the recommendations made by the World Bank. The group expressed its willingness to continue substantial support. But the donor nations had some areas of concern. For instance, there was a general consensus that the pace of tax reform had to be accelerated. Some undesirable taxes that actually led to inefficiency needed to be lowered. Now that the Chellaiah Committee Reports published implementation should get under way as soon as possible. Also, tax administration has to be streamlined to move in tandem with tax policy changes. It is common knowledge that the major cause of shortfall in revenue realization is the revenue leakage due to dishonesty, inefficiency and incompetence of the tax administration, effective toning up of tax administration is a vital step in the direction of larger revenue realization. Collection of long standing arrears from large income tax assesses will help reduce the fiscal deficit without much effort.

Political stability is, of course, beyond doubt. The Government has survived the No-Confidence motion moved by the opposition political parties in the Lok Sabha. Its continued stability and resilience are a foregone conclusion. The Government should be extremely cautious about implementing policies involving subsidies and labour. It would be more selective in its approach to pushing reforms. At the same time with the pace of reforms already slackening, any ambivalence would put external financing, in the required measure, at risk.

According to the Reform Agenda, the overall fiscal deficit of the Government is to be brought down to 3 percent of GDP by 1996-97 and the import tariff to an average of 25 percent. Fiscal balance will be sought to be achieved by reduction of subsidies, decontrolling the price of fertilizers, coal, petroleum products and other critical commodities, further reduction in budgetary support to public undertakings and completion of tax reforms which should become highly revenue positive. The States have to fall in line and do away with massive subsidies given for irrigation, electricity, public road transport and other activities. With these reforms on the agenda fiscal consolidation should not be a difficult task.

The World Development Report shows India's alarming plight. Though India came out of the balance of payments crisis of 1991, the impending crises could be much worse unless timely action is taken to avert them. China is moving ahead fast in its economic reforms despite some overheating of the economy. After the Tianmen Square tragic incidents of 1989 China decided to accelerate on the economic front and did so with remarkable success. In 1991 China had over $48 billion as foreign exchange reserves compared to India's $7.6 billion. Furthermore, the Chinese external debt in 1991 was only $60 billion compared to India's external debt of $71 billion.

If resort to external borrowing is easy, the Government would not have any qualms about running balance of payments deficits in the confidence that the external sources are there to finance the deficit. Seen in this perspective, the limit on the quantum of external borrowing is welcome. But this is not enough. It is necessary to impose a constitutional limit on external borrowing as a whole. At the same time there is need to impose a constitutional limit on the volume of domestic borrowing also. The case for the imposition of a constitutional limit on domestic borrowing is based on the imperative need to reduce the rate of inflation which, as the Cambridge Economic Policy Group (CEPG) has demonstrated, is the cause of balance of payments deficits. To impose a limit on external borrowing without, at the same time, imposing a limit on domestic borrowing is to tackle the symptom without tackling the disease. Therefore, imposing constitutional limit on both domestic borrowing and external borrowing simultaneously is the need of the hour. The Government of India will do well to undertake this task in order to save India from the inflation crisis and the balance of payments crisis. An expert group may be set up to make an indepth study of the problem and to determine the levels at which limits are to be imposed and then to bring it before the parliament for a debate and final approval. I am confident that this will meet with the approval of all the political parties and more so the approval of the Leftist parties which are up against foreign borrowing. If this is not done, there is the danger of India being tormented perpetually by, the inflation crisis and the balance of payments crisis with adverse consequences for economic growth and macroeconomic stability and the danger of a risk of entering the classic debt trap of the type in which the countries of Latin America are struggling. While foreign borrowing is necessary and desirable, excessive foreign borrowing on the scale contemplated by India is dangerous.

# 59

## Food Subsidies Cannot be Part of Plan Expenditure

Food subsidy at present, is an item of non-plan expenditure of the Union Government. It is estimated that the subsidy on food grains will be Rs. 4000 crore in 1994-95 against the revised estimate of Rs. 5200 crore in 1993-94. Since buffer stocks are at unprecedentedly higher levels, and heavier expenditure will have to be incurred on storage, interest and transport charges, a higher allocation will have to be made in the revised estimates for 1994-95. If bumper crops are again harvested in 1995-96, the subsidy will have to be further higher. In respect of nitrogenous fertilizers also the expenditure on subsidies will be rising as imports are being secured in larger quantities at higher prices. The consumption has also been rising as they are relatively cheaper than complex nutrients. The fixed subsidy on the latter is also being continued and the expenditure may be higher as consumption has risen despite higher prices. As in the case of food subsidy the estimate is lower at Rs. 4000 crore in 1994-95 against 4,400 crore in 1993-94 (RE). The expenditure will be higher by atleast Rs. 1000 crore in the revised estimate for 1994-95. The provisions for 1995-96 depends on the new decision that may be taken by the Government in the 1995-96 Budget. The 1995-96 Budget would have been framed under normal circumstances in a manner which would enable the Union Finance Minister to reduce or eliminate completely expenditure on subsidies under various heads and also relax control over prices and distribution of fertilizers and petroleum products particularly. In the changed political conditions the Union Finance Ministry may not be able to take major decisions about changes in the mode of subsidies, controls or adjustments in administered prices with modification of procedure. The Union Finance Ministry may be examining the implications of all issues and chalk out a strategy to be adopted. Various committees and Government departments have been keen on reducing the burden of subsidies and dispensing also with the system of administered prices wherever feasible in order to conform closely to the policy of liberalization pursued since July 1991.

It is agreed that changes in policy relating to foodgrains and fertilizers should be made in such a way that they do not give rise to difficulties to lower income groups or weaker sections of society. The question of dispensing with the food subsidies bristles with many difficulties as inflationary implications have been be borne in mind not to speak of political considerations. It is not expected that there will be any modification of subsidies on foodgrains for the weaker sections of the community. It was pointed out that subsidised sales of foodgrains could be discontinued for card holders having income above the stipulated limits. This exercise can be attempted only after the requisite data had been collected. For the time being subsidies have to stay whether anybody likes them or not. This is necessary in the context of the charge that the economic reform programme is anti-poor.

At present, there are three items of non-plan expenditure viz., subsidies, defence expenditure and interest payments on the public debt. If food subsidies are reckoned as part of plan expenditure there will be claims for treating defence expenditure and interest payments also as part of plan expenditure. If there could be a national consensus on treating food subsidies as plan expenditure there is no reason why there should not be a national consensus for treating defence and interest payments also as plan expenditure. If this is allowed it will create complications for the budget exercise. Unless the full implications of listing food subsidies as part of plan expenditure are explored, a decision in the matter needs to be deferred.

Subsidies cannot be continued indefinitely. They need to be phased out in gradual stages so that the people be prepared to meet a situation where there are no subsidies of any kind. But for the time being the Union and State budgets need to be pro-poor without being populist. For, in the long run populism and competitive populism will spell economic disaster. The political parties should desist from seeking immediate gains at the cost of the long run interests of the nation. It should be enjoined on all the State Governments to honour the financial code in letter and spirit if the nation is to be saved from ruin away inflation, social revolution and political instability.

# 60

## Can We Sacrifice Growth to Hold Prices in Check?

The high inflation rate and rising prices of essential commodities rocked both the houses of Parliament in the first week of December. The opposition political parties came down heavily on the Government for its alleged failure to check the rising prices. The Finance Minister in his reply to the debate excluded confidence that the prices would come down within a few weeks though the opposition maintained that this was an assurance difficult to realize.

The rate of inflation in 1995 has remained consistently over 8 percent since the end of July when it was 7.6 percent. From 8.13 percent in the middle of November 1995 it fell to 7.96 percent on 25 November 1995. This has made the Finance Ministry claim that this is due to the success of monetary policy. It is confident that the rate of increase in prices will decrease further in the next few weeks as the Reserve Bank of India continues to have a tight leash on money supply. As the provisional wholesale price index figures are generally lower than the final figures the inflation rate of 7.96 percent for the week ending November, 25, may finally turn out to be between 8.5 percent and 9 percent. The Finance Ministry states:

"Control over inflation has been the overriding priority of the government this year. All efforts are aimed at keeping inflation down to less than 10 percent".

The political observers hold the view:

"Double digit inflation in the country has always created political problems for the governments in power, and the present government would like to keep in single digit this year so that it could use it as an election plank in the coming months."

To what extent is the present fall in the inflation rate to 7.96 percent from 8.13 percent or from an earlier higher figure due to the tight monetary policy of the Reserve Bank of India? The Reserve Bank of India had envisaged a monetary growth rate or 15.5 percent for 1995-96 while keeping inflation control as the central aim of monetary policy. The available data show that the increase in money supply during the current fiscal year thus far has been much less than what was envisaged. Money supply with the public on a year-on-year basis increased by 14.19 percent as on November 10, 1995. This raises the question whether the reduction in money supply growth from the projected 15.5 percent to 14.19 percent and the following fall in the inflation rate are causally related.

The Classical Quantity Theory of money of the Fisherian and the Cambridge versions and the latest version given by Don Patinkin envisage a cause and effect sequence between monetary growth and the changes in the price level subject to the assumptions underlying these versions. A fall in money supply should lead to a fall in the price level. A fall in money supply, output and velocity of circulation of money remaining constant causes a fall in demand for output and to a fall in the price level. In the Patinkin version a fall in money supply, the price level being constant, causes a fall in real balances; this causes a fall in demand, and output being constant, it generates excess supply and causes a fall in the price level. In these mechanisms the fall in money supply and the fall in the price level are supposed to be instantaneous. No time lags are involved. But time lags are the essence of the sequence. It is estimated that a lag of six months is necessary to enable a monetary change to register itself in a price change. If this is so the decline in the prices on the inflation rate to 7.96 percent as on November 25, must be due to a fall in the rate of monetary growth six months earlier i.e., last week of May. This is on the assumption that output i.e., availability of goods was constant. But the availability of goods was not constant. Due to a policy of import liberalization there was a rise in imports which added to the availability of goods. This was also a cause of a decline in the level of prices. The question now is how to apportion the decline in the inflation rate between the rise in imports and the fall in the rate of monetary growth. This has to be decided before crediting the decline in monetary growth with a decline in the inflation rate. We cannot connect the two on the basis of the argument post hoc ergo propter hoc. This is not to deny the influence of a decline in monetary growth on the decline in the rate of inflation.

The policy of restricting the rate of monetary growth has led to complaints of a liquidity crunch. Both the Prime Minister and the Finance Minister have recently made it clear that the Government has kept a check on money supply since it has its impact on prices. This policy necessarily means restricting the rate of economic growth. The Finance Ministry officials say that "the government would not mind sacrificing growth to keep prices in check since inflation is the worst enemy of the poor."

It is the industrial and the agricultural sectors that are buoyant registering a high growth rate. It is these sectors that have felt the pinch of the credit crunch. The rate of growth of these sectors is bound to decline. It is true that inflation is the "worst enemy of the poor" for the simple reason that by causing a decline in real income it pushes the people just above the poverty line below it and aggravates their poverty. If, at the same time, the decline in the rate of growth of the productive sectors causes a fall in real income the share of the poor per capita also falls. In both the cases the real income falls and both are the "enemies of the poor". But if the momentum of growth is maintained by means of an adequate supply of money and credit to the productive sectors real output rises and causes a rise in the real income of the poor and pulls them out of the mire of poverty. At the same time, the rise in output counters any tendency for the prices to rise in which case the poor people are twice blast by a constant or even a declining price level and by a rise in output per capita provided the output is properly distributed. The time lag between a rise in output and the fall in prices is shorter than the time lag between the rise in monetary growth and the rise in the price level.

If the rise in the rate of monetary growth causes a rise in the price level by generating excess demand, the fall in the rate of monetary growth by inducing a rise in the interest rate causes a rise in the price level through its cost effect. This is what has happened in the Indian economy. Thus, demand inflation will yield place to cost inflation which is equally dangerous. There can be no escape from inflation. Inflation can also be caused by the rise in the prices of imports of consumer goods and industrial inputs because of the depreciation of the rupee. This inflation is unamenable to monetary restriction. There can also be inflation because of the fiscal deficit which, at present, stands at 6.5 percent of G.D.P. and fiscal deficit is likely to be larger on account of the interim relief granted to government employees and the salary hike in the wake of the implementation of the Fifth Pay Commission recommendations and the need to enhance food and fertilizer subsidies especially in the election year. Thus, while the sources of inflation are many and varied of which monetary growth is just one, the source of a rise in real income of the poor is just one—the rise in output of the industrial and agricultural sectors and the consequent rise in the rate of economic growth above the present level. Thus there is no guarantee that the reduction in the rate of monetary growth will be a blessing for the poor for the reduction in the price level, if any, due to monetary restriction may be more than offset by the rise in the price level due to fiscal deficit and the associated demand factors as well as the cost factors generated by monetary restriction and depreciation of the rupee.

The foregoing analysis calls for the need for the Government to reorder its priorities and to allow the growth mechanism to function unimpeded by credit crunch. When once the growth momentum slows down, it is not easy to make it pick up. The growth momentum must be self accelerating. It should not be put in reverse gear. Growth is also the best contraceptive. It keeps the rate of population in check and this causes a rise in per capita real output. The costs of slow growth are many and the benefits of fast growth are many more. The answer to the question in the title is too obvious to need emphasis. The Government will do well not to yield to lay pressure. It is necessary to bear in mind that a gently rising price level is necessary to increase profit prospects and to promote growth.

There is now increasing discussion of the relation between inflation and economic growth. The emergence of economic growth as a policy objective owes much to claims for the merits of economic growth as a counter to inflation. Faster growth of aggregate supply is the answer to the problem of aggregate excess demand. A rise in investment generates inflation; at the same time it generates output. And inflation is the price to be paid for a higher growth rate and when output rises it acts as a counter to inflation. What is needed is a high rate of economic growth consistent with price stability or a gently rising price level. But the former cannot be sacrificed for the latter. The problem of poverty can be reduced, even without any change in the distribution of income, by economic growth which would make all better off and a more equal distribution of income could be achieved more easily in a rapidly growing economy in which some could be made better off without any one being made worse off. If growth involves inflation in the short run, it is a price worth paying for; after a while growth generates output which counters inflation. President Eisenhower, in his Economic Report (1959), outlined " A Programme for Economic growth with Stable prices" by which "the economy should grow at the maximum rate consistent with primary dependence on free enterprise and the avoidance of marked inflation". It shall be the task of the next Government to prepare a plan of action in this regard. An expert committee needs to be appointed for this purpose.

# 61

## Reducing the Fiscal Deficit

This fiscal deficit has become the most important variable in the budgetary lexicon and is now the index of the success/failure of the fiscal adjustment programme currently underway. Initially the fiscal deficit as a proortion of GDP fell from 8.4 percent of GDP in 1990-91 to 7 percent in 1993-94. This means that the Government has not had much success in fighting it during the past four years. This view was discussed as ill informed and uncharitable. But now there is universal admission that the Finance Minister's efforts to reduce the fiscal deficit have not been much of a success. The Finance Minister himself has admitted that he has lost the battle against the fiscal deficit. He has averred that every year during the past four years there was election in one part of the country or the other and this did not allow him free hand in reducing the fiscal deficit to the targeted level.

In the first Memorandum to the IMF the Finance Ministry had indicated that the economy would move to a level of about 3-3.5 percent of the GDP. But now the fiscal deficit is nearly twice this. The existing level of fiscal deficit is clearly unsustainable, the situation being not very different from that existing in 1990-91. The fiscal deficit target for 1995-96 was 5.5 percent. This is unlikely to be met despite the Finance Minister's confidence that it will be met. He admits that the shortfall, if any, will only be marginal. The two sponsors of stabilization Vito Tanzil, Director of the Fiscal Attains Department of the IMF and Mr. Claude Smadja, the Senior adviser of the World Economic Forum admit that the Government's war against the fiscal deficit has not been much of a success. The decline in the fiscal deficit from 8.4 percent of GDP in 1990-91 to 6 percent now has been achieved on the revenue amount through systematic changes like the abolition of export subsidies and cutting food subsidies. There are one shot policy measures which, in technical terms, amount to changing the intercept without lowering the rate of growth. More significantly, the way in which stabilization and fiscal reforms have been pursued has created a number of macro distortions and anomalies in the system. As could be expected in the election year subsidies for food, fertilizers and oil have been going up along with all kinds of anti-poverty programmes. The food subsidy will be Rs. 6200 crore this year. The fertilizer subsidy is also likely to go up as the State Ministers of Agriculture are demanding the enhancement of fertilizer subsidy with all the vehemence at their command. The subsidy on oil has also to be raised in order to check the cascading effect of higher oil prices on the inflation rate. One has but to sympathise with the Finance Minister who has been putting a valiant fight against fiscal profligacy unaided. The truth is that he is isolated in the fight against fiscal profligacy.

One of the macro-distortions is the burgeoning interest payment on internal public debt. According to the latest country economic memorandum of the World Bank India's internal liabilities as percentage of GDP shot up from 22.7 percent of GDP in 1980-81 to 52.5 percent in 1989-90. The problem here is the rise in the interest rate on internal debt which has pursued up interest payments as a fraction of revenue receipts and GDP. For 1995-96 the interest payment on internal debt is Rs. 52,000 crore. Current monetary pressure makes it worse.

The Government hoped to gain a Rs. 7000 crore from the sale of public sector equity but the response to their sale is poor. The Government could get only Rs. 200 crore against the immediate target of Rs. 2000 crore and the eventual target of Rs. 7000 crore for this fiscal year. This signaled the inability of Government owned financial institutions (and of mutual funds belonging to Government owned banks) to bail out the Government. Evidently they too were short of cash to subscribe to the 2000 crore carrot which the Finance Ministry dangled out at discounted rates. Unless the Government manages to raise Rs. 7000 crore through PSU disinvestments it would end up with a massive budget deficit. This would upset the

World Bank tremendously. But India cannot afford to do it as it needs the Bank's like of credit. It is possible that it was for this reason that the Government rushed through the ordinance on the pension scheme. This would transfer Rs. 8300 crore from the Family Pension Scheme (FPS) to the Government subject to legal impediments being overcome.

The Government's proposed realization is Rs. 7000 crore from the public sector disinvestments this year. As the year goes by and the stock markets go deeper and deeper into slump this looks like an impossible dream. This calls for recasting the public sector disinvestments programme. The problem lies with the way the Government is handling disinvestments. As long as disinvestments in public sector undertakings is done in a piecemeal manner with no prospect of change in their managements the Government is forcing bidders to value its companies on the basis of the profits that are generated and not on the basis of the assets they own or the profit potential they hold. This may not be much of a problem in case of PSU monoplies but in the case of the PSUs operating in competitive markets this does become a problem. In a competitive market a company's valuation depends on the competence of the management and if the management is not efficient the price won't be good. If the Government is keen on maximizing its sale proceeds what needs to be done is the sale of control of management and not bits of shares. This is likely to upset labour. But labour can be pacified by issuing part of the higher price that the Government releases by selling management control for working out for an acceptable URS scheme. This is not an easy task to do but it requires political will on the part of the Government. It is not just the fear of labour that is forcing the Government to go in for piecemeal disinvestments. It is also the belief that the Government has to disperse the ownership of public sector undertakings among the maximum number of investors. The Ranagarajan Committee talked about shares being held "by the widest cross section of the Indian public". Where the PSU being privatized is a monopoly there may be sense in dispersing ownership but where it is in a competitive market there is no reason why dispersal of ownership should be an objective at all. If the dispersal of share ownership means that the Government realizes a lower value from the shares the disinvestment process will involve taxing the general public. This amounts to reducing the disinvestments programme into a revenue raising exercise. If this results in lower revenue it is very bad indeed.

This is a problem for the medium term. In the immediate present the Government has to sell the PSU shares at a discount. Even then it may not be able to realize the anticipated Rs. 7000 crore so necessary to reduce the fiscal deficit. If all goes well the pension fund of Rs. 8300 crore should come to the rescue of the Government. The Government's borrowing programme has not been much of a success. Its targeted borrowing has not been reached and is unlikely to be reached. In this situation it will be in trouble. The Finance Minister has begun to throw up his hands in helplessness. This will not make the fiscal malaise less acute. After five years of stabilization India has begun to see a fiscal crisis in the distant horizon. This is because the Finance Ministry has focused on revenue while ignoring expenditure though revenue has never been a problem owing to its buoyancy. The rate of growth of revenue receipts has been above 16 percent for the last decade. But expenditure has grown and is growing faster.

# 62

## Open Market Operations are Better Than Variation of Cash Reserve Ratio

The Reserve Bank of India has several weapons of monetary control at its arsenal; the Bank Rate open market operations, cash reserve ratio and statutory liquidity ratio. When it desires to reduce liquidity in the economy, it raises the bank rate, or sells securities in the open market or raises the cash reserve ratio or the statutory liquidity ratio and it does the opposite when it desires to increase liquidity in the economy. During the hey day of the gold standard the Central Bank would raise the bank rate in order to correct the balance of payments deficit. This would attract capital into the economy. Furthermore it would make borrowing costlier and would reduce the quantum of borrowing and spending and thus the price level. This would in turn stimulate exports, reduce imports and help to restore trade balance. In the years of a balance of payments surplus it would lower the bank rate with salutary efforts on the trade balance. But with the passage of time, the bank rate as an instrument of monetary policy was relegated to the background and its place was taken by other instruments of monetary control. In India the bank rate is being sparingly used to control the volume of liquidity in the economy.

In recent years, the Reserve Bank of India (RBI) has undertaken Open Market Operations (OMO) to control the quantum of liquidity. It undertook open market operation of over Rs. 9000 crore in 1993-94 equivalent to cash reserve ratio (CRR) of 2.8 percentage points illustrating that this was a better instrument of monetary control than the latter. Shri S.S.Tarapore, Deputy Governor of the Reserve Bank of India, said on Monday December 5, 1994 that the absorption of liquidity through open market operations was from where the liquidity is lodged rather than an across-the-board uniform tightening. This means that under the open market operations liquidity is reduced when those who have it purchase bonds from the Reserve Bank while under the CRR every banking institution is affected whether it has excess liquidity or not. This hurts the banks which have just enough liquidity and checks their lending ability and this adversely affects their profitability. Those with excess liquidity do not feel the pinch at all. They use the excess liquidity to purchase securities in the open market and this curbs their excessive lending.

In November 1994 the Reserve Bank of India undertook OMO of around Rs. 1500 crore equivalent to a CRR increase of a little less than 0.5 percentage points. According to Tarapore there was no mystery of afore the way in which the RBI conducted the OMO putting out a buying and selling list of government securities. Furthermore, all subsidiary general ledger transactions were recorded and made public daily. For this reason, the market players had a considerable amount of information made available to them.

It is now being recognized all this would over that the indirect instrument of monetary control through OMO is the most effective method of conducting monetary policy. In India also the same perception exists. To be effective the bond market must acquire considerable depth. There should be transparency, a system of primary dealers and a delivery versus payments system.

Tarapore maintained that through OMO the RBI was able to withdraw or inject liquidity in the system as part of a conscious policy. Large capital inflows as at present would generate unduly larger increases in domestic liquidity which had to be sterilized by means of CRR or OMO. With the opening of the economy to the international forces sterilization has become difficult as the effort to control liquidity might push up interest rates generating further waves of capital inflows which enlarge liquidity.

There is the risk of the rate of interest rising under the OMO and this higher rate might attract an inflow of capital. If the buyers of securities buy them at par there would be no risk of a rise in the rate of interest. In this event, an open market sale of securities by the RBI meant to reduce liquidity would be matched by an equivalent purchase of securities by those in possession of liquidity. There is no excess supply of securities, no fall in the price of securities and no rise in the rate of interest. But if there emerges an excess supply of securities offered by the RBI to absorb liquidity, there is bound to be fall in security prices and a rise in the rate of interest. This was the effect of attracting an inflow of capital which adds to domestic liquidity. What is absorbed by the RBI will be made good by the inflow of capital. If the buyers are to purchase securities at par, the demand for securities should be equal to their supply. But this possibility cannot be taken for granted. However, the OMO can be made effective if the supply and demand for securities match so that there is no excess supply of securities leading to a fall in security prices and a rise in the rate of interest.

Furthermore, there must be simultaneity between the sale and purchase of securities. The banks with excess liquidity may purchase the securities sold by the RBI but they may take time to make payment to the RBI. In this case the open market sale of securities does not immediately result in a reduction of liquidity. Despite the open market sale of securities excess liquidity continues unabated. Conversely, in the case of an open market purchase of securities there should be simultaneity between the purchase of securities by the RBI and the release of cash to enhance liquidity. Otherwise, an open market purchase of securities does not immediately enhance liquidity. This calls for the release of cash by the RBI as and when the securities are bought without any time lag.

When the CRR is raised in the attempt to absorb liquidity all banks whether they have excess liquidity or not will be uniformly affected and those with no excess liquidity will be hurt as their lending capacity is curtailed. But under the open market operations only banks with excess liquidity will be affected and their lending capacity will be curbed. Banks with no excess liquidity will not be affected and they will continue to lend as before. Thus the OMO is better than CRR as a weapon of monetary control.

# 63

## India and the WTO

The major trading partners of the world ratified the Uruguay Round and this ratification led to the emergence of the World Trade Organisation (WTO) which, along with the IMF and the World Bank, has begun to oversee the world economy. Despite substantial political opposition President Clinton managed to get the ratification in the United States. When India signed the treaty at Marrakesh last year, India made clear its opposition to social clauses and labour standards. But lately the developed countries led by the US have begun to demand the inclusion of environmental clauses and labour standards in the WTO as preconditions for access to markets. This goes to show that notwithstanding all the verbal support to free trade lent by these countries at the GATT and other fora, the plain fact is a lingering obsession with them. At the Uruguay Round negotiations, the US made no bones about inducting the social clause in the final agreement leading to the establishment of the WTO as it was successfully resisted by the developing world. The question of mandating a new precondition for multilateralism in trade by making uniform labour standards binding on all the contracting parties to the GATT despite the wide disparities in economic development is beyond the realm of acceptability by the developing world. The Prime Minister of India rightly told the Fifth Conference of Labour Ministers of the Non-Aligned and other developing countries in New Delhi on January 17, 1995 that the idea of linking trade with labour standards was not only wrong inherently but would also be fraught with dangerous implications for the developing countries. The demands to include labour standards and environmental clauses are aimed at poor countries, are largely protectionist in nature and reflect the unfounded fears that trade with poor countries will result in the emergence of a poor class in the developed countries. They seek to raise the cost of production in the poor countries by imposing high environmental and labour standards on them failing which their trade with them would be subjected to the so called "eco dumping" and "social dumping" duties. It needs to be remembered that these should have no place in the WTO.

The US and the developing world harp on the social clause which insists on the imperative that economic growth should lead to the amelioration of exploitative conditions of labour. This demand can be interpreted in two ways; genuinely ultruistic and purely commercial. If public policy is to focus on the enlargement of employment, labour welfare, continuous improvements in the conditions of work and wages commensurate with rising productivity, the elimination of child labour, and rendering gender justice in the matter of employment, the message of social clause cannot be misconstrued as it represents commitment to the abiding values of a humane society as opposed to the ruthless exploitation in the capitalist world, in the pre-war days. If this is how the US insistence on social clauses and labour standards is to be interpreted the question arises whether all these improvements should be worked out by the developing countries on the basis of democratic decisions taken in their respective sovereign parliaments or be forced down their throats in the name of an international covenant like the WTO or the ILO. In actual fact the US has been demanding that the ILO should move beyond "core labour standards", namely, freedom of association, the right to collective bargaining and the ban on forced labour and child labour and should start judging whether member countries were raising the living standards of their workers on par with the rise in their GDP. This has to be seen as a brazen attempt by the US to corner the developing world on the ground that it does not adhere to labour standards, particularly to wage levels sanctioned by international covenants. This indeed is protectionism in a new garb aiming to strike at the main competitive advantage of the poor countries, namely, the employment of cheap labour. The consensus arrived on January 17, 1995 at the New Delhi conference against the linking of international trade with adherence to the social clause dictated by the developed world led by the US represents a stern resolve of the poor countries not to submit to the bullying tactics of the affluent nations.

India, on her part, is right in opposing the insensate demands of the developing world. It is said that India has a comparative advantage in cheap labour whose wages are low. But seen in the context of low labour productivity this labour cannot be said to be exploited. Admittedly wages of labour in the developed world are higher than those in India but what is ignored is that the productivity of labour there is also higher. Seen in the context of productivity and not just in the context of wage rates, labour cannot be said to be cheap in the way it is made out to be. If labour in India is considered cheap, the abuse of migrant labour in the rich countries must lead to cheap labour. But the rich countries are discreetly silent on this issue.

The non-aligned countries 'Labour Ministers' conference held in Delhi indicated the industrialized countries for their attempt to influence world trade through linking it with labour standards and for advancing "neo protectionist arguments" and imposition of "extra territorial laws". The draft declaration expressed deep concern over the "threat of new and emerging forms of protectionism which have the potential for neutralizing comparative advantages of developing countries and benefits resulting from the Uruguay Round of trade liberalization". It also warned the US led industrialized world against the "use of unilateral economic measures".

There is unfortunately a dichotomy in the stand adopted by the industrialized world. This world which championed the cause of free trade against socialist controls was now raising the issues of labour standard and environment to influence the terms of world trade. This is to introduce a new form of protection through the back door surreptitiously. The conference called for all these concerns to be addressed by the individual developing countries and suggested that they be addressed at the world summit on social development at Copenhagen in March 1995.

India should oppose the demands made by the US led industrialized world. In addition India should balance this opposition at the WTO by arguing for an aggressive assault on important social problems such as the prevalence of child labour in poor countries and the abuse of migrant labour in the developed countries. Apart from the untenability of the social clause India and the countries of the developing world should pay greater attention to the appalling plight of labour in the unorganized sector in their economies. India, in particular, should aim at a conscientious implementation of existing laws relating to minimum wages, safety and conditions of work. In any scheme designed against exploitation of labour, the elimination of child labour must command paramount attention.

The ongoing economic reforms, their success and the appreciative references made to them by the world leaders, economist and foreign investors have restored the Indian image as a nation guided by sensible, progressive and forward looking economic policies. India has regained the respect and attention which is her due in world affairs. India should use its new status to act "proactively" rather than "reactively" and should utilize the splendid opportunities to play an important role at the WTO and at the world summit on social development scheduled to be held in Copenhagen in March 1995.

# 64

## Reserve Bank's Dilemma

After the announcement of the tight money policy the Reserve Bank of India in October, 1995 there emerged a liquidity crunch in the economy. The banks were unable to make the credit needs of industry and trade. In response to the bank's demand the Reserve Bank of India reduced the Cash Reserve Ratio (CRR) from 14.5 percent to 14 percent with effect from December 9, 1995. This was the fourth reduction in CRR in quick succession during November and December 1995. The Reserve Bank reduced the CRR by half a percent from 15 percent to 14.5 percent on November 11, 1995. This had the effect of releasing Rs. 2000 crore to the banking system which was short of lendable resources. It again reduced the CRR on FCNR deposits by 7 percentage points and this had the effect of releasing Rs. 1050 crore impounded funds to the banks. Subsequently the CRR on incremental FCNR deposits was waived. The final reduction from 14.5 percent to 14 percent was given effect to on December 9, 1995. Even this reduction has been found to be far short of the expectation of banks. The rates of industrial and agricultural growth are on the rise necessitating adequate finance to sustain their tempo. Furthermore, fresh credit of the order of Rs. 4000 crore is required in December 1995 to pay advance taxes. In view of this the latest release of Rs. 2000 crore is grossly inadequate. It appears as though a slight reduction of CRR is imperative. The CRR reductions represent a permanent release of funds to the commercial banks. This is violative of the earlier announcement of the Reserve Bank of India that the money market support would be provided by it "only for very short periods". This means that the Reserve bank has gone back on its announcement for reasons which are to do with the interest of industry and business.

In the liberalized monetary policy the Reserve Bank of India allowed freedom to the Commercial banks to raise the interest rates on deposits. The rise in deposit rates was not uniform. Each bank had its own deposit rate in mind and raised it accordingly. Some banks waited for the others to take the initiative in the matter of interest rates and after this they raised their interest rates either to be on par with the other banks or above the rates announced by others. Even so, these higher deposit rates have not been successful in accelerating deposit growth. Those which raised the deposit rates had perforce to raise the lending rates in order to maintain the spread between the two rates so as to keep their income unimpaired. The Reserve Bank of India did not take cognizance of the rise in lending rates. The higher lending rate did not reduce the demand for bank finance thus indicating that the demand for finance has increased enormously, during the past two months. If the Reserve Bank of India does not increase the supply of liquidity the bank lending rates are bound to rise. This will hurt some industry and business which are unable to foot the higher interest bill. Considering the fact that the Reserve Bank of India is also the banker to the Government, it cannot let the commercial interest rates to rise. For a rise in the commercial interest rates will cause a rise in the interest rate on borrowing by the Government. This will add to the interest burden which already is of the order of Rs. 52,000 crore in 1995-96. The banks find commercial lending more attractive than investment in Government bonds. During November and December 1995 the bond flotations by the Government have increased substantially. If the Government raises the coupon rate on its loans above the existing 13 percent it will attract funds towards itself. This reduces the supply of credit to the commercial sector whose demand for credit is on the rise. This will raise the interest rates on commercial credit and hurt the commercial sector. This, indeed, is a predicament in which the Reserve Bank of India finds itself and, in fact, it is unwilling to face this situation. It is for this reason that the Reserve Bank of India has chosen to nibble at the CRR at frequent intervals. This will moderate the rise in interest rates if it cannot reduce it at any rate.

A growing economy needs adequate finance to sustain the growth momentum and even to accelerate it. But the Government has declared its intention to hold down the rate of inflation even if it means sacrificing economic growth. But the Government will do well to maintain the momentum of growth even if it means a slight rise in the rate of inflation. It must be borne in mind that the increase in output made possible by a rise in the rate of economic growth will act as a counter to inflation in the medium term. A temporary hardship caused by inflation is preferable to a long run suffering caused by slow economic growth. If it is possible to realize faster growth with stable prices it is well and good. But if a gentle inflation is necessary to accelerate economic growth this should be preferred. The choice before the Government is clear and unambiguous. Faster growth is always preferable to stable prices. But to prefer stable prices to faster growth would be an anti-growth policy. This needs to be avoided.

# 65

## Impending External Debt Crisis

India's external debt profile is causing unmitigated concern to the Government and even to the common man. The external debt which was Rs. 72,000 crore in 1988 rose to Rs. 1,24,500 crore in 1990. Since then it has shot up to Rs. 2,76,000 crore. The Status Report on India's External Debt released by the Finance Ministry early in November, 1993 reveals that the debt service payments on India's external debt were $6.83 billion in 1992-93. The Report states that at this level the country's debt service is comparable to that of Brazil and Mexico which have almost graduated out of the debt crisis.

The Government maintained that there are countries in a worse situation than India but this is no consolation to the harried tax payer. India spent $7.4 billion in 1991 as debt service payments while Mexico, Brazil and Indonesia spent $14 billion, $11 billion and $10.8 billion respectively. It must be understood that a lower repayment liability for India was partly due to a larger component of concessional portion of total debt at 42 percent compared to 28 percent for Indonesia, 13 percent for Thailand, 12 percent for South Korea, less than 3 percent for Brazil and just 1 percent for Mexico. But at present the volume of concessional loans is shrinking. Unless the quantum of debt is brought down drastically, the repayment burden will be unbearable indeed.

Assuming that the debt-service burden remains at 10 percent of debt India has to repay $23 billion during the next three years including the current financial year. The annual average burden comes to $7.7 billion of principal repayment and about $3 billion of interest payment totaling $10.7 billion per year. The situation calls for keeping the interest burden within moderate limits. Therefore, during these years there is need for converting the commercial loans already taken from high rates of interest to low rates of interest bearing institutional loans. A re-scheduling of this sort will help to reduce the debt service burden. Besides this there is need to persuade the NRIs to invest in areas of import substitution and export promotion. The inflow of NRI deposits can mitigate the present external debt crisis but more effective than this would be to persuade them to invest in the production of goods for mass consumption. This will help to bring down the rate of inflation and make Indian exports competitive in world markets.

The Government is euphoric about the comfortable foreign exchange reserve position. At present foreign exchange reserves are of the order of $10.5 billion sufficient to pay for four months imports. But this comfortable position is over-exaggerated when it is remembered that 70 percent of these reserves could be withdrawn at a short notice of 24 hours forcing the country to the brink of default. The increase in foreign exchange reserves is due to the inflow of speculative external funds. For this very reason full convertability of the rupee is an unwise step at present.

India's foreign exchange reserves need to be consolidated as external debt has to be repaid in the coming years with debt servicing ratio reaching the height of 36-37 percent. This can be done by raising exports. In the year 1994-95 exports occupy the centerstage in the country's economy. A quantum jump can be achieved through exploration of new markets in Africa and Asia. With the market friendly forces succeeding free trade would be the order of the day. The fact that exports increased significantly during 1993 should not make us complacent on the export front. The analysis of exports reveals that the bulk of this increase was limit has to be raised to Rs. 48,000 in order to induce greater tax compliance and check tax evasion. The raising of the exemption limit is necessitated by the rapid rise in the price level and the depreciation of the rupee. The alleged loss of tax revenue resulting from the raising of the exemption limit will be more than made good by the gain in tax yield resulting from greater tax compliance. It is my fervent plea that this scheme of black money eradication and tax restructuring be examined, its implications be analysed and its feasibility be assessed. The crisis facing the Indian economy is grave and no palliative can resolve it. What is necessary is a radical measure. Of course, it goes without saying that it requires political will to implement the scheme.

# 66

# Monetary Policy of the Reserve Bank of India

The monetary policy announced by the Reserve Bank of India on Thursday October 8, 1992 has been received with mixed reactions by different sectors in the economy. The interest rate on bank deposits was reduced by 1 percent from 13 to 12 percent with effect from the following day. Simultaneously the Reserve Bank reduced the lending rates of commercial banks on credit of over Rs. 2.0 lakh from 19 percent to 18 percent. This is said to be part of the busy season credit policy for the second half of the current financial year. The Reserve Bank has also reduced the Statutory liquidity Ratio (SLR) of commercial banks from 38.50 percent to 37.75 percent to be implemented in three phases between January 9 and March 6 in 1993. By this measure, the banks will release Rs. 1650 crore in the system. However, there is no change in the SLR of 30 percent of incremental net demand above the level outstanding as on April 3, 1992. The Reserve Bank has also decided to release one-third of the additional cash balances maintained by the banks under the 10 percent incremental CRR amounting to Rs. 1,280 crore in installments between October 17 and December 12. Both the measures are expected to increase the availability of funds in the banking system. At the same time, there is a reduction in interest rate on the rupee export credit by 1 percent while a new refinance facility called the Government Securities Refinance Facility is being introduced from October 31. These measures have been taken following distinct signs of recovery of the Indian economy in 1992-93 with agricultural production likely to rise by 2 percent and industrial growth rate from 4 to 5 percent.

It must be understood that these measures have been taken in the context of a spurt in prices and a sluggish recovery from the recession of the preceding year. There is a great risk of upward inflationary pressure in the economy following the recent hike in the prices of petroleum products, fertilizers and other industrial raw materials. The cut in interest rates could have been larger had the prices of essential commodities remained constant at a reasonably lower level. After taking into account the possible impact of the recent hike in prices of petroleum and fertilizers the Reserve Bank had considered it appropriate to cut the interest rate by only 1 percentage point.

India is faced with a recession from which recovery is slow and sluggish and also with an inflationary situation caused by the fiscal deficit and compounded by the hike in the prices of petroleum products. The recessionary trend underlines the need for a reduction in interest rates and the inflationary trend underlines the need for an increase in interest rates. A reduction in interest rates causes a rise in investment activity and wards off recession but, at the same time, it stimulates aggregate demand and provides an upward thrust to the rate of inflation.

In the theory of the policy mix there are two instruments to reach two goals. The two goals are recovery from recession and a decline in the rate of inflation. There are two instruments; fiscal policy and monetary policy. Fiscal policy is intended to reduce the rate of inflation. Under the conditionality prescription of the IMF the fiscal deficit has been brought down from 8.5 percent of GDP in 1991-92 to 6.5 percent of GDP in 1992-93 and it is expected to be brought down to 5 percent of GDP in 1993-94. This continued reduction of the fiscal deficit through time exercises an anti-inflationary effect on the economy though this exercise is impeded by the pro-inflationary forces beyond the control of the Government. If the monetary policy is also restrictive this will exercise a drastic anti-inflationary effect but at the same time it deepens the recession and reduces the sectoral and overall rate of economic growth. Therefore, while the fiscal policy is restrict, the monetary policy must necessarily be expensive. The industrial sector is not happy with a 1 percent reduction in the rate of interest; it needs a 2 or 3 percent reduction in order to stimulate recovery but the fear is that it may exacerbate inflation in the economy. The rate of inflation was falling before the hike in the prices of petroleum products but after this the rate of inflation started to climb up. The Reserve Bank had, of course, concern for rapid recovery but it had the fear that a greater reduction in the rate of interest would provide a boost to the rate of inflation and frustrate the anti-inflationary effects of the reduction in the fiscal deficit. Seen in this light, the policy of the Reserve Bank in reducing the lending rate by just 1 percent is understandable. The recovery will be slow, of course, but inflationary forces will be held at bay.

There is a reduction in the deposit rate by 1 percent from 13 percent to 12 percent. At a time when the objective of policy is to mobilize deposits this reduction in the deposit rate has the effect of reducing the rate of deposit mobilization. With the removal of the tax on interest income from bank deposits in the Union Budget for 1992-93 the rate of deposit mobilization is on the increase. But the reduction in the deposit rate adversely affects deposit mobilization by reducing its competitiveness. What matters for deposit mobilization is the real interest rate. Empirical evidence has shown that the rate of savings varies directly with the real interest rate. The real interest rate is the money rate corrected for the rate of inflation. In an inflationary situation the money rate of interest must rise at a greater rate than the rate of inflation. But in India not only is there a rise in the inflation rate but also there is a fall in the money rate of interest. This reduces the real rate of interest and given the assumption of a direct variation between the real interest rate and the rate of savings, the rate of savings must fall. Since deposits are made from out of savings the rate of deposit mobilization will fall. The fall in the real rate of interest will make the depositors shift their deposits to investments in other lines of activity purchase of gold and real estate which are continuously appreciating in value and which, therefore, provide alternative outlets for their deposits and also to other instruments like company fixed deposits and debentures which offer a much higher yield. The consequence is a decline in deposit mobilization. This has the effect of reducing the profitability of banks and making some of them sick unless there is a reduction in administrative expenditure.

There is need to raise the money rate in a greater proportion than the rise in the inflation rate in order to raise the real rate of interest. This will not only stimulate savings and deposit mobilization but will also ensure an anti-inflationary effect as a rise in savings will be anti-inflationary being a leakage from the income stream.

There is another factor which reduces the profitability of banks. The cut in the lending rate is with immediate effect while the cut in deposit rates will be applicable to future deposits. On the deposits made already an interest rate of 13 percent has to be paid till the deposits reach maturity. The deposit rate in the meanwhile remains constant while the lending rate falls. This reduces bank profitability and renders them sick. Furthermore, there is the possibility that the banks may not reduce the lending rate in all cases as the reduction of the lending rate has not been made mandatory.

The limited reduction in the lending rate has been criticized by industry and business as they expected a 2-3 percent reduction. But this criticism loses its force when the context in which the limited reduction is made is considered. The Reserve Bank had to adopt a cautious approach in order not to exacerbate the inflationary forces. While the growth of Reserve Bank credit to the Government has falled to 6 percent in the first six months of the present financial year as against more than 10 percent in the same period last year, overall growth in money supply remains high. Money supply so far this year has grown at more or less the same rate as in 1991-92. And growth since September 1991 has been close to 19 percent while the target for 1992-93 is 11 percent. In the light of such rapid monetary expansion it would have been dangerous to reduce interest rates drastically. The substantial expansion of non-food credit between April and September 1992 suggests that the high cost of borrowing has not deterred the industrial and commercial sectors from approaching banks. The Reserve Bank's caution has not come in the way of expanding loanable funds. The reduction in SLR and release of 10 percent of deposits which had earlier been impounded under the incremental cash reserve ratio regulation (abolished in April 1992) will together add Rs. 4,000 crore to the pool of loanable funds. This makes the cautious approach of the Reserve Bank eminently understandable. At the same time, the token reduction in the SLR by 0.75 percentage point also points to the Reserve Bank's concern that the time is not propitious for a relaxed monetary policy.

The exporters have criticized the limited lowering of interest rate and the reduction in the bank refinance limits for export credit. They ignore the justification for the high cost of export credit. It reflects prevailing monetary conditions of excess liquidity besides, the high cost of export credit is meant to deter the exporters from delaying remittance of export proceeds. The continued expectation that pull convertibility of the rupee is about to take place, has persuaded many exporters that they will be better off waiting for that to happen than to remit export proceeds right away for in that event the exporters can sell the export earnings at a single rate instead of selling a part to the Reserve Bank at the official rate and another part at the market rate.

The industrial and business borrowers may expect the bank lending rate to be reduced further in the coming months but this depends on the current rate of inflation declining or atleast being maintained at the single digit level. But in view of the hike in the prices of petroleum products endangering a rise in rate of inflation one has to be skeptical about the possibility of the rate of inflation declining and the bank lending rate being cut further.

The assessment of the monetary policy leads to the conclusion that the Reserve Bank which has appreciated the need for adopting two policy measures to achieve two goals has been cautious. The reduction of the lending rate by 1 percent is meant to stimulate investment in order to revive economic activity from the recession; at the same time the small cut in the rate of interest is meant to hold the rate of inflation under check. This is a policy-mix in the theory of macroeconomic stabilization, using fiscal policy to control inflation and using monetary policy to revive economic activity from the recent recession. The Reserve Bank's policy is judicious in the prevailing circumstances.

# 67

## Pros and Cons of Liberalisation of Consumer Goods Imports

At present a controversy is raging between the Finance Ministry and the Commerce Ministry about the advisability or otherwise of liberalizing the import of consumer goods. Early in July 1994 the Finance Minister advocated and ably defended the idea of liberalizing the imports of consumer goods in order to fight the inflationary forces in the economy and to enable the domestic consumer goods industries to improve their competitive efficiency. He also argued that larger imports of consumer goods would result in larger yield of customs revenue so necessary to reduce the fiscal deficit. The surfeit of forex reserves will be there to finance these imports. On the other hand, the Minister of Commerce, opposed the import of consumer goods on the ground that they would hurt the small scale industries in the country. Let me make it clear that I am on the side of liberalizing the imports of consumer goods for good economic reasons.

The Raja Chellaiah Committee on tax reform had recommended that there should be freedom for the import of consumer goods that they should be imported under the open general licence system and that higher customs duty should be imposed on them. The Finance Ministry upholds this recommendation and the line of reasoning adopted by it and wants it to be fully implemented. The Commerce Ministry is vehemently opposed to it. This has become a prestige issue for both the Ministries and their presiding Ministers.

The salient feature of the policy of liberalization initiated in July 1991 is the removal of restrictions of all kinds on economic activity and to pave the way for ushering in a free market economy; to supply goods in quantities sufficient to meet the rising demand for them. It is common knowledge that in a competitive environment every industry tries to improve efficiency and to reduce the cost of production. When it is exposed to the rigours of competition, it will be under pressure to improve productive efficiency in terms of quality and price. This will be to the advantage of the consumers and of the industry itself. The entire economic system will have the chance to activate its inner dormant energies and to work efficiently. In a regime of globalisation, the country will be able to compete effectively in any country in the sale of its products. This is the ideological basis of the policy of economic liberalization.

It is also argued that the unadulterated implementation of liberalization will be harmful to the economy. When the imports are unrestricted the foreign goods will flood the domestic market and damage the domestic industries producing goods. The essential consumer goods are being produced by the small scale industrial sector. When exposed to the unmitigated rigours of foreign competition they will sag. As they are the main generators of employment, their closure will aggravate the problem of unemployment. For this reason, the Commerce Minister is opposed to the unrestricted inflow of foreign consumer goods.

There are also those who find fault with this line of argument. The domestic industries producing consumer goods have reached a stage where they can effectively face foreign competition. What they need at present is a competitive environment. Where they will achieve efficiency and cost competitiveness. Prices of goods will fall and this will be to the advantage of the consumers that the foreign companies in India will destroy domestic industry is far from truth. The domestic industrial companies are in collaboration with the foreign companies. The multinational companies of Indian origin are coming to the fore. Globalisation holds out the hope of achieving all round progress. The increased imports yield larger customs revenue which helps to reduce the fiscal deficit. It is argued that seen in this perspective increased inflow of imports will be beneficial.

Free import of consumer goods is feared to reduce India's forex reserves. But the present problem is not one of shortage of forex reserves, but one of surfeit. At present there is a surfeit of forex reserves which are of the order of $18 billion and which are expected to reach the figure of $25 billion by the end of the fiscal 1994-95. The foreigners bring money to India. There is also the hope that large sums of loans are available to India. They expect that their investments in India will be highly profitable. The foreign institutional investors are engaged in investing their capital in India. The inflow of investible funds has inflationary consequences. The rupee is prone to appreciate in the foreign exchange market. If this is allowed to happen, it will adversely affect India's exports as their prices rise under appreciation of the rupee. In order to avoid this danger, the Reserve Bank of India intervenes in the forex market to buy the inflowing foreign money. This has helped to keep the rupee exchange rate stable at Rs. 31.37 per US dollar. The country will also be able to retire a part of its external debt by using its surplus forex reserves. It is argued that imports of consumer goods will help to hold down the rate of inflation. This will also stimulate the domestic industries to improving their competitive efficiency, to reduce the cost of production, to reduce prices and to efficiency, to reduce the cost of production, to reduce prices and to reduce the burden on the harassed consumers. For these reasons, the World Bank has advised the Government of India to liberalise the imports of consumer goods. The payment for these imports is no problem as India has a surfeit of forex reserves.

The Commerce Minister opposes import liberalization for another reason. If the Government wants to promote exports, import liberalization should not be adopted. It is imperative that India's exports should grow. At the beginning of this year, the export growth was 20 percent. In recent months it has declined. The export subsidy offered to exporters has been withdrawn. The only incentive they have at present is the special import licence allowing the import of raw materials necessary to produce export goods. The exporting firms are making huge profits by selling these import licences to others. The Commerce Minister thinks that this is an incentive to exporters. He seems to condone the illegitimate sale of licences by the exporters. If there is import liberalization, the exporters will be denied the facility of special import licence and they will have to suffer losses. According to him the exporters should have atleast this one incentive. The fact of the exporters having misused this special import facility and of having caused a loss of Rs. 1200 crore of foreign exchange have recently come to light. Even though export subsidy has been there for the past 40 years exports have not shown any significant growth. India's exports were 1.5 percent of world exports 20 years ago. At present it is just 0.5 percent. Even though last year, the export subsidy was cut; our exports grew by 20 percent. For this reason it is through export competitiveness that our exports can be made to grow. Whatever be the merits of the arguments against import liberalization, India has set its foot on the road to liberalization and this step should not be reversed. Any reversal of liberalization will erode the credibility of India's policy and will spell disaster. In a system of mutual interdependence sectoral liberalisation will not do. Import liberalization will, on the one hand, help to bring down the inflation rate and to increase the customs revenue and on the other hand it will help to improve the efficiency of the industrial sector which is necessary in a regime of globalization.

# 68

## Export-Oriented Foreign Investment

It is a fact of recorded history that foreign investment was allowed to foster the economic development of the host country. Agreements were signed by the host countries about the terms of amortisation and interest payments and repayment of capital. Ordinarily foreign investment was made in industries producing goods for exports.

Under the policy of economic liberalization adopted by the Government of India in July 1991 foreign investment is freely allowed and it is expected that it will flow into the country in a larger measure than before. In this connection two questions arise: (1) will the expected inflow of direct foreign investment be adequate to meet the country's requirements? (2) will foreign investment boost the country's exports and increase export earnings? It appears that the Government is not so much concerned with the export-promoting aspect of direct foreign investment as with the need to fill the exceptional financing gap of the order of $3 billion (Rs. 9,000 crore) to $4 billion (Rs. 12,000 crore) a year in the country's external accounts.

The external financing gap did not occur during the Narasimha Rao Government. In the mid-eighties there was import liberalization which generated a trade gap and a deficit on current account. The foreign lenders were reluctant to cover the current account deficit. Therefore, the Government took recourse to commercial borrowing for the purpose. The rising debt service obligation aggravated the current account deficit. The Government continued its policy of import liberalization and to finance imports by means of commercial borrowings. As the foreign lenders were willing to lend to India exceptional financing gap did not arise. But in course of time the debt servicings and amortisation payments accelerated. This made the lenders reluctant to lend. This generated the exceptional financing gap. To cover the gap India approached the IMF for loans. Even these loans have to be repaid. The IMF loan is a temporary expedient and ultimately the exceptional financing gap has to be covered by direct foreign investment and by a rise in exports to exceed the rise in imports. But India is trying to cover the exceptional financing gap by means of inflow of foreign investment. Despite devaluation exports have not increased substantially. The Government, therefore, is relying on inflows of direct foreign investment to cover the deficit. But foreign investment is too inadequate to meet the needs of the situation. Hence, the resort to IMF on loans agreeing to its conditionality prescriptions.

The direct foreign investment is not without its costs. The new investment inflow must increase by 20-25 percent every year to cover the dividend payments in foreign exchange on investments in earlier years. In fact, the expansion has to be even larger as the foreign investor has the right to repatriate investment. If, however, foreign investment has to meet the exceptional financing gap it has to be of the order of 30 percent per year.

It must be stated that the quantity of foreign investment is inadequate not only in respect of its absolute size but also in respect of its rate of expansion in order to tide over the difficult balance of payments crisis. When once the foreign investment reaches the $3 billion (Rs. 9,000 crore) figure it will have to increase by more than $ 1 billion every year. If foreign investment does not grow at this rate there will emerge a foreign exchange crisis which can be averted by a rise in export earnings. The pattern of investment has, therefore, to be export oriented. Foreign investment cannot be a substitute for export earnings.

Foreign investment in India is not export oriented. The foreign investors focus their investment priorities on the domestic market rather than on the export market. The luxury goods they want to manufacture cater to 20 percent of the population or 200 million people and also to foreign tourists who demand goods of the type they consume at home.

Foreign investment in computer production does not earn any foreign exchange as it is used to strengthen the domestic infrastructural base. This will enhance managerial efficiency. Foreign investment in power generation, oil exploration and oil refining will produce the required inputs in a variety of lines of production. But they support domestic consumption and not export potential. This means that new investment is meant to produce goods for the domestic market. In the 1980s India resorted to foreign commercial borrowing in support of production for the elite classes. At present, India persists in doing the same unmindful of the imperative need to enlarge the export volume.

This calls for a new approach to foreign investment. It should be used not to fill the balance of payments gap but to produce goods for the export market and through them to earn foreign exchange. Foreign investment responds positively to the production of goods for the export market. It should be made in all the sectors in a manner that will produce more goods of better quality at lower cost than those produced by India's competitors. Foreign investment for the production of goods for the domestic market creates problems of dividend payments, amortisation and interest payments. This requires recourse to the IMF for loans accepting the conditionalities it prescribes. Therefore, foreign investment should be made in areas where it will increase the productive capacity of the nation and its export potential. What is necessary for India is not a consumption oriented approach to development but savings investment oriented approach with emphasis on export growth.

The Eighth Five Year Plan aims at a 13 percent growth of exports. If this target is to be realized, foreign investment should be made in areas with the greatest export potential. The foreign investment policy should be reoriented with this objective in view. But the foreign investors have expressed a desire to invest in India only if the rupee is made fully convertible on both current and capital accounts. This view has been expressed by the American, German and Japanese investors. Foreign investment policy cannot be viewed in isolation from the rest of the policy measures. It is to be viewed as an integral part of the totality of measures. Now that the full convertibility of the rupee on trade account is being contemplated, the foreign investors should not be weary of making investments in India especially in the export sector. Foreign investment to fill the exceptional financing gap may give temporary relief but overtime it creates problems for the country. But foreign investment to increase exports will ensure solvency of the balance of payments accounts. It is this that is necessary. The Foreign investment promotion board should shift its policy stance in favour of export growth.

# 69

# Wage Demands of Bank Employees

The employees of banks numbering about 7 lakh are to get a bonanza any time now. The employees of the banking sector get higher emoluments and perquisites than the employees with similar qualifications in other sectors of the economy. Therefore the dream of every graduate boy or girl is to get into the banking sector. They have become the envy of the employees in the other sectors of the economy. The bank employees enforce their demands for higher wages and allowances at frequent intervals and if they are not granted they go on agitations, hold demonstrations and bring the banking operations to a standstill causing inconvenience to the general public. Thus they hold the banking sector to ransom.

According to the latest agreement arrived at between the employees of the nationalized and private banks 7 lakh employees will get a hike in monthly pay ranging from Rs. 200 to Rs. 985. The agreement which is the sixth bipartite settlement was signed by the Indian Bank's Association (IBA) and four major unions on February 15, 1995. This entails an extra wage bill of Rs. 388 crore for the banks which is nearly 10.5 percent of the present wage bill. This 10.5 percent excludes superannuation benefits. What is important to note is that the settlement will have retrospective effect from November 1, 1992. This settlement is valid for a period of five years and its actual implementation will start within 90 days of the sealing of the document.

This agreement will cover the employees of 56 banks in the public and private sector—Indian and foreign. The settlement covers dearness allowances, other allowances and service conditions.

Under the agreement new pay scales for the clerical staff starts from Rs. 1750 and closes at Rs. 5500; for the subordinate staff it begins at Rs. 1600 and closes at Rs. 3020. Dearness allowance is payable for four points rise over 1148 points as per the following revised rates: 0.35 percent of pay upto Rs. 4800; 0.29 percent of pay above Rs. 4800 and 0.17 percent of pay above Rs. 7700. The House Rent Allowance varies between 8.5 percent and 12 percent. The City Compensatory Allowance has been fixed between Rs. 75 and Rs. 200 per month. In addition all sections of workmen will get a conveyance allowance of Rs. 100 per month. The clerical and subordinate staff will get an additional fourth stagnation increment.

While the bank employees get the foregoing benefits, the bank officers cannot remain far behind. The All India Bank Officers' Confederation (AIBOC) is "nearer to reaching a consensus" with bankers on the wage revision for the 2.3 lakh bank officers in the country. According to the present indications given by the President of the AIBOC, the rise of the present wage bill would not be less than 10.5 percent as in the case of the bank workmen. There is also an understanding reached with the IBA on the issue of computer increment in addition to the benefits of salary revision for the officers. The package of wage revision for the officers is subject to clearance by the Government and the next round of talks was likely before the end of February. If no hitch develops at the Government level, a settlement may be reached by mid-March 1995. This indeed is the saga of wage, salary, allowance escalation for the bank employees of all cadres covering the lowest of the low and the highest of the high. If the employees of the banking sector get the bonanza the employees of the other sectors are bound to enforce similar demands. Equity demands that their demands should be considered favourably too. If this is allowed the rate of inflation which at present stands at 11.55 percent rises further and it goes on rising with every successive wage revision exercise.

The inflation rate which was 17.4 percent in July 1991 was brought down to 7-8 percent in August 1994. Since then it has been rising slowly but steadily. The fiscal deficit, resort to borrowing which increases the interest cost of public debt, the monetary impact of the rising stock of forex reseves, hikes in administered prices of several commodities, enhancement of procurement prices have all had their contribution to make to the rising inflation rate. The revision of wages and allowances of bank employees will cost the banking industry over Rs. 600 crore and this much money will be pumped into the economy. The Fifth Pay Commission is holding its sessions. It has called for memoranda from various sections of the Government employees and the associations of these employees have asked for emoluments which are 3-4 times their present emoluments. Even if a part of their insensate demands is conceded, there will be a monetary deluge in the economy. The State Government employees will enforce similar demands. The State Governments appoint pay commissions which will be guided by the pay scales sanctioned by the Fifth Pay Commission. The pay revisions recommended by them will add to the monetary deluge. In consequence the inflation rate rises without limit disturbing macro economic stability. A rise in the inflation rate will adversely affect the international competitiveness of India's exports and occasion a balance of payments disequilibrium making it imperative for India to approach the Fund Bank duo for assistance with all the complications attendant thereto. In this event the Mexican Disease will contaminate the Indian economy. This is a danger which we should guard against.

Wages and salaries are an important contributor to inflation in any country. Under the traditional gold standard wages would not be enhanced for there would be no money to pay the higher wages. Monetary expansion would not take place unless gold flowed into the country through the balance of payments. But when the countries went off the gold standard and went on the paper standard. The monetary system became permissive and the supply of money would be expanded to meet the ever growing demands of the Governments. Inflation was the inevitable consequence.

The Finance Minister has been grappling with the task of reducing the fiscal deficit and through it to rein in the rate of inflation. But the upward wage revisions for the Government employees, for the bank employees and for the employees in the other lines of activity will make the task of reducing the fiscal deficit very difficult. In fact, despite the buoyancy of Government revenues, the danger of the fiscal deficit becoming bigger is imminent in which case the rate of inflation is bound to rise.

In this connection the Keynesian prescription comes to mind. During the Second World War when Britain was seized with the task of finding resources to finance the war, the demands for compensatory wage revisions became strong and insistent. Britain, at the time, was facing the inflation crisis. Lord Keynes published a book titled: "How to pay for the war" where he suggested several ways of mobilizing resources for the war effort. One of them was the "Deferred pay scheme". Under this scheme the revised wages would not be paid as and when they became due but their payment would be deferred to a subsequent date when fiscal stability would become a reality. This would check the monetary deluge in the economy. This holds lessons for India. The additional wages and allowances recommended for the bank employees and officers and by the Central and State pay commissions for their respective employees need to be held up and their payment to them should be deferred. This will check the monetary deluge and save the economy from the inflation crisis. Even the pay commissions should exercise self restraint in recommending wage scales and allowances which the country can ill afford at present.

From this follows the suggestion for deferring the payment of higher wages to the bank employees and officers. The payment of arrears with retrospective effect should be held up. The Government should, instead, issued bonds of the value of the arrears due to the bank employees and officers and these bonds should carry a low rate of interest. While the labourers are demanding the payment of higher wages and allowances, they do lack work ethnic in the areas where they are functioning. While the Government pays higher wages deferred though their payment might be it has got to enforce work culture. If this is not done productivity suffers and this gives rise to productivity related inflation. All these considerations point to the need for the adoption of the deferred payment scheme of the Keynesian variety. At present the Mexican Disease is miles away from India. But if India does not bring down the rate of inflation India's progress towards the Mexican Disease will be accelerated. Economic statesmanship demands capping the rate of inflation at a level of not more than 6 percent.

The Indian stock market has received a severe drubbing in the past few months from the foreign institutional investors (FIIs). The selling spree in the stock market is attributed in some circles to the uncertainties about political stability and fears over the continuity of reforms. There are also apprehensions in some quarters that the FIIs are worried about the possibility of a Mexican type debacle surfacing in India and are resorting to quick liquidations. But these fears are discounted as overreactions to a cyclical price movement in the stock market and these price movements are normal in bourses. Some FII luminaries concede that the Indian economy is much stronger in fundamentals and is better managed. The Finance Minister and the Prime Minister have assured the nation that the economic reforms programme is irreversible. Furthermore what happened in the Southern State elections will not happen at the centre as the issues governing the elections to the State Assemblies and the Parliament are far different. A recent issue of *Business Week* lists out Argentina, Canada, France, Italy, Mexico and Spain as possible catchers of the Mexican Disease but it omits India and rightly too. It was the absence of liquidity in the stock markets after the abolition of badla and periodical booking of profits that are found to be the causes of the stock market upheaval in India. This made the Government wake up from the inertia. The SEBI has now been empowered through an ordinance to address the various deficiencies in the market and effectively deal with the intermediaries who do not fall in line. It is now left to the SEBI to act fast and firm to rectify the inadequacies and replace the punitive practices with modern systems. This is enough to allay the fears of the FIIs and to stabilize their investments. This means that there is no danger of the FIIs shifting their capital outside India in the same way as they did in the case of Mexico. However abundant caution is necessary.

Wage escalation poses a danger to macro economic stability in India. This makes the poor poorer and makes the people think that the economic reforms are anti-poor and makes them apathetic and even anti-pathetic to the reform programme. If the inflation rate goes above the tolerable limit it affects the balance of payments stability and this becomes a cause of capital outflow. This is the harbinger of the debacle of the Mexican variety. Seen in this light there is a strong case for adopting the deferred payments scheme.

# 70

## Can the Subsidies be Cut to Reduce the Fiscal Deficit?

The problem of fertilizer prices has been vexing the Government, the fertilizer manufacturers and the farmers. The Government of India introduced several economic reform measures meant to accelerate the rate of economic growth. These reform measures are said to be market-friendly. One of them is the abolition of subsidies on food and fertilizers. The abolition of subsidies is conceivable in a free enterprise, market economy where the prices are market determined and changes in relative prices duly correct excess supplies and excess demands and the system reaches stable equilibrium and remains there unless some disturbance gives a jolt to the system.

The IMF prescribes a reduction in Government expenditure in order to bring down the fiscal deficit. Another expedient is a rise in tax rates. But tax rates cannot be raised beyond a certain limit as the economy is tax resistant and the taxes have virtually reached a stage of disminishing returns. The other alternative is a reduction in Government expenditure. The expenditure reduction which commends itself and which the IMF prescribes is a cut in food and fertilizer subsidies. The consequence that is claimed is a reduction in the fiscal deficit and through it a reduction in the rate of inflation.

Recently, the Government partially reduced the fertilizer subsidy. This led to a rise in fertilizer prices. This rocked the farming sector and generated a furore—a virtual revolt among the farmers. In the wake of this the Government announced a new set of fertilizer prices which have come into effect in the market. The anxiety generated by the partial reduction of fertilizer subsidy seems to have been allayed by the new prices. Even so, any relief that has accrued to the farmers is illusory and notional but not real. The heat generated by the reduction of subsidy has not been alleviated.

This means that the expected evil effects emerging from the phased reduction of subsidies are self-evident already. It is estimated that there will be a 20 percent decline in farm output. It appears that it is for this reason that the Central Government has advanced subsidy assistance to farmers with intent to reduce the burden of higher fertilizer prices. But unfortunately the new concessions are not likely to yield expected results.

It must be admitted that the fertilizer subsidy had assumed colossal proportions of Rs. 6000 crore per year; it must also be admitted that this sum of subsidy led to a diversion of resources from developmental expenditure and caused a slump in the rate of economic growth. It is in this context that the Fund Bank duo prescribed the abolition of the subsidy as a precondition for the extension of the loan. The Government in its anxiety to obtain the loan, erred in agreeing to this condition without examining the manifold consequences of subsidy abolition. Before the abolition/reduction of the subsidy the Government could have evolved policy measures necessary for the proper and effective utilization of fertilizers, like reorganization of the fertilizer industry, cost reduction and the utilization of the savings for schemes of poverty alleviation. Along with this it could have taken measures to reduce the cost of production of fertilizers; it could also have discovered alternatives to fertilizer input in the conduct of farming operations. Finally, it could have taken precautions to prevent the untoward effects on the farming community. It was also possible to reduce the subsidy in a phased manner. The policy measures adopted by the Government in unseemly haste have created a critical situation on the fertilizer front. The Government should therefore give up its palliatives of showing transitory concessions and should undertake a thorough examination of the problem of fertilizer prices.

There are those who oppose subsidies on grounds of equity. The medium and large farm households constitute less than 8 percent of the total rural households but own about 50 percent of the cultivated area. The fertilizer, power and irrigation subsidies, it is argued, mostly benefit a minority of the rural rich. At the level of Rs. 6,000 crore the fertilizer subsidy is more than the total of the central and state plan outlays on agriculture. The dampening effect of the price rise on fertilizer demand has been much exaggerated. Its demand responds more to the availability of water than to its price. This means that the availability of water being given a rise in the price of fertilizer due to the abolition / reduction of subsidy does not cause a perceptible fall in the demand for fertilizers.

The small and marginal farm households constitute over 90 percent of the total farm households and they own 50 percent of the cultivated area. They intituate the large and medium farmers in the use of fertilizers. The input of fertilizers in their farms may not be as intensive as the input of fertilizers in medium and large farms but they do farming by using fertilizers. As they are prone to increase their output they are averse to reducing their demand for fertilizers. Even in this case, if the demand for fertilizers falls it is due to unavailability of adequate water rather than to the rise in fertilizer prices. As they have to produce food for their consumption and to generate a marketable surplus which is necessary to enable them to purchase non-food items in the market whose prices are rising they are under a compulsion to increase food supply. This deters them from reducing the purchase of fertilizers when their prices rise. Having paid higher prices for fertilizers they have to raise the prices of farm output to be able to recover the higher cost of production. This necessitates the payment of higher procurement prices which cause a rise in the final market prices of food articles. In a situation where the food prices govern the general price index and so the rate of inflation; a rise in food prices cause a rise in the rate of inflation. A rise in food prices raises the cost of living index which generates demands for higher wages to compensate for the higher cost of living index and this leads to a vicious circle of wages chasing prices with no end in sight. The elimination of this vicious circle demands that the food prices should not be allowed to rise in the market. If this is to be possible, the food subsidy equivalent to the difference in the price of food before the enhancement of procurement prices in the aftermath of the abolition of fertilizer subsidy and the price of food after the enhancement of procurement prices should be paid. Thus, what is saved by the abolition of fertilizer subsidy is lost due to the enhancement of food subsidy. There will be no net budgetary savings and no relief to the fiscal deficit. This fact strengthens the case for retaining fertilizer subsidy. But there are alternatives.

The food subsidy is necessary to hold down food prices and through it to help the poor sections of society. But it needs to be better targeted in order to cushion the impact of higher food prices on the poor. The beneficiaries of food subsidy are more than twice the number living below the poverty line. For example, in Andhra Pradesh 80 percent of the population is covered by the rice subsidy even though according to estimates, only 30 percent are below the poverty line. The Government of Kerala has decided to spend Rs. 180 crore from State funds on food subsidy. Similar is the case of Karnataka and other States. In all these cases, the concern of the State Governments has not been for the poor; the motivation is to gain partisan political advantage.

The subsidies can be reduced effectively on the basis of a political consensus. This is particularly true of hidden subsidies like those of electricity, irrigation and higher education. Given the nature of resistance to the reduction of subsidies the policies have to be designed so as to link the reduction of the subsidy to a concrete counter balancing advantage. Such trade-offs will create constituencies for reform. Thus, if the fertilizer subsidy is reduced, a part of the savings so made could be allocated to rural work programmes and the balance to additional investment for irrigation. This policy will benefit landless workers, poor farmers and urban consumers and will lead to a higher rate of economic growth and greater social welfare.

In like manner electricity and irrigation rates could be raised to a level that would yield reasonable return on capital invested in these undertaking. This will release resources to provide irrigation and electricity facilities to the poor farmers. Policies of this type may render the subsidies unnecessary to help the poor for the burden of abolition of the subsidies will fall on those shoulders able to bear it. At the same time, the price of fertilizer, irrigation and electricity could be brought down by means of improved efficiency. Thus, an increase of just one percent in the plant load factor will yield an additional output of 500 MW of power from the existing capacity or save about Rs. 700 crore worth of new investment. The improvement of efficiency reduces the need for subsidies. In a similar manner better targeting of food subsidies and greater cost effectiveness of the public distribution system will result in savings which could be used to expand the system and to help a larger number of the poor and the needy.

Thus, while the continuation of the subsidies is necessary for some more time, the quantum of subsidies can be reduced gradually and this will be a substantial gain to the budget. This will result in a reduction in the fiscal deficit which is necessary to satisfy the conditionalities prescribed by the IMF and to hold down the rate of inflation.

The burden of this song is this: Fertiliser subsidy can be reduced by making fertilizer production cost-effective. This requires a reorganization of the fertilizer industry. The food subsidies can be reduced by better targeting of subsidized food towards those who are below the poverty line. Irrigation and electricity subsidies can be reduced by improving the efficiency of their production so as to yield a reasonable return on capital invested in these undertakings. It is the inefficiency of the operations of Government agencies and public sector enterprises that has partly rendered the case for subsidies strong. This justifies the farmers demand for subsidies in several cases.

The Government is committed to reducing the fiscal deficit to 6.5 percent of GDP in 1992-93 and to 5 percent of GDP in the following two years. But there is nothing sacrosanct about these figures so long as the trend is in the right direction and there are other advantages to be gained by not reaching these figures. The IMF is not unaware of the costs of structural adjustment programmes. It is aware of them and is showing greater understanding of the costs of adjustment programmes than heretofore. The President of the World Bank, in his report on structural adjustment loans, has called for analysis of the short term impact of the adjustment programmes on the Urban and rural poor and for measures to alleviate their negative effects. This means that the subsidies should be done away within stages using the resulting savings to alleviate the sufferings of the poor. Otherwise, the policy of liberalization will become meaningless.

# 71

## Dumping of Steel Wire Rods by India in the United States Market

The Government of India has taken strong exception to the dumping of steel goods by the United States Steel manufacturers on the ground that it has adversely affected the prospects of the Indian steel industry. Dumping which involves the sale of goods in another country at a price below cost of production with intent to obtain monopoly control over the market and after the control is established to raise the price with intent to recoup the losses made earlier and also to reap monopoly profits has been identified by the GATT as an unfair trade practice and against its accepted convention. The Indian steel industry, in this situation, has demanded tariff protection against the deleterious consequences of dumping.

But it is surprising that the Indian manufacturers of steel wire rods are found to be exporting their wares in the US market and selling them at a price below domestic cost of production. The US International Trade Commission (USITC) has observed that this constitutes dumping. In a preliminary finding against India, Brazil and France on their exports of steel wire rods to the US, the USITC has identified evidence of injury to the US steel industry caused by dumping by these countries. While India has rightly objected to dumping its steel goods in India for its damaging consequences to the Indian Steel industry and has demanded protection against this unfair trade practice it is beyond anybody's comprehension why India should resort to dumping of steel wire rods in the USA. India is thus guilty of an unfair trade practice.

As it is, the Indian steel industry which is no match to the US steel industry cannot compete with them it in terms of price or quality. The cost of production of steel goods is rising and it is poised to rise still higher because of the rise in coal prices after the price of coal is decontrolled. In a situation like this, India cannot afford to dump the steel wire rods at a price below cost of production. India now and for the foreseeable future is unable to drive out US steel manufacturers from the US market and to establish monopoly control over it—much less to reap monopoly profits to make good the earlier loss caused by dumping. In the second place, it is unable to face the wrathful glance of the GATT council. Even so, it has undertaken dumping in the US market. There must be strong reasons for this action.

Under the partial convertibility dispensation those who earn foreign exchange by exporting goods have to sell 40 percent of it to the Reserve Bank of India at the official rate and they have to sell the balance of 60 percent in the open market at the market rate. The market rate is higher than the official rate the gap between the two at present being over Rs. 7. The sale of 60 percent of the foreign exchange earned by the exporters at a price of Rs. 7 above the official rate may partially offset the loss they incur by selling steel rods at a price below cost of production. There is another stronger reason. The exporters of steel wire rods to the United States who get paid in dollars may use these dollars to pay for the imports of other goods which they can sell in India at the black market prices. The black market prices may be many times higher than the CIF prices. These prices may more than offset the loss they incur because of dumping. To be able to assess the gain the exporters of dumped goods make, it is necessary to identify the items of goods they import and the prices at which they are sold in India. The demand for luxury consumer goods like TV sets, video sets, sophisticated cameras and the like is highly income elastic and this swamps the price effect of black market prices and on balance causes a rise in demand for them. Furthermore, under the liberalized import trade dispensation the tariffs on these goods are reduced from 255 percent to 150 percent on 35 baggage items and this has considerably reduced the cif prices of these goods. The rise in the prices of these imports in the black market, will to some extent, be offset by the new cif prices and in many cases the new prices reflecting the black market prices will be less than the prices before the reduction of tariff duties. In view of this, the price effect is unlikely to be dominant as a determinant of import demand. What matters is the income effect which remains dominant as a determinant of import demand. This means that the use of foreign exchange proceeds from the export of steel wire rods as dumped goods are likely to be used to purchase electronic gadgets and to sell them in the domestic market at black market prices in order to make a profit which will wipe out any loss sustained by dumping of goods at a price below cost of production. The Indian steel industry will not be able to establish a monopoly in the US market but it will be able to get foreign exchange which can be used to import luxury items that could be sold in the domestic market for a profit. This seems to be the motive prompting the Indian steel manufacturers to dump their steel wire rods in the US market. This no doubt, is an unfair trade practice which must be eschewed forthwith. India which complains of dumping by other countries cannot indulge in this practice itself. If it does, its action is bound to be counter-productive.

# 72

## Streamlining the Public Distribution System

It is a matter of great satisfaction that food production in 1992-93 has exceeded the previous record. In 1990-91 India produced 174 million tonnes of food. The Economic Survey for 1992-93 expects food production to be 177 million tonnes. This year the Khariff food production is 98.7 million tonnes while rabi food production is 78 million tonnes. Though there is a rise in aggregate food production the production of different items of food articles has not risen uniformly. The production of paddy has delivered to 73.7 million tonnes. The reduction in the area under paddy cultivation is the main reason for this decline. The production of wheat has risen from 55 million tones to 56 million tonnes. Though the area under wheat cultivation has declined by 4.9 percent, the rise in wheat output can be explained in terms of the rise in the per acre yield of wheat, coarse food grains, pulses, oil seeds have also recorded higher output. The output of sugar cane has declined. This is due to the reduction in the area of sugar cane cultivation is due to the sugar mills not paying the arrears to the sugar cane cultivators. However, the favourable monsoons in 1992-93 has helped India to realize a record production of food grains. It is necessary to maintain this output in the coming year also by means of providing irrigation facilities, adopting scientific methods of cultivation and reforming the agricultural operations in general.

Quite apart from increased production of food what is necessary is the procurement of what is produced and distribution of what is procured; furthermore what is of greater concern is the determination of procurement prices and the provision of subsidy on food. However much the food production may rise, unless their prices are within the reach of the consumers they are bound to get agitated. Further, unless the procurement prices paid to the farmers are remunerative they find food production unattractive. The prices paid for food must be such as to provide sufficient income to the farmers so that their savings and investment in agricultural operations may rise. Time is past when agriculture was regarded as a way of life and not a business. Empirical evidence has shown that cropping pattern is responsible to price incentives indicating that the farmers are sensitive to price incentives.

When compared with 1991-92 the procurement of food in 1992-93 appears to be satisfactory. In 1991-92 the procurement of rice was 11 million tonnes; in 1992-93 it is 12 million tonnes. In 1991-92 wheat procurement was 10.5 million tonnes; in 1992-93 it is 11 million tonnes. As the food prices started rising in 1991-92 it was feared that more food would have to be released from the stock and in consequence the food stock would decline. In the current year the release of rice and wheat from the stock was of the order of 20 million tonnes. The procurement of food for holding stocks has increased by 18 lakh tonnes. Moreover in 1992-93 wheat was also imported. For these reasons it is hoped that the situation in 1993-94 will not be alarming.

But viewed from the side of the government, the situation is not satisfactory. As the Government has to pay subsidies in order to hold down the food prices, the burden of subsidy rises. But the Government intends to reduce subsidies in order to hold down the fiscal deficit. The international financial institutions also prescribe the same conditionality. But this year, owing to special circumstances the food subsidy payment has increased. In 1992-93 the food subsidy rose to Rs. 2800 crore. The reason for this is the delay in the enhancement of market price of food in line with the hike in procurement prices. The two food items which are given the benefit of subsidy are paddy and wheat. The procurement price of paddy has been raised by 22.2 percent in 1992-93. Whatever may be the Government's calculation the food subsidy is bound to rise in 1993-94. The Union Budget for 1993-94 has provided for food subsidy of Rs. 3000 crore. In 1992-93, the Government would have had to pay a subsidy of Rs. 127.71 per quintal of wheat and Rs. 86.97 quintal of rice. As the procurement prices are hiked, the

Government has to pay a higher subsidy in order to hold down the market price of food. The storage cost of rice (including interest rate) will be Rs. 501.65 per quintal; the storage cost of wheat will be Rs. 431.35 per quintal. To be able to sell these two items of food at the price prescribed by the Government there is need to pay a subsidy of Rs. 140.83 per quintal of rice and Rs. 220.85 per quintal of wheat. At the same time the Government which desires to reduce the burden of subsidy has to limit the distribution of food to the really poor segment of the population. But this is easier said than done. For this reason the possibility of a rise in the subsidy burden cannot be ruled out.

The subsidy payment in 1993-94 will be as under:

| | |
|---|---|
| Food subsidy | Rs. 3000 crore |
| Domestic fertiliser subsidy | Rs. 3000 crore |
| Imported fertiliser subsidy | Rs. 500 crore |
| Export subsidy | Rs. 500 crore |
| Total | Rs. 7000 crore |

This is 80 percent of the total subsidy to be paid by the Government. The aggregate subsidy is Rs. 8376 crore. The actual subsidy payment can be expected to be higher than the estimate.

In the attempt to reduce the burden of food subsidy on the budget the Government has contemplated a scheme of ruling out the creamy layer of society from the benefits of subsidized food distributed through the fair price depots. To this end it has set up a committee of three members. In the light of the report of this Committee which is due before April 30, 1993 the Government will formulate a national policy regarding food distribution through the fair price depots the public distribution system (PDS).

The Government revamped the PDS in January 1992 and this system covers a total of 1700 blocks. Under this scheme about 1000 new godowns and 11,000 new ration shops were proposed to be opened. The revamped PDS aimed at improving the system through delivery at the door steps through the fair price shops. The Government claims that it has been providing food grains at affordable prices to the poor residing in remote areas of the country.

But the analysis of the data of on the actual beneficiaries of the revamped PDS and the grain allocation reveals certain interesting trends. The Government claims that it has issued about 2.36 million additional ration cards. These ration card holders demand food grain from the fair price depots. But what is the quantum of grain allocation? An official note on the revamped PDS says that the Centre has "earmarked two million tonnes per annum of food grains for specific allocation to the revamped PDS areas, in addition to the normal allocation". If this is so, the per ration card allocation of food grains in the revamped areas works out to be a ridiculously low level of 0.83 kg a year. Again, in the absence of data on the actual allocation of food grains to the revamped PDS, let us assume that the entire grain offtake by the PDS is for the revamped PDS areas. In April 1992 to January the offtake by the PDS is 7.9% lower when compared to the 15.80 million tonnes of grain lifted by the PDS in 1991. If the offtake increases at the same rate for February-March 1993 we get a total offtake of 17.4 million tonnes for the entire year. Even if all this grain goes to the revamped 1700 blocks the per card ration allotted will be 7.25 kg per year.

It is further claimed that the revamped PDS covers 160 million people nearly one-fifth of the population in the tribal majority states, hill areas and other places where the draught-prone area programme and integrated tribal development programme are operating. The per capita allocation to these areas is most revealing.

Even assuming that the entire PDS grain supply is going to these areas the per capita allocations of food grains works out to a meager 0.11 kg per year. This means that the actual per capita allocation of food gm is only 110 gm annually. As the total grain supply is not entirely directed to these areas, the actual per capita allocation is much lower than this. If the allocation is 2 million tonnes for the revamped PDS, the per capita allocation is as good as nothing.

This is the dismal scenario in the current year (1992-93). But in 1993-94 the real allocation would be much less than this because of the declining trend in grain procurement. In 1992-93 procurement has fallen by 17.7 percent from the level prevailing in 1991-92. A poor monsoon and the consequent rise in food prices would result in strain on the procurement of food grains. This causes a further decline in the per capita allocation of food grains. This means that the revamped PDS is not of much help.

The need to exclude the creamy layer of society from the benefit of subsidized food or cheap rationing is being underlined for quite sometime, but it is only now that the resolve has become operational. That the Government means business this time can be gauged from the facts that the high powered three member committee has been given a time-bound mandate up to April 30. It is apparent that the rich ration card holders comprising nearly 40 percent of the beneficiaries will have the ration cards only for the sake of identification and not for drawing rations. This move may hurt some but it has become inevitable under the present circumstances when reduction of the fiscal deficit below the present level is absolutely necessary. The rationing system dates back to the days of food scarcity when the country depended on imports and virtually lived from ship to month. Since then the situation has undergone a sea change. The population has increased steeply since then and food procurement of food has hardly kept pace despite an increase in support prices. This has resulted in either a denial of benefits to the real targeted families the urban and semi-urban poor or availability of inferior quality items. To cap it all it has occasioned a subsidy bill of Rs. 3000 crore per annum at present a burden which the country is not in a position to bear.

Ironically, the main beneficiaries of the overburdened system are the procurement agencies and depot holders who siphon off various items to the open market and make huge profits. The legitimate ration card holders are told that as the stocks have not arrived they should wait. The hurried consumers have to purchase food in the open market or in the black market by paying a higher price than the one they have to pay to the fair price depots as they cannot go hungry. For this reason the fair price depots have earned the name "unfair price depots". One reason for this is the heavy burden on the depots. Under these circumstances, pruning of food availability to the people has become unavoidable. The affluent and middle class segments especially in the urban areas should not grudge this small sacrifice as they, by and large, use better quality items purchased in the open market. Furthermore, this should not impose any sacrifice on them. There are complaints that the rich and middle class families which hold ration cards do not buy food articles from the ration depots but instead make the ration cards available to the poor families for a consideration and find the present system a source of income. Therefore, the new policy will be meaningful only if the benefits of curtailing the number of beneficiaries are passed on to those for whom the subsidized rations are the life line. This should be reflected in the expansion of the network in rural, border and hill areas and the improved quality, quantity as well as the availability of levy sugar, wheat and rice etc. In this regard the definition who dwells on the creamy layer is very important. It is held in certain quarters that the exclusion of pensioners from the benefits of the PDS is unfair. But this needs careful examination. Not all pensioners are poor deserving of the benefits of cheap food supplied through the PDS. The poor employees become poor after retirement as their pension income is reduced by over half of their regular salaried income. In this case, they need the benefits of cheap rations and they should be included in the category of people deserving the benefit. But those who retire after holding highly paid jobs accustomed as they are to using high quality food articles purchased at a high price in the open market do not suddenly take to the consumption of cheap, low quality food articles supplied through the PDS. As their pension income is high they can afford to purchase high quality food articles in the open market. Therefore this class of pensioners does not deserve any benefit of subsidized food supplied through the PDS. They can also be excluded as part of the creamy layer of society. Admittedly the criterion of identifying. The creamy layer of society is a controversial one in the case of backward classes and this may lead to an unsavoury row in and outside the Parliament. No criterion is hundred percent perfect. The consolation is that justice is rough.

In January 1992 Public Distribution System was revamped and special emphasis was laid on opening1700 blocks in the certain identified backward areas. Emphasis was also laid on opening of new ration ships, door step delivery of rationed articles and supply of more essential commodities and construction of more godowns. Even so, the problem remains as unmanageable as ever.

If 40 percent of the ration card holders who constitute the creamy layer of the population are excluded from the public distribution system 40 percent of the food subsidy of 3000 crore viz., Rs. 1200 crore can be saved. To this extent the burden of subsidy on the budget will be reduced. Those pensioners who held highly paid white collar jobs earlier also have to be excluded. There is no need to issue ration cards for the purpose of identification for these ration cards are liable to be abused. As the legitimate card holders are found to be selling sugar which is their quota to the nearby hotels and restaurants at the black market prices the supply of sugar to these card holders has to be stopped; in the alternative vigilance squads are to be deployed to detect such card holders and to delete sugar from the ration cards. These vigilance squads must also be deployed to detect the sale of food articles in the black market by the employees of the fair price depots and to award punishment to these employees. As there are complaints of sale of substandard and refractory food articles by the fair price depots care must be taken to stop the sale of such food articles in the interests of maintaining health standards of the population. The exclusion of the creamy layer of the society from the benefits of the public distribution system is necessary to promote equity and justice. The criterion of identifying the creamy layer of society is difficult and controversial but this criterion must be employed to exclude them from the benefits of the public distribution system. Justice is always rough and it must be used, to exclude them. Their exclusion is necessary to reduce the burden of food subsidy on the budget.

The appointment of the committee to target supplies from the PDS to the genuinely needy, shows a welcome concern for equity under structural reform. The mere exclusion of income tax payers from the benefits of PDS as suggested in certain quarters is, at best, a token economy considering the fact that they number less than 30 lakh out of 5 crore ration card holders. The claimants for rationed supplies include a vast number who by no stretch of imagination can be deemed to be needy. How to find out who the needy consumers are. The answer to this question can be found by taking up the vulnerable sections of urban and rural society covered by special employment programmes for protection under PDS. The entitlement of subsidized rations of food, kerosene and cloth should be limited to those assisted under the Jawahar Rozgar Yojana and the IRDP. Outside this core group supplies should be extended to the disadvantaged groups covered by schemes for training for self employment and spreading literacy. Many purchase rationed supplies rice and wheat because the PDS does not supply jowar, bajre or maize. The better-off sections do not buy these coarse food grains and go in for finer varieties. This demands that the PDS should cover the supply of coarse grains to regions where they are in demand.

Small and marginal farmers who lack holding power sell their crop immediately after harvest and use the proceeds to meet their umpteen items of expenditure and they buy grains for consumption in the loan season when the prices are higher than in the harvesting season. They need protection. Procurement prices are hiked before the harvest. But if the crop yield turns out to be poor the marketed surplus shrinks. This causes a further rise in food prices. Factory workers holding temporary jobs need to be protected from high food prices stocked by high procurement prices in the years of scarcity. Improved targeting of rationed supplies will enlarge the scope of the PDS. This causes a rise in food subsidy but the consolation is that it will benefit the really deserving segments of society. There is talk of marketisation of food distribution place of the PDS. But this scheme is dangerous with high interest rates stocking costs, which account for 30 percent of total cost, the market prices will be pushed up. This means that at present giving up PDS in favour of marketisation of food distribution is highly dangerous as it will stock the inflationary fires.

Over 30 percent of India's population is wallowing below the poverty line. With the continuing rise in prices eroding the value of the rupee even those slightly above the poverty line sink below it as it causes a fall in real income. Unless these people are protected against the rise in food prices their lives become miserable. Poverty alleviation is one of the indices of economic growth. If growth has any meaning, poverty has to be alleviated, extending the scope of the PDS to cover all vulnerable sections of society and not marketisation of food supply is the answer to the question of poverty alleviation.

The PDS at present is known for its inefficiency. The most eloquent testimony of this is the Rs. 3000 crore food subsidy in the 1993-94 budget. Such a hefty magnitude of subsidy is due to the persistent financial leakage caused by inordinately high storage and transport costs. On account of this misspent money the poor, the legitimate targets of the system, are denied their share. As a solution to this problem there is a demand for overhauling the Food Corporation of India. This solution ignores the fact that a more useful policy would be to reorient the entire mechanism of procurement and distribution. This will do away with the centralized scheme of procurement and distribution under the acquis of the Food Corporation of India. Procurement of food grains could be done at the local levels and the distribution centres could also be locally manned. This smacks of people's participation which in the present context is the only effective answer to the problem.

Ensuring the efficient working of the decentralized system requires careful and imaginative monitoring The government is reluctant to do away with the food corporation of India. But happily the government has shown more interest in proposals to abolish the absurdity whereby almost 40 percent of the present beneficiaries belong to income groups that should disqualify them from any manner of benefits under the scheme of food subsidies. The governments proposal to keep the creamy layer off the subsidy list has provoked the advisory council to refer the issues to a sub-committee. This has been done despite the existence of several comprehensible means to determine the cut-off point. The most identifiable means are the tax paying income of consumers in the urban areas and the people living below the poverty line in the rural areas. The PDS needs the implementation of these reforms rather than the setting up of advisory panels and sub-committees which because of their dilateriness undermine the workability of the scheme.

## POSTSCRIPT

The planning commission has contemplated a new method of identifying the creamy layer who could be excluded from the benefits of the PDS. Those who hold more than two hectares of land and use electricity above a prescribed limit are to be construed as those not deserving benefits under the PDS. But even this method is fraught with many uncertainties. In the first place, the families with more than two hectares of land cannot be so easily excluded. If a family has five members and if it owns 10 hectares of land, this family is to be excluded. But if the family splits the land holding and registers two hectares in the name of each person while they continue to live under one roof, they will be entitled to five ration cards and this method fails to exclude the family. Further more even the prescription of the limit on electricity consumption cannot be said to be of much success. The family may economise on the use of electricity and reduce its consumption to the limit prescribed. This will save on the electricity bill and will also entitle the family to the benefits of the PDS. In view of these complications it would be ideal to take precautions against the misuse of these restrictions.

# 73

# Tariff Protection for the Steel Industry

The steel industry the world over is facing a serious recession. Most of the steel plants in India including the private sector TISCO is saddled with unsold stocks. In the post-decontrol period steel industry is facing competition in the liberalized economy. The steel industry demanded decontrol on the ground that it would solve most of its problems. The Government conceded this demand but the industry finds itself in deep trouble. There are several reasons for this state of affairs. When the Government liberalized the economy, it was believed that industrial production would pick up which would mean consumption of more steel domestically. But there is a demand recession in the market for all industrial goods including the market for steel and steel products. The structural reform also generated problems. The producers found it difficult to adjust themselves to the new situation created by structural adjustment. Another reason is the dumping of steel and steel products by the countries of the West and Japan which find themselves in possession of surplus stock.

The Indian steel industry which is employing and providing sustenance to lakh of workers is at present in doldrums because of the dumping of steel and steel products in India by countries like the USA, Japan, Hungary, Sweden, Belgium, Hungary and other countries which are accumulating surplus stocks of steel. Between April and June the Government of India spent Rs. 1,180 crore of foreign exchange for the purchase of steel even though such steel and steel products were available in the country.

As it is, the steel industry in India is facing a recession consequent on a fall in the demand for its products. The purchase of dumped steel will hit the steel industry hard and lead to unemployment of labour employed in the industry. The steel exporting countries which have accumulated steel and steel products are faced with a grave situation. The way out for them is to dump their surplus steel in India at a price below cost of production. The strategy of dumping involves the sale of surplus products in another country at a price below cost of production. This makes the dumped goods cheaper than the domestically produced goods and makes the consumers shift from domestic goods to imports. The domestic industry which is faced with a decline in the demand for its products will have no alternative to closing down. After it is closed down, the foreign exporter of the dumped goods establishes a monopoly in the domestic market and as a monopolist raises the prices of his products in order to recoup the losses he made earlier by selling his products as a price below cost of production. This is a variant of international exploitation which the GATT rules out as impermissible under its rules.

The dumping of cheap steel in India by the steel manufacturers of the European countries, the USA and Japan has crippled the Indian steel manufacturing industry. Many countries which are the victims of dumping have enacted anti-dumping legislation in order to save their industries from collapse. The Indian steel industry is facing such a situation at present. It needs to be protected by means of anti-dumping legislation and also be means of protective tariff the policy of trade liberalization notwithstanding.

Under the new Export-Import policy the Government has liberalized its import trade. It is offering import concessions which have rendered imports cheap and have increased the demand for them at the cost of domestic goods. In the Union Budget for 1992-93 the peak-tariff level was brought down to a maximum of 110 percent and the Government is committed to reducing it to not more than 25-30 percent within 3-4 years. Over Rs. 2,000 crore of customs revenue was lost in 1992-93 and despite new excise levies of over Rs. 2,200 crore the Centre was left with a net revenue loss of Rs. 517 crore.

The Union Budget for 1993-94 will carry forward the process of lowering import tariff though no drastic reduction seems possible because of the necessity of reducing the fiscal deficit as agreed to by the Government in its letter to the IMF. However, reduction of tariffs at the present time is impermissible. It is true India is committed to pursuing the policy of liberalization. But if liberalization results in the ruination of domestic industries such liberalization needs to be amended. Liberalisation necessary to enhance the competitiveness of Indian industry is welcome but liberalization that is ruinous to domestic industry needs to be amended. A World Bank paper on India's trade regime has said that high tariffs and excise taxes on capital goods are damaging the competitiveness of Indian industry. It states that the extremely high tariffs do not fulfill their primary purpose of providing reasonable protection and incentive signals but are primarily aimed at generating revenue. If the tariffs are yielding revenue it means that the demand for imports is price-inelastic and the tariffs fail to protect the domestic industries; they yield revenue. They are called revenue tariffs. If the tariffs do not yield revenue, it is because the demand for imports is elastic and so tariffs which raise the domestic prices of imported goods cause a fall in demand for them. Such tariffs are called protective tariffs. The Government has to choose between these two types of tariffs. If the tariffs are revenue tariffs they yield more revenue but as the demand for imports is price-inelastic demand does not fall in which case these tariffs fail to protect the domestic industries. If the tariffs are protective tariffs, the demand for the goods bearing the tariffs falls causing a fall in revenue but the domestic industries will be protected. The Government has to strike a balance between revenue tariffs and protective tariffs. The protective tariffs do not yield revenue and revenue tariffs do not afford protection.

The Government cannot pursue a general policy in the matter of tariffs. Tariffs are to be imposed on those goods for which the demand is inelastic so that the revenue yield rises and the tariffs are to be raised on those goods for which the demand is elastic so that higher tariffs cause a fall in demand for imports and protect the domestic industry. In the instant case of the steel industry tariffs are to be raised in order to reduce the demand for imported steel so that the domestic steel industry may be protected against the competition from steel imports. Quite apart from this, appropriate legislation must be formulated to prevent dumping of steel products or any products for that matter. If, in the name of liberalization, dumping is allowed, domestic industries will come to grief. Even those countries which have adopted a policy of trade liberalization have, at the same time, adopted anti-dumping legislation in order to protect the domestic industry. A distinction has to be drawn between fair competition and unfair competition. Fair competition can be allowed under a policy of liberalization as it enhances the international competitiveness of domestic industry; but unfair competition of the type that flourishes under dumping must be checked by means of anti-dumping legislation. It is in this context that the steel industry is to be protected by means of anti-dumping legislation.

The Indian steel industry needs support, certain protection for a period during which it adapts itself to the changes. Any country even without much import duty does make sure that dumping does not take place. Even the USA which believes in liberalized trade does it. This is unexceptionable. It will be in the interest of the Indian steel industry and of the nation as a whole to ensure that while we liberalise the economy dumping does not take place.

One argument in favour of purchasing cheap dumped goods is the consumers will be benefitted by it. This is no doubt true. But a country which wants to build an industrial base of its own has to make some sacrifices in the short run in order to strengthen the industrial base in the long run. The cost of production of the Indian steel industry is cheaper than international cost. If the import duty on steel and steel products is brought down the imported steel becomes cheaper than the domestic steel and the latter suffers in consequence. For this reason the import duties on steel imports must be higher than they are at present.

# 74

## Should India Opt for IMF Loan

India's balance of payments scenario in 1989 is more disquieting than it was in 1981 when India obtained an IMF loan of $ 5.6 billion, to be disbursed in three instalments, to tide over the balance of payments crisis. India drew only two instalments of the loan but said that it did not need the third instalment in 1984—the election year—partly for political reasons. At present, there are speculations that in view of the disquieting balance of payments situation, India will go in for fresh IMF loan, at the same time, there are half-hearted official denials of any initiative in that direction. This article analyses India's balance of payments scenario and assesses the possibility or otherwise as well as the desirability or otherwise of India approaching the IMF for a loan to tide over the present crisis.

Under the impact of fiscal deficits, the balance of payments gap has gone on widening continuously with marginal reductions in certain quarters. At present it is of the order of Rs. 6,601 crore. This is due to the rise in imports at a greater rate than the rise in exports. Imports rose by 27.4 percent from Rs. 20,200 crore in 1987-88 to Rs. 22,390 crore in 1988-89 and exports rose by 22.47 percent from Rs. 12,462 crore to Rs. 15,741 crore. Foreign exchange reserves declined from Rs. 7,687 crore in 1987-88 to Rs. 5,967 crore in 1988-89. The surplus on invisible account is too small to cover the trade gap. On capital account there is a rise in interest payment on external debt and a bunching of repayments to the IMF on its 1981 loan. Foreign borrowing has been increasing at the rate of $.7.0 billion per year adding to the debt burden and leading the country to the classic debt trap of the Latin American variety. The long and medium term external debt has soared from Rs. 25,000 crore in 1985 to Rs. 55,000 crore in 1989. This has necessitated the earmarking of Rs. 2,700 crore or 24 percent of foreign exchange earnings to debt servicing in place of 13 percent in 1985. The 1989-90 Union Budget proposes to raise an external loan of Rs. 3,722 crore net of repayment and servicing of external loans. With a reduction in the quantum of concessional borrowing the country is constrained to resort to commercial borrowing at market rates of interest which are higher than those on concessional borrowing thus adding greatly to the burden of debt servicing. External borrowing accounts for over 10 percent of Government borrowing for investment. This trend is patently dangerous. This was how the build-up of Latin American debt problem began : foreign borrowing not so much to cover the trade gap as to provide resources for domestic investment.

India has become a high-cost economy due to the decline in productivity on the one side and the rise in wages and the costs of inputs on the other. As a result, India's exports are unable to face competition in foreign markets. The sluggish rise in exports is due to the cosiness and attractiveness of the domestic market where, under the impact of fiscal deficits, income is rising diverting tradeable exports to the domestic market. According to the Economic Survey for 1988-89, sustaining the present dynamism on the export front in the coming years would have to be the key feature of balance of payments management. However, considering the likelihood of the pace of economic activity decelerating in the industrialized countries in 1989, one can expect a deleterious impact on India's export performance in 1989-90. Imports, especially bulk imports like food and edible oils, are rising to meet rising domestic demand. Other imports too rising encouraged by indiscriminate trade liberalization measures. The most significant among the imports is petroleum whose price and quantity have gone on progressively rising adding to domestic inflation and the import bill.

In view of the steady depreciation of the Indian rupee based on purchasing power parity calculations, the authorities have come to feel that a further depreciation should be avoided. Efforts are afoot to maintain the stability of the external value of the rupee after allowing it to sink over the past few years. This is because the Indian economy has now reached a stage where any further depreciation will not promote exports or hinder imports owing to what is technically called the "J-Curve Effect". At the same time, the Government is running fiscal deficits which depreciate the rupee further. This will only lead to the aggravation of imported inflation and loss of foreign exchange reserves without much effect on exports thus further heightening the crisis.

The Government of India has been under incessant pressure from the World Bank and the IMF to devalue the rupee believing it to be able to correct the balance of payments deficit. They argue that the value of the rupee is kept at an artificially high level and this has contributed to slow growth of India's exports. India's exports have risen rapidly over the past few years in nominal terms increasing by over 20 percent during 1985-89. The feeling now is that devaluation will no longer help boost exports and that stability of the value of the rupee should now be maintained. The effect of devaluation is only to increase the prices of imports without reducing the demand for them, to give an upward thrust to the price level and to cause a drain on foreign exchange reserves.

India is faced with the problem of repaying and servicing the mounting external debt. The situation is bound to get worse necessitating new initiatives and reforms. What is needed is a comprehensive programme comprising policy reform at home, new inflows of private and public capital restructuring of external debts in order to minimise the possible impact of future increase in interest rates and international agreement at interest rate reduction. The Baker strategy for managing the international debt problem announced in 1985 broadly accords with this line of thinking. The Baker Plan sets targets for bank and private agency lending to indebted countries which would in turn implement economic reforms intended to boost exports and increase competitiveness. The baker strategy has been backed by President George Bush. However, the Baker Plan, in the case of India, is to be supplemented by measure to induce capital which has flowed to foreign countries to avoid the loses caused by depreciation of the rupee to flow back into the country. The success of this effort depends on maintaining the stability of the value of the rupee and the offer of competitive interest rates on loans. This Government has to realize that the stability of the value of the rupee depends on fiscal balance.

Even the foreign aid provided by the United States through the scheme of International Development Assistance (IDA) is too meager to provide any substantial relief to India. According to the latest report of the Agency for International Development, India gets only 3 cent per head of its population (i.e., $ 24 million) as aid while Israel gets $ 1,000 per capita followed by Turkey and Pakistan in that order. The Bush Administration is negotiating cuts in its IDA aid in view of the tight budgetary position. This makes the old scenario somber indeed.

In view of the disquieting balance of payments scenario, speculation is rife about the Government approaching the IMF for a fresh loan. The foreign exchange reserves at present are sufficient to finance just three months imports. This is a critical level of foreign exchange reserves considering the fact that the reserves should be of the value of four months' imports as a factor of safety. But, with the growing trade deficits and with the aid climate being unfavourable, the situation is bound to worsen in the near future.

This situation should make recourse to the IMF loan imperative under normal circumstances. However, the Government has decided (or so it says) not to obtain a fresh loan from the IMF to solve the crisis situation. Political calculations are manifest in this decision. The Government instead, is contemplating other measures for the purpose. The reason is its concern for maintaining atleast a semblance of solvency in the election year.

Negotiating a loan from the IMF will provide unmistakable evidence of unsatisfactory economic management and growing external indebtedness which may give a handle to the Opposition to mount its intemperate attacks on the ruling party. Furthermore, there is the grave possibility that the IMF, convinced that the Government of India approached it for a loan in a critical situation, would certainly impose stiff conditonality clauses which the Government is not prepared to accept and view with equanimity in the election year as it may be charged with mortgaging the country to foreign interests with adverse effects on its election prospects.

When, in November 1981, India obtained a loan of $ 5.6 billion from the IMF, the balance of payments situation was not as critical as it is now and so the conditionality clauses imposed on India for observance were not as severe as they could perhaps be now. In 1981, the Government which anticipated a crisis, obtained a loan before the crisis actually occurred and so India was able to avoid the prescription of harsh conditionality clauses. Now that the balance of payments situation has all the ingredients of an incipient crisis, the conditionality prescriptions are bound to be harsh and therefore unacceptable. The IMF is bound to prescribe a drastic reduction and eventual elimination of subsidies on food, fertilizers and exports, its policy being guided by the supply-side economic philosophy. However, in the election year the Government finds itself unable to accent these harsh conditionality clauses for political reasons if not for any other.

Judged in the light of world trade projections, the trade deficit is likely to reach a record figure of nearly Rs. 9,000 crore in the present fiscal year. The reduction of this deficit requires a considerable rise in exports by over 25 percent every year. This is certainly a stupendous task considering the declaration of economic activity in the West and its adverse impact on India's exports in 1989-90. It also requires a drastic reduction in or elimination of inessential imports which may not be easy as imports are bound to rise under the impact of fiscal deficits. There is also need to attract more concessional aid from the World Bank and other lending countries. But, this cannot be relied upon because of poor aid climate. This makes the scenario more disquieting and makes it necessary to adopt a policy of fiscal balance without which all other policies are bound to be blighted. For the first time, the Government has understood the causal connection between fiscal deficits and the balance of payments deficits. The analysis of the Cambridge Economic Policy Group (CEPG) has shown that fiscal deficits are at bottom a cause of balance of payments deficits. That this analysis has influenced official thinking is borne out by the warning contained in *The Economic Survey* for 1988-89 that domestic fiscal imbalances would have to be set right if the balance of payments position is to improve. Despite the awareness of the crucial connection between fiscal deficits and balance of payments deficits, the Government has budgeted for a deficit of Rs. 7,337 crore in 1989-90. An example of Voodoo economics.

Any tough stance either in the domestic sphere or in the external sphere is considered politically inexpedient in the election year. Even if any tough stance is adopted, it takes a long time to bear fruit. In the medium term, the balance of payments position steadily drifts from bad to worse and it may not be improbable that just on the eve of the election the Government will inevitably approach the IMF for a loan in which case the damage to the Government's credibility will be graver than it would be if as loan is negotiated now as the conditionality clauses are bound to be harsher and their implementation more unpopular. The "wait and see" attitude of the Government will in the end, prove damaging to the solvency of the nation. So why not an IMF loan now with soft conditionality clauses attached to it than at a later date when the balance of payments crisis of graver proportions warrants harsher conditionality prescription? This question is uppermost in the minds of economists, bankers, financiers and politicians.

The IMF has been taking the initiative to mould its loans into attractive packages. It introduced the "enhanced structural adjustment facility" (ESAF) which became operational in April 1988. This facility seeks to provide concessional assistance to low-income countries to low-income countries facing protracted balance of payments problems; it is meant to strengthen the country's exports and relieve the foreign exchange crunch in the medium term and it would also carry a lower rate of interest than the 1981 loan. In view of these considerations the apprehension that the conditionality clauses would be unduly harsh are unfounded. The case for opting for a loan now is stronger than ever. What is necessary is the adoption of appropriate measures of structural adjustment and fiscal reform. What will ultimately happen, the future alone can unfold.

# 75

## The Entry of Foreign Banks to the Indian Financial System is Desirable

The Narasimham Committee on Financial Sector Reform has recommended the opening up of the Indian financial system to the entry of foreign banks. But discordant voices are heard even from responsible quarters that the entry of foreign banks would thwart the progress of the Indian banking system as the foreign banks with their superior customer services, sophisticated operations and computerisation would wean customers away from the Indian banks and would adversely affect their deposit mobilisation programme, reduce their profitability further and erode the already thin capital base. These apprehensions are overly exaggerated. At present there are only 150 foreign bank branches operating in India and their aggregate assets are less than 5 percent of those of the Indian banks put together. Even if, under the Narasimham Committee dispensation, the numbers of foreign bank branches are doubled, there is unlikely to be any threat to the Indian banking system. But, instead, the positive gains are many and they should be considered while examining the issue of entry of foreign banks to India.

All said and done, the Indian banking system is a byword for inefficiency. Quite apart from diversion of funds to priority sectors at concessional interest rates, the loan mela and loan waiver schemes have landed the Indian banking system in doldrums. There is overstaffing of banks, there is unrestrained opening up of branches in areas which are not bankable; in an area where there is not enough business even for a single branch there are 5-6 branches of different banks with the result that administrative expenditure is on the rise. The bank employees are opposed to computerisation of banking operations as it is likely to displace labour. The quality of customer service is very poor. In the absence of alternative abode for their deposits the customers have, per force, to go to these banks to deposit their savings. The banks, therefore, are continuing their inefficiency in the thought that their supremacy is unchallenged and they are not under any pressure to improve their operations or the quality of customer service rendered by them.

The objective of the policy of liberalisation is to expose the Indian economy to the bracing winds of competition in order to enable every sector of the economy to be cost-effective in the global environment. The financial sector is an important segment of the Indian economy and unless this sector is liberalised the programme of liberalisation would be incomplete.

The foreign banks presently operating in India have been rendering quick and efficient customer service with the help of sophisticated electronics gadgets. Their deposit mobilisation and lending operations are a model for Indian banks to emulate. The computerization of their operations enables them to attend to customer problems and needs with efficiency and quickness. They are highly profitable entities and they are free from labour troubles. These virtues make them attractive to Indian customers. The capital adequacy of these banks renders them safe abodes for the deposits. It is these that are held to constitute a danger to the viability of the Indian banking system. To think so is to make the Indian banks lead an ostritich-like existence.

The Reserve Bank of India has asked the public sector banks to get themselves rated by a credit rating agency. The credit rating of banks is necessary to prepare them to mobilise funds from the market in order to reach the prescribed capital adequacy ratio. Those which are rated high have no problem at all except that they have to improve on the present satisfactory credit rating. But those which are rated low have to make strenuous efforts to enhance their credit rating to be able to convince the lenders that they are solvent in the strict financial sense. This advice of the Reserve Bank of India is in the best interests of the Indian banks. Excessive protection accorded to the Indian banks has made them lethargic and to remain in a state of perpetual inefficiency rendering the financial sector unable to meet the challenges posed by the on-going economic reform measures. When they are exposed to the competitive forces emerging from the foreign banks operating in India they get into an atmosphere of challenge and opportunity and make efforts to reach the standards of efficiency attained by the foreign banks. Seen in this light, the entry of foreign banks into the Indian financial systems is desirable and the recommendation of the Narasimha Committee has to be implemented.

Admittedly, the loan mela and loan waiver schemes have to go for good. But the concessionary lending to the priority sectors has to remain for some more time. The Narasimham Committee recommends a reduction of this lending from the present 40 percent to 10 percent in stages. But this reduction should be gradual. However, it is a moot point whether the foreign banks could be persuaded to toe the line of Indian banks in the matter of concessionary lending to priority sectors. If they agree there will be homogeneity in lending operations. But if they do not agree there will be two parallel systems. This does not augur well for the progress of the financial sector and the financial sector reform will have no meaning. But the foreign banks operating in India have to be governed by the law of the land. It is a reasonable surmise that they will abide by whatever regulations are applicable to Indian banks considering the desperate need to ensure a competitive atmosphere the entry of foreign banks to the Indian financial system is highly desirable.

# 76

## Indian Banks in a Handicap Race

The Narasimhan Committee report on financial reforms has recommended that foreign banks be allowed to set up their branches in India in order to infuse a spirit of competitiveness in the Indian banks. This recommendation has been accepted by the Government of India. The acceptance of this recommendation is in consonance with the philosophy of liberalization and globalisation which has become the philosophical basis of the economic reforms initiated by the Narasimha Rao Government in July 1991. The policies founded on this philosophy are being pursued with unabated vigour.

As it is, the Indian banks which also serve a social purpose have to advance loans to the sectors labeled priority sectors at concessional interest rates. This by itself has reduced the profitability of the Indian banks. At the same time, they have not been allowed to raise the deposit rates in order to attract deposits to meet deposit mobilization targets.

The foreign banks do not suffer from either of the two handicaps. They are not to serve a social purpose in their loan operations. As a result, they charge competitive rates on loans advanced by them irrespective of the sectors to which the loans are advanced. Furthermore, they are free to pay competitive interest rates to the depositors with intent to maximize deposit mobilization. These factors place the foreign banks at a great advantage when compared with their Indian counterparts.

The foreign banks are found to be circumventing the regulations framed by the Reserve Bank of India. A foreign bank, namely, the City Bank is found to be offering a higher rate interest for deposits on current account in the name of money management. In contrast, the public sector banks in India are not allowed to raise the interest rates charged on loans because of their commitment to social purpose lending to the priority sector at concessional interest rates. The Indian banks are therefore denied a level playing field so necessary in a competitive environment.

Competitiveness in banking demands that the rules and regulations prescribed by the Reserve Bank of India be made applicable to all the banks whether foreign or Indian. If the foreign banks are allowed freedom in the matter of the interest rates offered to depositors and in the matter of the interest rates charged on loans, the Indian banks should also be allowed the same degree of freedom. To allow freedom to foreign banks and not to the Indian banks in the matter of interest rates would harm the interest of Indian banks. If the foreign banks are free to offer any interest rate they consider necessary to attract deposits and the Indian banks are not free to do so, depositors choose to keep their deposits in the foreign banks. This will adversely affect the deposit mobilization efforts of the Indian banks. In a similar way, if the Indian banks are asked to lend a certain part of their funds to the priority sectors at concessional interest rates and the foreign banks are free from this commitment to social purpose, the Indian banks will suffer a cut in their profitability while the foreign banks increase their profitability. This is the meaning of the statement that Indian banks are denied the facility of a level playing field. In this situation the Indian banks will have to function on a competitive disadvantage while the foreign banks enjoy competitive advantage and prosper.

A competitive economy functions on the principle of normality of profits. If the profits of firms in the industry are normal there will be no entry of new firms into the industry and there will also be no exit of the existing firms from the industry. Normality of profits keeps the number of firms in the industry stable. If the existing firms are making supernormal profits the other firms enter the industry. This causes a fall in the profits to the normal level and the entry of firm into the industry stops. Thus, supernormality of profits is a sign of disequilibrium which can be corrected by the entry of firms into the industry. Conversely, if the existing firms in the industry are making below normal (subnormal) profits they leave the industry and go elsewhere. In this matter subnormality of profits is a sign of disequilibrium which can be corrected by the exit of firms from the industry. If the firms which make subnormal profits cannot leave the industry as the capital they have sunk cannot be thrown to the scrap heap, they continue in the industry putting up with subnormal profits or even losses hoping for better days to come. This situation is called *pliopoly*. Thus, the theory of the competitive firm/ industry can be applied to banking treating banks as firms functioning on the principle of competitive efficiency.

While the foreign banks in India are allowed to set up branches and are allowed to function as competitive firms, the Indian banks do not have the privilege. They have to function under severe restrictions which makes them incapable of competing with the foreign banks in the matter of deposit mobilization and of making loans and advances. As a result, while the foreign banks make super normal profits the Indian banks make subnormal profits. The foreign banks, in the event, set up fresh branches to take advantage of the profit prospects. But the Indian banks cannot set up branches as these branches become unviable and therefore sick. They have to be closed down throwing the bank employees out of job or they have to continue in business putting up with subnormal profits or losses as in the case of *pliopoly*. This situation is not conducive to competitive efficiency of the banking system.

As it is, the Indian banks do not satisfy the test of competitive efficiency. They have to fulfill a social commitment in the matter of lending to priority sectors at concessional rates of interest. This commitment cannot be thrust on the foreign banks: while in the matter of lending the foreign banks charge competitive interest rates and make profits, the Indian banks, committed as they are to a social purpose, have to charge interest rates on lending which are far below the competitive rates charged by the foreign banks. Furthermore, the Indian banks are burdened with loan melas and loan waivers with which the foreign banks are not concerned. Thus, the Indian banks are competing in a handicap race and in such a race they are bound to lose. The extent of freedom allowed to foreign banks in the Indian money market is detrimental to the Indian public sector banks. This is bound to hinder the development of banking in the country.

If the Indian banks are to survive in business, they should be allowed the same degree of freedom as the foreign banks in the matter of deposit rates and loan rates. At the same time, they should also be freed from the social commitment which, at present, has reduced this profitability. Many are against freeing the banks from the social commitment. They with their present output, are unable to compete with the foreign banks in the matter of customer service. This is one of the factors which make people prefer Havala traders to Indian banks in the matter of remitting foreign exchange. If the Indian banks are to achieve the degree of competitive efficiency characteristic of foreign bank, they should go in for computerisation of their operations and work culture. But the bank employees are up against computerisation of their operations on the ground that they will be thrown out of jobs. They have also held out threat of agitation and demonstrations against the Narasimhan Committee Report on Financial Reforms. The Government should not hold up this report buckling under the pressure of the bank employees. As in the case of exit policy in regard to industry where a social safety net is provided in the National Renewal Fund there should be a Renewal Fund to provide a social safety net for the bank employees thrown out of jobs as a result of the computerization of their operations. This will allay the apprehensions of the bank employees and allow smooth sailing to computerization which is going to enhance competitive efficiency of the banks. Even so, the main problem remains the problem of freeing the Indian banks from the social commitment. Given the Indian psyche this problem does not admit of any easy or universal acceptable solution. If this problem is not solved the Indian banks are sure to lose the race in favour of foreign banks.

# 77

## Foreign Direct Investment and Technology Transfer Hurdles Need to be Removed

India's economic policy since Independence has been one of the autonomy and import substitution within a mixed economy outfit. Public sector and private sector coexisted and operated side by side. The public sector occupied the commanding heights of the economy and the private sector was controlled through, controls, licences and permits. In the post-Nehru era this policy came in for a good deal of valid criticism. It was held that licences and controls constricted economic advance and made it impossible for the economy to realize its full potentialities.

The Government recognised the imperative need to give a new thrust and orientation to economic policy. It adopted the policy of liberalization implying delicensing, de-regulation, disinvestment, privatisation, fifty-one percent of foreign equity, opening national doors to the NRIs and to the multinational corporations. In July 1991 when the economy was in a serious balance of payments crisis it resorted to a massive two-stage devaluation and in consequence the rupee value depreciated by 22.8 percent. The two-stage approach to devaluation made the exports cheaper and imports dearer though it must be noted that the expected improvement in the balance of payments did not come about as the conditions on which devaluation depends for its success were not met. Gold was pledged to overcome the crisis in the balance of payments, the foreign exchange reserves at the time being only Rs. 2,606 crore in May 1991.

Under the policy of liberalization India is committed to inviting foreign capital and is integrating itself with world market which on its part is also integrating itself with India. With foreign capital rendered free to come to India, the old bureaucratic rule book has become irrelevant. Under the New Economic Policy all the existing rules and regulations which allowed the licence permit raj to flourish need re-examination. This is particularly imperative if foreign capital is to come to India to foment industrial advance and induce economic revival in general.

It is possible to distinguish between three stages in the evolution of the foreign direct investment (FDI) policy in the post-independence period. Between 1950 and 1980 the policy was inward looking. This was for two reasons: (1) there was the genuine fear of neo-colonialism resulting from the invasion of multinational companies. This fear was genuine when viewed in the context of British exploitation of the Indian economy for 200 years; (2) the Government of Independent India was committed to a policy of self-reliance and was determined to make the economy grow with domestic resources, foreign support being only marginal. Foreign capital had to play the supplemental role for the domestic capital base in private sector projects on terms designed to protect the industrial structure.

As India wanted to compete in foreign markets her goods had to be price and quality competitive. To be able to produce such goods India needed technology more than capital. But foreign capital could came only with foreign technology. Technology transfer thus became a necessity and technology could be transferred in free foreign exchange. The foreign firms could supply technology and could participate in Indian industry with minority equity holding limit of upto 40 percent. All such participation could be only with government approval. There was thus considerable technology transfer to India but not much of direct foreign investment.

With the progress of industrialization and the change in the investment climate in the country the policy towards direct foreign investment entered the second stage. By this time the Asian tigers viz., South Korea, Taiwan, Singapore, Hong Kong, Thailand and Malaysia had considerably benefitted from foreign capital and technology. The Government of India took some bold decisions in the matter of encouraging direct foreign investment and technology transfer. It initiated a process of liberalization. The procedures governing foreign investment were liberalized to enable it to flow in large quantity. Though the policy became more flexible it remained vague. The main concessions were in foreign equity limit and technology supply. In respect of high technology areas and export linkages the question of allowing higher than 40 percent foreign equity was kept open. The oil exporting developing countries were allowed to invest in Indian industry without having to meet technology supply condition as, though they were flush with capital. They lacked advanced technology. They were allowed to set up 100 percent export-oriented industries and also units in export processing zones with 100 percent ownership. Administrative redtapism was reduced considerably. Single window clearance and fast track mechanism for speedy disposal of cases were introduced. All these measures aroused foreign interest in India. As a result there was a spurt in the number of foreign collaborations with equity back up and the corresponding foreign direct investment. In 1981 there were only 51 foreign collaborations involving Rs. 11 crore of foreign capital but in 1990 the number of approvals rose to 194 involving foreign capital of Rs. 128 crore. During the decade of the 1980s the quantum of foreign investment amounted to Rs. 1274 crore in respect of 1839 collaborations. Thus India could get, as an average, foreign investment of just Rs. 127 crore a year during the 1980s. This was an insignificant fraction of nearly $ 150 billion global foreign direct investment flow per annum.

Since 1991 when the economic reform package was initiated by the Narasimha Rao Government and when the globalization of the Indian economy got a boost foreign investment became a source of foreign exchange reserves necessary to meet the balance of payments crisis. The earlier restrictive and discriminatory policy gave way to a liberal and transparent foreign investment regime. Foreign investment came to be delinked from technology transfer. Foreign investors could bring just their capital which need not be in free foreign exchange and can also come in the form of plant, machinery and capital goods.

The foreign investors began to demand majority ownership of the companies floated with their capital. This demand was readily conceded. Automaticity has ended discretion in priority areas. Furthermore, the foreign equity limit was raised from 40 percent to 51 percent. The earlier case by case approval has yielded place to automatic approval of direct foreign investment upto 51 percent foreign equity holding in high priority, capital intensive, high technology industries subject to certain conditions including "Dividend Balancing" in the consumer goods sector as a precaution against drain on foreign exchange.

At present, the Reserve Bank of India has been vested with powers of automatic approval. A special foreign investment promotion board has been established to look into large foreign investment projects where foreign equity of more than 51 percent may be permitted. The facility of portfolio investment has been extended to foreign investors thus giving partial access to the capital market. This represents a major break with the earlier policy.

In keeping with the spirit of liberalization the Government has opened the economy to foreign investors in promoting industry, trade tourism and capital market. In a market friendly, competitive environment the earlier prejudice against foreign investment is disappearing. Under the scheme of industrial delicensing, the MRTP and FERA regulations have been relaxed and the initiative has shifted from Government to industry giving freedom of decision making to Indian and foreign businessmen. The earlier hurdles like official discretion, bureaucratic delays and uncertainties have been removed. This has created a bracing foreign investment climate.

The political parties in the Parliament charge the Government with a "sell out" to foreign multinational corporations. This charge is unfounded. The Indian industrial structure, as it has evolved, reflects the maturity of Indian companies and their ability to withstand any possible onslaught by the multinational corporations. Time has come when the need to encourage direct foreign investment and technology transfer to India is imperative in order to strengthen the productive and export base of the economy. China which is pursuing a liberal economic policy and has thrown its doors open to foreign capital and technology provides an inspiring example for India. Many Asian nations are competing with India for foreign capital and technology. They flow in directions which are remunerative. For this reason, it is necessary for India to offer investment opportunities which are better than those offered by the emerging Asian tigers. This requires the adoption of a new strategy to encourage free flow of foreign capital and technology.

It is necessary for India, like China, to open up the economy no matter whether it is dictated by the World Bank or the IMF. India cannot afford to remain isolated from the countries like China, Thailand, Singapore, Malaysia and even Vietnam which have been developing fast besides the developed countries of the West.

In this context the example of China should inspire India. China's stable political situation and the move to remove bureaucratic hurdles have helped it to attract foreign investment. China offers a lot of incentives to the foreign investors in the form of tax reliefs. Initially, the foreign investors in China were not allowed to enter into areas such as railways, airlines, telecommunications, banking and finance and those industries which are prone to environmental hazards. However, at present, all sectors except those which can create environmental pollution have been thrown to foreign investment. Automobile and electronics industries also remain out of bounds to foreign investors as the Government still protects the domestic entrepreneurs in these areas.

Between 1979 and 1991 foreign investments worth $121.7 billion were negotiated in China and $79.6 billion were realized. Out of 41,000 joint venture proposals approved during this period 20,000 have already been set up. The US, Japan, Germany, Italy, France and the UK are the major trade partners of China. In 1992 China exported goods worth $ 71.9 billion and imported goods worth $ 63.79 billion. The nature of the goods exported has also changed. The export of primary goods fell from 50.3 percent in 1988 to 22.5 percent in 1991 while the export of manufactures went up from 49.7 percent to 77.5 percent during the same period. The eighth five year plan of China for 1991-95 has revised the annual average growth rate from 6 percent to 9 percent. Ever since the economic reforms were introduced in the 1980s, in terms of purchasing power the Chinese economy has already second or third largest in the world after the US and Japan and in any case, certainly bigger than Germany's.

It is forecast that if current growth rate differentials are maintained the Chinese GDP is likely to exceed that of the United States. Life expectancy at birth is 70 years (India 59 years) and illiteracy is 27 percent (India 52 percent). A decade ago China's foreign trade ranked 20th in the world and in 1993, at $200 billion, it will be the tenth largest trading nation accounting for a larger share than even South Korea or Taiwan. The boom in foreign trade is mainly because of its open door policy on foreign direct investment and it is here that China has to offer a valuable lesson for India. The quiet march towards a free market economy is also underlined by the Government's decision to raise grain production to 475 million tonnes by 1997. This is indeed a spectacular achievement. The optimism of the Chinese leadership is perfectly justified by a favourable investment climate and a burgeoning foreign trade volume which has touched a staggering $ 165.6 billion volume. The success of China can be attributed to the open door policy which is favourable to foreign investment. India can as well follow Chinese example.

In a major liberalization move and a step to attract foreign investment the Government has opened up Indian Capital market to foreign institutional investors on highly attractive and liberal terms. A concessional tax regime of a flat rate of 20 percent of dividend and interest income and a tax rate of 10 percent on long term capital gains have been given to the foreign institutional investors. They can now invest in all securities traded on the primary and secondary markets including equity and other securities instruments of companies which are listed or will be listed on Indian stock exchanges. They will be required to be registered with the Securities and Exchange Board of India (SEBI) and also have to obtain permission of the Reserve Bank of India under the Foreign Exchange Regulation Act (FERA). The Reserve Bank's general permission will be obtained by SEBI before granting initial registration under a single window approach. The permission will be valid for a period of five years and renewable thereafter. They will be allowed to open foreign currency denominated accounts with designated banks permitted by the Reserve Bank. There will be no lock in period for any investments made by the foreign institutional investors in the primary and secondary markets. The total holdings of all registered investors is 24 percent excluding foreign investments under financial collaboration permitted upto 51 percent.

Indian rupee is made fully convertible. The question that is still being asked is whether coupled with full convertibility exchange control regulations too will be substantially lifted to make rupee convertibility meaningful. The question assumes relevance in view of the recent FERA ordinance. This ordinance has shed some stale and obsolete provisions. But draconian punishments and cumbersome regulations continue to find place. For example even after the deletion of Section 27, Reserve Bank's permission for setting up joint ventures will continue to be necessary. Permission is limited to the extent of capital contribution abroad. But is this necessary? What then is the sanctity of President's power under Article 123 of the constitution of India? Can it be stultified by an executive press release by the Reserve Bank of India?

In a similar manner two of the most cumbersome regulations, namely, Sections 19(1)(d) and 29(1)(b) of the FERA continue to be operative. Some old regulations with regend to carrying on commercial, trading, industrial activities in India continue to apply on NRIs, non-resident foreign nationals and non-resident companies incorporated outside India. Similarly, the power of police officials to "arrest without warrant" etc., have not been removed. Against this background, the jargons like "full convertibility", 'liberalisation' and 'deregulation' are meaningless. There is no visible sign that exchange control will be liberalized. Without this rupee full convertibility is a meaningless slogan. If the Government is keen to liberalise and make the rupee fully convertible, the only way out is to allow free rupee trading beyond the national barrier. Rupee must be allowed to find its rightful plan in the forex market. FERA should be fully liberalized so as to attract foreign investment.

In the context of the New Economic policy all the existing rules and regulations which had paved the way for the emergence of the 'licence permit' raj need thorough examination and screening. India does not yet have a clear, consistent exit policy making a nonsense of liberalization. India's statute book and the underlying subordinate legislation must be rewritten to fall in line with the, structure, style and spirit of liberalization and market economy. Indeed the whole harmony of laws in India is basically of colonial origin suiting the imperial regime. It must be market friendly in letter and spirit.

There is a case for purging bureaucracy of its pathological ailments. The permit licence raj created a culture of corruption in public administration. If the prevalent attributes like corruption, delay, harassment etc., continue even under liberalization potential investors are bound to be deterred from investing in India.

So far, no evidence is in sight to suggest that India's bureaucracy is prepared to accept the logic of liberalization. Twenty months after the inauguration of the new economic policy an entrepreneur faces as many as 18 agencies for clearance and is confronted by as many as 51 inspectors from as many statutes relating to industrial laws. Getting funds from financial institutions still requires clearance from five authorities. Each agency has its own complex and time consuming bureaucratic procedures. For instance, the form to be submitted for appointment as a managing director of a company has 55 questions to be answered. Industrial licensing entails 60 questions; pollution control board seeks answers to 82 questions and an import licence for capital goods in some cases needs 61 answers in an application form. Things are no better with excise duty regulations. There are 385 rules. The tariff rates, for instance, are given in 96 rambling chapters. This is the limit. The whole exercise is frustrating in the extreme.

India is often called a "soft state". There is urgent need to transform it into an hard one so that public policies get implemented quickly and honestly. For the first time since Independence India finds itself on the brisk of a debt trap. Worse days are ahead if the bureaucracy and the political leadership fail to reform themselves and to change their mind set in time. Foreign corporations are of late, visiting India but many go back without risking investment of their capital. They prefer investment in other countries of Asia including China, alleging the unhelpful behaviour of Indian bureaucracy. These things have to change expeditiously.

The reactions of the foreign investors need to be recorded as they help the country to restructure its attitude towards foreign investment while the Government bureaucratic elite is toeing the official line in expressing satisfaction with the process of liberalization, the foreign investors have expressed doubts about the continuity of the reform process. They have the perception that the Government of India has become complacement after announcing the policy changes and is not doing more to promote itself, as a competition with various countries (in East Europe and Latin America) to attract foreign investment becomes intense. The Government harbours the impression that since the doors have been opened by India, foreign investors should actually be queuing up. But nothing of the sort happened as the Government has not done enough to tell the world about the on-going changes in the economic reform process. The Indian diplomatic outfit overseas needs to be used in a proactive manner and the Government should send more political delegates abroad for promoting India.

Data collected by the independent agencies seem to corroborate the view of inadequacy of effort to sell India abroad and for this reason India still is not as attractive to foreign investors as other South East Asian countries. An audit conducted by an independent agency which interrogated senior executives of companies listed in the Fortune 500 and who are present in India showed that India is ranking a lowly 10 among competing countries for attracting foreign investment. Many foreign investing firms feel that only the major policies were in place and the Government must now initiate the process of simplifying the procedures. Many foreign investors have found it easy to get clearance from the Government but have had a rough time while implementing the project. They feel that India should further reduce direct taxation as well as the tariff structure although a beginning has been made in the Union Budget for 93-94.

In the eyes of the foreign investors India really counts for less with Asia effectively meaning the "tigers". If, inspite of this, they want to do business with India it is, no doubt, because of the reform measures the New Delhi has adopted. The process of liberalization and opening up is seen as a gateway to investment growth in India and they see some light at the end of the tunnel. But now the Government is more flexible as it has realized the importance of foreign investment and technology to modernize its industrial outfit and to increase industrial productivity. The foreign investors want business and not idle talk or unmeaning drama. This New Delhi should not ignore. When the foreign investors say "fast" they really mean fast and would not settle for less. They would not tolerate hurdles, bureaucratic or otherwise. They are waiting to get into the act and would not like a long wait. It is, therefore, necessary for the Government of India to intensify the drive for liberalisation so that foreign capital and technology may enter India unimpeded unlike in the past. The Government should identify the hurdles, if any and remove them with no loss of time. Competitiveness which is a major objective of the measures of liberalization should now become sharper through relaxation of licensing and free entry of firms.

# 78

# Autonomous Status for the Reserve Bank of India

Of late the Reserve Bank of India and the Finance Ministry do not seem to be seeing eye-to-eye with one another in the matter of fiscal monetary policy. The Governor of the Reserve Bank (Dr. C. Rangarajan) has gone public with his displeasure about the Central Government's fiscal management. He has sounded the warning of a limit to which the Reserve Bank can support the Government's borrowing programme. While admitting that the Reserve Bank, as lender of last resort, should lend, he has stated that there is a definite limit to the quantum of lending. The limit to lending is set by the targeted rate of monetary growth.

In the current year, the budget deficit is running at the extraordinary level of Rs. 19,000 crore. This is far in excess of the gain from the most distinguishing feature of fiscal reform reduced monetisation of the fiscal deficit. At the end of 1994-95 this was less than Rs. 2000 crore. This was the result of the change in the mode of financing Government expenditure from deficit financing to debt financing. There is again a recourse to monetisation. The Finance Ministry holds the view that recourse to monetisation is due to difficulty of borrowing in the debt market. Why is the debt market so saturated? The existing conditions in the debt market are actually a consequence of the Government's own borrowing programme. According to the Reserve Bank Governor this "highlights the problem faced in placing increasingly larger amounts of Government debt in the market and the crucial need for pruning the fiscal deficit."

The persistent and growing deficits emerging from the Central Government's fiscal operations negate the monetary policy efforts of the Reserve Bank and are eroding monetary stability. Neither the quarterly ceiling introduced from 1992 nor 10 days' ceiling on adhoc treasury bills during the current year have helped discipline the Government for the Reserve Bank has no power to enforce the observance of these limits. Unless these limits are enforced there will be no limit to the extent of Government borrowing from the Reserve Bank and no safeguards for monetary stability.

It is in this context that the case for greater autonomy for the Reserve Bank becomes strong and unassailable. Apart from monetary policy compulsions which are important in their own right, the thrust towards financial liberalization also makes it imperative that the Reserve Bank of India be vested with full authority to regulate the functionally varied and spatially diversified financial system. Given that the basic motivation for vesting the Reserve Bank with greater authority is to ensure consonance between the fiscal and monetary policies, what is required is functional autonomy in order to achieve the objective of price stability.

In this connection, the case of the German Central Bank appears relevant. German law states: the Deutsche Bundes Bank shall be obliged, in so far as is consistent with its functions, to support general policy of the Federal Government". What makes the Bundes bank strong and independent is the provision that " in exercise of the powers conferred on it under the law, it shall not be subject to instructions from the Federal Government".

In the light of this, the question arises: should the Reserve Bank of India be independent of the Government? If the two authorities do not see eye to eye in matters of general economic policy what is the way out? If there are major disagreements between them in the matter of macro-economic objectives there can be legislative provisions to resolve them. The experience of the major central banks, namely, the Federal Reserve of the USA, the German Bundes Bank and the Bank of England does not indicate that such a conflict can arise. If there have been such cases, it is because the authority of the Central Bank has not been clearly delineated.

At present, the Reserve Bank of India lacks an autonomous status and, is in fact, a department of Government subserving its fiscal interests. The Government which, at times, comes under populist compulsions has to exceed the limits of fiscal prudence thus upsetting economic stability. In a situation like this the Reserve Bank has to play an accommodative role however much it does not like to play this role for fear of causing inflation. It is this that is causing uneasiness in the mind of the Governor of the Reserve Bank of India. It would be in the interests of monetary stability and stable growth to confer autonomous status on the Reserve Bank of India. This will ease the task of fiscal stabilization.

# 79

# A Case for Retaining Fertilizer and Food Subsidies

The question relating to the fertilizer subsidies has been a headache to the Government of India. The World Bank and the International Monetary Fund have been insisting on removing the subsidies of all hues and they have made this the condition precedent to the credit/loans being extended to India from time to time. Their contention rests on two grounds: (1) that they are inconsistent with the market-friendly policies being pursued by the Government and (2) that they exacerbate inflationary pressure as they widen the fiscal deficits which are inflationary. These arguments need to be examined.

The Government of India appointed a committee to go into the question of fertilizer prices which has also to examine the need for and the desirability of continuing fertilizer subsidy. The policy in this regard is expected to be announced in September 1992.

Admittedly the economic reform measures initiated by the Government of India over a year ago are market-friendly. This does not mean that India has adopted the free market approach of classical conception. India is on the road to a free market economy and the progress towards this goal is slow and sluggish considering the structural and institutional imperfections inherent in the Indian economic system. In a system like this, it would not be in order to scrap the fertilizer subsidy or any other subsidy. It must be remembered that the economic system of the United States and of Western Europe approach the classical free market economy. Even so, they have retained agricultural subsidies. When this is the case it is incomprehensible why the Fund-Bank duo insists on India scrapping the subsidies. This insistence lacks logical force.

It is true that the subsidies involve a rise in Government expenditure. Given the revenue from sources the payment of subsidies increases the non-plan expenditure of the Government and widens the budget deficit. Whether the budget deficit is financed by borrowing or by money creation the consequence is inflationary though money financing of the deficit is less inflationary than debt financing. The Fund-Bank combine insists on the fiscal deficit being reduced from 6.5 percent of GDP to 5 percent of GDP. If this is to be possible the subsidies should be scrapped. So far so good. But this argument does not go far enough. The reason for advocating the scrapping of subsidies is the need to reduce the rate of inflation. If scrapping of the subsidies which results in a reduction of the fiscal deficit acts in a disinflationary manner, there can be no opposition to its scrapping. But the things are not so simple as this. The scrapping of the fertilizer subsidy would push up the prices of urea and phosphate base manure widely used by farmers by 60 percent and 100 percent respectively. Even at the current subsidized prices it is difficult for the farmers to buy fertilizers. The free market price of fertilizers is bound to render fertilizers absolutely unaffordable to the farmers. If the demand for fertilizers is elastic the demand for it falls, the input of fertilizers falls causing a fall in farm productivity and farm production. The demand for farm products being constant, the fall in their supply is bound to generate excess demand for them which pushes up the prices of farm products. As a consequence, the market prices of farm products including those of food articles rise. This has the effect of exacerbating inflation which the scrapping of the fertilizer subsidy is supposed to hold down. If, on the other hand, the demand for fertilizer is inelastic the input of fertilizers will not fall and, in consequence, farm productivity and farm production will not fall (assuming no change in the weather conditions). But as the higher prices of fertilizers push up the costs of production, the farmers have, perforce to raise the prices of their farm products. Thus if the demand for fertilizers is elastic there will occur demand-pull inflation and if the demand for fertilizers is inelastic there will occur cost push inflation. In either case inflation is the consequence though the scrapping of the fertilizer subsidy results in a reduction of the fiscal deficit. If the subsidy is retained there will be inflation generated by the fiscal deficit; if the subsidy is scrapped there will be demand-pull or cost-push inflation depending on whether the demand for fertilizers is elastic or inelastic. In any case inflation is inevitable. But inflation caused by retaining the subsidy is preferable to inflation caused by scrapping it. In any case the argument of the Fund-Bank combine that the scrapping of the fertilizer subsidy is necessary to hold down the fiscal deficit and through it to hold down the rate of inflation is, on the face of it; unsustainable. Besides this there is a noneconomic argument against the scrapping of the fertilizer subsidy. The farmers are used to buying subsidized fertilizers. If all on a sudden, the subsidy is scrapped it would be difficult for them to make the necessary mental adjustment to the new situation and there is bound to be a popular upheaval against the scrapping of the fertilizer subsidy. Already there are many social, political and economic tensions and the scrapping of the fertilizer subsidy will add to them and make the situation grossly intractable.

The dilatory attitude of the Government in adopting a firm policy has put the fertilizer industry in an embarrassing position and has rendered it incapable of designing future plans. The industry has been pressing the Government for sometime, albeit in vain, to clear the arrears due to it. The industry argues that the delay on the part of the Government in paying back the subsidy amount and unscientific method adopted in computing subsidy have had a crippling effect on the industry. The subsidy arrears at present amount to Rs. 1600 crore. Within a few months they would rise to Rs. 2,000 crore. Even if the Government pays up the arrears without delay it will be Rs. 5000- Rs. 6000 less than the industry's expenditure.

The subsidy being paid on fertilizers was calculated on prices fixed in 1990. Though the rate is being hiked by 5 percent every year, the actual rise in real terms works out to 10 percent. There are several other factors which have put the fertilizer industry in doldrums. The Gulf War which caused a hike in oil prices, the devaluation of the rupee and the EXIM Policy adopted on

01.04.1992 have caused a tremendous rise in the cost of production of fertilizers but the Government has not taken these factors into account while determining the price of fertilizers and the rate of subsidy.

Besides this, there are several anomalies in the official policy stance. Fertilizers are exempted from the hiked railway freight rates but many of the vital inputs of the industry do not enjoy this advantage. The imported fertilizers are not subject to import duties but the import of certain raw materials used in fertilizer production attract duties. In the second place, the subsidy has to be calculated on a scientific basis. In the third place, the vital inputs required by the industry should be exempted from the hike in railway freight rates in the same way as fertilizers. In the fourth place, the import of raw materials required by the fertilizer industry should be free from import duties in the same way as imported fertilizers. These measures will go long way in placing the domestic fertilizer industry on a sound footing and enhance its viability.

The Fund-Bank combine is also insisting on scrapping of subsidies on food. It is true that food subsidies cause a rise in Government expenditure, increase the fiscal deficit and occasion inflation. But the scrapping of food subsidies will cause a rise in food prices in the market in India. It is the food prices that govern the general price index and therefore the rate of inflation. If following the scrapping of food subsidies, food prices rise, the cost of living rises. This engenders demands for higher wages which, if granted, will generate demand-pull and cost-push inflations which get entwined and become difficult to disentangle. This creates a situation where there will emerge a vicious circle of prices and wages chasing one another. This type of inflation is worse than the inflation generated by fiscal deficits caused by the payment of food subsidies.

The Fund-Bank combine want the Government of India to reduce the rate of inflation. For this reason it wants a reduction of the fiscal deficit to 5 percent of GDP in 1992-93. If the reduction of the fiscal deficit results in a reduction in the rate of inflation one would lend support to the argument advanced by the Fund-Bank combine. But the scrapping of the subsidies, while reducing the fiscal deficit, has the unwelcome effect of generating inflation of the type which is worse and more vicious than the inflation generated by the enlarged fiscal deficit caused by the retention of the subsidies. In view of this, subsidies on fertilizers and food have to be retained for some more time and their phased scrapping should be pragmatic and not doctrinaire. But at present and for some time to come the case for retaining the fertilizer and food subsidies is strong indeed. Given the foregoing arguments the Government of India should resist any demand for scrapping subsidies. Subsidies are there even in the economies approaching the market economy of the classical conception. When India is gradually moving in that direction why scrap subsidies. The time is not yet propitious for it.

# 80

## Enhanced Support Prices for Food Grains

Recently the Government of India has enhanced the support price of food grains to facilitate the transfer of Rs. 335 crore to the farmers. As a consequence the prices of rice and wheat in the market have risen. The price of rice and the price of wheat, the two food grains used in the public distribution system, has gone up by Rs. 40 and Rs. 50 per quintal respectively. The Minister for Agriculture, has maintained that the support prices of rice and wheat have been raised in order to reduce the financial burden imposed on the farming community by the rise in fertilizer prices consequent on the reduction of fertilizer subsidy. This means that the burden which would rest on the farmers is shifted onto the shoulders of the consumers.

The IMF and the World Bank insist on the removal /reduction of subsidies of all hues as they feel that subsidies are anathema to a market oriented economy. The consequence of implementing, albeit partially, the conditionality prescriptions is to impose a burden on the common man. When the fertilizer subsidy was reduced, the Government had mollified the farmers who were sore with the policy. But it had not given any assurance that it would take action to prevent a rise in prices. Even so, it had given the assurance that it would check the rise in the rate of inflation. Now that the prices of rice and wheat have risen this assurance has been falsified. In November and December 1992 the price of rice was falling. This was due mainly to the removal of zonal restrictions on the movement of rice. But now as a consequence of the enhancement of the support price for rice the price of rice in the open market has begun to rise again. The Government of India had earlier raised the support price. But it had not raised the support price by Rs. 40-50 per quintal. This rise appears to be steep indeed.

It was possible for the Government to shift the burden of Rs. 335 crore to the fertilizer industry itself. It was also possible for the Government to reduce the price of fertilizers by making the subsidy payment for production and holding of fertilizer conditional on raising the price of fertilizers. This is not a difficult task if only the Government takes measures to streamline the distribution of fertilizers. Without doing any of these things the Government has only shifted the financial burden from one sector to another as if it is not its concern. In future whenever the Government takes action to reduce the subsidy or to remove it, the harried consumer has inevitably to bear the burden of the price rise in consequence.

It must be remembered that it is the food price that holds the key to the rate of inflation in the Indian economy. On the one hand, it takes measures like the reduction of the fiscal deficit and the reduction of the rate of monetary growth with intent to reduce the rate of inflation to a level specified in the Fund's conditionality prescription; on the other hand, it takes measures that would raise the rate of inflation. These two sets of measures are mutually contradictory.

The Fund-Bank combine is underwriting India's transition to a market economy and the transition is fairly rapid. But this should not make the Fund-Bank combine insist on the removal of all subsidies on the ground that subsidies are inconsistent with a market-oriented economy. The American and the European economies are more market oriented than the Indian economy. Even so, subsidies are the mainstay of American and European agriculture. When this is the case there appears to be no reason for the Fund-Bank combine to prescribe the removal of subsidies as a condition of making the loan available to India.

Removal of the fertilizer subsidy causes a rise in fertilizer prices. As the fertilizers are an essential farm input, the cost of production rises. To be able to meet the higher cost of production, the Government has to enhance the support prices of food grains so far so good. But what are the further consequences. The market prices of food grains rise. The consumers have to buy food grains by paying the higher market prices. This causes a rise in the cost-of-living index which governs the wage rate. The labourers enforce their demands for higher wages. If they are not granted there will be strikes and lockouts which through a reduction in mandays reduce output and through supply deficiency raise the price of output. On the other hand, if higher wages are granted, as they have to be granted they generate both cost-push inflation and demand-pull inflation which get intertwined and become difficult to disentangle. Thus, a removal of the fertilizer subsidy may help the Government to reduce the fiscal deficit but the rise in the support prices of food grains at the farmer's level causes a rise in the prices of food grains at the market level and generates inflation. This can be checked by offering food subsidy. But what is saved on fertilizer subsidy is lost on food subsidy so that there is no net saving to the Government to enable it to reduce the fiscal deficit and through it to reduce the rate of inflation.

This means that the removal of fertilizer subsidy, by reducing the fiscal deficit, reduces the fiscal deficit induced inflation rate but it engenders the cost-induced and demand-induced inflation due to the enhancement of the support price. In either case there is no relief from inflation.

India is not yet a free market economy through it is on the road to reach this goal. For some more time fertilizer subsidy is necessary. When the fully market-oriented American and European economies are offering fertilizer and other kinds of subsidies to their agricultural sectors it would not stand to reason to demand the removal or even reduction of the fertilizer in the Indian economy. Subsidy fertilisers should, of course, be phased out in stages. But at the present stage of the evolution of the Indian economy fertilizer subsidies are a necessity. To remove them at present is to cause a social upheaval in the agricultural sector and also to defeat the Government's efforts to reduce the inflation rate. At the end of December the rate of inflation reigned at 7.84 percent. But the consequence of a spurt in support prices for food grains due to the reduction of fertilizer subsidy is to provide an upward thrust to the inflation rate. Therefore, the reduction of the fiscal deficit, the reduction of the rate of inflation and the removal of fertilizer subsidies are not a coherent package of measures.

The burden of this song is that the fertilizer subsidies must be retained as an antidote to inflation for some more time. The support prices can be enhanced if warranted by the rise in other input costs so as to provide incentives to farmers to step up production.

# 81

## It is Wrong to Connect the Securities Scam with Liberalisation

The Government of India appointed a Committee under the Chairmanship of Shri. M. Narasimham to suggest reforms of the financial sector. The objective of reforms of the financial sector as enunciated by the Finance Minister in his Budget speech on 24.7.1991 is to "preserve its basic role as an essential adjunct to economic growth and competitive efficiency, while improving the health of its "institutions". In pursuance of this enunciation a High Level Committee was appointed in August 1991 to consider all relevant aspects of structure, organisation, functions and procedures of the financial system. This Committee, which submitted its report to the Government on 20.11.1991, has suggested a reform package for strengthening the system through measures aimed at enhancing productivity, efficiency and profitability. In particular, its aim is to provide protection to depositors and investors in an increasingly competitive environment, to enlarge the scope of private and foreign banking in the economy in order to expose the Indian financial system to the bracing winds of competition. The financial reform is an integral part of the reform package meant to give a boost to the Indian economy. Serious efforts have been launched to cry halt to the spending proclivities of the Government; the industrial policy has been liberalized to free the industrial system from bureaucratic controls and licensing procedures which thus far had impeded industrial progress, controls were loosened in order to help the foreign exchange regime move closer to a market determined ethos; the worst foreign exchange crisis was effectively tackled and conditions favourable to a larger inflow of foreign equity investment were created. However, in order to control inflation and to overcome the foreign exchange crisis import curbs had to be imposed, credit squeeze had to be resorted to, steps had to be taken to mitigate the recessionary trends in the industrial sector. These were necessary in order to render the structural adjustment policies prescribed by the Fund-Bank combine successful. In the Memorandum on economic policies for 1992-93 sent on June 2, 1992 by the Finance Minister to Mr Michael Camdessus, Managing Director of the IMF, it was stated that the country's GDP is expected to increase by 3.5 percent to 4.0 percent. In 1991-92 the estimated actual rate of growth of GDP (which shows the rate of growth of the economy as a whole) was 2.5 percent against the original expectation of 3.0-3.5 percent. The Memorandum further states: "Consistent with our twin objectives of a substantial reduction in inflation and a revival of economic growth, monetary policy will aim at a substantial slow-down commercial sector receives adequate credit. Thus, broad money growth is now targeted to decline sharply from 18.5 percent in 1991-92 to about 10.5 percent in the current year". Broad money is the generally accepted primary indicator of the amount of money available in the economy. One of the major tools of inflation control, as per the monetarist logic, is reduction in the growth of board money. The Memorandum goes on to say: "In order to allow the bulk of the fiscal correction in 1992-93 to be reflected in lower bank credit to the Centre and to ensure adequate growth in credit to the business sector, further measures as needed will be considered during the course of the year. This should permit an increase of about 12 percent in bank credit to the commercial sector during 1992-93". According to the Memorandum, inflation control and revival of economic activity are the "twin objectives" of the Government this year. In order to realize these objectives it must be assumed that the monetary policy will give equal importance to both the objectives. It is in this context that the proposed financial reform package assumes importance. The financial reform package is an integral part of the entire package of reform measures. If the reform measures are to succeed the financial reform package must be implemented in the manner proposed in the Narasimham Committee Report.

At a time when the reform measures were making great headway the securities scam involving some high street banks and leading brokers surfaced to convulse the economic system. Those who were opposed to the reform measures for ideological or other reasons have lost no time in attributing the stock scam to the deregulation and de-bureaucratisation process set in motion by the Government and to argue for holding at bay the Narasimham committee package as its implementation would further aggravate the scam. This indeed is bad logic.

They argue that if the scam could occur under the tight control exercised by the Reserve Bank of India and the Finance Ministry, those who perpetrated the scam will have a field day under a policy of deregulation and liberalization. They suggest that the Government should suddenly stop the ongoing reforms especially of the financial sector. Obviously, they have not understood the import of the Narasimham Committee package. It must be mentioned here that this package is not revolutionary. It does not recommend that the financial sector should be free from all controls and all types of controls and should be brought on par with the financial systems prevailing in the USA or Japan. All that it says is that the banking system and the capital market institutions which are subject to tight bureaucratic rules and constant political interference should be allowed to function according to business norms in the interests of competitive efficiency.

In the second place, even though the Indian financial system was subject to tight bureaucratic control it was, in fact under governed. The stock market crash of the mid 1980s took place when the capital market was literally under the thumb of the controller of capital issues in New Delhi. When the loans made under the loan mela scheme were not recoverable, the Government waived loans amounting to thousands of crore of rupees especially those advanced to the so called farmers who misused the funds lent to them ostensibly for agricultural operations. These practices like at the root of the present stock scam in which banks have transferred crore of rupees to brokers accounts in camea and with practically no collateral.

In the third place, none of the reforms contained in the Narasimham reform package are implemented. They seek to return to the bankers their own norms of prudence and transparency in financial transactions. The SLR and CRR have been reduced from their former high levels in order to increase the profitability of the banking system and to make bank loans cheap to enable the industries to borrow more in the attempt to mitigate the severity of the on-going recession in the economy. Loan and deposit rates have been rationalised. The banks are now free to open or close their branches depending on the intensity or otherwise of, banking business. The office of the Controller of Capital Issues has been abolished and its powers are shifted to the Securities and Exchange Board of India. In the attempt to increase the operational efficiency of the banking system the Reserve Bank of India has been speeding up the process of computerization of its operations despite threats of demonstrations held out by the bank employees. The banks have been given fresh instructions about treasury operations and management of investment portfolios.

The stock scam is being investigated by the Janakiraman committee. This committee has found four foreign banks fingering in the scam. This has made some anti-reformers to advise the Government to do away with the liberal approach adumbrated by the Narasimham Committee Report and to demand the resignation of the Finance Minister and the Governor of the Reserve Bank of India. However, they are not necessary. The scam took place without their knowledge and it is unfair to blame them. As it is, there are several checks and balances to ensure that they function according to the Banking Regulation Act. What is necessary is for the Reserve Bank of India to exercise effective supervisory powers over the operations of the foreign banks. It is possible that if the powerful political forces had not been involved, the scam would not have occurred.

That the scam occurred is no reason for abandoning the financial reform package contained in the Narasimhan committee Report. The reform measures pertaining to several sectors of the Indian economy are an interdependent whole. They are mutually reinforcing. If the financial reform measures are abandoned the other reform measures will be weakened and the progress being made by the Indian economy will be retarded. In view of this, the financial reform measures underway should be pursued with unabated vigour while taking effective action to stall the occurrence of scams in future. It would be illogical to connect the stock scam with the policy of deregulation and liberalization. The origin of the scam lies elsewhere but not in liberalization. To demand the resignations of the Finance Minister and the Reserve Bank Governor is to demand punishment for the innocent. This is grossly unfair.

# 82

## Full Convertibility of the Rupee—We should Hasten Slowly

The Finance Minister of India, took a decision on March 1,1992 to make the rupee partially convertible deferring the issue of full convertibility to a later date. Under the partial convertibility dispensation 40 percent of the foreign exchange had to be surrendered to the Reserve Bank of India at the official rate and the balance of 60 percent of the foreign exchange had to be disposed of by the exporters at the market rate. Expectedly, the market rate is higher than the official rate. In my earlier Memoranda on the subject I opposed the "dash to convertibility" as being premature and on the ground that it would lead to inflation in the economy as the imports financed by foreign exchange purchased at the market rate would inject inflationary impulses through higher costs. The Finance Minister contended that this was an integral part of the strategy of liberalization of the economy and so the partial convertibility experiment came to stay. It was also argued at the time that this was only a transistory measure towards full convertibility on trade account at an opportune time. Now the Finance Ministry study shows that the average exchange rate of the rupee in terms of SDRs (which consists of a basket of five major currencies US dollar, Pound, Sterling, German DM, Japanese Yen and French France) depreciated by 3.3 percent during the first quarter of 1992-93. The premium average over official exchange rate which had ranged around 19-20 percent in April 1992 declined to around 17-17.5 percent in May and further to about 16.5-17 percent in June 1992 for these major five currencies.

This goes to show that the foreign exchange market has fully stabilized and the rupee has got its own footing vis-à-vis the major international currencies in a short period of five months after the introduction of partial convertibility. The Government now feels that the first experiment has stood the test and the time has come to take a plunge in full to globalising the economy by resorting to full convertibility of the rupee.

Full convertibility of the rupee may be announced anytime now. The Finance Ministry has already started advocating early implementation of full rupee convertibility on trade account since the rupee is prepared for this step. Two considerations have influenced the Government is thinking in favour of early announcement of full convertibility on trade account; in the first place, the annual rate of inflation has declined to a single digit figure of 9.28 percent as on July 25, 1992; in the second place, foreign exchange reserves have reached a high and comfortable level of $6,457 million by the end of July 1992. Foreign exchange reserves excluding gold and SDRs which had declined to $ 1,141 million at the end of August 1991, increased to $ 5,631 million by the end of March 1992 and to $ 6,224 million by June 1992. These reserves rose further by $ 233 million during July 1992. Thus, during the first four months of the current fiscal year, the foreign exchange reserves rose by $ 826 million and their level at the end of July 1992 was $ 6,457 million.

This level of foreign exchange reserves is sufficient to finance three months' imports. But what has added to the Government's confidence is the decline in the outflow of NRI funds from the country. The monthly outflow from NRI accounts during June 1992 was of the order of $62 million as against $ 312 million in June 1991. The total outflow of these deposits during the first quarter of 1992-93 comes to $375 million as compared to a substantially higher outflow of $952 million during the corresponding quarter of 1991-92.

The improvement of the foreign exchange reserve position is due to larger inflow of funds from the international agencies and not to the rise in exports. Exports have risen only in a slow and sluggish manner. In dollar terms they increased by 0.3 percent in May 1992 as against a decline of 7.9 percent in April 1992. However, during April-May 1992 exports recorded a decline of

4 percent against a higher decline of 5.8 percent during April-May 1992.

The decline in exports was mainly due to the fall in exports to rupee payment areas by 57.7 percent. Exports to general currency areas increased by 3 percent. Imports in April-May 1992 in dollar terms increased to 24.7 percent. The Government has projected that the exports would pick up from September onwards and the Government can boost exports through full convertibility of the rupee. Furthermore, free convertibility would also be able to take in its fold capital account transactions. The rupee being made fully convertible into foreign currency and vice-versa, market forces are expected to ensure a stable rate structure.

It is argued that when the rupee is made fully convertible on current account, its value will be determined by the purchasing power parity of currencies. Under this system the new rate of exchange will be equal to the old rate multiplied by the quotient of the degrees of inflation in India and in other countries. If the exchange rate of the rupee is to remain stable, the Indian inflation rate has to be brought down to the levels of the inflation rates in other countries. If the inflation rate in India is higher than in other countries, the exchange rate of the rupee depreciates. Inflation rate can be brought down by a dear money policy and a reduction of the fiscal deficit. In this event, the interest rates in India will be higher than those abroad. In the regime of capital mobility higher interest rates may help the capital account by attracting funds from abroad and generating a capital account surplus. But it will have other effects also. Foreign companies are waiting for the full convertibility of the rupee before entering India to expand their operations. It is held by them that the two-tiered exchange rate operating in India now and even the full convertibility covering only the trade account creates disincentives to expand trade and investment because of the wide gap between the official and the market rates. Foreign investment can be attracted if the rupee is made convertible on capital account also. This is the view held by the American, German and Japanese investors who are otherwise anxious to invest in India.

When the rupee is made convertible on capital account also, the exchange rate will be determined by interest rate differentials as distinct from inflation rate differentials (as under the purchasing power parity dispensation) and this bears on the current account. If the exchange rate of the rupee on capital account is to be held steady the interest rates in India must be equal to the interest rates abroad allowing a margin for risks and uncertainties. In order to attract capital from abroad, the rate of interest in India must be held higher than those abroad. This creates a dilemma; higher interest rates attract foreign investment but they reduce domestic investment. Thus, the stability of the exchange rate of the rupee depends on two conditions: the rate of inflation should be contained and the rate of domestic interest rate should be kept at an adequately high level. This can be done by reducing the fiscal deficit and imposing restrictions on credit availability.

Credit restriction and fiscal discipline may land the economy in a recession as the two together have an excessively contractive effect on economic activity. To the extent that higher interest rates attract foreign funds they will give a relief to the balance of payments. But as the dividend, amortisation and interest payments are made, the external accounts would come under severe strain. It is possible to stimulate demand by increasing public investment to make good the fall in private investment brought about by high interest rates. But the policy of policy-mix enjoins on us mixing a contractive fiscal policy with an expansive credit policy.

The Indian economy has come under severe strains partly due to mistaken policy measures and partly due to inefficiency and corruption in high places. The market cannot resolve all the rigidities and imperfections inherent in the economic system. The Indian economy is far from the Walrasian general equilibrium model which is self- adjusting; there are several frictions in adjustment and so the adjustment to equilibrium is neither smooth nor quick. In order to realize growth with stability and to implement the fully convertible rupee, India needs a zero inflation rate and a low interest rate. The market is as yet unable to provide the correct signals for the policy markers. The economic policy in India is said to be market-friendly. But at the present moment, we cannot be too sure of market friendliness. There is uncertainty of market friendship. The fully convertible rupee can function efficiently in an economy where market signals are trustworthy. In their absence the free rupee will behave erractically. The government should therefore be cautious about making the rupee fully convertible. There is need to hasten slowly.

# 83

## Wage Freeze is Inevitable

The International Monetary Fund has advanced the badly needed structural Adjustment Facility to India on the condition that India fulfills certain conditionality prescriptions. Early in July 1992 the IMF released a further $ 681 million. This has been used to meet the critical balance of payments situation caused by the outflow of NRI deposits. This facility was advanced by the IMF in view of the Government of India adhering to the domestic borrowing target for the first quarter of the 1992-92 fiscal year. This means that the fiscal deficit for the first quarter is contained to roughly one-third of the target set for the full fiscal year. This leaves two-thirds of the deficit financing to play around within the remaining three quarters of 1992-93. The second quarter of the year is holding out the possibility of an ordeal. In the first quarter of 1992-93 several factors helped to contain the fiscal deficit viz., (1) the release of plan and tax funds to the States was postponed; (2) the payment of subsidies including the payment of arrears to the fertilizer producers was deferred. The honouring of these commitments in the second quarter of 1992-93 will widen the fiscal deficit. If the economy had registered a vibrant growth the matter would not have been serious. The withdrawal of import compression measures under the new Export-Import policy announced on April 1, 1992 has caused a rise in imports and this has caused a rise in customs revenue. But these imports are used up in keeping the economy going and they do not result in accelerated growth. This is one of the reasons why the exports are not growing. As a result there is no likelihood of a revenue buoyancy from excise duties and income taxes to bring down the fiscal deficit in the second quarter and subsequent quarters of the present fiscal year.

The fiscal adjustment in the first quarter was relatively painless. But it is unlikely to remain so in the subsequent quarters. As a result, in order to contain the fiscal deficit to the targeted level the Government has to rely less on the growth of tax revenue and more on drastic expenditure cuts. But expenditure cuts should not involve a scrapping of fertilizer and food subsidies as such scrapping generates demand-pull and cost-push inflations. As it is, the Government is yet to be successful in controlling inflation. In view of this the Government has perforce to yield to the pressure of labour unions to enhance wage rates. The need to raise the wages in the organized sector has been recognized and this will be given effect to shortly. This is bound to result in inflation which offsets the price effect of devaluation on exports, imports and the balance of payments. If the Government finds it difficult to control expenditure it has to reduce its investment expenditure budgeted for the current year with deleterious consequences on the rate of economic growth. But the rate of economic growth can be sustained if the reduction in Government investment is made good by the rise in private investment. But this prospect is dull during 1992-93. There are several reasons for this. In the first place, the rates of interest are too high and they have to be high because of continuing inflation. In the second place, the stock exchange is hit by the recent security scam and this has resulted in a liquidity crunch. It takes some time for the stock exchange to recover from the shock. It was expected earlier that the stock exchange would serve as a new window for significant foreign investment. But this expectation is belied by the scam. As a result, the present fiscal year 1992-93 is bound to experience high inflation, low investment and low economic growth and low growth of income and employment.

The Government is committed to bringing down the fiscal deficit to 5 percent of GDP. This commitment is grossly overambitious. For it cannot be brought down to 5 percent of GDP by scrapping the subsidies for this would mean a higher inflation rate; it cannot be brought down by reducing investment for this would mean low rate of economic growth and reduced revenue buoyancy. It has to be brought down by reducing wasteful expenditure and by going in for a wage freeze. The wage freeze is bound to be resisted by the labourers and the Government employees. But an appeal to their patriotic sentiment may be of some help. Several State Governments have appointed Pay Commissions in order to recommend new (higher) scales of pay and dearness allowances. If they are allowed it becomes impossible to control inflation. Therefore, the State Governments should be directed to keep in abeyance the reports of the Pay Commissions. The Central Government, on its part, should keep in abeyance the report of the H.N. Ray Committee which is currently examining the question of equalizing the pay and dearness allowances of the Central Government employees, employees of nationalized banks and employees of public sector industries. If these reports are implemented the money supply in India will be on the so-called "Labour Standard" with deleterious consequences on the rate of economic growth, the balance of payments and social harmony. For this reason a wage Freeze appears necessary and inevitable if the Government wants to slow the rate of inflation.

The tight anti-inflationary policy of the Government brought about by higher interest rates considerably reduced output growth and brought in recession. But slowing the rate of inflation by wage freeze should permit greater latitude for economic expansion. The decline in 1991-92 affected most major industries but the relatively better performance of the service sector and infrastructure industries other than petroleum sector suggests scope for a quick rebound in output if inflation is brought under effective control. This is also necessary to reduce the balance of payments gap and heavy external indebtedness which has lowered India's credit rating. Fiscal deficit cannot be reduced below 5 percent of GDP in the attempt to reduce the rate of inflation; restrictive monetary policy cannot be employed for the same purpose as it generates recessionary tendencies. Therefore, non fiscal-monetary measures are necessary to bring down the rate of inflation. The policy of wage freeze appears to be the only alternative.

# 84

## Renewal Fund

The Labour Union in the country are opposed to the New Industrial Policy (NIP) apprehending the generation of unemployment as a consequence of the expected closure of chronically sick units under the policy of liberalisation and the entry of multinationals to India. These actions of the Labour Unions are bound to disturb industrial harmony and to result in fall in industrial production, productivity and failure to achieve international competitiveness. If the NIP is to achieve its objective of accelerated industrial growth the co-operation of the Labour Unions is absolutely essential and this co-operation is forthcoming only when the labourers are assured that there would be no unemployment or, if any unemployment occurs, it would be alleviated at short notice.

The businessmen in the country looked for the highest profit margin whereas those in Korea worked on a nominal margin. The high margin of profits was possible in India because of the protection given to industry resulting in technological innovation being slow. It is in this context that liberalisation is to be understood. The criticism that liberalisation policy meant throwing open the flood gate to multinationals is unfounded. In Singapore—a small country with a population of hardly 2.5 million—there are 700 multinational companies but they are not able to dictate terms to local industries or to the Government. When this is the case how can any body apprehend danger to the Indian economy from the multinationals when India is a big country with 850 million people. Indian industries have the capacity to ensure quality of products and this would ensure their success and their survival. But in the process there may be some unemployment of a transitory nature.

It is in this context that the proposal of the Finance Minister made in Bombay on November 16, 1991 to create a Renewal Fund gains relevance. This Fund will be concerned with modernization of industries, particularly sick units, in the public and private sectors. This Fund will be set up with the financial assistance from the World Bank and the International Monetary Fund. The Renewal Fund is to be utilised only to improve industries while safeguarding the interests of the labourers who may face the prospect of unemployment due to closure of sick industrial units.

This proposal is remarkable for its ingenuity and thoughtfulness. India is an integral part of the global economy and as such it must participate effectively in the global trading system. This participation is possible if India takes steps at modernization and technological upgradation of its industries. India which is faced with a yawning trade gap has to achieve a significant breakthrough in export promotion. This India can hope to do only if the industries achieve price and quality competitiveness of their products. This is possible only if they are modernized and technologically upgraded. This exercise may result in closure of certain industries which are technologically backward throwing the labourers employed there out of jobs. This fear is genuine and this is the cause of labour unrest. It is here that the Renewal Fund has a part to play in allaying and apprehensions of labourers.

It is not known how many industries are facing closure and what the magnitude of the unemployment will be in the event of their closure. Many industries are already sick. With imminent technological upgradation many more will enter the list of sick industries. This requires a Renewal Fund of quite a large dimension. One suspects whether the international financial institutions are willing and prepared to provide financial assistance of the required magnitude. Assuming that the financial assistance of the required magnitude is forthcoming, the Government has to prescribe the modalities of its utilizations. Should the Renewal Fund be used to revive the sick units to pink health or should it be used to retrain and rehabilitate the labourers who become unemployed as a consequence of the closure of industries due to technological upgradation. Furthermore, the terms and conditions of assistance have to be specified. Before employing the Fund to revive sick industries the causes of sickness have to be identified and criteria of renewal have to be specified. It is alleged that several industries are deliberately rendered sick by their managers in order to get the benefit of subsidies. Assisting such industries to remain in business will not be of much help. It is possible that even after financial assistance is given they may be rendered sick again in order to get more assistance. Thus, they may turn out to be Oliver Twists situation will not solve the problems of sickness, closure and unemployment. If the international financial institutions which extend assistance find that their assistance is misutilised, they may stop this assistance aggravating the problems of sickness, closure and unemployment. The unemployment alleviation programme has, perforce, to be stopped halfway resulting in wastages of financial resources.

This calls for the creation of an agency to monitor the use of assistance by the industries so that the assistance is properly utilised for the good of the country. This agency should be vested with powers to examine the accounts of the industries concerned and to award punishment to those found guilty of deliberate misutilisation of the Fund. An agency of this type should be a necessary adjunct to the Renewal Fund. The Fund can be used in this way to assist accelerated industrial growth in the country. The Finance Minister deserves credit for formulating this ingenious proposal though he is yet to work out its operation details.

# 85

# The Dunkel Package and Indian Industry

The Dunkel package, in so far as it concerns industrial development in India, is one which does more harm than good to India. Already under the New Industrial Policy announced by the Government of India foreign capital with 51 percent equity participation is allowed to enter the Indian economy to set up industries and to start production. But under the Dunkel package India forfeits its right to limit equity participation for direct foreign investment. This means that equity participation may go above the 51 percent limit prescribed by the New Industrial policy.

Under the Dunkel package foreign entrepreneurs are free to enter any area of production. Naturally, they choose the area of high-tech consumer goods production in order to cater to the kit culture of a thin top stratum of Indian society. At present many small scale industries with great employment potential have been catering to the needs of consumers. The high-tech consumer goods with their sophistication and technological perfection will conquer the market now held by the small scale industries and spell their ruin generating unemployment in the process. However much the small scale industries may strive to remain in business, they will not be able to do so as the jaggernaut of foreign companies will crush them out of existence.

The foreign companies that will be set up in India will have to be given the following privileges:

- They will bring their raw materials.
- They will bring their own technical personnel and others to work in the industries.
- They will be free from the obligation to export goods outside India.

The consequences of each of these privileges to accord to the foreign companies will be analysed hereunder.

The foreign companies are free to import raw materials from the country of their origin in order to produce goods for the Indian market. This means that they will not purchase the raw materials available in India. As a result, the prices of raw materials will be depressed and their Indian producers will suffer production losses. Not being able to put up with these losses for more than a couple of years they will have to make an exit out of business. The labourers employed in these businesses will be unemployed and they add to the existing unemployed population, making nonsense of the country's unemployment alleviation programmes.

The foreign companies will be free to import labour from the country of their origin. There is a difference between importing highly specialized technical staff not available in India and importing the staff skilled, semi-skilled, unskilled and employing them in place of the locally available labour force. The purpose of any enterprise is to provide employment to the local labour force but under the Dunkel dispensation employment opportunities are created for the foreign labour force and not for the Indian labour force. This is to aggravate the problem of unemployment in India.

The foreign companies will be free from the obligation to export goods outside India. This means that they will confine themselves to the Indian market. They are free to import capital goods and raw materials from abroad by using India's foreign exchange resources but they will not contribute to them. This constitutes a strain on India's scarce foreign exchange reserves. Furthermore, these companies with their superior competitive advantage conquer the Indian market and drive out the domestic industries which are at present catering to it. This represents an economic conquest of India by the foreign companies reminiscent of the economic conquest of India by the British East India Company. As a result, India's economic sovereignty will be in jeopardy.

At present the United States of America is faced with a deep recession with demand for goods and the demand for labour falling. This is compounded by the fierce Japanese competition in the U.S.

market which is virtually conquered by Japanese companies. It is aware that the Indian market is vast and expanding. The free import of capital goods, raw materials and labour from it to run the companies in India will generate demand and help to ward off the recession. At the same time, there will be recession in the Indian economy with demand for Indian goods, demand for Indian raw materials and demand for Indian labour falling. There appears to be a clever design in the Dunkel package to make the USA boom at the expense of India.

The Indian economy is already in the grip of a recession, the rate of industrial growth being zero as averred by the Government of India Economic Survey for 1991-92. The acceptance of the Dunkel package would deepen the recession and make the lives of million of Indians miserable.

The Government of India has not yet given its definite views on the Dunkel package. It has only asked for time to examine the package. In the meanwhile, a Cabinet Committee headed by the Commerce Minister has been constituted to look into the Dunkel package. This committee has invited the leaders of political parties and the representatives of trade and industry for discussions. This is not enough. There is need for an open and in depth debate in the Parliament about the wider and long run implications of the Dunkel package for the Indian economy.

The expert teams of the National working group have made deep examination of the Dunkel package. The reports of these groups on TRIPS (Trade Related Intellectual Property Rights) and TRIMS (Trade Related Intellectual Property Measures) as well as trade in services and farm commodities show that the Dunkel package, when embodied into an international agreement, will subvert India's laws which protect India's interests and promote development and curtail the sovereign rights of India.

It is reassuring that the Hon'ble Minister of State for commerce, told the Lok Sabha on February 28,1992 that the matter would be placed before the Parliament for a debate before communicating the Government's views to the GATT on the Dunkel package. The debate will throw light on the consequences of accepting the package in the present form and suggest ways and means of modifying it in a manner that does not harm India's interests. It is in the light of the debate that India's views are to be formulated for communication to the Uruguay Round of multilateral negotiations.

# 86

## Liberalisation of Consumer Goods Imports

The rate of inflation for the week ending January 28, 1995 climbed to a new high of 11.55 percent. With all the other macro fundamentals evidencing a turnaround in the economy, as the cumulative result of reforms, the failure to bring down the rate of inflation to 6-7 percent level envisaged in the Union Budget for 1994-95 is extremely disquieting. The diagnosis of the factors causing inflation is incomplete. The argument that the inflation is caused by the deficiencies on the supply side of sugar, edible oils and cotton is flawed for the reason that the high rate of monetary expansion steaming from a large fiscal deficit is also an important factor. Apart from the supply factors it is the Government's fiscal policy or the slippage in fiscal corrections which had a decisive impact on the unmitigated inflationary trends. The money supply ($M_3$) has been literally surging during the current year since July 1994 at an average of 20 percent compared to 1993-94. Though there is a welcome contraction in the Reserve Bank credit to the Government the bank credit to the commercial sector has been 14.3 percent increase at the end of December 1994 compared to the previous year. What has triggered the expansion of money supply is the pronounced increase in foreign exchange assets of the banks from Rs.53,727 crore at the start of the fiscal year 1994-95 to Rs.70,103 crore at the end of December 1994. The indications are that the rate of accretion of capital inflows is coming down because of the new Euro-Issue Guidelines which obligate the companies raising funds in the European capital market to park them there until they actually require them in India. It must be noted that the damaging impact of their stock on prices has already become a fact to live with.

There is another factor to be reckoned with the trade deficit. The trade deficit of $ 2.5 billion will be reflected in an increase in the current account deficit. This is expected to rise to over $ 1.0 billion as compared to $ 400 million in 1993-94. This gap may not be reflected in a net reduction in foreign exchange reserves though it remains to be seen whether there will be capital outflows as a result of repatriation by foreign institutional investors or the disposal of underlying shares against GDRs in the companies concerned by the foreign holders. However, it is pointed out in industry circles that there will be inflows on account of direct investment in some directions and borrowing in foreign currencies may also be attempted by many enterprises requiring funds in foreign currencies, not necessarily in the form of GDRs. In this context the reduction of the current account deficit becomes of paramount importance. The revival of economic activity noticed in 1994-95 is likely to remain in evidence in 1995-96 also despite political uncertainties. There will be scope for raising industrial output in particular directions with the completion of modernization and expansion schemes by existing enterprises in many cases and the commencement of production by a large number of entirely new enterprises. To realise this goal, there will have to be a proper planning for boosting exports and avoiding inessential imports. As it is imperative that the current account deficit should be kept within reasonable limits a determined effort needs to be made to minimise the trade gap through necessary incentives to exports and for avoiding imports of products that can be provided by domestic suppliers.

The existence of the tyranny of twin deficits—the fiscal deficit and the trade deficit—has raised the question of the desirability of liberalisation of consumer goods imports. The Finance Minister has supported the idea of liberalisation of consumer goods imports in order to cap the rate of inflation emanating from the fiscal deficits and the accretion to forex reserves with their impact on monetary growth. The trade deficit that may be caused by a policy of import liberalisation constitutes no problem as the vast forex reserves can be drawn upon to pay for these imports. This will reduce the rate of inflation through the supply side and through the demand side. The imports will add to supply and overcome the supply deficiencies so necessary to reduce the rate of inflation. At the same time, the drawing down of forex reserves will lead to a reduction of monetary growth and check excess demand which is behind the price spurt. The argument advanced by the Finance Minister and by the Finance Ministry is logical and impeccable. At the same time it is argued by the Commerce Minister and by the Commerce Ministry that the policy of import liberalisation will hurt the domestic small scale industries which manufacture consumer goods for the domestic market as the consumers go in for sophisticated imports which they hold, are substitutes for domestic goods. The issue is highly debatable and the economic profession is sharply divided over it. The issue needs to be analysed objectively.

This question of liberalising the import of consumer goods by easing quantitative restrictions and reducing import duties has assumed significance on the eve of the presentation of the Union Budget for 1995-96. The issue has found more supporters than opposers. The recent World Bank paper: "India: Issues in Trade Reforms" has come out in support of a policy of import liberalisation. The focus of economic reforms is on the efficient allocation of resources and so, it is held that liberalisation of consumer goods imports will increase the efficiency in resource allocation and resource use. In a situation where the other sectors of the economy have undergone a process of liberalisation and globalisation allowing for foreign competition protection to domestic consumer goods industries has the effect of diverting resource from the efficient lines to the protected inefficient industries. The policy of import liberalisation will increase the supply of better goods and better quality goods and result in a more efficient allocation and use quality goods and result in a more efficient allocation and use of scarce resources. Allowing foreign investment to enter the domestic consumer goods industries instead of importing consumer goods from abroad will not be of much avail so long as the domestic industries are flourishing behind the protective wall. The production will be high cost and low quality. In this situation, the allocation of resources will be sub-optimal despite high profits for the entrepreneurs.

The policy of import liberalization leads to a rise in imports and thus a rise in the customs revenue which helps to reduce the fiscal deficit. At the same time the imposition of higher duties on imports will also result in larger revenue. The policy of import liberalisation will help to contain the inflationary forces let loose by the accretion of forex reserves through their monetary impact. But there are arguments against the policy of liberalising consumer goods imports. It is argued that the imports of consumer goods will be at the expense of essential imports of capital goods, raw materials and others necessary for producing goods for the exports considering the fact that a large part of the exports are import intensive. This is not to advocate liberalising all kinds of imports like potato chips and cosmetics which can be produced at home. The case is for liberalising the import of essential consumer goods of quality which cannot be produced in India. If this argument is considered valid in the case against liberalising the import of essential consumer goods becomes weak. In like manner the case against import liberalisation on the ground that it adversely affects the small scale industries is weak. The small scale industries cater to the needs of the lower middle class and poor segments of the population. The products are crude and unrefined and as such the affluent sections of the society, by and large, do not buy them. They prefer imported consumer goods of high quality and sophistication. Seen in this light the imported consumer goods cannot be considered to be substitutes for the goods produced by the domestic small scale industries. The imported consumer goods and the consumer goods produced by the small scale industries cater two different segments of society. For this reason, it is not correct to say that consumer goods imports hurt the small scale industries. If the case against the import of consumer goods is valid the case against the opening up of the other sectors of the economy is equally valid. In this sense the case for globalisation looks ridiculous and globalisation going ahead in the other sectors for good. Seen in this perspective the case for liberalising the imports of essentials consumer goods which do not affect the import of capital goods necessary to accelerate the growth of exports is firm, valid and unassailable.

The Finance Minister is more than right in advocating the policy of liberalising the import of essential consumer goods. This policy will not affect the import of capital goods so necessary to promote import intensive exports; this will also help to absorb the inflationary forces unleashed by the growth of forex reserves and by the supply shortages. It is hoped that the Finance Minister will rationalise the case for liberalising the import of consumer goods in the Union Budget for 1995- 96 to be presented on 15-3-1995.

# 87

## Import and Sale of Gold

The Government of India allowed the sale of confiscated silver quite successfully. In 1993 the customs officials sold silver of the order of 33 tonnes. The interesting point is that the sale of this entire quantity of silver took place in Bombay. In 1993 the customs officials confiscated 1.19 tonnes of gold, according to our estimate. It is also reported that they are having the stock of gold carried forward from last year. But the quantity of this stock is not known.

Even though the sale of confiscated gold is, in principle, the same as the sale of confiscated silver it is a debatable point whether the Reserve Bank of India will give its consent to such a sale of gold.

It must be remembered that in the past the practice was to transfer all the gold confiscated by the customs officials to the Reserve Bank of India. In 1993 a quantity of 3.75 tonnes of gold was transferred to Reserve Bank of India. The gold stock in the Reserve Bank of India at present is 356 tonnes. If the confiscated gold is transferred to the Reserve Bank it enhances the international confidence in the solvency of the Reserve Bank. Again the Reserve can get foreign exchange as it did in June-July 1991 by pledging its gold stock. For these reasons Reserve Bank is unlikely to agree to the sale of confiscated gold by the customs officials.

Nepal and Pakistan have liberalised the import of precious metals. It is expected that India may also liberalise the import of Gold. A Nepalese citizen who spends atleast a month abroad is allowed to bring in to the country 10 kg of gold and 150 kg of silver. The customs duty to be levied on the import of these precious metals is 5%. But it is incumbent on the part of the individual who bring these metals to Nepal to declare the source of these metals and mode of financing their purchase. In like manner Pakistan which has liberalised the import of precious metals has reduced the customs duty from 5% to 3%. Furthermore, the tax on the transactions in gold is abolished.

In view of the policy adopted by the neighbouring countries the Government of India will do well to liberalise the import of precious metals and raise the gold import from 5 kg to 10 kg and the silver import from 100 kg to 150 kg. At the same time the Government can raise the duration of stay abroad above 6 months and reduce the customs duty on gold and silver imported.

The Reserve Bank of India, at present, is in possession of 356 tonnes of gold. If it is considered necessary, it can be raised to 400 tonnes of gold which will be more than enough to meet any emerging situation. Any import of gold after the target of 400 tonnes of gold is reached can be allowed to be sold in the market. This will have the following advantages:

- As the purchase of gold in India is to be financed in rupees, the rupee holding in the hands of the gold purchasers will decline and this will exercise an anti-inflationary influence.
- This will check smuggling of gold into India
- This will reduce the domestic price of gold
- Whenever the Reserve Bank of India needs gold, it can issue gold bonds and obtain gold which can be put to any use it likes. After the gold bonds mature, the holder of the bonds can surrender them to the Reserve Bank and get his gold back with interest; if the Reserve Bank needs gold for further term it can retire the old gold bonds and issue fresh bonds in their place.
- The possession of gold will lend strength and stability to the rupee and enhance international confidence.

It may be argued that those who bring gold will purchase it abroad by using foreign currency in which case the flow of foreign exchange into India will stop and India will get gold instead. But if the gold import is not allowed, there is no guarantee that the foreign exchange will flow in for they may purchase expensive consumer durables and bring them to India. This argument may be countered by the argument that if heavy import duty is levied on the import of these articles they will have no incentive to import them. In this case, they may keep their foreign exchange in the Bank of the Countries where they earned them. This will swell their bank balances abroad but will not increase the flow of foreign exchange into the country nor will it increase the import of gold. In view of these possibilities, it is necessary to allow the import of gold into the country. The chances of the gold value appreciating in future will give them an added incentive to import gold. It behoves the Finance Minister to liberalise the import of gold and to allow for its sale in India.

# 88

# Is the Keyesian Remedy of a Free Rupee Suited to Domestic Instability?

Ordinarily, there is a choice between exchange rate stability and domestic price stability. In the context of the continuing upsurge of foreign exchange reserves causing monetary expansion and domestic inflation, this has assumed special significance. Some economists and financial journalists have cited the great authority of Lord Keynes to support the case for a free rupee in order to maintain domestic price stability. But the circumstances under which Lord Keynes advocated a sacrifice of exchange rate stability for the sake of domestic price stability are different from the circumstances obtaining in the Indian economy and in the global economy in general.

Under the traditional gold standard the exchange rate was stable allowed to move within the narrow band set by the gold points. The stability of the exchange rate was maintained at the sacrifice of domestic stability. The supply of money was determined by the gold flows. An inflow of gold caused by a favourable balance of payments would cause monetary expansion; conversely an outflow of gold caused by an infavourable balance of payments would cause monetary contraction. In the former case, there would be inflation and in the latter case there would be deflation. But the exchange rate remained stable moving only within the gold points. Thus under the gold standard domestic stability was sacrificed for exchange rate stability. But while a gold inflow caused monetary expansion and generated inflation, a gold outflow was not allowed to effect monetary contraction and deflation. This made Mr. Joan Robinson say that the gold standard has a "built-in inflationary bias". For this reason Lord Keynes characterized the gold standard as "a barbarous relic". His preference for domestic price stability was coloured by the damage done to it by the gold standard which maintained exchange rate stability.

In 1926 Indian opinion sought to move away from a currency based on the value of silver to one based on the value of gold. It was considered desirable to have gold rather than silver as backing for the Indian rupee. Though the arguments are not relevant today, there was one aspect which is germane to the present situation; the choice between domestic price stability and the stability of the exchange rates.

In March 1926 when the Royal Commission on Indian Currency and Finance set to discuss the question of the rupee exchange rate Sri Purushotamdas Thakurdas put the following question to Lord Keynes:

"Can you tell me what you think is the ideal system of currency for India in the circumstances in which you know India is at present?"

Lord Keynes' answer was the following:

"I think a system like the present in which the stability of the exchange is aimed at in normal circumstances but in which India is free to depart from the present level of exchange if it is in the interests of the internal stability of prices for her to do so. I would not have her allowed the question of the rate of exchange to overbear every other object, but I think she should have the liberty to have a different exchange from the present one if the maintenance of the present exchange would cause internal prices to rise and fall to a marked extent."

Keynes clarified this argument in his Memorandum to the Royal Commission: "stability of internal prices in India is, in my opinion, much more important than stability of foreign exchange's. He wanted India to avoid the worst effects of booms and depressions after the First World War by allowing the rupee exchange rate to fluctuate as this would allow her to maintain internal price stability. During the boom of 1919-20 when world prices soared, the rupee was allowed to appreciate. In consequence domestic prices rose by 12 percent as compared to a 29 percent rise in British prices. In the following year when world prices collapsed the rupee was allowed to depreciate and Indian prices fell only by 16 percent in comparison with a 50 percent rise in British prices.

What is said above is a misreading of the economic history of the times. The Indian rupee was tied to sterling and it could not move up and down independently. The 1920s and 1930s were years of violent exchange rate changes. There was post-war inflation in the western world and the rates of inflation were different for different countries. The determination of exchange rates was a difficult problem. In order to explain the determination of exchange Gustal Cassel propounded the purchasing power parity principle. According to this principle, the new exchange rate would be equal to the old rate multiplied by the quotient of the degrees of inflation in the countries concerned. This was also a period of inflammatory capital movements across national borders disrupting exchange rates and upsetting domestic economic stability. The Western World found the exchange rate mechanism in these years highly disturbing to economic stability. Those who assembled at Bretten Woods to establish the Brettonwoods Twins opted for stable exchange rates. They designed the "adjustable peg" in the area of exchange rates. The countries suffering from "fundamental disequilibrium" could apply for permission to devalue their currencies to the extent required but they could not act unilaterally. The I.M.F would permit the countries to devalue only after it was satisfied that the country concerned had a fundamental disequilibrium which had to be corrected by means of devaluation.

On 18.09.1949 the Pound sterling act devalued with intent to remedy the balance of payments disequilibrium, on 19.07.1949 the Indian rupee was devalued by the same percentage as Pound sterling. The rupee was devalued in June 1966. It was devalued in July 1991. India was reluctant to devalue the rupee as it would enhance the value of external debt. In July 1991 the rupee was devalued in order to remedy the balance of payments deficit to close which India did not have sufficient foreign exchange reserves and it had to pledge its gold reserves and arrange for emergency financing. But devaluation did not have the intended effect immediately as the "J- Curve Effect" was in operation. There were other factors which did not allow devaluation to have its full effect on the trade balance for the conditions necessary for the success of devaluation did not exist. These conditions are: (a) the import demand elasticities should be greater than unity; (b) there should be no rise in the budget deficit, (c) wages should remain constant. No estimates of import demand elasticities have been made in India but it is a fair presumption that they are not greater than unity. Budget deficits were rising and under the impact of inflation the wage rates were also rising. In these circumstances, the price effect of devaluation on the demand effect generated by the rising budget deficits and rising wage rates. The Cambridge Economic Policy Group (CEPG) posits a direct relationship between budget deficits and balance of payments deficits. This relationship is valid in the case of India as my own researches have so conclusively demonstrated. But the effect of devaluation was an enhancement of the burden of external debt in proportion to the degree of devaluation. It was this factor which made the authorities think twice before undertaking devaluation.

Is the present exchange rate the cause of on-going inflation?

There are three most important reasons for inflation today: (a) the recent rise in the prices of several commodities like foodgrains and steel; (b) the budget deficit which keeps coming back with nagging regularity every year and (c) very high level of foreign exchange holdings which has caused a sharp increase in the supply of money. The prices of several commodities including food articles like rice and wheat were raised to provide minimum support prices for the farmers. The rise in the cost of production of steel led to a rise in its price. These added to the rate of inflation. The financial year 1993-94 ended with a budget deficit of Rs. 9000 crore. But that was in end March 1994. The deficit was much larger during a greater part of the year crossing Rs. 21,000 crore in September, 1993. For 1994-95 the Finance Minister had announced that the deficit, broadly defined as the borrowing from the Reserve Bank will be limited to Rs. 6000 crore and at no time will it be allowed to go above Rs. 10,000 crore for more than 10 days. The position has been generally maintained since then. As of May 13, 1994 the net Reserve Bank credit to the Government stood at Rs. 10,366 crore Rs. 840 crore less than the level at the same time in 1993.

The factor causing concern to the Government is not so much the budget deficit as the fiscal deficit which is a more comprehensive indicator of the health of Government finances. An increase in the fiscal deficit has a bearing on future Government expenditure because of higher repayment liabilities and interest payments. The importance of this indicator is such that today just the interest obligation on the past borrowings make up 35 percent of the centre's revenue expenditure. Though the direct budget deficit i.e., Government borrowing from the Reserve Bank has been kept within stated limits, the fiscal deficit has been increasing. Against the target of 4.7 percent of the GDP for 1993-94 the actual fiscal deficit for the year rose to 7.3 percent of GDP. This has been attributed to burgeoning Government expenditure and to lower revenues due to sluggish performance of the industrial sector. This year also the position is very serious because though the borrowings from the Reserve Bank have been contained there has been a sharp rise in the Government borrowing from the commercial banks. Statistics for April 1994 show that there has been a massive increase of Rs. 9,492 crore in the credit released by the commercial banks to the Government. The magnitude of this increase can be judged from the fact that the total credit from commercial banks to the government during the whole of 1993-94 was Rs. 27,000 crore. During April 1993 there was a decline of Rs. 235 crore in the commercial banks credit to the Government which worked out to a percentage reduction of 0.3. In comparison was 9.1 percent in April 1994. Official figures are not available for the subsequent period. In view of this the Centre's claim to have contained the budget deficit lacks relevance since it has not been able to curtail expenditure much. The World Bank has not accepted the inclusion of the proceeds of the sale of public sector equity as a deficit reducing measure because income from the sale of assets cannot be constructed to be part of current revenue. But the Centre has no choice in the matter. Even during 1994-95 it has planned to sell Rs. 5000 crore worth of public sector equity to help to meet the deficit.

This and the expected rise in revenues as industrial growth hikes up will be the two important factors in containing the budget deficit. But one has to wait and watch keeping one's fingers crossed.

There is a massive inflow of capital into the Reserve Bank's vaults. The Reserve Bank of India intervenes in the foreign exchange market to prop up the sagging dollar and to prevent the appreciation of the rupee. The forex reserves which were just $1.0 billion have now crossed the $ 17 billion mark. They are funds sent by the Foreign Institutional Investors (FIIs), direct foreign investors and the NRIs. A considerable part of this capital inflow is volatile being interest sensitive. These forex reserves have led to a rise in monetary growth of the order of 18 percent per annum. This undoubtedly is a source of inflation. But if the weights are assigned to the three factors causing inflation foreign exchange reserves get the lowest weight.

Those who are against a stable exchange rate regime, considering it to be a source of domestic instability advocate a free exchange rate following the logic of Lord Keynes. In the present context a free exchange rate regime emerges if the Reserves Bank of India abstains from intervening in the foreign exchange market. This means that in the face of massive inflow of capital abstaining from intervention will lead to an appreciation of the Indian rupee. It is admitted that an exchange rate appreciation encourages imports and discourages exports and generates and widens the trade gap. It is true that appreciation makes the imports of capital goods, raw materials, and intermediates which are essential inputs into exports cheap and expands the volume of import-intensive exports. This has to be weighted against the other factors causing an enlargement of the trade gap.

Normally a currency is devalued to a balance of payments deficit. Conversely a currency is upvalued to correct a balance of payments surplus. India has a balance of payments deficit. In this situation appreciation is not the right remedy. It may reduce the inflow of dollars or/and cause an outflow of the dollars in the vaults of the Reserve Bank of India and thus cause a depletion of the stock of forex reserves and thus reduce the rate of monetary growth which is supportive of inflation which was governed by the balance of payments and the supply of money governed the price level. A rise in money supply caused a rise in the price level in the same proportion as per the mechanism underlying the Classical Quantity Theory of Money. This is no longer the case at present.

Under the gold standard a balance of payments deficit would be the occasion for a rise in the domestic rate of interest. As the capital flows were interest-sensitive capital would flow in and this would be used to meet the payment deficit. This inflow would not be inflationary. Even if the rupee is appreciated and the inflow of foreign exchange reserve is abated there will not be let up in the rate of inflation caused as it is by more fundamental factors, namely, hikes in the prices of several commodities and the fiscal deficit. This means that even if rupee is made free and is allowed to appreciate as Lord Keynes advocated nearly 70 years ago, there will not be domestic stability. In the days of the gold standard the supply of money would be expansionary, one of the reasons for the inflow of capital into India is the high interest rate offered in India. In the developed countries the rate of interest varies between 3 percent and 9 percent. But in India it is as high as 15 percent. This is an attraction for foreign capital. If the interest rate is reduced the interest-sensitive capital leaves the country and reduces the stock of forex reserves and its inflationary potential. A reduction in inflation will have favourable effect on the balance of payments. A low interest rate will reduce cost inflation though it may generate demand inflation. But the anti-inflationary effect of reduced stock of forex reserve will more than offset the inflationary effect of a low interest rate. In view of this appreciation which is considered to be a remedy for a trade surplus is not the remedy for a trade deficit. If anything it will make the trade deficit worse. Even the freely floating exchange rate is not ideal for India for by generating destabilising expectations it further disturbs domestic economic stability.

The international economic and financial relationships at the time when Keynes wrote were not as complex as they are today. The remedy considered good for the beginning of the 20th century is not good at the end of the century. The case for fixed exchange rate is strong at present. In the event of a balance of payments deficit due to fundamental disequilibrium the rupee can well be devalued to the extent necessary; conversely, in the event of a balance of payments surplus the rupee can be appreciated to the extent necessary. When domestic instability is caused by other more fundamental factors appreciation of the rupee or a freely moving exchange rate is not the remedy. In fact, a freely moving exchange rate may turn out to be an unstable exchange rate. It would therefore be hazardous to revert to the Keynesian remedy which was efficacious at the beginning of the present century. The remedy for domestic instability lies elsewhere and not in the exchange rate. What is necessary is to hold in check commodity prices and the fiscal deficit.

# 89

## Half Hearted Approach to Financial Sector Reforms

In June 1991 the economic situation was dismal indeed. Inflation was raging at the rate of 17 percent ; the balance of payments was in a state of crisis. Industrial stagnation threatened to slow down economic growth. The financial sector was in doldrums. The banks were labouring under capital inadequacy. Some of them were sick or unviable and their profitability was very low. The administrative expenses were high and rising. The bank employees were militant in their demand for higher wages and perquisites. The Government was convinced of the imperative need to reform the financial system. It therefore appointed the Narasimham Committee on Financial Sector Reform. This Committee submitted its report over a year ago making far reaching reforms of the financial sector. Though the Government sounded euphoric about implementing these reform measures, it did not do it. It only hesitated. In the meanwhile the bank employees who did not find these reforms to their advantage threatened to stage nation-wide demonstrations protesting against these reforms. The Government obviously did not want to precipitate the matters. The Narasimham Committee Report was, therefore, kept in abeyance. The Securities Scam involving over Rs.5000 crore (some say over 10000 crore) forced the Government to take a serious look at the financial sector and to consider implementing the reforms.

Given the magnitude of the securities scandal the Finance Minister could hardly have been expected to have the banking system exposed to all the risks that have surfaced in the light of the various irregularities committed in securites transactions. In his budget speech the Finance Minister categorically stated that

"Exports must be made a truly high priority national endeavour so that we can move as quickly as possible to control the balance of payments without the need for confined exceptional financing from abroad. This is the only meaningful route to self reliance". How can self reliance be achieved? It is possible only when Indian industries are able to satisfy domestic requirements. For this, the industrial sector needs adequate credit facilities with reasonable rates of interest. The reduction of SLR from 36 to 25 percent over a period of three years announced in the budget speech represents the Government's partial acceptance of responsibility for providing for bad and doubtful advances of banks and proposal for banks tapping the capital market as a step towards capital adequacy were entirely in order. These measures might have been postponed but for the securities scam and the Government might have sat on the Narasimham Committee Report for a little longer if the scam of a grave magnitude had not erupted, but with a problem exposure of over Rs. 5000 crore as estimated by the JPC the expectation was that the Finance Minister would address himself at the earliest opportunity to a strategy that would put the banks on a more orderly course than what the scam suggested.

The factor mainly responsible for the inadequacy of credit for the commercial sector is that the levels of SLR and CRR have been progressively increased over the past several years. In the case of SLR this happened because of the Government's desire to mobilize even larger resources through the market borrowings in support of Central and State budget. In the case of the CRR this happened because of the need to counter the expansionary impact of large budget deficits on the supply of money. These two together preempted a large part of bank resources into low income. Earning assets thus reducing bank profitability and pressurizing banks to charge high interest rates on their commercial advances. The high interest rates charged on the corporate sector make them raise funds from the market directly by paying higher rates than the ones which the banks can offer. This makes the banks to take recourse to disintermediation. The high SLR and CRR are in effect a tax on financial saving the banking system and helps to direct flows into markets where this tax does not apply. Therefore, it appeared imperative to change the financial system to make it more healthy. For this reason, the Government had decided to reduce the SLR and the CRR.

In order to release a larger volume of resources for commercial sector lending the Finance Minister announced a further reduction in SLR to 25 percent from an average level of 36 percent in a phased manner. The decision has to be formally announced by the Reserve Bank of India later. Even so, this reduction will create a positive impact in the minds of the entrepreneurs and bankers. It is expected that this will have a favourable impact on production.

Even then some questions remain. While the proposed reduction in the SLR should normally contribute to a weakening of the base that was responsible for the strains on the banking system, the Government was under pressure to depend on the banking sector. Even at 25 percent the SLR will impose a heavy burden on banks. Moreover, as the burden of disinvestment in public sector equity is largely passed on to them, they will have to operate in tight conditions.

Another step towards financial sector reform is the reduction in the bank lending rate and the deposit rate by the percentage point in each case—from 18 percent to 17 percent in the former case and from 12 percent to 11 percent in the latercase. The reduction in the deposit rate will slow down the rate of deposit mobilization and will divert deposits to the speculative activity in the real estate sector and gold. Further, the banking system will suffer a loss of viability following a cut in the minimum lending rate though it may be necessary to assist the industries hit by the recession. The possibility of loss to be incurred by the banks because of the reduction in the lending rate and the deposit rate was not of any concern for the finance minister. He justified the reduction in the two rates of interest on the ground that the rate of inflation had come down. It is the monetary return on investment that matters in respect of saving and investment. The Fund-Bank combine may not like administered interest rates and the borrowers will always complain about the interest rate being at uneconomic levels. But when the banks find that the deposits are not rising and resources for lending are not easily available, the reduction of deposit and lending rates appears indiscreet. The securities scam not only revealed "certain weaknesses" as the Finance Minister put it but also reflected the strains on the banking system caused by the Government policies with regard to SLR, interest rates and credit deployment. However, these weaknesses will remain as a result of the reduction of the deposit rate and the lending rate.

The major part of the financial sector reform concerns the permission given to banks to raise equity from the public—the case of privatization to a certain extent. The Narasimham committee went into the question of capital adequacy and provision for bad and doubtful advances. The Finance Minister in his budget speech noted:

"A major reform initiated last year was the introduction of new norms for income recognition, and providing for bad debts and the presumption of new capital adequacy requirements in line with internationally accepted Basle Committee norms. The new norms will ensure that the books of the banks will reflect their financial position more accurately and in accordance with internationally accepted accounting practices. These changes will improve our ability to evaluate the performance of the banks and will also make for more effective bank supervision.

" Because of the new norms, however, banks will have to make large provisions amounting to over Rs. 10,000 crore for bad and doubtful advances in their portfolios. As the provisioning norms are being introduced in two stages the first impact will be felt in the year ending 31, March 1993, with a further impact next year. The resulting losses will eat into the capital of the banks which is already inadequate given the new capital adequacy norms. In order to protect the viability and financial health of the Indian banking system. I am making provision for large capital contribution of Rs. 5700 crore to the nationalized banks in 1993-94 to meet the gap crossed by application of the fist stage of the provisioning norms".

The Government has decided to retain majority ownership of the nationalized banks while allowing the banks to mobilize funds in the form of equity from the public. As prescribed by the Reserve Bank of India the banks have to maintain a provision for bad debts under the new norms of upto Rs. 10,000 crore. This is to be implemented in the stages and first stage is ending on March 31st, 1993. If banks are to make provisions for bad debts they must also be in a position to realize the security on their bad debts. But at present the legal processes for realizing bad debts is for tribunals to enforce legal action by the banks regarding recoveries. In future unless the banks make their securities more flexible to meet their bad debts injecting any amount of money by the Government will remain as unfinished task.

In the context of the securities scam, the Reserve Bank of India is going to set up a new supervisory board for looking after the various functions of the commercial banks. The budget pays due attention to the functioning of the capital market which is part of the financial sector. The Government has made it possible for the capital market to mobilize large funds for investment. The Securities and Exchange Board of India Act has been amended to give more powers to the SEBI which is the watch dog of capital market operations. The provision for Rs. 5700 crore might match the exposure as calculated by the JPC but what worried the Finance Minister was its budgetary implications. For this reason he has decided that the State Bank of India and other nationalized banks should tap the capital market. How are these requirements to be met ? One bank may contribute to the equity of another and the foreign banks also may play some part in it. But when the market outside the bank is reluctant to take Government securities the threat of another scam is real when banks go to the market for meeting the capital adequacy norms.

A major reform envisaged in the budget speech is the full convertibility of the rupee on current account. Under the new dispensation all exporters and foreign exchange earners including the Indian workers abroad will be allowed to convert all their earnings at the market rate exchange. The Government expects it to give a boost to exports and will encourage the inflow of foreign exchange into official channels.

The risks inherent in the abolition of the dual exchange rate will become evident in the near future. Under full convertibility the value of the rupee will be determined by four factors: the growth of exports compared to the growth of imports, the value of the rupee in the havala (illegal) market, inflation rate and the foreign exchange reserves. Even with this incentive it is difficult to see how exports can register a fourfold growth of 12-16 percent a year from the 3-4 percent registered between April and December 1992. A low export growth will further widen the trade deficit as import growth can be expected to surge consequent on the reduction of customs duties. A widening of the trade deficit will tend to depreciate the rupee further. Of course, this can be controlled by a larger inflow of remittances through the legal channels. Without an appreciable increases in remittances there is little covered. This means that with an excess demand for dollars the value of the rupee will drop. A drop in the value of the rupee may be of some advantage to exporters. At the same time, it will make imports more expensive and will push up the rate of inflation. This will make Indian exports more on domestic inflation cannot be discounted. India's dependence on oil imports is increasing every year and all such imports will have to be financed at the market rate exchange compared to 1992-1993. When, under partial of convertibility dispensation they were purchased at the official rate. A depreciation of the rupee and a finishing up of a oil prices which is likely will give a self sustaining upward momentum to inflation. In this situation the value of the rupee can be held up by intervention by the Reserve Bank of India. But its ability to do so depends on the foreign exchange reserves in its possession. This is where the Government's plans to seek $ 2.5 - $ 3 billion a year of exceptional financing come in. The loans from the International Monetary Fund and the World Bank will provide the necessary cushion. But this exceptional financing facility was supposed to cover the trade deficit not support the value of the rupee. If exports do not increase as expected the country has to countenance a reversal of the recent trend in the rate of inflation.

The financial sector reforms extend to the various fields like to private sector banks, the foreign financial institutions, private financial companies, development banking institutions and so on. The operation of certain private sector banks wanted a level playing field in the context of the entry of the foreign banks into the financial sector. But the Finance Minister in his address to the members of the Indian Bankers' Association in Delhi on Saturday March 13, 1993 stated that the operation of certain private and foreign banks weakened their case for a level playing field for all banks. He wanted them to make extra efforts to demonstrate that they would operate in conformity with the rules of the country. He lamented the loan of credibility of the banking system and urged the Indian Banks' Association (IBA) to restore the credibility of the banking system and regain public confidence. He said; "collectively we have a responsibility to develop a banking system which is sound, viable and deeply committed to our social and economic goals". He favoured strategic scrutiny by the RBI and the Government in place of detailed scrutiny. He directed the banks to rise to international standards to fulfill the tasks, which are socially necessary and economically profitable.

In recent years the quality of consumer service is on the decline and it is no match to that rendered by foreign banks. He wanted the IBA to conduct public opinion surveys about the quality of banking service in order to rate them in terms of the quality of customer service. The improvement of the quality of customer service is necessary in order to encourage the inflow of foreign remittances under full convertibility dispensation. This requires the improvement of work technology which is possible by developing computerized and fully automatic branches. To start with he recommends the starting of 200 such branches. He also cautioned the banks against entering into unrealistic wage settlements which the banks are unable to meet.

Despite the far reaching nature of the financial sector reforms envisaged by the Finance Minister in his Budget speech (1993-94) his announcements regarding the financial sector can be said to be timid. The most important announcement viz., the setting up of special tribunals to ensure speedy disposal of civil suits for recoveries of banks dues is a measure which was recommended by the Narasimham Committee and has been in cold storage for some time. Given the urgency of the matter and the impact it would have on bank balance sheets all that has been achieved is a mere statement of intent to set up the tribunals. This measure should not have been delayed for so long. The setting up of the board for financial supervision has also been announced. The Narasimham Committee which recommended such a board had emphasized that it should be autonomous. What the nature and the structure of the board would be is not made clear. The decision to contribute Rs. 5700 crore towards the capital of capital adequacy norms in 1993-94 will merely delay the day of reckoning for some banks. The reduction in the lending and deposit rates by 1 percent each will not be of more than marginal significance considering the fact that the change in the normal lending rate by 1 percent has been offset by the decline the rate of inflation leaving the real interest rate either constant or higher than before. Admittedly, many private sector banks are allowed to be set up but their operations are too much restricted. The SLR and CRR have been reduced but there is no significant augmentation of the lendable resources of the banks. Nothing is said above winding up of the banking division in the Ministry of Finance. The same is the case with the structural changes like free recruitment policy, exit policy, computerization of banking services. The Government, of course, realizes that divestment of 49 percent of equity or pumping of Rs. 5700 crore worth of capital would not lead to a change in the functioning of banks. The Government claims that "specific commitments will be required from each bank to ensure that their future management practices ensure a high level of portfolio quality so that the earlier problem does not recur" but it is forgotten that the government itself is, in large measure, to blame for the ills of the country's banking system what with loan melas, loan waiver schemes and directed credit to priority sectors at concessional interest rates. It is true that the profitability of the banks has declined and some of them are sick or unviable but profitability cannot be improved unless the banks are free to determine their own policies including credit policy, pricing policy, recruitment policy. These structural reforms are to implemented with no loss of time. If this is not done the banks will sink deeper into the red with grave consequences for the financial system and serious results for the Government as the owner of banks.

The Narasimham Committee recommendations for financial sector reform constitute a coherent package. To be able to realize their maximum effectiveness they must be implemented together as they are a mutually interdependent set. To pick and choose those which are politically convenient to implement would not come to grips with the long standing problems plaguing the Indian financial sector. The financial sector has come of age and it can sustain the reforms. India is moving fast on the road to a market economy. The benefits of a market economy can be reaped by integration of the Indian economy with the global economy. The Narasimham Committee reform package are intended to achieve financial integration. Financial integration is possible only with a wholehearted implementation of these reform measures together. They cannot be implemented part by part. The Finance Minister will do well to implement them together (bearing the one relating to directed credit which can be implemented in a slow and phased manner).

The bank employees are out to hold the banking system to ransom. They enforce unreasonable wage demands unmindful of the low profitability of the banks and their own productivity. They are also opposed to computerization of banking operators under the apprehension that they would be rendered jobless. Unless the banking operations are computerized and the customer service is improved, the customers will shift to the foreign banks equipped with sophisticated operational techniques. The Indian banks will thereby lose in the process. Therefore, computerization of banking operation should be enforced. The Government cannot go by the whims and fancies of the employees of banks. There should be an exit policy in respect of sick and unviable banks with provision for retrenched labourers being retained and redeployed. These issues cannot be deferred. When India is faced with international competition it must work with speed and dispatch. India can no longer afford to perpetuate inefficiency.

# 90

## India's Forex Reserves and the Trade Deficit

India's balance of payments scenario is anything but encouraging. But the distress is held at bay by the comfortable forex reserve position. The Commerce Minister projected an export growth of 25 percent for 1994-95. But in actual fact exports are slated to lag behind the high growth of 20 percent of 1993-94. In April-May 1994 export growth plummeted to just over 9 percent, The rise in farm exports which contributed to high overall exports in 1993-94 can hardly be sustained. There is no building up of a range of agricultural surpluses in a variety of commodities. At the same time domestic demand is picking up rapidly. There is perceptible improvement in the utilization of manufacturing capacity. The increase in output is absorbed by the domestic market with a consequent decline in exports. The economic reform measures aim at making the domestic market attractive to foreign direct investment. The export of steel has also fallen because of the lure of the domestic market. In the wake of the devaluation of the rupee there was a rise in exports and this increased the rupee receipts from exports. But the exports have now lost their advantage because of the rise in domestic costs under the impact of the rising rate of inflation.

In April-May 1994 imports rose by 12 percent over the same period in 1993. In 1993-94 import growth was just 7 percent. Imports are now rising because of lower import duties, dumping by foreign suppliers and rising domestic demand under the impact of fiscal deficit. This, of course, will increase Government revenues from customs duties. The Government also has resorted to a large commodity imports, edible oil, sugar and cotton to bring down their high domestic prices. The cost of imported crude and oil products has also tended to move up.

As a consequence accelerating imports and sluggish export growth the trade deficit will widen. This scenario will not cause any alarm as India has a comfortable foreign exchange position. In fact, a large trade deficit will bring down the forex reserves which will siphon some of the excess supply of rupees that is driving up the supply of money which is a source of inflationary pressure. Thus, the enlargement of trade deficit will help to reduce the supply of money and ease the monetary pressure on prices. The excess of imports is thus used to counter the inflationary effects of fiscal deficits. The slowing down of exports reflects a rapid loss of competitiveness.

The remedy for inflation is the achievement of an excess of savings over investment or an excess of imports over exports, or an excess of tax revenue over expenditure. They are all leakages which help to stem the tide of inflation. In the Indian context there is an excess of investment over savings; there is also an excess of Government expenditure over tax revenue. These two variables are pro-inflationary. The excess of imports over exports representing a foreign leakage helps to hold down the rate of inflation—the price effect—and to hold down the rate of monetary growth—the monetary effect. In the instant case of India the trade deficit has a contractive price effect and a interactive monetary effect. There is a catch here. The use of forex reserves may help to hold down the rate of monetary growth and the rate of inflation. But the forex reserves are not the ones earned by India through our excess of exports over imports. They are resources lent by the multilateral financial institutions and the foreign investors. If the forex reserves are used to meet the trade deficit and if, after this, the foreign lenders recall their funds, India will be in trouble. Though the surge of imports leads to rise in customs revenue and helps to reduce the fiscal deficit and also reduces the rate of monetary growth, it has an unwelcome side effect the danger of default on external loans. In view of this, it is dangerous to be euphoric about the contractive price effect and monetary effect of the trade deficit. Efforts are to be made to achieve the export target and also to use the forex reserves to repay external debt and to accept only those inflows of capital which will remain in India for a specified period. This means that volatile capital should not be allowed to enter India for volatility of capital contains the danger of sudden withdrawal necessitating fresh borrowing to meet this withdrawal. External solvency is necessary and it has to be achieved by promoting exports to the targeted limit. This requires the restriction on domestic demand for goods in order to increase the exportable volume.

# 91

## The White Paper on India's External Debt

Soon after the adjournment of the winter session of the parliament on December 22, 1995 the Finance Ministry brought at the "White Paper on External Debt" highlighting the growth of external indebtedness and assuring the nation that it is not or cause for concern. According to it, the external debt at the end of March 1995 was $ 9904 crore. In just one year it increased by $ 634. At the end of 1991 it was $ 716 crore. In the following year it jumped to $ 9268 crore. Such a rapid growth of external debt should ordinarily cause concern. But the Government is of the view that this is not a cause for concern at all. The next Government, whatever its political complexion, has to inherit this debt. When the Britishers were in power the subject of external debt was the exciting talk of the political leaders fighting for India's Independence. It was hoped that with the dawn of independence the burden of external debt would decline. But what is happening is contrary to what was expected. It is held in the theory of external debt that it represents an inter-temporal transfer of resources from the future to the present generation unless at the same time, the debt is used to create productive assets which will benefit the future generation and compensate it for the burden of debt it bears.

If external debt is invested productively and if the debt can be repaid through the increment of income from it, the growth of debt does not cause any anxiety for the debt, in this case, is self liquidating. However, if new debt is contracted in order to repay an old debt and if a situation emerges where the debt cannot be repaid at all the country enters the debt trap. Many Latin American countries have reached this stage. In India we have reached a stage where we have to consider seriously whether India is at the doorstep of the debt trap.

The white paper assures the nation that there is no danger of India reaching or having reached that stage. The review of debt statistics holds out the threat of the stage having been reached. But in fact it is claimed that stage is not reached. All that is necessary is to take precautions against that stage being reached. The entire debt has to be viewed against the background of the income, Viewed in this context there is no danger of India defaulting on either debt repayment or interest payment. It is held by the Government that the debt service ratio is not unsatisfactory. We have to assess the quantum of debt repayment and interest payment and its ratio to our external receipts. This ratio is at present far outside the danger zone. The fact of the Latin American countries having reached this stage can be seen from the debt statistics of those countries. The white paper claims that during the decade of the 1990s this ratio will decline. This was 33.5 percent in 1990-91 but by 1994-95 it declined to 26.7 percent. But this is not the case with the other debt ridden countries. Their debt services ratio has been rising. That such a situation will not arise in the case of India is the stand taken by the white paper.

However, it can be stated that the other debt ridden countries have managed their debt scenario far better than India. In 1991 India was the fourth bigger borrower. By the end of 1993 it moved to the status of the third biggest borrower. The debt burden experienced by India during these two years was not experienced by the other countries. The Government is of the view that as the dollar declined in terms of pound sterling, D-Mark, Japanese yen the Indian debt in terms of the US dollars increased. Even so, it is to be regarded as debt and the burden has to be regarded as the debt burden. As the external value of the dollar declined in terms of the other currencies, its value should decline in terms of the Indian rupee also. However this did not happen. The US dollars which declined in terms of the other currencies. Its value should decline in terms of Indian rupee also. This means that the rupee has depreciated. It is for this reason that in terms of the dollar India's debt burden has increased. According to the Economic Survey published by the Government in March 1995, in the first half of

1994-95 India's external debt had declined. But, of the subsequent rise in debt by $ 600 crore, 88 percent was due to the decline in the external value of the US dollar in terms of other strong currencies. About 39 percent of India's debt is dollar denominated. If it is expressed in terms of the dollar it is natural to expect a rise in the volume of debt. It is also held by the Government that by next year there is the possibility of this debt burden declining. The nation has to keep its fingers crossed.

It is held by the Government that India's debt scenario is healthy. In 1990-91because of political uncertainty India was not in a position to raise external loans. It was necessary to raise a short term loan in the market. This was 10.2 percent of total debt. The long term debt was 89.8 percent of total debt. The new economic policy adopted by the Government in 1991-92 lent a new vigour to the Indian economy. The quantum of long term loans advanced by the international financial institutions and the concessional loan increased. The foreign exchange reserves mounted. On account of these factors there is a welcome change in India's debt profile. The Government holds the view that though the debt burden has registered an increase because of the depreciation of the rupee in terms of the dollar and depreciation of the dollar in terms of other currencies the debt-service ratio has declined. For this reason the debt burden is no cause for concern. However, the fact remains that the debt-burden in terms of the US dollar has mounted and this should serve as a red signal to India.

How to meet this debt burden?

- The debt has to be used to increase productivity and output. But a significant part of this debt is being used to finance consumption goods and imports oil. If the imported oil is used in the industrial and farm sectors there will be rise in industrial and farm output and the monetary proceeds can be used to repay debt. But oil is imported to meet domestic consumption needs. Oil is sold to the users of vehicles who do not exercise any restraint in the use of this vehicle. If oil is rationed as in Japan it saves a large part of foreign exchange outgo and this can be used to repay external debt.

- The use of debt meant to increase production needs to be of the long term variety. A large part of the existing debt is of the short-term variety. The justification advanced in support of short-term debt is that the interest burden of debt is low. But we have to see the other side of the picture also. Short term debt involves repayment of maturing debt. In the event of the country not being in a position to repay the debt when it matures the country has to borrow in order to repay it. This results in frequent borrowing to repay earlier debts. Furthermore the short-term debt cannot be invested in projects with long gestation periods. Rapid increase in productivity and production requires that the debt should be invested in projects with long gestation periods. The interest cost of long-term debt may be high but this avoids the necessity of going to the market at frequent intervals to borrow for repaying earlier debts. Furthermore, the existing short term debt needs to be converted into long term debt.
- Foreign exchange can be increased apart from the device of export promotion by eradicating the evil proactive of over invoicing imports and under invoicing exports. By eradicating under invoicing of exports the country can save $ 5 billion per year. Furthermore, a sum of $ 6 billion per year can be saved by banning the import of gold into the country. What is necessary is the reduction of the burden of external debt and not the escalating glitter of gold. There is enough gold in the country already.
- It is necessary to impose a constitutional limit on external borrowing. This will restrain the Government from excessive resort to external borrowing this limit can be relaxed, depending on compelling circumstances by the parliament. A similar constitutional limit on internal borrowing is also necessary. These limits are necessary to prevent the country from entering the debt tap. Internal and external.

"The white paper on India's external debt" despite the burgeoning volume of external debt holds out a rosy picture allaying all fears of the external debt trap. If the actual picture is as rosy as the one depicted by the Government all will be well. Nobody knows what the future will bring forth. To be forwarned is to be forearmed. In view of this it is imperative to hold down the burden of external debt and to invest whatever is borrowed in long term projects which enhance the productivity of the economy and production which help to repay the debt so that it no longer constitutes a burden on the present and future generations. The acceptance of the suggestions offered above will help to hold down the burden of external debt.

# 92

## How to use the Bulging Forex Reserves

The inflationary impact of bulging forex reserves is too obvious to bear repetition. The Reserve Bank of India which desires to keep the external value of the rupee stable at Rs. 31.37 per dollar is buying the inflowing dollars. These dollars are prime cause of monetary growth. The money supply has been literally surging during the current year, since July 1994, at an average of 20 percent compared to 1993-94. Although there has been a welcome contraction in Reserve Bank credit to the Central Government practically throughout the current year because of the shift to debt financing of the deficit the bank credit to the commercial sector has shown 14.3 percent increase at the end of December 1994 compared to the previous year. What has really triggered the expansion of money supply is the pronounced increase in foreign exchange assets of the banks from Rs. 53727 crore at the beginning of the current fiscal year to Rs. 70103 crore at the end of December 1994. Indications, however, are that the rate of accretion of capital inflows is coming down because of the new Euro issue guidelines which lays down that the Indian companies raising capital in the European capital markets should park these funds abroad until they are actually required in India. But the damaging impact of this on prices has already become a fact to live with.

In order to deal with this situation, Dr. Raja Chellaiah has recommended that Indians should be allowed to invest in foreign stock markets and US treasury bills to relieve the pressure of dollar inflows. But this recommendation sidelines the possibility of capital outflows caused by the market sentiment. A large part of the forex reserves is volatile capital or "hot" money. This can be withdrawn by the investors instantly without giving any notice. If the forex reserves are invested in foreign stock markets and are tied up there,

India will find it difficult to meet the outflow of capital. It will have to sell the stock in the foreign capital markets at a capital loss which will have to be borne by India. Even the US treasury bills mature after 90 days. If, in the meanwhile, the need to meet capital outflow arises, these treasury bills will have to be sold. Though the loss involved is not as big the loss involved in the sale of stocks, the fact of loss has to be borne in mind. In view of this, the proposal to invest the bulging forex reserves in the foreign stock markets and US treasury bills does not seem to be a viable proposition unless the reserves so invested are stable ones.

There is another proposal to mitigate the pressure on prices brought about by the exchange inflows. This is to run down the reserves for well planned imports of equipment for labour intensive projects such as extensive road construction and expansion of port facilities. The questions that arises and needs to be answered is with regard to the availability of equipment necessary for labour-intensive projects. In the first place, they may not be available considering the fact that the equipment manufactured in the West are for the most part suited to capital intensive projects. Even if they are available the gestation period may be too long before these projects yield results. Even then, their effect on productivity is indirect. If in the meanwhile capital outflow takes place India will not be in a position to meet the demand. India will be constrained to stop these projects when they are half way through and in consequence the projects will not be completed. The investment made thus far will be colossal waste. This imposes a loss which India is unable to sustain. In fact, this is an avoidable loss. Furthermore, even if these imports are possible, the outgo of foreign exchange reserves to finance these may be only a trickle which does not cushion the economy against the inflationary impact of the reserves. Even on the assumption that the imports of labour intensive equipment are possible and if these investments generate employment and additional income these incomes are bound to generate additional demand which pushes up the rate of inflation unless there is a sufficient quantity of wage goods in the economy to absorb the excess demand and to hold the price line. Even then the time lag involved between the generation of additional employment and income and the production of supply is bound to be long. Professor Evesy Domar's "Sigona Effect" comes into play. Investment is both income generating and output creating. Income is generated immediately after the investment is made but output is created after a time lag. In the meanwhile there will be inflationary pressure. The experience of the second Five Year Plan when the economy faced the inflation crisis because of the time lag between income generation and capacity creation is too obvious to need elaboration here. However, it must be said that the second Five Year plan failed to match income generation and output expansion and proved to have an in-built inflationary bias. The employment to be generated will be among the illiterate and semi-literates groups of unemployed labourers whose contribution to productivity is only marginal. Their employment will to some extent mitigate the prevailing social unrest but its immediate anti-inflationary impact is in doubt. The social tensions are generated by the widening inequalities between the poor on the one side and the rich and the super rich on the other side. What is necessary to eliminate this inequality is the imparting of the technical skills to the labourers, raising their productivity and their standard of living. This type of leveling up will eliminate the prevailing social tensions. But at present there is the danger of the social tensions aggravating. The employment prospects brought about by the investment of inflowing forex reserves will benefit the professional classes possessing marketable skills. The affluence of this class of professionals and entrepreneurs becomes an eyesore to the under privileged who constitute the majority. They live in squatter settlements by the side of the palatial buildings occupied by the new breed of professionals and others who are the beneficiaries of the new economic policy. This is bound to aggravate inequality which breeds social tensions. In view of this, the employment potential of the investment of forex reserves incomes suspect though its potential for generating social tensions is great.

The Government seems to be in a fix about the mode of utilization of the bulging forex reserves which, at present, stand at

$ 20.00 billion. The investments of these reserves in the stock markets of foreign countries and in the US treasury bills is alright provided the foreign investors do not withdraw these funds. If they are withdrawn due to changes in market sentiment the Government will be hard put to meet this demand. This demand can be met, if at all, by selling them in the market at a loss to be borne by the Government. There is no assurance that the foreign investors will not withdraw their investments. If they do the crisis of the Mexican variety will crop undermining confidence in the viability of the on-going reform programme. The anti-inflationary effect of the investment of these reserves in labour intensive projects is a chimera considering the time lag between income generation and capacity creation and during this time lag inflation is bound to rage.

As far as possible the hot money inflows should be discouraged by reducing the interest rate attached to them. This serves as a market disintensive to the inflow. The stable part of the inflow could be used to repay external debt carrying a higher interest rate. This will reduce the external debt burden of servicing of the debt. This will take away the inflationary impact of the bulging forex reserves.

# 93

# The Paradoxes Around the Falling Rate of Inflation

Inflation based on the Wholesale Price Index (WPI) has declined to 5.08 percent. The Finance Minister has been holding this as the target rate to be achieved. But the harried consumers dismiss this achievement as a statistical contrivance. They argue that the basis of calculating the rate of inflation should be Consumer Price Index (CPI) as it takes note of the prices of commodities consumed by the consumers. The wholesale price index on the other hand, is based on the prices of capital goods also. And as the capital goods prices have fallen, the inflation rate based on the WPI should indicate fall. In fact, they argue, the rate of inflation based on the consumer price index is even now in the double digit range. This of course, is a moot point admitting controversy.

Even going by the inflation rate based on the WPI one cannot resist the conclusion that there is suppressed inflation in India indicating that inflation has actually not been brought under control but is only deferred to future date. The Government has refrained from raising the administered prices of oil and coal. The issue prices of rice and wheat have not been raised and in consequence the Government itself has absorbed the higher issue price by enhancing food subsidy. The Government has deliberately withheld the injection of funds to the banks for recapitalisation and has thus used the funds to finance non-developmental expenditure. These factors have suppressed inflation which will rise with a bang as soon as factors have suppressed inflation which will rise with bang as soon as the administered prices of oil and coal are raised, the issue prices of rice and wheat are raised and the funds are injected into the banks to help them to go ahead with recapitalisation. This won't be long.

At the same time the supply side factor has also worked to reduce the rate of inflation. It consists of a buffer stock of food grains of 27 million tonnes compared with the buffer stock norm of 16 million tonnes and the growth rate of 8-9 percent in industry since October 1995. It is also possible that the liquidity crunch in the economy has caused a fall in demand and thus a fall in the rate of inflation.

Fiscal deficits represent an injection of demand into the income stream and they go with a rise in prices. The center for monitoring the Indian Economy (CMIE) has estimated that the fiscal deficit in 1995-96 will be more than Rs. 65000 crore or 6 percent of GDP. The decline in the inflation rate at a time when the fiscal deficit is rising has created a paradoxical situation. It is possible that the reduction in the rate of monetary growth from 20 percent to 14 percent has caused the fall in the rate of inflation. If this is so the credit policy must be deflationary. There is a time lag of six months between a fall in money supply and fall in the price level. If the price level has fallen before the completion of the time lag can it be said that the time lag has become shorter? If the inflation rate has actually fallen the external value of the rupee must appreciate as per the purchasing power parity paradigm. But the external value of the rupee is, in fact, going down. Statistics show that the dollar has pierced the psychological barrier of the Rs. 36 as the exchange rate and the rupee is going down. The fall in the rate of inflation and the depreciation of the rupee do not go together. Due to the liquidity crunch the cost of borrowing is rising and is causing a fall in the rate of investment which adversely affects the rate of economic growth and employment generation. The question arises, if the rate of inflation has actually fallen is there is no need for relaxing the tightness of the monetary and credit policies in order to accelerate the rate of economic growth. These questions naturally arise and present discovering paradoxes. The fall in the rate of inflation does not square with a rising fiscal deficit or with depreciation of the rupee in the exchange markets. There is something, wrong somewhere. It is for the Finance Minister to find out and to offer explanation for the paradoxes. It appears desirable to calculate the inflation rate on the basis of the consumer price index rather than on the basis of the wholesale price index. What matters for general welfare is the prices of consumer goods at the retail level and not the whole sale prices of goods including capital goods which take long to be reflected in the consumer prices.

# 94

## Checking the Slide in the Rupee

The external value of the rupee has been causing concern to the Government and to the Reserve Bank of India. The dollar-rupee exchange rate had remained stable between August 1993 and February 1995 at $ 1= Rs. 31.37. Despite minor slips the exchange rate remained stable upto the middle of July 1995. During the period upto October 1994 when the capital inflows into India were heavy the Reserve Bank found that the effective exchange rate had appreciated significantly between March 1993 and August 1995. This called for a correction involving the purchase of dollars. The Reserve Bank stood ready to offer to purchase dollars in exchange for rupees at the declared rate and it gave hint that if the economic fundamentals required, a depreciation of the rupee which stood at the rate of $ 1 = Rs. 31.37 would not be defended. In the last quarter of 1994 the inflow of foreign funds tapered off but the rupee did not depreciate in respect of the US dollar as the latter was weak. From July 1995 the dollars strengthened against the major currencies and the rupee depreciated vis-à-vis the dollar. Upto the third week of August 1995 the rupee held its own against the dollar. After this the rupee began to slide and it slided to $ 1 = Rs. 35.69 towards the end of October 1995. Between the middle of October and the end of October the Reserve Bank of India intervened strongly in the forex market. Since the beginning of November 1995 there has been only limited intervention in the spot forex market to even out temporary shortages. However, in view of the two-way intervention there has been no net loss of foreign exchange reserves as a result of the intervention operations.

However, of late the rupee is in trouble. It nosedived to a historic low of Rs. 36.70/73 vis-à-vis the US dollar on January 31 1995 during the course of the trading at the inter bank forex market in

Bombay. However, the rupee later recovered to close at Rs. 36.42/47 after repeated interventions by the Reserve Bank of India in support of the rupee. Though the rupee staged a late rally, the closing quote was still a record low and a sharp fall from overnight levels of Rs. 36.11/14 since recovering liberalise exchange rate management system in early March 1993. In the last week of January the rupee depreciated by about 65 paise against the dollar and Rs. 1.29 over the month of December 1995. The main reason behind the hectic fall of the rupee was the heavy all round demand for dollars on the part of the corporation and importers. Furthermore, the Reserve Bank of India attributes this appreciation of the dollar against currencies across the world. The fear that the dollar will go to Rs. 40-45 per unit are causing problems in the external market.

An appreciation of the rupee makes exports dearer and imports cheaper. If appreciation takes place when the balance of payments is in deficit, it enlarges the deficit and if left uncontrolled leads to a crisis conversely, a depreciation of the rupee makes exports cheaper, imports dearer. If depreciation takes place when the balance of payments is in deficit, it corrects the deficit and helps to restore equilibrium if the price elasticities of trade are high. But if the price elasticities of trade are low greater movements in the exchange rate will be required to overcome external stocks. Excessive variability of the exchange rate in either direction will dampen capital mobility especially when the entire burden of adjustment is on the exchange rate. The assessment of the external competitiveness requires a consideration of the real effective exchange rate index adjusted for relative price movements. Thus, an appreciation of the real effective exchange rate indicates deterioration of the country's external competitiveness; conversely, a depreciation of the real effective exchange rate indicates an improvement of the country's external competitiveness. But a depreciation beyond a point generates expectation of a further depreciation which plays havoc with external equilibrium.

A sustainable exchange rate requires the support of monetary policy which is consistent with the exchange rate policy. In India at present despite the ongoing liquidity crunch the rate of monetary growth has been brought down from 18 percent to 14 percent. This, along with higher interest rates has caused a decline in the inflation rate to 5.08 percent. A reduction in the money supply and a fall in the rate of inflation appear to be inconsistent with a depreciation of the rupee to the present level. For, as per the purchasing power parity paradigm a fall in the domestic inflation rate should cause a rise in the exchange rate. That has not happened. This raises the question whether the supply of money and the rate of inflation can be reduced further. If it is necessary to reduce them further, the question is whether it is possible to do so. These are questions which it is difficult to answer.

Whatever it is, the fact is that the external value of the rupee has pierced the psychological barrier of Rs. 36 per US dollar and it is expected to slide further down. The rate of monetary growth has declined from 18 percent to 14 percent and the interest rates have risen. These two factors which are contractive may responsible account for a decline in the rate of inflation. At the same time, the fiscal deficit is of the order of Rs. 65000 crore or 6 percent of GDP. This is an expansive factor which should push the rate of inflation up. But this has not happened. This is indeed a paradoxical situation. Despite a decline in the rate of inflation, there has been a depreciation of the rupee which should be considered excessive.

The effect of depreciation on the trade balance needs to be considered. Ordinarily, if the price elasticities of trade are high depreciation should increase exports by enhancing their competitiveness. At the same time, depreciation should reduce imports by making them costlier. But the effect of depreciation on the trade cannot be considered to be significant. The prices of imports do rise following depreciation. To the extent that the demand for imports is price inelastic the expected decline in imports will not come about. About 35 percent of imports are meant to be inputs for exports. If their prices rise the prices of exports also rise. This reduces the competitiveness of exports. At a time when the income are rising the income effect on imports swamps the price effect on imports and on balance, imports rises. This means that depreciation is no remedy for the trade imbalance in the short run, at any rate. Unless the price elasticity of trade are very high and the are high enough to offset any income effect of a rising income due to the fiscal deficit.

That the present depreciation of the rupee is excessive needs no emphasis. The depreciation upto a Rs. 35 per dollar is sufficient and it should not be allowed to exceed this limit. If it exceeds this limit, it generates expectations of a further depreciation which causes an acceleration of import flow and a declaration of export flow and widens the trade deficit which causes a further depreciation of rupee. This also impedes the inflow of foreign funds and aggravates instability. Therefore, there is imperative need to intervene effectively so as to keep the exchange rate stable at Rs. 35 per US dollar. This of course, requires the availability of dollars in sufficient quantity. If the inflow of foreign funds through various channels is not sufficient to meet the demand for dollars they can be mobilized by eradicating under invoicing of exports and over invoicing of imports which together save $ 4.5 billion and also by banning the import of gold which saves $ 6.0 billion. At the same time the exporters need to be asked to repatriate their export earnings promptly. Therefore, the rupee-dollar rate needs to be stabilized at $ 1=35 which is enough to promote exports by enhancing competitiveness of exports and by reducing imports and thus by reducing the current account deficit. In 1995-96 the current account deficit will not be more than $ 4.0 billion or 1.5 percent of GDP which can be easily financed.

The rupee dollar rate should not be allowed to move outside a pre-determined band. If the rupee depreciates outside this limit, the Reserve Bank of India should intervene to sell dollars to keep the rate at Rs. 35; if, on the other hand, the rupee goes outside this limit in the opposite direction, this is an indication of an appreciation. In this event, the Reserve Bank of India should stand ready to buy the dollars to keep the exchange rate within the band. This system combines the virtues of both a fixed exchange rate system and a floating exchange rate system: fixed exchange rate at the limits of the band and floating exchange rate within the limits of the band. This is an exchange rate mechanism which the Reserve Bank of India can experiment within the interest of stability.

# 95

## Capital Inflows need not Cause Worry

India's foreign exchange reserves have been on the rise. Though this may be a source of satisfaction viewed from the balance of payments angle, it has become a source of worry also to the monetary authorities. During April and May 1994 the first two months of the present fiscal year India's forex reserves registered the fastest rate of growth. At the end of April 1994, forex reserves (excluding gold and SDRs) stood at $ 15.073 billion and at the end of May 1994 at 15.50 billion. This balance is after repayment of $ 1.13 billion loan to the IMF during 1994-95, a year ahead of schedule. The repayment of the IMF loan of $ 1.13 billion was done on April 22 in a single transaction. On that day the reserves were reported at $ 14.5 billion compared to $ 15.068 billion at the end of March 1994 and $ 15.073 billion at the end of April 1994. If this large transaction is kept aside, actual addition to forex reserves during April were of the order of $ 1.127 billion. Final figures for May have yet to come in. Addition to the reserves during the first three weeks of May were about $ 0.50 billion. The fast rate of growth of forex reserves has lent strength to the rupee vis-à-vis the US dollar. The steadiness of the nominal rupee-dollar exchange rate implies that the real (inflation adjusted) rate of exchange of the rupee has appreciated since inflation has been 7-8 percentage points higher in India than in the United States of America. It is, however, likely that the Reserve Bank of India will continue its policy of passive absorption of dollars by purchase in the Indian foreign exchange market (in case of lack of demand from importers). By implication, the reserve bank does not consider the appreciation of the rupee to be viable option even though it could serve to curb growth of money supply and hence the rate of inflation.

A sudden upsurge of inflow of capital into the developing countries in general has characterized international capital markets in the late 1980s. Capital inflows are always welcome for capital scarce countries like India as they provide avenues for higher investment and growth besides their vulnerable balance of payments. Such inflows have a side effect: they cause distortions in the domestic sector which may, and often do, outweigh the gains in the external sector. This is of particular significance to India as the economic performance in 1993-94 was dominated by a large inflow of capital into the country which, in fact, was not prepared for this unexpected event.

Inflows of capital come in the form of foreign direct investment, remittances, foreign institutional investment etc. and are directed primarily to the private sector. The country receiving these inflows has to strike a paradoxical balance between "accommodation" and "restraint" of these inflows. There are two forces causing inflows of capital of such large dimensions: pull and push. The former include change in domestic economic policies especially as they concern the external sector, attitude towards direct foreign investment and domestic credit policies. The latter are exogenous to the performance of the economy but for their sustenance they depend on the operation of the pull factors. The push factors consist of declining interest rates in world capital markets and an economic slow down in the industrial countries.

These inflows can be countered in three ways. The first one has to do with "sterilization" of the inflows of capital meant to control the growth in money supply by the Reserve Bank of India engaging itself in open market operations, changes in reserve requirements, curbing rediscount facilities and raising discount rates. This measure operates spontaneously and avoids the prospect of enlarging the current account deficit as it has the effect of locking in a large part of the forex reserves. But this policy measure involves a cost which involves issuing bonds with high interest rates while investing in foreign exchange assets carrying lower interest rates. Open market operations involve a rise in the domestic interest rates which attract more and more foreign funds. This entails a vicious circle capital inflows, higher interest rates, more capital inflows and so on. Thus this measure deprives the economy of the benefits of the capital inflows. Furthermore, when the economy is faced with a serious recession capital inflows coupled with credit curbs would aggravate the situation. This is particularly relevant to the Indian context.

The second policy alternative is the control of exchange rates. In the past countries maintained rigid exchange rates as they felt that the sustainable real exchange rates were not higher than they were before the capital flowed in. As capital inflows push up the rate of inflation, the real exchange rate rises. The question that arises is whether capital inflows should be pre-empted through nominal appreciation. Countries like Chile, Columbia, Mexico and Spain undertook nominal appreciation to control the capital inflows. Nominal appreciation is preferable to real appreciation through inflation as it avoids domestic distortions. In the case where the exchange rate is flexible there is the danger of speculation which may cause the real exchange rate to overshoot.

The third measure concerns the reduction of the Government deficits. If this is done, inflation can be held down and the real appreciation can be avoided. The reduction of Government deficits means a reduction in aggregate demand which causes a downward pressure on the price level. But this policy is not very popular especially when it results in a reduction in expenditure on infrastructural development with adverse effects on the rate of economic growth.

The Government can consider three policy measures though they are effective in the sort run. They are : (a) restricting the capital inflow by means of taxes and physical impediments; b) adopting financial reforms aimed at strengthening the banking system by introducing strict norms for provisioning and capital adequacy. This would strengthen the economic system against risks in lending and against exchange rate fluctuations; (c) a policy of trade liberalization could be adopted in order to increase imports which have the effect of absorbing capital account surplus.

The Reserve Bank of India has made use of monetary policy in order to contain the ill-effects of capital inflows into the country. The use of open market operations has serious consequences for the banking sector if it has to invest its funds in Government securities rater than in traditional credit activities. Even if this is accepted as being prudent there is the problem of rising interest rates. In order to make the Government securities attractive the interest rates have to be raised. But in an environment where there is a general demand for a reduction in the interest rate this option does not find supporters.

The use of monetary policy has become inevitable. Net Reserve Bank credit to the Government is already on the decline as the Government has shifted to public borrowing in order to finance the deficit. Ordinarily a capital inflow causes an appreciation of the exchange rate but the Reserve Bank of India policy of intervention does not allow the exchange rate to appreciate. The Reserve Bank intervention is prompted by a desire not to hurt export growth which an appreciated exchange rate does. In a free market system the rupee should have been allowed to appreciate in the wake of capital inflows and settle at the market determined level. But the Reserve Bank of India is concerned with increasing the foreign exchange inflows and monetary policy has been assigned the task of sorting out these problems.

The Reserve Bank Governor has expressed concern about the massive inflows of capital but is wary of allowing the market forces to determine the exchange rate for in this case the rupee is bound to appreciate with adverse consequences on export growth and on the trade balance. He considers it imperative to purchase the dollar inflow in order to prevent the rupee from appreciating. But this has got serious inflationary consequences. There has been no sizeable outflow of forex reserves so far on account of an increase in imports and the emergence of a large trade gap. In actual fact, there was even a small surplus in April 1994 even in the face of a big rise in imports. There was a decline in the balances held abroad from Rs. 36,886,49 crore to Rs. 36,587.91 crore in the week ended 3, June 1994. But this might have been due to debt-servicing obligations with new Euro issues being floated by Indian enterprises and reports of fresh purchases by foreign institutional investors in the stock markets these balances should tend to rise in the coming weeks.

Dr. Prabhakar Narvekar a Deputy Managing Director of the IMF has indicated that the surge of capital flows into India is fine as long as it is appropriately channeled and has maintained that "one certainly hopes it......... will be sustained". "The thing to do is to make sure it is used correctly. He has further added: "we have to make sure that India's environment remains sufficiently receptive to the inflows........ so that it will stay and not panic and go away." However, the IMF including its Managing Director Michael Camdessus has raised concerns over the surge of capital inflows into India. It must be admitted that India's need for additional forex reserves is not pressing. The improvements in India's external accounts—both current and capital—has exceeded the most optimistic forecasts. With exports rising by 20 percent in 1993-94, modest growth of imports and an improvement in the service account the current account deficit declined to $ 0.8 billion in 1993-94 from $ 10 billion in 1990-91. The World Bank, in a report on India titled: "Recent Economic Developments and Prospects" for the India Development Forum meeting to be held in Paris towards the end of June 1994, has said that at $ 4.7 billion foreign investment (largely portfolio investment) surged to unprecedentedly high levels. As a consequence, reserves rose from $ 1.0 billion in June 1991 to over $15 billion by the end of March 1994. The monetization of reserves, has led to sharp expansion in base money to 25 percent in march 1994 in relation to March 1993. Together with significant increases in administered prices this has led to inflation. After declining from a peak of 17 percent in August 1991 to around 7 percent in mid-1993, inflation has increased again exceeding 10 percent in the first week of June 1994.

Quite apart from the purely domestic factors exacerbating the rate of inflation in the country, the rate of monetary expansion engendered by the surge in forex reserves has acted as an accommodating factor sustaining the high rate of inflation. The issue has to be placed in the right perspective. If the capital inflows are allowed to enter the Indian capital market the forex reserves rise causing monetary expansion and exacerbating inflation. If, however, the reserve Bank of India does not intervene in the forex market and allows the market forces to determine the exchange rate, the rupee appreciates adversely affecting export growth, stimulating imports and widening the trade gap. A widening of the trade gap will use up the existing forex reserves and occasion a decline in the rate of monetary growth and a decline in the rate of inflation. Though the decline in the rate of inflation is welcome the financing of the trade gap necessitates resource to the Fund-Bank duo for a loan which increases the volume of external debt and the associated burden of interest payment. Thus both the options allowing capital inflows by intervention in the foreign exchange market and abandoning the present policy of intervention to keep the exchange rate steady have unwelcome side effects. What is to be done?

The Reserve Bank of India can intervene in the foreign exchange market to prevent the exchange rate from appreciating and thus allow capital inflows into the country. In order to avoid the inflationary effects of surge in capital inflow the country can use it to repay external debt. This will help to reduce the burden of external debt and also reduce the burden of interest charges. As the capital that is flowing into India is of a short-term variety the utilization of it to repay external debt may cause embarrassment to the authorities in the event of foreign investors withdrawing their capital. In this case the country will have to resort to external borrowing to meet the sudden and unexpected withdrawals. The relief thus obtained will be transitory and no lasting benefit will accrue to the country. Such volatile or inflammatory capital movements will disturb the exchange rate and will be a source of instability as the European experience in the inter-war period has made it so distressingly obvious. In order to impact an element of stability the Reserve Bank of India can allow only those capital inflows which will be held in the country for a specified period and disallow those capital inflows which are volatile and speculative in character. The capital inflows thus allowed into the country can be used to repay external debt carrying a higher rate of interest than the capital flowing into the country. This will reduce the burden of external debt and also the burden of interest cost.

Apart from this, a part of the forex resources can be invested in gold through direct purchases in world markets. However, a decision in this regard cannot be easily taken as world prices for the yellow metal have not been exhibiting and decisive uptrend lately. The value of gold may tend to rise only when there is a softening of US dollar and a shrinkage of floating gold stocks. If stocks held by the Government are made available to the Reserve Bank only the former will get credit in terms of Indian currency and there cannot be any use of forex resources. Gold coin and gold bullion held in the Issue Department of the Reserve Bank increased slightly from Rs. 10365.6 crore to Rs. 10418.97 crore only on account of the revaluation exercise being carried out at the end of every month. Aggregate foreign exchange reserves excluding gold coin and bullion are around $ 15.5 billion. The total including gold reserves will be easily $ 20 billion. This comfortable level of reserves is an indication that the pressure on the balance of payments has eased significantly. In fact the main worry of the Reserve Bank of India is to prevent an appreciation of the rupee by effecting purchases of dollars in fairly large volume from the open market. As averred above, this has got inflationary implications thought the adverse effects of rupee appreciation on the export growth can be avoided. But the reserves accumulated in this manner can be used to purchase gold which has a proneness to appreciate in value. This does not entail the prescription of any condition to the foreign investors about the duration of the time span during which they cannot shift their capital. In the event of the capital being shifted outside the country, gold can be pledged and resources can be mobilized to meet the capital outflow. But there is a hitch here. There will be no return on investment in gold while the country has to pay interest on the capital held. But so long as this gold is appreciating in value the appreciation can be used to offset the interest payment on the capital held here. But the behaviour of gold prices is uncertain. In the event of the price of gold being constant or declining the country has to suffer a loss. But this possibility is remote. However. It is a risky business.

In view of the above, the use of capital inflow held for the specified period to retire high cost external debt is desirable. This avoids appreciation of the rupee and its ill effects on export growth. This also avoids the inflationary effects of capital inflow. This option merits serious consideration.

Quite apart from this, the fiscal deficit of the Government has to be reduced in order to bring down the rate of inflation. The world Bank has stated that about one to 2.6 percentage points of GDP fiscal deviation in 1993-94 is estimated to be result tax revenue shortfalls from a weak economic recovery. The remaining 1.6 percentage points are accounted for by expenditure overruns mostly on subsidies (0.5 percent of GDP), defence (0.3 percent) loans to states (0.3 percent) and public enterprises (0.1 percent). The worsened fiscal performance in 1993-94 could undermine the creditability of the fiscal adjustment process. Unless in 1994-95 fiscal deficit target of 6 percent of GDP is met and decisive steps are taken to reduce it further in 1995-96 the Central Government's fiscal deficit may dim India's economic prospects. The Central Government, for its part, has been carefully watching the budgetary position constantly as there has been an increase in non-plan expenditure due to heavier burden of interest charges, subsidies and payment of additional dearness allowances to Government employees. But it is hoped that there will be an increase in revenues with a higher level of economic activity. The Finance Minister is optimistic that by October 1994 the seasonal factors which have raised the rate of inflation will weaken and the rate of inflation would come down to the single digit figure provided the monsoon are favourable.

With the expected rise in tax revenues resulting in the reduction of the fiscal deficit to the target level of 6 percent of GDP, with the onset of favourable monsoons resulting in a rise in agricultural output and the utilization of the capital inflows to repay external debt/to purchase gold thus avoiding the monetization of the capital inflows, the rate of inflation might hopefully come down to the single digit level. If the capital inflows are used in this manner the present upsurge in them will not be a source of worry at all. As averred above India has to balance between "accommodation" and "resistant". That part of the capital inflow that can stay stable in India for atleast a stipulated period of time should be accommodated and the other part which is volatile in character should be restricted. India cannot be a haven for volatile capital as this proves to be a source of instability which frustrates all efforts at macroeconomic stabilization.

The World Bank in its latest country Report on India warns the Government of India against the danger posed by the inflation induced by Capital inflows and fiscal deficit. It says:

"Unless the monetization of the inflows is sterilized, there is a loss of control over the money base, inflation and appreciation of the real exchange rate".

It points out that the challenge to the Indian authorities is to formulate a policy which protects the competitiveness of the real exchange rate and translates the unexpected surge in capital inflows into higher investment. The base money growth rose to 25 percent basically as a consequence of the monetization of capital inflows. This along with the fiscal deficit of 7.3 percent of GDP against the target of 4.7 percent of GDP caused a rise in the rate of inflation to the double digit figure. The fiscal deficit escalated to 7.3 percent of GDP as a result of both revenue shortfalls (40 percent of deviation) and expenditure over runs (60 percent). The options indicated above are intended to prevent the capital inflows from contributing to monetary growth and to the inflation rate. If the rate of inflation is reduced the appreciation of the real exchange rate will be prevented. Quite apart from neutralizing the inflationary effects of capital inflows policies on the domestic front are also necessary.

# 96

# Guidelines for the Non-banking Financial Companies

Narasimham Committee Report on Financial Sector Reforms was submitted to the Government in September 1991. Two years later, i.e., in September 1993, the A.B. Shah working Group submitted its report to the Reserve Bank of India. The Reserve Bank had implemented the first phase recommendations of the Committee which related to inter-corporate deposits, minimum and maximum period of deposits and maintenance of liquid assets.

On Monday June 13, 1994 the Reserve Bank of India announced detailed guidelines containing prudential norms for non-banking financial companies and residuary non-banking companies covering the entire areas of income recognition, accounting standards, provisioning for bad and doubtful debts, capital adequacy and concentration of credit and investments. In a statement the Reserve Bank stated that the guidelines would be applicable to those non-banking financial companies which have net owned funds of Rs. 50 lakh and above and are registered with the Reserve Bank of India. The guidelines are generally on the lines prescribed for commercial banks and are a part implementation of the recommendations of the Dr. A.B. Shah working group.

According to the guidelines, income due to a company but not yet received by it within a period of six months, is not to be regarded as income until it is actually received. The assets of the company are required to be classified as non-performing assets (NPA) based on recovery record. If the payment of principal or instalments is due but not received within a period of six months such loans or advances are to be classified as NPAs. The companies have to follow all accounting standards and guidance notes issued by the Institute of Chartered Accountants of India dealing with lease accounting and depreciation.

As per the guidelines, investments are to be classified into two categories current investments and long-term investments. The current investments are those which are readily realizable and are intended to be held for not more than one year from the date of investments. Long-term investments are not current investments. The long-term investments are to be valued at cost but current investments are to be valued at the lower of cost and market value.

The assets of a company are to be classified into four categories. They are standard assets, sub-standard assets, doubtful assets and loss assets. Provisioning norms for bad and doubtful debts have been prescribed for the last three categories of assets as their realisation is shrouded in uncertainties of different degrees. The Reserve Bank has also prescribed risk weights on the on-balance sheet assets and credit conversion factors for off-balance sheet items of exposures. Cash, bank balances and investments in Government and approved securities have been given "zero" weightage but the other assets have been given weightage of 100. The off-balance sheet items of exposures carry credit conversion factors ranging from 50 to 100 percent.

The financial companies have been asked to attain capital adequacy ration of 6 percent based on the risk-weighted assets and conversion of off-balance sheet exposures by March 31, 1995 and 8 percent by March 31, 1996. Capital of a company will be divided into two tiers: paid-up equity capital and free reserves and preference shares, revaluation reserves, general provisions and loss reserves in excess of the required amounts and hybrid debt capital instruments or subordinated debts, if any,. Tier-II capital is not to exceed Tier-I capital. While arriving at Tier-I capital, investments, loans and advances in subsidiaries and companies in the same group and other non-banking financial companies in excess of 10 percent of the owned fund of the registered financial companies will be deducted.

The registered financial companies should not lend more than 15 percent of their net owned funds to any single party or 25 percent of their net owned funds to a single group of parties. Advances made in excess of these limits are to be brought down in the course of repayment of the dues as scheduled. A financial company should not invest more than 25 percent of its owned funds in shares and debentures of another company. The financial companies are advised to bear in mind the attendant risks in regard to investments in companies belonging to a group or in a particular industry and should try to diversify their portfolios.

The registered companies are to compulsorily get credit rating done by the credit rating agencies in a phased manner. They have to have their first credit rating completed by March 31, 1995 and submit it to the Reserve Bank of India long with the relevant half-yearly reports. A fresh rating has to be obtained atleast once every year. Companies owning a net fund of below Rs. 2 crore have been given the option to get the rating done latest by March 31, 1996.

The existing restrictions regarding deposit acceptance including the limits on deposits vis-a-vis owned funds will continue for the registered financial companies till the Reserve Bank is satisfied that the company has met all the norms and has obtained a satisfactory credit rating. When the Reserve Bank is thus satisfied, it will issue a specific advice to the company concerned withdrawing some of the present restrictions.

The Reserve Bank of India has allowed a higher limit of acceptance of deposits (including money raised through the issue of non-convertible debentures/bonds) to a financial company other than an equipment leasing or a hire purchase company (such as a loan or an investment company) registered with it. The deposit to be accepted by it should be equal to its net owned funds instead of 40 percent of its net owned funds as at present. These companies will be required to maintain liquid assets to the extent of 10 percent of their deposit liabilities by the end of December 1994 as against 5 percent at present.

The Reserve Bank of India has further proposed to bring down the volume of deposits (including inter-corporate deposits/ borrowings) in a manner in respect of all categories of finance companies which are not registered with it from the present levels prescribed in the directions to the levels of 25 percent and 15 percent of their net owned funds from public and share holders respectively.

On the face of it, the guidelines issued by the Reserve Bank of India for non-banking financial companies seem pretty tough. The reflect the same approach as has been followed in the case of nationalized banks and financial institutions. Considering the fact that non-banking financial institutions are an important segment of the financial sector. They could not be left out of the reform process especially when more than 50 percent of their funds come from public deposits. The protection of the interests of these depositors depends on the regulation of the operations of these institutions. Equally important and also welcome is the stipulation that these companies should obtain a minimum credit rating from recognized credit rating agencies. The Reserve Bank advice to them not to lend more than 15 percent of the funds to a single group of parties, though seemingly restrictive, should help to reduce the risk factor. It is understandable that the new guidelines do not apply to leasing and hire purchase companies for these companies continue to own their assets even after leasing them out and hence need to be treated on a different footing. It can be asserted with confidence that these guidelines will go a long way in enhancing the viability and stability of the non-banking financial companies. The guidelines permit them to accept deposits equal to their net owned funds as against 40 percent at present. This is a fair reward for adhering to the rigorous norms and is bound to boost their operations. The guidelines are forward looking and they need to be implemented in letter and spirit. There shall be no dilly-dallying as in the case of the Narasimham Committee Report.

# 97

## The Inflation Muddle

The Indian economy is poised for stability and growth. The days of anxiety are gone for good. Food production has exceeded the 185 million tonnes. It has become difficult to procure and store the food grains. The rate of industrial growth is expected to reach 8 percent in 1994-95. A factor that was a source of anxiety concerned the external accounts. India's exports are rising, imports have raised greatly this year. Though their growth is 12.3 percent there is no cause for anxiety. Furthermore, the supply of oil, sugar and other essential commodities was not satisfactory. This caused a rise in imports of these commodities. Their imports were necessitated by the need to prevent the prices from rising. The trade deficit this year is estimated to be $ 250 crore. It is therefore necessary to stimulate exports as a means of reducing the trade deficit. The forex reserve position is satisfactory. India has accumulated forex reserves of $ 20 billion and this is expected to reach $ 25 billion by the end of the fiscal 1994-95. The rate of economic growth this year is expected to be 5-6 percent. All these are evidence that the economy is poised for sustainable growth. The Government is beaming with satisfaction that the economic reform programme has yielded the expected results.

But when compared with the experiences of other countries certain factors which are not entirely satisfactory become evident. Of these one is conspicuous by its presence. This is the rate of inflation. The rise in the inflation rate is proof, if proof is needed, that there is disequilibrium in the economy. This means that the income distribution is being shifted from the weaker sections to the affluent sections of society. This generates social tensions. Three years ago the rate of inflation was 17.5 percent. This started declining. This reached 7 percent and showed signs of a further decline. But this situation was temporary. In 1991-92 the rate of inflation was 13.6 percent. In 1992-93 it fell to 7 percent but in 1993-94 it rose to 10.2 percent. In October of 1993 it was close to 8 percent. Subsequently it rose steadily and touched the 10 percent figure. In April 1994 it was 11 percent and it declined steadily in the following months. In September 1994 it touched the 8 percent figure and in recent weeks it has resumed its upward trend. At present it is 9.41 percent holding out the threat of a further rise.

The foregoing figures refer to the wholesale price index. But if we examine the movement of the consumer price index things look different. The consumer price index is even now 11 percent. In 1994-95 it is hoped to bring down the inflation rate by 4 percentage points as per the pronouncements made by the Finance Minister and the Reserve Bank Governor. But one wonders whether it is possible at all.

There are two reasons for this. In the first place the fiscal deficit of the Government has not yet come under control. The finance minister has admitted that it is not easy to bring down the fiscal deficit. Though the Government is restricting the borrowing from the Reserve Bank, the clear picture about the magnitude of the fiscal deficit becomes available only towards the end of 1994-95. In the second place there has been a steady rise in the rate of monetary growth exercising an expansionary effect on the price level as per the classical quantity theory of money. The quantum of money in the economy a year ago was Rs. 3.85 lakh crore. At present it is Rs. 4.68 lakh crore. A year ago the loan advanced by the banks to the Government was Rs. 1.99 lakh crore. At present it is Rs. 2.12 lakh crore. The aggregate bank deposits in the country have risen from Rs. 3.04 lakh crore to Rs. 3.66 lakh crore. These statistics are evidence of incipient instability. Furthermore, the inflow of foreign exchange is also a cause of monetary growth and economic instability. The Government has made it a policy to increase exports. But the rate of export growth depends on price and quality competitiveness of Indian goods in foreign markets. When their value in rupees were converted into foreign currencies, should become cheaper to foreign buyers. This means that the exchange value of the Indian rupee should not be high. At present the dollar-rupee rate is $ 1 = 31.37. There is an incessant inflow of foreign funds into India. Ordinarily the value of the rupee appreciates. If it appreciates the Indian goods become costlier to foreign buyers. This causes a fall in exports. Therefore, in order to keep the dollar-rupee rate stable at $1=Rs. 31.37 the Reserve Bank is purchasing dollars in exchange for rupees. This is a reason for monetary growth and the rise in the rate of inflation. This has occasioned a dilemma for the authorities. Some have suggested devaluation of the rupee in order to stimulate exports and to curb imports. This is a matter of internal contradiction. As a result of inflation the rupee is becoming weak. For this reason the foreign experts advocate a devaluation of the rupee. The reason is that it will stimulate exports. This has created a confusing situation. If the rupee is allowed to appreciate, it will reduce exports, stimulate imports and widen the trade deficit. If the rupee is devalued it may stimulate exports and reduce imports. But his outcome depends on several conditions which it is not easy to satisfy. At the same time even the policy of stabilizing the dollar-rupee rate at $ 1 = Rs. 31.37 is also problematical. At the same time imports are rising. This is said to be an indirect boon as it helps to reduce the forex reserves and to bring down the rate of inflation. The finance minister has advocated liberalization of consumer goods imports as these imports meet excess demand and help to reduce the rate of inflation. At the same time the payment for these imports by drawing down the forex reserves reduces the base for monetary growth and helps to reduce the supply of money in the economy which, at present is excessive.

In the second week of November 1994, the Government raised the minimum support prices of various food articles. These are bound to be passed on to consumers in the form of higher market prices. They give an upward push to the inflation rate. But there is a restraining factor at the same time. The Government has recently introduced fresh Euro-Issue guidelines on what to do with funds raised from Global Depository Receipts (GDRs) and these guidelines help to keep the proceeds abroad until utilization will reduce the supply of dollars and thereby lower the need for RBI intervention in the foreign exchange market. Already, this move had an impact on the domestic inter-bank market. For the first time since May 1993 the rupee fell against the dollar without being able to recover. The rupee dropped to a low of Rs. 31.43 per dollar before ending the fortnight at Rs. 31.4150. The decline in the exchange value of the rupee is likely to have a salutary effect on the trade deficit.

A factor causing anxiety is the fiscal deficit. The Finance Minister was confident of reducing the fiscal deficit to 7 percent of GDP. The buoyancy of tax receipts held out the hope of the fiscal deficit falling even below 7 percent of GDP. But the Finance Minister averred on 13.11.1994 that "the reduction of the fiscal deficit is not an easy task". If this is so there is cause for anxiety. It is in this context that he came down heavily on the rising subsidies which are the prime cause for fiscal deficit. He made out a strong case for their drastic reduction. The greater challenge will be on the expenditure side. The recent panic following the outbreak of a plague epidemic in some parts of the country underscores the need to spend more on basic social sectors like health, education and welfare. The pay commission for Government employees is about to begin its labours and during fiscal 1995-96 it can be expected to make an interim award, one that will be eagerly awaited by the civil service. There is every case for paying the Government employees a better wage but, if this is not to beggar the Government, all wage increase must be matched by a corresponding cut in the overall number of Government employees. If the UK could slash the size of its civil service by something like 40 percent over the past decade, there is no reason why India should not make a beginning in this direction. The first step will be to ask whether each function being performed by Government needs to be performed any more and if so, whether it needs to be done by Government. The next that need to be addressed is whether the purpose can be served more efficiently and at a significantly lower cost. There is considerable flab in the civil service and this needs to be cut only to reduce public expenditure but also to make the remaining part of the expenditure cost effective. Fiscal deficit has to be brought down as a means of reducing the rate of inflation by using all methods though some of them are patently unpopular. Inflation is also unpopular. We have to use less unpopular remedies to cure a more unpopular diseases.

# 98

## The Entry of Private Banks into the Indian Financial System

The Reserve Bank of India has recently announced the guidelines concerning the establishment and the management of the banks in the private sector. In India banks are, for the most part, in the public sector. Of the 60,000 bank branches in the country there are only 3,800 branches in the private sector. Twenty-four private banks are merely regional banks. It is alleged, not without reason, that the Government has adopted a step-motherly attitude towards them. Ever since 1969 when the 14 major banks were nationalized, the Government has not permitted the establishment of even a single private bank. Even the number of banks has not increased during this period. On the other hand, some private banks are merged with the nationalized banks. This does not mean that all the nationalized banks are in pink health. As many of the deficiencies and defects of these banking systems are unexposed to public view, their weaknesses have not come to light. Of late, they are all coming to light. Owing to Government interference and the politicalisation of their management, the banks have become a butt of public criticism and even ridicule. The recent securities scam has tarnished the image of the banking system as a whole including the public, private and the foreign banks.

Not all the private banks are new. Of them as many as 14 banks were established over 60 years ago. About 15 banks have over 100 branches each. It is stated, quite rightly, that the Government monopoly of the public sector banks is the main cause of their malfunctioning. The Narasimham Committee on Financial Reform has expressed the opinion that these banks would be able to fare better in a competitive environment. A year after this Committee submitted its report the Government of India and the Reserve Bank have both designed regulations in the matter of establishment of private banks. This committee also recommended that the foreign banks should be allowed to set up branches in India. It is feared that the domestic banks may be unable to face the competition of the foreign banks which render efficient customer service equipped as they are with advanced, sophisticated electronic devices. Globalisation of the economy is the declared policy of the Government and this being so even the financial sector is to be globalised. The Dunkel Draft Text (DDT) prepared under the auspices of the GATT and the conditionality prescriptions of the Fund-Bank duo emphasize the need for globalisation of the Indian economy and exposing it to the bracing winds of international competition.

Prior to bank nationalisation important banks in the country were in the hands of a few industrial houses. There was the danger of the bank funds flowing freely into these industries starving the other sectors. With the fall of these industries the banks would also face the prospect of insolvency. Under the Banking Companies Act which was enacted in 1949 this tendency was checkmated. The nationalised Reserve Bank of India was given special powers. With the naitonalisation of the banks it became possible to use the bank funds for social purposes. The priority sectors came to obtain concessionary finance. But as the Government began to use the banks as their obedient servants and directed them to use their funds for purposes which did not satisfy the commercial banking norms, the banks came to trouble. The permission to the private banks to establish themselves in the country is meant to correct the present deficiencies in the banking system.

The Reserve Bank of India has adopted certain measures to prevent a recurrence of the ills the banking system suffered from all these years. The rule that nobody should own more than 1 percent of the total number of shares will continue. This is a process of democratisation of the ownership and management of banks. But if a group of people or members of a family get 1 percent of the shares each it is possible for that group or that family to control the bank. This danger can be averted by an amendment that each person/

family should not get more than 1 percent of the shares. The present capital resources of many banks are not in proportion to the size of their transactions. For this reason of capital inadequacy these banks are weak. The Reserve Bank has stipulated that the capital of these banks should be atleast 8 percent of their resources within the next 2-3 years. The private banks to be established anew have to have so much of capital from the beginning. Apart from this, they are required to have a minimum of Rs. 100 crore of capital. Under these stipulations the banks will be free from the clutches of vested interests, and their activities will be multi-faceted and further they will be free from the risk of insolvency.

Following the recommendations of the Narasimham Committee on Financial Sector Reform the foreign banks are to be given access to the Indian financial system. This access was held in abeyance in the wake of the multi-crore securities scam that rocked the Indian financial system last year. The Fund-Bank duo has made its assistance to India conditional on the entry of foreign banks and the way is open for their entry. Concurrently the way is being cleared by opening up banking to the domestic private sector. Thus, parity is established between the foreign banks and the domestic private banks. These banks will have to employ electronic gadgets from the start to make the financial system, "vibrant, dynamic and competitive". This is the objective of the Reserve Bank of India. But it would be a facile view to regard the computer-intensive Indian Private Sector banks as a competitive force against the foreign banks which employ sophisticated electronic gadgets. It is pertinent to observe that foreign banks in India registered a deposit growth of 69.9 percent during the year ended September 1992 while the scheduled banks registered a deposit growth rate of 24.6 percent. This means that the playing ground is not even.

The domestic private banks take time to learn the tricks of the trade before they can engage themselves in competition with the foreign banks which have achieved a high degree of mastery over it. The domestic banks must be able to earn profits high enough to attract capital from the market to finance their operations. The new banks will have to sell shares which are not in a position to offer attractive dividends comparable to those offered by the non-banking sectors. Furthermore, they will also not be able to adopt the convertibility debenture route to build up reserves to conform to prudential norms. Thus, the strategy of using the private banks to level the playing field will be murky. Under the policy of financial liberalization, the Reserve Bank of India has decided to allow free run for the foreign banks.

Despite these handicaps the private banks are likely to make the grade. This is clear from the eagerness of the select industrial houses to acquire private banks. The reluctance of the markets to subscribe to the equity of the new banks is to be overcome with the support of the public financial institutions. The role of the new private banks is to be defined and the needs which the nationalized banks have failed to meet have to be identified and they have to be assigned to the private banks. Admittedly, banks in India are not competitive but this is not the consequence of the shortage of players. Indian and foreign banks work as a cartel under the Indian Bank's Association in a financial system administered by the Reserve Bank of India. The entry of a number of private banks will strengthen this system. However, the Reserve Bank owes to the nation the announcement of its banking policy.

It is apprehended that the entry of private banks will affect the growth of public sector banks. But this apprehension is unfounded despite its *prima facie* plausibility. On the contrary, it is expected to intensify competition and pave the way for a new work ethic in the public sector banks. Mr. J.V. Shetty, Chairman, Indian Banks Association, has this to say on the subject:

"We have the relative advantage of large physical presence, which the new private sector entrants cannot achieve overnight.... But our boys will have to stand up and face the challenge in terms of automation and improved customer service the private sector may pose".

However, the sudden entry of a large number of private banks can create a situation similar to the one which emerged in Indonesia where a large number of new private sector banks are having a difficult time. Several banks are overburdened with bad debts and the banks have to deal with them individually on their own. The banks should initiate steps to adjust themselves to the changes taking place in the economic environment taking place in the country and also globally. The banks have begun to classify their asset portfolio to the internationally accepted prudential norms. The banks are considering various options to raise fresh capital to achieve the capital adequacy norms as per the Basle Committee recommendations.

The bank employees are opposed to computerization of banking operations on the apprehension that they would be thrown out of employment. This apprehension is not entirely unfounded when the Indian banks have to compete with foreign banks they have to reach the standards of international competitiveness in their operations as otherwise they will not succeed in the game. The foreign banks render quick and efficient service to the customer with the assistance of the sophisticated electronic gadgets. If the domestic banks do not match the foreign banks in respect of the efficiency of quickness of customer service, the customers go to the foreign banks. In this event, the domestic banks lose their business, become sick and may ultimately go out of business. If this eventuality is to be stalled the banks must computerize their operations. The Indian Banks Association should resume talks with the bank employees union and discuss the issue of computerization of their operations and the issue of pay hike sought by them. An exit policy of the type envisaged for the industrial sector must be envisaged for the banking institutions also. In this case, the banks should not be allowed to be closed down but the employees eased out of banks because of computerization should be retrained and redeployed after they acquire the requisite skills. In the meanwhile, they should be given compensation. As the banks enter the banking business the demand for skilled employees increases and those who acquire the requisite skills should be redirected to these banking institutions. But the period of training should not be unduly long. A fund similar to the National Renewal Fund set up for retraining the workers retrenched from the unviable industrial units that are closed down should be set up with contributions from the

Government, the banking institutions and the international financial agencies. If the bank employees are given such assurance, they will not oppose computerization. At the same time, the salary and perquisites of the bank employees should be suitably raised so that they do not lose real income on account of the on-going inflation. Computerization of banking services is essential and it should be undertaken with the active co-operation of the bank employees.

Under the bank nationalization scheme the banks were expected to fulfill certain social obligations like lending to the prior sectors at confessional interest rates. The banks were asked to lend 40 percent of their resources to the priority sectors. The Reserve Bank of India now insists on the private sector banks meeting the priority sector lending targets. But as the new banks need time to adjust to the new situation calling for lending to all categories of the priority sector, the Reserve Bank is prepared to modify the composition of priority sector lending.

The Narasimham Committee recommends a reduction of priority sector lending from the represent 40 percent of bank resources to 10 percent. This priority sector lending at conversional interest rates has no doubt, reduced the profitability of the banking system. But recommended reduction of lending to 10 percent of resources is too steep. The priority sectors, especially agriculture, are used to borrowing at a concessional interest rates. But to reduce it to 10 percent would be to drive the farmers to the clutches of money-lenders who lend money on the security of land at exorbitant interest rates. This will reduce investment in agriculture and farm output in consequence. At a time when the need of the hour is provision of food security, the reduction of priority lending to 10 percent of bank resources will come in the way of reaching the goal. Therefore, while the reduction of priority lending is unexceptionable given the low profitability of the banking system one has to underline the need to reduce it in a phased manner. The priority sector lending norms applicable to public sector banks should be applicable to the private banks also.

The low profitability of the banking system coupled with high and growing non-performing assets and low capital base is a cause of anxiety. The factors responsible for low profitability are the preemptions in the form of Cash Reserve Ratio (CRR) and Statutory Liquidity Ratio (SLR) and the administered structure of interest rates. This calls for a reduction of the CRR and SLR so that the resources may be freed for use by the banking system in order to earn higher interest income. With the projected reduction in the fiscal and budgetary deficits in keeping with the conditionality prescriptions of the IMF the possibility opens itself of reducing CRR and SLR which release funds which the banks can lend at their discretion. Due to the changes made in these ratios preemption of incremental deposits which were 63.5 percent in 1991-92 fell to 45 percent in the first half of 1992-93 and would fall to 25 percent in the Second half of the year. This means that in the second half of 1992-93, 75 percent of the incremental deposits would be available for lending.

The securities scam has underlined the need to strengthen the supervisory system. The scam revealed gross violations of the guidelines prescribed by the Reserve Bank of India. The finance minister stated that the scam was due to "the failure of the system". The Government of India and the Reserve bank of India are designing an optimal model of supervision which envisages the establishment of a supervisory board within the Reserve Bank of India which would attend exclusively to the supervisory functions. This board would be vested with powers to ensure implementation of regulations in the areas of credit management, asset classification, income recognition, provisioning, capital adequacy and treasury operations. This supervisory structure along with shifts in supervisory focus and policies would undoubtedly strengthen the supervision of the Indian banking system.

At present, the interest rate structure is for the most part administered. The deposit and lending rates are specified and the depositors have to deposit their money in the banks at the specified interest rate and the borrowers have to borrow at the specified rate. The gap between the two rates is very wide over 10 percent. The administered interest rate structure is anathema to the competitive financial sector which the Narasimham Committee envisages. If the deposit rates are freed they will be higher than the present specified interest rates and this will increase bank deposits. The lending rates, except in the matter of lending to the priority sectors, should also be freed so that those who want to borrow at the going rate can borrow and invest. The International Food Policy Research Institute in Washington has warned of a food crisis in the developing countries inclusion India due to a decline in investment in agriculture. This has to be reversed to stall the impending food crisis. As the interest rates free form their administered outfit, are higher than the present rates the interest cost component of the cost of production will rise raising the total cost of production and hence the prices of the products. This is unavoidable and this is the side effect of a competitive financial system.

The Indian banking system is even now tradition-bound operating under a system of controls which are out of tune with the emerging economic scenario domestically and globally. India is moving fast in the direction of the market economy. The closed entry of private banks, the administered interest rate structure and the priority sector lending at concessionary interest rates have jointly caused a reduction in the profitability of the banking system and have made some of the banking institutions unviable and even sick. The high CRR and SLR have impounded a large part of bank resources and have reduced the credit potential of the banks. The entry of both foreign and domestic private banks into the financial system is necessary to strengthen the competitive forces in the economy. But the domestic private banks may initially be unable to compete effectively with the foreign banks given to computer-intensive banking operations. This calls for computerizing the banking operations by enlisting the co-operation of the work force. This can be done by introducing a safety valve in the form of a fund to retrain the retrenched employees and to pay them compensation during the period of re-training. As the number of banks in the system increases the re-trained employees can be re-employed there. In these ways, the Indian financial system can be rendered more competitive in keeping with the spirit of the times.

# 99

## Salaries Paid by the Indian Companies to their Personnel

In the absence of indexing wages have a notorious upward flexibility but lack downward flexibility. Wage rates are linked to the rate of inflation. When the inflation rate rises, the cost of living rises engendering enhancement of the wage rates and dearness allowances. This is prevalent in all the sectors of the economy. A rise in wage rates engenders inflation: demand inflation and cost inflation. When wage rates rise the labourers get larger incomes which they spend on goods and services thus generating demand inflation. The employers who pay higher wage rates pass them on to consumers of their products in the form of higher prices. This is called cost inflation. In an inflationary process the two kinds of inflation get entwined and become difficult to disentangle. There emerges a wage-price-spiral-higher prices occasioning higher wages and higher wages occasioning higher prices with no end in sight.

In India one sees this scenario. In all sectors of the economy wages have been rising with the rise in prices and the rise in wages causes a rise in prices. The Union Government appoints pay commission at frequent intervals and these pay commissions are found to be recommending higher salaries and dearness allowances. The state governments are not far behind. They too appoint pay commissions which also recommend higher salaries and dearness allowances. They add to Government expenditure which, in the absence of a proportionate rise in tax revenue enlarges the budget deficits which are patently inflationary. The industrial sector cannot stay behind. Of late the labourers have become militant unlike their predecessors who were docile and timid. Labour militancy is one of the factors which engenders demands for higher wages and if these demands are not met, labourers go on strikes or adopt go-slow methods which have the effect of reducing labour productivity and production. These wage escalations generate inflation in their turn. The banking sector is an important sector which concedes demands for higher wages and salaries more frequently than do other sectors. Wage revision adversely affects profit margins of the public sector banks. At present the bank employees are demanding wage revision. The managements are already committed to staring discussions on the subject now. If the employees are allowed to have their way even partially it would mean a drain of Rs. 900-Rs. 1000 crore towards the increase in wages and salaries. These increases in wages, salaries and dearness allowances push up the inflation rate. But there is another aspect of the problem. The pay commissions recommend wage and salary enhancement with retrospective effect. In consequence, the employees get arrears of large amounts which they are prone to spend rather than to save. This generates demand -push inflation wit a thud.

The higher level of prices has to be sustained by monetary expansion and monetary expansion is occasioned by budget deficits. Under the old gold standard wage revisions were few and far between as there was no money to pay higher wages and governments were committed to running balanced budgets. But at present balanced budgets are the exception rather than the rule. Budget deficits are met by money financing and debt financing. Money financing expands money supply which, under the assumptions, underlying the classical quantity theory of money generates higher prices. Debt financing activates idle savings into active money and through a rise in income velocity also causes a rise in prices. Money financing of the budget deficit is possible if the Reserve Bank of India creates more money. As a result the monetary system has come to be based on what Professor J.R. Hicks calls the "Labour Standard". This is what is happening in India at present.

There is another aspect of the problem which is highlighted by the Finance Minister. The Finance Minister has, of late, expressed concern over the rapid increase in the salaries of senior personnel in the corporate sector. It must be remembered that this development is a consequence of the very policies that the Government has been pursuing in the name of economic reforms. The industrialists owing the corporations have pointed out that globalization of the Indian economy means the movement of capital and labour between India and the rest of the world. Such movement which has to be allowed freely will necessarily lead to an equalization of salaries and profits. This is akin to the factor-price equalization thereon in international trade so ably propounded by Heeksucher and Ohlin. Any move to restrict this development will either not work or will lead to a totally counter-productive work environment or will render the talk of globalization a farce. The attempt by the civil aviation ministry to bind down the senior pilots is a good example of the vitiation of the work environment. The personnel want a level playing field and the Finance Minister seems to have ignored the importance and the necessity of ensuring a level playing filed to the Indian professionals.

The economic reforms programmes, necessary as they are, have been found to be proving to be an expensive proposition. Under the policy of liberation imports of consumer goods are allowed freely. These imports are more expensive than their domestic substitutes. This is true of the whole range of products from cars to soft drinks. It is small consolidation that the products incorporate the latest technologies. The Indian car owners today opt for the old model Ambassador cars but they are reluctant to do it because the producers like so many others in the field have taken the cue from market leaders to increase prices. Furthermore, a large segment of the meritorious medical and engineering graduates migrate to the west in pursuit of better opportunities on higher emoluments and status. Not many return to India for jobs unless the multinational corporations which are their employees post them back on salaries which their counterparts in India cannot even dream of. The only way to reduce this exodus of talent is not to interfere when the corporate employers in India are prepared to offer them sufficient incentive to stay in India. It behoves the Government to formulate a rational wage policy acceptable to all concerned which assures to all sections of the organized sector a fair deal. Level playing filed is the core slogan in a regime of liberalization and globalization. When an Indian employee of a multinational corporation gets salary and status which are attractive it is natural for an Indian employee employed by an Indian company possessing equal talents to aspire for equal salary and status. It would be unfair to blame him for emigrating abroad if he fails to get them. Many talented technocrats are committed to serving Indian and staying in India too as they find the socio-cultural milieu conducive to their happy living. But they need to be given salary and status which approximate, if not equal, those given to the Indians employed by the multinational companies. It is true that this engenders inflation but this is inevitable. When the Government employees and the employees in the industrial and banking sectors get upward revisions of wages at frequent intervals, notwithstanding, the inflationary consequences of these wage revisions, there is no point in expressing concern over the Indian corporate sector paying higher salaries to its personnel in the context of the higher salaries and status enjoyed by the Indian personnel employed by the multinational corporations.

# 100

## Controlling India's Foreign Exchange Boom

Presently, India is faced with the foreign exchange boom which is an embarrassment of riches. In July 1991, when the new Government took over, India's forex reserves were precariously low - $1.1 billion (then worth about Rs. 2300 crore). In the third week of October 1994, they were about $ 18.75 billion (Rs. 58000 Crore) excluding gold coins and bullion worth $ 4.08 billion (Rs. 12000 crore). At present, they are estimated to be $20.0 billion (Rs. 62000 crore). By the end of the fiscal year 1994-95 they are expected to reach $ 25.0 billion (Rs. 77500 crore). It is a worry that this boom has come about in a very short time before the administration could arm itself with sufficient measures to neutralize its evil effects. The rupee is riding high against the US dollar and the Reserve Bank of India (RBI), despite its periodic pronouncements of restraint, continues to buy dollars to prevent an appreciation of the rupee. In fact, the rupee has appreciated already. By maintaining the rupee dollar exchange rate constant at $ 1 = Rs. 31.37 the rupee is allowed to appreciate by the difference between the rate of inflation in India and the rate of inflation in the U.S.A. The purchase of dollars by the RBI spawns more and more money supply in the economy.

The sources of foreign exchange are many and varied. They are, a sharp increase in exports during 1993-94, rise in receipts of invisible Global Depository Receipts (GDRs) funds raised by the Indian companies in the European and US markets, foreign direct investments (FDIs) and funds brought in by foreign institutional investors for portfolio investments. These sources are unlikely to dry up in the next 18 months. Instead, some of them may provide an enhanced flow. For example the flow of both foreign direct investments and foreign institutional investments will increase in the near future. Indian companies are optimistic about raising more funds through the GDR route.

The foreign exchange boom has to be managed for insulating the economy from the inflationary influences emanating from it and also for minimizing the volatility of these fund flows. A similar situation had arisen some years ago in the case of Mexico, Spain, Thailand, Egypt, Columbia and Chile in the wake of economic reforms initiated by them. At present there are many developing countries which have a higher level of forex reserves than India. They are Brazil ($35.7 billion) Malaysia ($33.8 billion) and Singapore ($55 billion), South Korea ($25 billion) China ($35 billion). But these countries do not find the foreign exchange boom problematical. The reserves have to be seen in relation to the volume of foreign trade. Usually reserves are measured against import requirements and three months' import requirements are considered adequate. But India has to live with increasing reserves which are estimated to cover six months' imports. Most of the developing countries have provided such a foreign exchange cover for their import needs like this: Brazil for ten months, Argentina for seven months and Singapore for over six months. In the Indian case, the overflowing reserves growing in volume almost everyday have become a cause for concern to the Government in the same way as in 1991 when the position was the worst. The question which is agitating the minds of the Government and the Reserve Bank of India is the mode of utilization of these reserves in a manner that would be of benefit to the country.

The Government has been adopting several measures since the middle of 1993 in order to check the adverse effects of the forex accumulation. It has reduced the quantum of short-term debts, especially those on which the exchange risk was borne by the Government or the RBI. The scheme under the foreign currency non-resident India deposits (FCNR) with less than one year maturity was withdrawn in May 1993 and the scheme with maturity of one year and above but less than two years was withdrawn in October 1993. In August 1994 the scheme was withdrawn in its entirety. This measure and others like the elimination of foreign currency deposit scheme in July 1993 resulted in a reduction in the share of short-term debt in the total stock from 10.2 percent in March 1991 to 7 percent by March 1993. For this reason the Government was able to pre-pay the IMF loan in 1994.

The Government of India announced the full convertibility of the rupee in August 1994. This will have the effect of limiting the flow of foreign exchange directly to the RBI and to this extent will reduce the problem of foreign exchange management. There were other relaxations relating to the foreign exchange deposit scheme, under the non-resident non-reptriable (NRNR) rupee deposit scheme both the principal and the interest are not to be repatriated. But from October 1, 1994 while the Principal remain non-repatriable interest income will become repatriable. The Government also abolished the foreign currency (ordinary) non-repatraible (FCONR) deposit scheme but the interest accrual will become payable from October 1, 1994. These measures help to reduce the foreign exchange reserves. The income on investments by NRIs and overseas corporate bodies (OCBs) is now repatriable in a phased manner over a three-year period. In the middle of September 1994 the Reserve Bank of India removed the lock-in period on investment made by NRIs / OCBs under the portfolio investment scheme for repatriation of the sale proceeds or sale and transfer of shares and convertible debentures. They can now be sold freely with no loss in a period of one year as earlier. This measure was prompted by a favourable foreign exchange position.

The Government of India has also invested a part of the forex reserves in the United States. But this investment which is expected to earn interest at the rate of 7-8 percent will add to the stock of forex reserves. The World Bank has offered certain important suggestions regarding the management of the forex boom : (1) companies in possession of excess forex reserves should park them in financial institutions and (b) they can be lent to companies which need them but are unable to raise them on their own. But the problem is that in this case, there is bound to be mismatch of maturities. This is because of the fact that while the companies invest their excess reserves only short-term the institutions in which they are invested will lend long-term. There is also the question of the companies unwilling to invest their excess forex reserves with the financial institutors. The companies and Indian banks could be advised to invest their forex reserves in overseas markets. The individuals also could be allowed to invest in overseas markets through mutual funds. The Reserve Bank of India has so thoughtfully raised the limit on India direct investment abroad from $ 2 million to $ 5 million. This is seen as a first step towards capital account convertibility which is already on the cards ready for introduction any time now.

The World Bank has proposed a method of neutralizing the inflationary effects of the forex inflows purchased by the RBI in exchange for rupees. This method is intended to reduce the pressure on the RBI to purchase dollars in order to prevent the rupee from appreciating in the forex market. If this is achieved, it will help to reduce the monetary expansion and the consequent inflation. In 1993-94 the RBI sold Government securities worth Rs. 9047 crore in the open market meant to check inflation. The RBI also raised the cash reserve ratio (CRR) from 14 percent to 15 percent and this immobilised Rs. 2000 crore and this resulted in a withdrawal of that much of money from circulation. The recent Euro Issue guidelines permitting the companies to keep the proceeds abroad until they are actually required by them for use in India has helped to check the inflationary impact of Euro issues. But the majority of companies which raise funds by means of Euro issues are not keen on transferring the proceeds to India as the interest rate overseas is as low 4 percent while it is 15 percent for commercial loans in India. This can be corrected if the rate of interest offered overseas is as high as 15 percent or if the Government of India pays the difference between the overseas interest rate and the interest rate in India. But this is bound to be unduly burdensome to India. The right course of action is to direct the companies to make Euro issues at the time when they need funds and not before they need them as at present.

Earlier, the companies used to avoid taking bank credit as it was found to be expensive. They preferred the cheaper route of

Euro issues and commercial papers (CP). They were reluctant to offer cash credit below 15 percent. After the announcement of the busy season credit policy this seems to have changed. The Indian companies have begun not to rely on CPS and foreign currency loans. Added to his is the apprehension that global interest rates which are attractively low at present may go up and the cost of raising such loans will be higher than raising debt finance in India. Companies with high credit rating are now expected to negotiate with banks for competitive interest rates. After the Euro-issue guidelines curbs are imposed on Euro-issue funds being transferred to India immediately whether or not the Indian companies need theses funds, the companies and corporate bodies, specially blue chip companies, have to come to banks for their funds requirements. This has the effect of reducing the inflow of foreign funds to swell the forex reserves. However small the reduction of the inflow of foreign funds it is bound to reduce the rate of monetary growth and the rate of inflation to some extent.

The Reserve Bank of India can either influence monetary policy or the exchange rate but it cannot do both simultaneously. If the exchange rate is maintained at Rs. 31.37 per dollar by means of purchasing the inflowing dollars, it will have to sacrifice its control over the supply of money unless it resorts to sterilization of incoming dollars, issuing bonds or through open market operations. At present the rupee-dollar exchange rate is not conducive to export growth. This rate is unrealistic. The US dollar is continuously depreciating against the major European currencies and the Japanese Yen. As the rupee is linked to the US dollar, the rupee has also been falling against these currencies. As India's imports from the European countries (in value terms) are large than India's exports to them, the present exchange rate is affecting the interests of India. The Indian exporters do not find the present rupee-dollar exchange rate attractive enough for them to increase exports while the importers find the level too high. There is need to find a mean between the two rates. Though the rate of exchange is fixed, imports and exports are not equal as the rates of inflation are different. The rate of inflation in the USA is 3 percent while that in India is just under 9 percent. If the real exchange rate is to be kept unchanged the rupee must depreciate against the dollar by 6 percent. However, the RBI is keeping the rupee-dollar exchange rate fixed by means of purchase of incoming dollars. For this reason, the rupee is appreciating against the dollar by 6 percent. This makes imports from the USA cheaper by 6 percent every year.

If the RBI stops purchasing the incoming dollars the rupee will appreciate and this will affect India's exports by reducing their competitiveness in world markets. The RBI is purchasing dollars in order to keep the rupee-dollar exchange rate stable at $ 1- Rs. 31.37. The dollar inflow inevitably increased the supply of money and triggered inflation. If the exchange rate is allowed to be determined by the market forces the exchange rate might settle at $ 1 = Rs. 25-26. But this would be harmful to India's exports. This will also upset the trade balance by reducing exports and increasing imports. As India has a comfortable forex reserve position, it is argued that this will be an acceptable alternative. But the increase in imports caused by the appreciation of the rupee will harm domestic production and strengthen the recessionary trends in the economy. There will also be tremendous rise in unemployment. Capital will also free from India as exchanging rupees for dollars at the new exchange rate will yield windfall profits. But this has a side effect which is favourable: it sucks out the rupees and eases inflationary pressures.

It is in this context that this Finance Minister has persuasively argued for liberalizing the imports of consumer goods in order to reduce the stock of forex reserves and to increase the supply of consumer goods in India. In July 1991 the Government set a five year schedule and promised that consumer goods would be allowed at the end of the structural adjustment and stabilization programme. And so. 1996-97 should remain as the year when quantitative restrictions on consumer goods would be removed and their imports put on a tariff basis. This would, of course, give time for domestic industry to enter into strategic alliances or gear up to face foreign competition. But considering the uncomfortably high level of forex reserves and the domestic inflationary pressures there would be no harm in advancing the time-table for liberalizing the import of consumer goods. Liberalization of consumer goods imports will compel domestic industry to improve quality and to reduce costs. At the same time, the forex reserves should also be utilized to import capital goods and advanced technology so necessary to improve price and quality competitiveness of the Indian industrial sector so that it may increase exports and supply high quality goods to the Indian market at reduced prices.

During the past two years, the Government has been able to retire the costly and volatile of foreign exchange reserves. India has also become much more dependent on portfolio capital and Euro-dollars. This is also risky though less volatile than NRI deposits. Speculative as these capital inflows are, they can flow out at short notice. If, per chance, this outflow coincides with the peaking of India's debt repayment next year, the balance of payments situation will come under stress and strain and cause concern for the authorities.

The foreign capital inflows into India are rising putting pressure on the exchange rate. In the past Indian economy used to absorb less than 0.5 percent of GDP in capital inflows. This rose to 2 percent in the mid-eighties. In 1993-94 the inflows were estimated at 4 percent of GDP. This figure could well double in the next few years. If this happens and monetary fiscal policies remain unchanged, the exchange rate of the rupee will significantly appreciate in real terms. This appreciation can be absorbed in two ways: (a) by allowing domestic prices to rise. The RBI has to buy dollars with matching rupees. This money adds to money supply and fuels inflation. (b) by allowing the prices of imported goods to fall. This can be done by allowing the nominal exchange rate to appreciate or by cutting import tariffs. But for an economy which wants to push up exports and appreciation in the nominal exchange rate may be counter-productive. Therefore, the Government has to cut import tariffs. This will lower the prices of imported inputs and increase the relative profitability of exports. But if capital inflows are unmanageable, the required real exchange rate appreciation will lead to domestic inflation even if monetary and fiscal policies are neutral. In this case, the choice of an appropriate nominal exchange rate regime becomes a vital policy matter for the future.

At present China and Singapore rely on direct foreign investment (DFI). The most likely form of capital inflow into India will be foreign equity holdings. This unfortunately can be volatile and can be liquidated much faster than DFI. If investors are given an implicit or explicit exchange rate guarantee, the country can suffer a foreign exchange crisis every time there is a change in the international risk perceptions of India. If the nominal exchange rate is flexible, investors will not withdraw their money as easily as they share both the investment and currency risks. If they unload their equity holdings suddenly, share prices will depreciate and investors will suffer losses. A fully flexible exchange rate will choke off capital inflows by appreciating and depreciating if the market turns bullish or bearish about the country's prospects. This will dissuade the investors from selling their equity holdings. But unless the domestic financial system has been reformed and the Government has attained a balance in public finances it may not be wise to let the rupee float freely. In view of this other options are to be considered.

It is suggested in certain influential quarters that the problem could be solved from the standpoint of supply side by devaluing the rupee in nominal terms. It is argued that this would improve the profitability of exports, would stimulate exports, curtail imports and help or restore trade balance. But the beneficial impact of devaluation cannot be taken for granted. Devaluation raises the prices of imports. A large part of India's exports is import-intensive. Devaluation, by raising the prices of imported capital goods, raw materials and technology, will raise the cost of production of exports making use of imported inputs. This reduces the profitability of exports. This also raises the prices of exports while devaluation itself lowers these prices. If the two are of equal strength, the net effect of devaluation on exports will be zero on balance. Furthermore, we have to take into account the income effect of rising income on the trade balance. When the income in the country is rising it generates fresh demand for imports and exportable items.

This effect increases imports, reduces exports and has a negative effect on the trade balance. In the context of a high fiscal deficit and wage escalation the rate of inflation rises and this works against the improvement in the trade balance. If the fiscal deficit is held constant and the wage rates are held constant, the price effect of devaluation may, if at all, improve the trade balance. But the fiscal deficit and the wage rates are unlikely to remain constant. Furthermore, the success of devaluation depends on the fulfillment of the Marshall-Lerner condition that the sum of the two import elasticities is greater than one. No precise estimates of the elasticities of demand for imports are available. For this reason, no definite conclusions can be drawn about the effects of devaluation on the trade balance. Devaluation as a remedy for the balance of payments deficits depends for its success on the fulfillment of several stringent conditions which do not exist in India. The major outcome of devaluation is certainly inflation which it is the objective of policy to avoid. Therefore, devaluation has to be ruled out.

At present, India's external debt has reached staggering heights. The need of the hour is to reduce it and thus to reduce the burden of external debt and the interest burden. The burgeoning forex reserves can be used to retire high interest debt and thus to save on the interest cost. The forex reserves are said to be volatile and their continuation in the vaults of the RBI is characterized by uncertainty and indefiniteness. If, after the debt is retired, the owners desire to shift the reserves abroad the Government will have to face embarrassment if the reserves are not available. Therefore, that part of the forex reserves which is fairly stable in India should be used to retire external debt. At the same time, the volatile part of the forex inflow should be discouraged by means of a strict ban on it or by offering a lower rate of interest. This will check the inflow of volatile capital. At the same time, the companies should be asked to raise money by means of Euro issues only at the time when they need capital and not long before they need it. In these ways the forex boom can be mitigated The finance Minister has to bestow some attention on the foregoing options failing which inflation emanating from the forex inflow becomes immitigable upsetting macroeconomic stability.

# 101

## Devaluation of the Rupee or Increasing the Conversion Ratio to 80 Percent

In his budget speech presenting the Union Budget for 1992-93 the Finance Minister announced that the rupee would be partially convertible. Under the partial convertibility dispensation, two rates of exchange for the rupee were envisaged. There is an official rate for transactions for Government imports and for foreign exchange upto 40 percent of the amount. The exchange rate for the balance of 60 percent is left for the market forces to determine. However, there are reports that the rupee would be made fully convertible in the Union Budget for 1993-94. This has triggered speculation about the future value of the rupee.

The dealers in foreign exchange expect a devaluation of the rupee in the next few weeks following depreciation of the market rate in the last two months. This depreciation has been caused by speculation in the market that full convertibility of the rupee is on the anvil. The fluctuation in the external value of the rupee has coincided with the volatility of the major currencies in the world money markets following the European currency crisis in which the US dollar has gained. The pound sterling, particular, has come under pressure and the other European currencies and the Japanese. You have also fluctuated widely as the dollar gained strength. This is another reason for the falling value of the rupee. The foreign exchange dealers feel that the slight devaluation will both reflect the realities of the world currency market as well as pressure on the rupee owing to domestic speculation over convertibility.

There was a two-step devaluation of the rupee in July 1991 and then by just over 1 percent in November 1992 when it came under pressure with the rise of the dollar. The rupee has been depreciating since November 1992 when the market rate was

I$1=Rs. 29.50. It came down to Rs. 30.20 in December 1992 and further to Rs. 30.30 in January 1993 and fell sharply to Rs. 32.18 on January 4, 1993 and to Rs. 32.78 on January 5, 1993 and to predict a further depreciation of the rupee in the next few weeks and this is another reason why they expect the Reserve Bank of India to order a devaluation of the official rate soon.

The Finance Ministry Officials say that the Finance Minister has not yet made up his mind on whether the rupee would be made fully convertible. This would depend on whether the balance of payments situation has improved and whether the rate of inflation has come down sufficiently. On the trade front, though exports increased by 6 percent during October 1992 the trade deficit during April-October touched $2.72 billion which is an increase of 103 percent over last years' deficit figures for the corresponding period which was $ 1.34 billion. This is the result of an increase of 18 percent in imports during October mainly because of increased imports crude and petroleum products. While a failure to increase exports significantly over the next year would tell adversely on the balance of payments position, unfortunately the rising oil import bill also does not augur well for the country's balance of payments situation. During the first four months of 1992-93 imports of crude oil and petroleum products has gone up 72 percent over the previous corresponding period to Rs. 5,626 crore. While this remains so, the foreign exchange reserve position hovers at a comfortable $ 5000 million after decreasing by $ 770 million during the first eight months of 1992-93. This would, however, be a misleading yardstick as the foreign exchange position has been shored up with borrowings from the IMF and the Asian Development Bank which actually means that the debt burden will increase over the next few years. The oil pool account estimates have done awry with the need for additional $ 500 million for fresh imports to meet demand for oil. According to estimates India will have to provide for a total of $47.2 billion towards repayment of Principal and interest over the next few years. The country's total external debt is put at $ 92 billion. Apart from the balance of payment problem, the higher petroleum imports, resulting from a shortfall of 2 million tonnes in domestic production could also lead to problems in meeting the fiscal deficit targets agreed to by the Government under the stand-by programme of the IMF. The Finance Ministry is reported to be hard-put to meet the conditionality on the budget and fiscal deficits for the next year as part of the macro-economic adjustment programme.

Even with modest current account deficits India's foreign exchange needs will be substantial largely due to the large scheduled repayments of debt. This is the opinion expressed by the World Bank Report on the Economic Reforms and Development Trends in various Developing countries 1992. On the challenges facing India on the balance of payments front the Reports says that India's foreign exchange reserves are still insufficient to cope with any exogenous stock such as drought related agricultural productions shortfalls or adverse developments in the external environment. In addition the management of the capital account will continue to be difficult because of the large share of volatile NRI deposits ($11 billion) and short-term debt ($3 billion) in India's external debt of $ 73 billion. Thus considerable vulnerability to liquidity crises remains. So decline in reserves could precipitate a confidence crisis.

The budget deficit of the Government is Rs. 13,000 crore. This will have to be brought down by Rs. 7,600 crore before the budget is presented on 27-2-1993 to meet the target of Rs. 5389 crore. While part of this is sought to be made up through the disinvestment of public sector equity to the extent of Rs. 3,500 crore, the lackluster response to the bids floated by the Government will place an additional burden on the Government in meeting the targets. A much more difficult task would be to bring down the fiscal deficit which reflects the total net borrowings of the Government. The 1992-93 budget had provided for a target of Rs. 34,408 crore for the fiscal deficit which is about 5 percent of GDP. While the tax revenues have been buoyant and collections have gone up considerably. The weak financial position of several state Governments would place an additional burden on the exchequer. While only 62 percent of the target budget deficit is sought to be met through borrowings from the Reserve Bank the rest is expected to be made good through market borrowings which will further raise the interest burden making it difficult to meet the fiscal deficit target.

The rate of inflation is fluctuating. The rate of inflation measured in terms of wholesale price index on a point-point basis was always in two-digit level each month during 1991-92; in 1992 it remained almost at a single digit level and in the first week of February 1993 it stood at 7.8 percent. Though the wholesale price index is expected to increase marginally following the increase in fertilizer prices and the enhancement of procurement prices, the record oil seed production and the Government's decision to go in for wheat imports coupled with brisk rice procurement is expected to contain inflation.

In view of the precariously comfortable foreign exchange reserve position the Finance Minister can confidently go in for reducing the customs duties as recommended by the Chellaiah Committee Report. The maximum import duty rate which was as high as 400 percent some years ago had been settled down to 100 percent by the Narasimha Rao Government. The Trade and Industry had been pressing for a further sealing down of import duty rates to bring it in line with the rates prevailing in other countries where the maximum import duty rates were around 40 percent. The Chellaiah Committee recommended that by 1997-98 the structure of advalorem rates of duties should be 5,10,15,20, 25 and 30 percent. In the case on non-essential consumer goods there should be another "slot", namely, 50 percent. The Committee suggested that a minimum rate of 5 percent should be applied to those items which were exempt. While it might not be possible to apply this rate immediately to fertilizers, ammonia and phosphoric acid, these commodities should also be subjected to duty at the earliest. The rate on other goods should be reduced so as not to hurt the domestic industries.

If the rupee is devalued as demanded by the industrialists it will be of much effect on the balance of payments front for several reasons: (1) the reduction in the import duty following the adoption of recommendations of the Chellaiah Committee Report will make imports cheaper and counter the price effect of devaluation on imports. Since the reduction of import duty is going to be massive it will more than offset the contractive effect of devaluation on imports; (2) the reduction of the budget and fiscal deficits are unlikely to reach the targets fixed by the Government. Furthermore, the increase in the procurement prices of rice and wheat are bound to unleash inflationary forces on the economy. In view of this the rate of inflation which is 7.8 percent at present is likely to rise; (3) the wage rates in the industries are poised for a rise. The pay commision appointed by the Central Governments and several state governments are sure to recommend higher pay scales and dearness allowances. These will unleash a fresh bout of inflation. These factors effectively counter the effect of devaluation of imports. The recession in the Western countries and the protective wall raised by them are another factor which are not conducive to an expansion of exports. Furthermore, any devaluation of the rupee will increase the rupee value of external debt and of the interest and amortization payments which will impose a burden on the capital account of the balance of payments. In view of all these considerations devaluation of the rupee is unlikely to be effective in remedying the balance of payments deficits.

In view of the uncomfortable balance of payments positions and the possibility of a rise in the rate of inflation the full convertibility of the rupee may not be a feasible alternative to partial convertibility in vogue at present. It is therefore, possible that the Finance Minister rather than opting for full convertibility will increase the conversion ratio from the present 60 percent to 80 percent at the market rate. If this is done what are the consequences?

If this is done, the price of foreign exchange in terms of rupees rises in the same way as it does under devaluation. The importers have to buy foreign exchange at the new market rate by surrendering more rupees per dollar or Mark than they did before. As the prices of imports are dominated in foreign currency, they will rise in terms of rupees. If there is no reduction in import duties, the prices of imports rise and to the extent that the demand for imports is price-elastic, this demand will fall. But the reduction of import duty as recommended by the Chellaiah Committee will reduce the prices of imports more than the new market rate of exchange raises them. There will thus be a net reduction in the prices of imports causing rise in the demand for them. There will thus be no relief on the import front even when there is an increase in the conversion ratio. What of the export front? The exporters have to import raw materials and capital goods to produce goods for the export market. As there will be a rise in the prices of these imports, the cost of production on the prices of exports rise rendering them uncompetitive in the international markets. This makes it difficult to reach the export target. Added to this the difficulty of meeting the budget and fiscal deficit targets and possibility of a rise in the rate of inflation also militate against a significant expansion of exports.

A comparison of the consequences of devaluation of the rupee and an increase in the conversion ratio under partial convertibility leads us to the following conclusions:

Devaluation has the effect of raising the prices of imports and lowering the prices of exports and to improve the balance of payments if the sum of the elasticities of demand for imports and the demand for exports is greater than unity. No reliable estimates of these elasticities are available at present and therefore all that can be said is that in respect of essential raw materials, petroleum and petroleum products and capital goods the demand is inelastic while in respect of consumer goods for which perfect domestic substitutes are not available the demand is inelastic. It is only in respect of consumer goods for which domestic substitutes are available that the demand is elastic causing a fall in demand following devaluation of the rupee.

Devaluation makes exports cheaper in terms of rupees and if the demand is elastic exports rise. But if the importing countries are facing a recession in their economies the demand for exports falls; furthermore, if they raise the tariff wall the prices of their imports rise and the protective tariff nullifies the favourable effect of devaluation on exports.

If in India prices rise under the impact of fiscal deficits or wage escalation and if, in consequence, the prices of domestic substitutes rise or if the level of income in the country rises the demand for domestic substitutes falls in the first case and the demand for import substitutes rises while the rise in income causes a rise in the demand for imports and, to some extent, a rise in the demand for domestic substitutes. The rise in the demand for domestic substitutes will not be significant. The net effect of the fiscal deficit and wage escalation is to increase the demand for imports through the income effect and to reduce the demand for imports through the price effect. If the income effect swamps the price effect there will be a net increase in imports. But the projected reduction in import duties makes the imports cheaper and this further offsets the price effect of devaluation and causes a rise in imports. Furthermore, a rise in the level of income because a rise in the demand for exportables and reduces the volume of exports; a rise in the prices of exports caused by fiscal deficit and wage escalation causes a fall in the foreign demand for India's exports. Thus, both the income effect and the price effect reinforce one another and reduce the volume of exports. These are the consequences of devaluation. These consequences are common to a raising of the conversion ratio under partial convertibility with the difference that under it only those goods exported and imported are affected.

There is one fundamental difference between devaluation and raising of the conversion ratio under partial convertibility. Under devaluation there will be a rise in the value of external debt and value of the interest and amortization payments and this imposed a burden on the capital account of the balance of payments. But this does not exist when the conversion ratio is raised under partial convertibility. This difference which is crucial to the burden of external debt should make the Government prefer raising of the conversion ratio to devaluing the rupee. It is hoped that if the Finance Minister is to choose between devaluation and raising the conversion ratio, he will choose the latter as it is the lesser of the two evils.

Full convertibility of the rupee can wait till the balance of payments position improves and inflation is brought down to the targeted level with no possibility of a rise. At present, the balance of payments position is weak, the rate of inflation is poised for a rise and the foreign exchange situation is not uncomfortable. Resort to full convertibility of the rupee now will make the rupee weak in the foreign exchange market with no assurance of any improvement in the balance of payments and no abatement in the rate of inflation. Full convertibility can wait till the situation improves. Raising of the conversion ratio to 80 percent where the exchange rate will be market-determined means that only 20 percent of the foreign exchange will be sold to the Reserve Bank of India at the official rate. This is close to full convertibility. In the light of the performance of this exercise full convertibility can be considered. Dash to full convertibility is not warranted now.

# 102

## Export Sluggishness and Strategy for Export Promotion

In India it is the export front that holds the key to the behaviour of the balance of payments. Despite the new EXIM Policy announced by the Government of India on April 1, 1992 exports are lagging behind the target. Though exports increased by 6 percent (as against the projected 13.5 percent) during October 1992 the trade deficit during April-October touched $ 2.7 billion which is an increase of 103 percent over the last years' deficit figure for the corresponding period which was $ 1.34 billion. This is the result of an increase of imports by 18 percent during October mainly because of increased import of crude and petroleum products. At the same time, it is estimated that the export target of $ 20 billion set for 1992-93 may be missed by about a billion dollars on account of the present unfavourable political climate in the country and the recession in major Western economies. While the failure to reach the export target next year adversely affects the balance of payments, the rising oil import bill has its contribution to make to making the balance of payment adverse. During the first four months of 1992-93 imports of petroleum products and crude oil had risen by 72 percent over the corresponding period of 1991-92 to Rs. 5626 crore. The foreign exchange reserve position hovered round $ 5770 million after decreasing to $ 770 million during the first eight months of 1992-93. This would of course, be a misleading index considering the fact that the forex position has been shored up with borrowing from the IMF and the Asian Development Bank which means that the debt burden will increase. The oil pool account estimates have been upset with the need for additional $500 million for fresh imports to meet the demand for oil. Furthermore, according to estimates India has to provide for a total for $47.2 billion towards repayment of principal and interest over the next few years. The country's total external debt is estimated to be $ 93 billion. Apart from the balance of payments problem, the higher petroleum imports resulting from a shortfall of 2 million tonnes in domestic production could lead to problem in meeting the fiscal deficit targets agreed to by the Government under the stand-by programme of the IMF. The Finance Ministry is hard put to it to meet the conditionalities on the Budget and the fiscal deficit next year as part of the structural adjustment programme.

In the mid-eighties the average export growth was 16% but now it is only 5% against the projected growth of 13.5%. The unsuccess of the export policy supported by the Liberalized Exchange Rate Mechanism (LERM) is due to several factors. The Government explains this phenomenon in terms of the following: (1) trade with the erstwhile rupee payment areas (RPA) has almost collapsed. In the first two quarters of 1992-93 RPA exports were down by 56% over the previous year and (2) world recession has caused a decline in the demand for goods in the recession-hit countries. The Commerce Ministry has sought refuge in these explanations. Many rupee payment areas have switched to dollar trade. Russia, the largest of the former RPA countries, is now a General Currency Area (GCA) country. Secondly, dollar exports to the United States and Germany have grown by 20.9 % and 7.9% respectively. This means that the world recession has not hit exports as much as the Government has made out. World recession and the collapse of the RPA trade had a sectoral impact on commodities like tea, leather and garments but they did not affect the export trade overall. In fact the cause of sluggish export growth is to be found in the dual exchange rate regime established by the partial convertibility of the rupee.

Under this regime the export earnings and expenditure on imports have been structured in the manner prescribed by the LERMs. Under the partial convertibility dispensation, the exporters have to convert 60% of their earnings at the market-determined rate and the balance of 40% at the official rate. Imports have to be financed entirely at the market determined rate. The imports of raw materials accounts for 15 to 25 percent depending on the import content of exports. The purchase of imports at the market rate results in high input cost and this has the effect of out-pricing Indian exports from the world market and making them lose competitive advantage. This has the effect of causing import compression as many importers defer their import decisions. This observation is grounded in official statistics. Between April and September 1992 the growth in total imports in dollar terms was just 0.8% over that in 1990 when there was no officially sponsored import compression. Comparative figures for non-oil imports are revealing. They are many of the inputs that feed exports like non-ferrous metals, iron and steel, cereals and newsprint. Non-oil imports in April-September 1992 fell by 5.6 percent compared with the same period in 1990. The high input costs are compounded by the high interest rates which ruled at 14 percent during the busy season credity policy. Though this is lower than the commercial rate of lending of 17 percent, exporters consider this rate unduly high. In some cases, (cashew exports) interest cost shave soared from 6 percent to as high as 32 percent of total cost. But exporters argue that since exports are considered to be a thrust sector, they are entitled to concessional credit at interest rates of 7-8 percent and that exports should be considered priority sector like agriculture. The problem of export credit is a complex one. Recently a committee was set up under the Chairmanship of Shri. Sundaram, Additional Secretary in the Commerce Ministry, to review the question of export credit. The problem is complex as there is a conflict of interests between the Commerce Ministry and the Finance Ministry. The Finance Ministry looks at the macro-balance. There is a mis-match between export promotion and the balance of payments crisis. In order to attract NRI investments the interest rate offered has to be high. But high interest rates adversely affect investment in the industrial sector and this has an adverse effect on exports. It is also possible that if the interest rate on export credit is reduced the banks may be unwilling to lend. This would adversely affect export trade. But the Commerce Ministry argues that the rate of interest reflects the distortions in the economy and the exporters should be compensated for this. There is thus utter confusion and uncertainty operating in the export sector.

It is admitted by the exporters that partial convertibility of the rupee has simplified the procedures. But they argue that the delay in claiming subsidies like cash compensatory support (CCS) reduces the cash flow. Many export houses are owed considerable sums of money but there is inordinate delay in realizing this and, in consequence, there is a reduction in the cash flow. There is also delay in the issue of licences for the import of goods listed on the negative list. The issue of licences for the import of goods listed in the negative list was announced in April 1992 when the EXIM Policy was announced. But the notification was issued in September 1992. The uncertainty also flows from the dual exchange rate regime. In fact, the exporters have to deal with three exchange rate systems the official rate, the market rate and the illegal or the hawala rate. It is true that partial convertibility has reduced the margin between the legal and the hawala rate from 15 percent to 5 percent. Even this discrepancy acts as an irritant. In order to avoid the uncertainty and confusion implicit in this exchange rate regime, many exporters opt for full convertibility. But it must be realized that full convertibility may improve the profitability but it also the increases in costs of POL and fertilizer imports in rupee terms. This would give a 2-3 percent cost push to inflation. However, there is one advantage in the present regime. This is the change in the norms for advanced licensing scheme. Advanced licences are made value-based instead of quantity based. This gives a chance for higher profitability. With the value-based advanced licence the exporters are able to adjust their import mix to better advantage instead of being constrained by the quantities stipulated by the government. But the procedural advantages of this type cannot hide the fact that the present export regime is not as effective as the policy makers think it is. It is held in certain quarters that the Exim scrip was better than the present arrangement for promoting exports. The reason is that the Exim scrip system tied the bulk of imports to a percentage of imports and this would serve as an automatic check on the strain on the balance of payments. This was conducive to enlarged foreign investment flow. But as there is no such automatic check to the strain on the balance of payments, the Government has to resort to devaluation and to the consequent cost increase.

Confusions reigning in the export front at present. This explains why two quarters into 1992-93, the export regime which was supposed to boost exports like never before and iron out the country's balance of payments problems yielded a paltry 6 percent growth in dollar terms. The EXIM policy announced on April 1, 1992 targeted for an export growth of 13.5 percent, but the actual achievement has taken far short of the target. This is too inadequate to close the trade gap. In view of this, the Government has formulated a short term action plan keeping in view the export target of $ 20,132 million or roughly Rs. 57,850 crore set for the year 1992-93. This plan includes the further simplification and streamlining of policies and procedures enunciated in the Exim Policy. This also includes the improvement of export environment such as full convertibility of the rupee on trade account, better terms for export credit, more efficiency duty drawback systems, wider coverage of income tax benefits and the like. These are routine remedies of not much consequence. What is necessary in the light of experience is the adoption of the following package of measures:

Under the partial convertibility dispensation the exporters have to surrender 40 percent of their export earning to the Reserve Bank of India at the official rate of exchange and the balance of 60 percent of their earnings they have to sell at the market rate. The market rate is higher than the official rate. The importers of inputs in the export industries have to purchase the inputs at the market rate of exchange. This has the effect of raising the input cost and consequently the price of final output. Therefore, pending the adoption of full convertibility arrangements could be made for the exporters who need imported inputs in their industries to finance these imports by purchasing foreign exchange at the official rate of exchange. This will reduce the input cost of export goods and reduce the prices of final output that is to be exported.

A related action to reduce the prices of export goods is the reduction of the rate of interest on borrowing for investment. At present it is as high as 14 percent. If this is reduced the volume of investment in the export sector rises causing a rise in the export volume. The case of lending at concessional interest rate to the export sector is strong indeed. Furthermore, the remedy for recession in the industrial sector producing goods for the export market is a low interest rate. While the reduction in the fiscal deficit is necessary to reduce the rate of inflation, a reduction in the rate of interest is necessary to remedy the recession. The theory of the policy mix stipulates a combination of fiscal deficit reduction as a remedy for inflation and a policy of interest rate reduction as a remedy for recession. In view of this, a reduction of interest rate is necessary to promote investment in the industries in general and in the export industries in particular. Furthermore, a reduction of interest rate on export credit is also necessary to promote exports. The apprehension that the banks may be unwilling to make export credit available to exporters when the interest rate of export credit is reduced is unfounded. The banks have been found to be financing the priority sectors at concessional interest rates. The export sector being an important thrust sector viewed in the context of the balance of payments gap needs to be encouraged to expand so as to enable it to take care of the balance of payments. The balance of payments gap has to be closed in order to reduce India's dependence on external financing. The right strategy is to increase exports. This cannot be done by devaluation for the conditions on which its success depends do not obtain in India.

# 103

## A Case for Retaining Fertilizer and Food Subsidies

The question relating to the fertilizer subsidies has been a headache to the Government of India. The World Bank and the International Monetary fund have been insisting on removing the subsidies of all hues and they have made this the condition precedent to the credit/loans being extended to India from time to time. Their contention rests of two grounds : (1) that they are inconsistent with the market-friendly policies being pursued by the Government and (2) that they exacerbate inflationary pressure as they widen the fiscal deficits which are inflationary. These arguments need to be examined.

The Government of India appointed a committee to go into the question of fertilizer prices which has also to examine the need for and the desirability of continuing fertilizer subsidy. The policy in this regard is expected to be announced in September 1992.

Admittedly the economic reform measures initiated by the Government of India over a year ago are market-friendly. This does not mean that India has adopted the free market approach of classical conception. India is on the road to a free market economy and the progress towards this goal is slow and sluggish considering the structural and institutional imperfections inherent in the Indian economic system. In a system like this, it would not be in order to scrap the fertilizer subsidy or any other subsidy. It must be remembered that the economic system of the United States and of Western Europe approach the classical free market economy. Even so, they retained agricultural subsidies. When this is the case it is incomprehensible why the Fund-Bank duo insists on India scrapping the subsidies. This insistence lacks logical force.

It is true that the subsidies involve a rise in Government expenditure. Given the revenue from various sources the payment of subsidies increases the non-plan expenditure of the Government and widens the budget deficit. Whether the budget deficit is financed by borrowing or by money creation the consequence is inflationary though money financing of the deficits less inflationary than debt financing. The Fund-Bank combine insists on the fiscal deficit being reduced from 6.5 percent of GDP to 5 percent of GDP. If this is to be possible the subsidies should be scrapped. So far so good. But this argument does not go far enough. The reason for advocating the scrapping of subsidies in the need to reduce the rate of inflation. If scrapping of the subsidies which results in a reduction of the fiscal deficit acts in a disinflationary manner, there can be no opposition to its scrapping. But the things are not so simple as this. The scrapping of the fertilizer subsidy would push up the prices of urea and phosphate based manure widely used by farmers by 60 percent and 100 percent respectively. Even the current subsidies prices it is difficult for the farmers to buy fertilizers. The free market price of fertilizers is bound to render fertilizers absolutely unaffordable to the farmers. If the demand for fertilizers is elastic the demand for it falls, the input of fertilizers falls causing a fall in farm productivity and farm production. The demand for farm products being constant, the fall in their supply is bound to generate excess demand for them which pushes up the prices of farm products. As a consequence, the market prices of farm products including those of food articles rise. This has the effect of exacerbating inflation which the scrapping of the fertilizer subsidy is supposed to hold down. If, on the other hand, the demand for fertilizer is inelastic the input of fertilizers will not fall and, in consequence, farm productivity and farm production will not fall (assuming no change in the weather conditions). But as the higher prices of fertilizers push up the costs of production, the farmers have, perforce to raise the prices of their farm products. Thus if the demand for fertilizers is elastic there will occur demand-pull inflation and if the demand for fertilizers is inelastic there will occur cost push inflation. In either case inflation is the consequence though the scrapping of the fertilizer subsidy results in a reduction of the fiscal deficit. If the subsidy is retained there will be inflation generated by the fiscal deficit; if the subsidy is scrapped there will be demand-pull or cost-push inflation depending on whether the demand for fertilizers is elastic or inelastic. If any case inflation is inevitable. But inflation caused by retaining the subsidy is preferable to inflation caused by scrapping it. In any case the argument of the Fund-Bank combine that the scrapping of the fertilizer subsidy is necessary to hold down the fiscal deficit and through it to hold down the rate of inflation is, on the face of it; unsustainable. Besides this there is a non-economic argument against the scrapping of the fertilizer subsidy. The farmers are used to buying subsidized fertilizers. If, all on a sudden, the subsidy is scrapped it would be difficult for them to make the necessary mental adjustment to the new situation and there is bound to be a popular upheaval against the scrapping of the fertilizer subsidy. Already there are many social, political and economic tensions and scrapping of the fertilizer subsidy will add to them and make the situation grossly intractable.

The dilatory attitude of the Government in adopting a firm policy has put the fertilizer industry in an embarrassing position and has rendered it incapable of designing future plans. The industry has been pressing the Government in paying back the subsidy amount and unscientific method adopted in computing subsidy have had a crippling effect on the industry. The subsidy arrears at present amount to Rs. 1600 crore. Within a few months they would rise to Rs. 2,000 crore. Even if the Government pays up the arrears without delay it will be Rs. 5000-Rs. 6000 less than the industry's expenditure.

The subsidy being paid on fertilizers was calculated on prices fixed in 1990. Though the rate is being hiked by 5 percent every year, the actual rise in real terms works out to 10 percent. There are several other factors which have put the fertilizer industry in doldrums. The Gulf war which caused a hike in oil prices, the devaluation of the rupee and the EXIM Policy adopted on 1-4-1992 have caused a tremendous rise in the cost of production of fertilizers but the Government has not taken these factors into account while determining the price of fertilizers and the rate of subsidy.

Besides this, there are several anomalies in the official policy stance. Fertilizers are exempted from the hiked railway freight rates but many of the vital inputs of the industry do not enjoy this advantage. The imported fertilizers are not subject to import duties but the import of certain raw materials used in fertilizer production attract duties. These two factors have put the domestic fertilizer industry at a great disadvantage. This calls for the following policy measures. In the first place, the arrears due to the fertilizer industry must be paid in full and without delay in order to avoid the industry becoming unviable. In the second place, the subsidy has to be calculated on a scientific basis. In the third place, the vital inputs required by the industry should be exempted from the hike in railway freight rates in the save way as fertilizers. In the fourth place, the import of raw materials required by the fertilizer industry should be free from import duties in the same ways as imported fertilizers. These measures will go long way in placing the domestic fertilizer industry on a sound footing and enhance its viability.

The Fund-Bank combine is also insisting on scrapping of subsidies on food. It is true that food subsidies cause a rise in Government expenditure, increase the fiscal deficit and occasion inflation. But the scrapping of food subsidies will cause a rise in food prices in the market. In India, it is the food prices that govern the general price index and therefore the rate of inflation. If following the scrapping of food subsidies, food prices rise, the cost of living rises. This engenders demands for higher wages which, if granted, will generate demand pull and cost push inflations which get entwined and become difficult to disentangle. This creates a situation where there will emerge a vicious circle of prices and wages chasing one another. This type of inflation is worn than the inflation generated by fiscal deficits caused by the payment of food subsidies.

The Fund-Bank combine wants the Government of India to reduce the rate of inflation. For this reason it wants a reduction of the fiscal deficit to 5 percent of GDP in 1992-93. If the reduction of the fiscal deficit results in a reduction in the rate of inflation one would lend support to the argument advanced by the Fund-Bank combine. But the scrapping of the subsidies, while reducing the fiscal deficit, has the unwelcome effect of generating inflation of the type which is worse and more vicious than the inflation generated by the enlarged fiscal deficit caused by the retention of the subsidies. In view of this, subsides on fertilizers and food have to be retained for some more time and then phased scrapping should be pragmatic and not doctrinaire. But at present and for some time to come the case for retaining the fertilizer and food subsidies is strong indeed. Given the foregoing arguments the Government of India should resist any demand for scrapping subsidies. Subsidies are there even in the economies approaching the market economy of the classical conception. When India is gradually moving in that direction why scrap subsidies. The time is not yet propitious for it.

# 104

## Population Growth and Unemployment

Unemployment has remained a serious problem in the country. Despite several plans to alleviate unemployment, it has developed resistance. At the beginning of 1990, the number of unemployed including severely unemployed was 28 million which would be likely to go to 57 million by 1995. Between 1995 and 2000 another 41 million would be added to the Jobless Roll taking the total tally of the unemployed to 106 million by the turn of the century.

The problem is not an easy task. Every day 44,635 babies are born. Development means nothing unless the rate of population growth is checked.

Unemployment in India is related to population growth. India's population has been growing at an alarming rate so much so that India has to run fast in order to remain in the same place. At present the rate of population growth is 2.2 percent. This is a conservative estimate. Presently India contributes more to world population growth than China or any other country and will continue to do so till the year 2150 according to the world bank report entitled "World Population Projections". India's eventual stationary population is projected in the Report at 2.3 times the 1985 population which was 765.147 million. By 2150 India's population is projected at 1756.718 million by then India's expected to overtake China as the most populous nation in the world between 2050 and 2075.

What are the causes of this alarming rate of population growth in India? In the first place family planning programmes are applicable to only one section of the population and the other section is free from it under Personal Law. Even that section to which they are applicable especially in the rural areas is averse to it. As professor Colin Clark has stated in India babies are considered to be gifts of god, then why refuse these precious gifts. This belief is pervasive and it militates against the effectiveness of family planning. In the second place Children are regarded more as producers of wealth than as a burden on the limited resources of the family. Greater the number of Children the greater the family income as children when they come of age, earn income for the family/income. Therefore every family wants to get as many children as possible.

Food supply for the growing population is inadequate even at sub-normally low nutritional standards. This leads to undernourishment, ill health reduced longevity and destitution. Further a growing population has more consumers than producers. Savings are used up in their maintenance, causing a fall in the savings ratio on which investment and the rate of economic growth depends. As a result the growth of population has pushed India to low level equilibrium trap. As the growing population adds to the labour force more than the jobs available for the fruitful employment, the rate of unemployment rises. This makes more and more people sink below the poverty line. Thus rapid growth of population generates the problems of unemployment and poverty. Considerable resources which would otherwise have gone to faster economic growth are used up in alleviating poverty and unemployment.

It is therefore, necessary to aim at a zero population growth (ZPG) by applying family planning programme to all sections of society irrespective of their caste or religion by the use of stick and carrot method.

# 105

## India's Balance of Payments

The Government of India has recently appointed a committee to examine India's balance of payments, the nature and size of its gap and to suggest measures or remedying this gap. The committee has started its work already under the Chairmanship of Shri Rangarajan.

Mrs. Joan Robinson developed the twin barrier theory of economic development and argued that every developing economy (India not excluded) faces two barriers: inflation barrier and the balance of payments barrier. The same idea was elucidated by Professor Jan Tindbergen in terms of the two-gap model the savings gap and the trade gap. These two gaps have been in operation in India since the beginning of the Second Five year Plan with different degrees of intensity. The Government has been trying several ineffective expedites without tackling the real problem.

The main cause of domestic inflation is the budget deficit, financed partly by money creation and partly by domestic borrowing. Both are inflationary in consequence though the latter is more inflationary than the former. This is due to the fact that domestic borrowing increases interest payments which add to budget deficit and generate inflation in the economy. Casualty tests have established causal connection between the budget deficits and balance of payments deficits. This means that the cause suggests the remedy. The remedy for the balance of payments gap in the reduction in the size of the budget deficit.

During the period of planning since 1956 the budget deficits have gone on rising with the exception of a few years when they were brought down. The Government tried other expedients to close the balance of payments gap without closing the fiscal gap. But these expedients proved ineffective. They were devaluation, import controls, import substitutions, export promotion, higher import duties, export subsidies and all other measures of their genre. When the fiscal gap persisted these measures were neutralized. In 1981 the Government approached the International Monetary Fund for a loan of $ 5 billion and got it. It had to be paid to India in three installments. The Government drew the first two installments of the loan but did not need the third installment. The Government also continued to borrow from other sources like the I.D.A. Exim Bank, Asian Development Bank etc. As a result, India's external debt mounted up and now it is of the order of over Rs. 20,00,00 crore. The interest payment on this debt uses up over 30 percent of India's export earnings.

The Government in Delhi pledged India's gold with the Bank of England and the Bank of Japan in July 1991 in order to mobilize foreign exchange to meet the balance of payments deficits. The gold so pledged has since been redeemed making Indians heave a sigh of relief. Furthermore, under advice of the IMF the Government devalued the rupee by 18 percent through the effects of the devolution in the trade balance are uncertain at best. There was some decline in the trade deficit providing some relief on the balance of payments front. But this does not indicate that a trend marking a break with that of chronic deficit has begun. The trade deficit between April and August 1991 was, in dollar terms, 44 percent lower than during the same months in 1990. The most important reason for this substantial decline was the reduction in imports which were lower by 15 percent during this period. However, the fall in imports has been solely because of Reserve Bank of India's steep enhancement of cash margins which have been in operation since March 1991. Once the margins are reduced, as is expected after the $ 2.5 billion loan from the IMF become available, imports are certain to rise again. The Finance Minister has already given hints at import liberalization measures in view of the so called comfortable foreign exchange reserve position which is said to be of the order of Rs. 6,000 crore. The problem of chronic trade imbalance can be resolved first by adopting measures that curb the country's appetite for imports over a long period. The adhoc margins currently in force do more harm than good in the long run. The second and more important path lies in substantially raising exports. This of course requires the enhancement of price and quality competitiveness of India's exports. The most crucial measure to adopt is to reduce the fiscal gap. If this is not done, other measures will not be of much avail.

It is here that the trend in the current financial year is disquieting. Exports, instead of rising, have been declining. Between April and August the value of exports was lower by almost 8 percent that in the same period in 1990. In August 1991, the first month after the 18% devaluation of the rupee, exports declined by more than 10%. Devaluation which was expected to make India's exports more price-competitive cannot show immediate results. As inflation at home continues to rule at 14% generating wage escalation, the expected results of devaluation cannot be realized. The one silver lining to the export performance this year has been that within an overall decline, exports to the general currency areas (with which trade is conducted in convertible currencies) grew by 5% in April August 1991. The decline that has taken place is in exports to rupee trade areas, where the fall has been over 50%. It is the economic crisis in the Soviet Union which is responsible for this dramatic drop in rupee valued exports. If the future of the rupee trade is going to be bleak, then exports to the general currency areas must grow much more rapidly than at present. This again is conditional on India enhancing the price-quality competitiveness of its exports.

This is by the way the most important measure to be adopted is the reduction of the fiscal deficit. The Finance Minister is committed to reducing the fiscal deficit from 8.5% of GDP to 6.5 percent of GDP. The Fund-Bank combine has suggested a reduction of the fiscal deficit to 5% of GDP in the 1992-93 budgets. This advice though imported is well taken for that is what is necessary to control domestic inflation and to reduce the balance of payments gap as the casualty tests have demonstrated.

Again, there is need to act on the monetary and exchange rate fronts also. At present monetary growth is of the order of over 15%. This is too excessive and has enhanced the liquidity of the economy which serves as a base for inflation. This calls for monetary targeting in India to limit monetary growth within the range of 3-5% per annum. This has to go with an exchange rate policy. What kind of exchange rate is suited to India? A freely fluctuating exchange rate regime has to be ruled out. A fluctuating exchange rate requires a highly flexible economic system. But the Indian economy which is plagued by structural and institutional rigidities cannot contain a freely fluctuating exchange rate regime. Furthermore, historical evidence supports the view that it generates destabilizing capital movements which harm India's interests. At a time when India needs direct foreign investment to make a success of its new industrial policy, a freely fluctuating exchange rate regime is harmful. For this reason it is proposed to adopt the band proposal according to which the exchange rates move along and within the prescribed band.

Monetary targeting and the band proposals have to be emphasized together in order to get the maximum effectiveness. At a time when the income velocity of money rises, productivity falls, the growth rate falls and the exchange rate depreciates the money target should move towards 3%. At a time when the income velocity of money falls, productivity rises, the growth rate rises and the exchange rate appreciates the money target should move towards 5%. In this manner it is possible to get the benefits of fixed and fluctuating exchange rates without their unfavorable effects. This scheme, of course, requires precise measurements of economic magnitudes. But at present measurements of economic magnitudes are in a rudimentary state. We should not wait for statistical perfection to precede the adoption of policy measures. Policy has to be adopted in a pragmatic manner provision for correction being made in the lights of unfolding deficiencies. This is how economic policy in India should be evolved and implemented. Thus, the measures for the correction of balance of payments gap must act on the trade front and the monetary front. The two are complementary.

Finally, a word about India's external debt. This has been growing unabated and the interest payments on this debt are also growing and they are using up over 30% of India's export earning.

India has not been able to repay its external debt as per schedule. This necessitates external borrowing to repay an earlier debt. This has caused acute embarrassment to the Government and the people of India. In view of this, it is suggested that the short term debt should be converted into long term debt so that the repayment of debt can wait till India's repaying capacity improves. It is true that long term debt involves a higher rate of interest than short term debt. But this is a price worth paying for the latitude India gets in the matter of repayment.

At the same time, it is necessary to hold down India's oil imports which use up 30% of export earnings and which impart inflationary impulses to Indian economy. This can be done by increasing domestic production of oil and reducing domestic consumption by rationing of oil in the private sector and by enforcing accountability for the use of oil in the public sector.

What is sketched above in this memorandum is only the skeleton. Each of these points can be elaborated. But time and space do not permit me to do it.

# 106

## Tax on Income from Bank Deposits : A Case for Withdrawal

This has reference to the statement made by the Hon'ble Minister of Finance in the course of his speech presenting the Union Budget for 1991-92 on Wednesday 24-7-1991 that the interest income of above Rs. 2,500 from bank deposits would be taxed and the tax would be collected at the source. In my memorandum forwarded to the Hon'ble Minister of Finance over a month ago I highlighted the deleterious effects of this measures on the banking system and pleaded for its withdrawal. But the government hard pressed as it is for funds in order to bring down the budget deficit from 8.5% GDP to 6.5% of GDP remind unimpressed by my plea and is going ahead with this measure unmindful of its consequences.

Newspapers publish disturbing reports about the flight of deposits for two reasons: (1) Collection of tax on interest income at source and (2) the necessity to disclose the sources from which the depositors got money to deposit in the banks. Already, the banks have begun to enforce the new income tax rules and this has created panic among the depositors and has accelerated the withdrawal of deposits. The panic stricken depositors are hurrying to the banks to secure premature withdrawal of their term deposits as the banks have begun to implement the new income tax rules after weeks of hesitation and dilly dallying.

It is confirmed by the bankers that the flight of deposits has begun. The excess work pressure on the bank brought by the new situation is enormous. The rush for withdrawal of deposits is so great that the banks are contemplating the opening up of special cells to deal with the additional work load.

The depositors have already, in many cases, withdrawn term deposits and transferred their money into savings accounts just to avoid the problems with the income tax authorities. A few of the depositors have been diverting their money into real estate and even purchase of virgin gold and gold jewellery. After the new income tax law come into force, gold prices have registered a spurt expectedly.

The depositors have not only to suffer a cut in their interest income but they have also to run the additional risk of being questioned by the income tax authorities about the sources of their savings. This has made the depositors wary and this has led to a big flight to investment from banks to other sectors. The bankers are also alleged to be advising the depositors to split the lump sum amounts and scatter them out in various bank branches in right quantum to circumvent the income tax rule. This advice may be heeded by the small depositors, but the big depositors, ingenious as they are, have the apprehension that the Government may evolve a device from which it is possible to combine all accounts of the same depositors and to bring them into the tax net. This plan may prompt them to withdraw their term deposits and divert them to real estate and gold. Thus pushing up the prices of real estate and gold further. Real estate and gold in boom condition prevailing in India today, register an appreciation in value every day and investment in them is considered to be a worthwhile business and profitable too. At the time of devaluation of the rupee in July 1991 the price of gold was ruling at Rs. 3,740 per 10 grams. But after devaluation the price jumped up by 14 percent to Rs. 4300. Now it is in the neighbourhood of Rs. 5020. This spurt in gold price is due partly to the diversion of deposits to the gold market. If the demand for gold continues to rise as it is bound to rise in future, the government will be frustrated in its efforts to get revenue from this source. Revenue from this source is uncertain at best.

This scheme is discriminatory. The union budget for 1991-92 introduced a scheme under which deposit could be made by any person with the National Housing Bank on or before 30-11-1991 without any obligation to disclose the source of funds for such deposits. Under the Income Tax Act tax payers can avail of the facility of a waiver of penalty and interest on the amount disclosed once in a life time. To those who have already availed of this facility, one more opportunity is to be given to disclose their unaccounted incomes.

When the black money holders are given this concession, it is understandable that those who have deposited their savings in bank deposits are asked to disclose the source of their savings. This obligation to disclose the source of their savings makes them wonder why they should disclose the source of their deposits which, being deposited in the banks, are white money. They ask the legitimate question why the Government, which exempts the black money barons who invest in housing from disclosing the source of their money holdings, should ask the depositors of white money as to how they got it. In view of these questions the provision that the depositors should disclose the source of their deposits is blatantly discriminatory. This is to treat the corrupt and the honest alike. Quite apart from the payment of tax on interest income from deposits, this discrimination is a factor which has accelerated the process of withdrawal of term deposits even before maturity.

Therefore it behaves the Government to annul the provision relating to income tax on interest income from bank deposits. The Indian banks are labouring under low profitability already. The withdrawal of deposits will erode their profitability further and cause irreparable damage to the banking system. The solvency of the banking system is more important than the uncertain yield from this tax.

# 107

## Deferring Capital Account Convertibility : A Wise Decision

While presenting the 1994-95 Union Budget in the Parliament the Finance Minister sounded euphonic about the unexpected spurt in India's foreign exchange reserves from $1.1 billion in July 1991 to $13 billion at the end of February, 1994. The Finance Minister is obviously under an embarrassment of riches. Others feel that the time is propitious for ordering full capital account convertibility of the rupee. This requires a close examination of the forex reserve profile.

The forex reserves are composed of export earnings, borrowings from the International Monetary Fund, the World Bank and other multinational financial agencies, portfolio investment by foreign institutional investors, direct financial investment, invisibles in the form of remittances and corporate funds raised abroad through flotation of issues. The Reserve Bank of India has been buying dollars in the market in order to maintain the exchange rate stable which means preventing an appreciation of the rupee which would render the exports uncompetitive and reduce the rate of export growth.

The question of whether the present foreign exchange reserve position can be regarded as comfortable can be answered after an analysis of the outflows during the next four years.

Starting from 1995 and ending with 1998 the annual debt repayments will be of the order of $8 billion per annum. Though the import demand is slack because of sluggish industrial growth at 1.8 percent, import demand may surge not only because of the projected industrial growth rate of 4% but also because of the reduction of customs duties in the 1994-95 budget. This calls for an estimate of the import demand and the foreign exchange reserves necessary to meet this demand. This analysis in necessary in the light of the fact that the foreign exchange crisis of 1991 was brought about by the bunching of debt repayments and spurt in imports under the liberalized import regime.

Of the $ 13 billion forex reserves 70% is made up of foreign funds which are volatile, speculative and are recallable within 24 hours and the balance of 30% is made up of export earning. Given the expected outflow the reserves will not be sufficient to meet the surging import demand. The current account deficit in balance of payments in 1993-94 is said to be 0.5% of GDP compared with 3% in 1990-91 and 2% in 1992-93. The is the cause for cheer. But the cheer is bound to be transitory.

The Reserve Bank's action in buying dollars is to prevent the rupee from appreciating. There is a general perception that the currency of a developing country under a fixed or nearly fixed exchange rate system is always over-value. The Reserve Bank's action in buying dollars has the effect of preserving an under-valued rupee. It is expected that as soon as the Reserve Bank stops purchasing dollars, the rupee will appreciate with adverse consequences on the balance of payments.

India's exports have been rising since 1991 under the favourable impact of successive devolutions of the rupee. Indian firms have been raising money from abroad through the sale of equities. Bank schemes have also raised over $ 11.5 billion foreign financial institutions have been pouring in dollars for the stock market. An extra $5 billion is expected to flow in the middle of 1994. Convertibility of the rupee in the trade account and the bullish upsurge in the stock market coupled with low import growth strengthened the case for full convertibility on current account. The Finance Minister is right in announcing full convertibility of the rupee on current account and in assuring that India fulfills the conditions prescribed by the IMF thereto.

But there is no equally strong case for full convertibility of the rupee on capital account. The money that is being brought in by the foreign financial institutions is not money which is migratory in character. As soon as they find that the returns elsewhere are more attractive or when they find that the Indian stock market turns doubtful, that money will flow out. Furthermore, import growth is bound to surge up at present in order to enable output growth. This boosts demand for foreign exchange. The huge debt burden and the likely increase in debt servicing obligation in the near future will call for higher inflow than the amount anticipated. For the time being, therefore, the Finance Minister is right in deferring the capital account convertibility of rupee. But generally speaking there does not seem to be any concern about the increasing reserves. Obviously people have underestimated the volatility of foreign funds which are a major component of forex reserves.

The *London Economist* has warned against resorting to capital account convertibility at the present stage of India's macro-economy. Admittedly full convertibility of the rupee constitutes a crucial component of the liberalization programme. But the EXIM Bank in its recently published study "Rupee Convertibility: Issue and Implications" has warned that full convertibility will not succeed unless both macroeconomic stability and microeconomic preconditions are satisfied. But in the present Indian context they are not satisfied. Macroeconomic stability is yet a far cry. The rate of inflation at present is 8.5%. With the pre-budget hikes in administered price of LPG cylinders, sugar, rice and wheat, hikes in railway fares and freight rates with their cascading effect on the price level and the fiscal deficit of 6% of GDP India is to go to the zone of double-digit inflation. This will make Indian exports uncompetitive in world markets. The EXIM Bank study points out that the microeconomic benefits of protection cannot be brushed aside altogether in the opening up process and "the withdrawal of protection must be gradual and pre-announced." In the opinion of the Bank this is important because the efficiency of the industrial sector cannot be improved in the short run nor is resource reallocation possible due to low resource mobility because of structural and institutional rigidities. If, on opening up, large sectors of domestic industry become uncompetitive the loss of industrial output and employment would occur. The study reminds all concerned that the newly industrializing countries introduced convertibility long after they achieved export-led growth: South Korea in 1988, Taiwan in 1980, Indonesia in 1988 and Thailand in 1990. It is further noted that the costs of imports have gone up substantially even after the tariff reductions in the 1993-94 budget. This is due to substantial nominal depreciation of the rupee during 1986-92.

At present the rupee has remained solid and stable. Forward premia on the dollar purchases have been moving down and at present they have moved down to all time lows. In the foreseeable future, the rupee is expected to be caught in a narrow band against all major currencies. A major threat to this rosy outlook is the prospect of an inflationary special arising from the recent hikes in administered prices, hikes in railway fares and freight rates and petrol and diesel. More analysts fear the resurgence of a double-digit inflation fuelled by the fiscal deficit of 7.3 percent of GDP. Another factor is the volatility of foreign capital which has contributed to the so called "Comfortable" forex reserve position. The situation needs to be constantly watched.

# 108

## The Report of the Narasimhan Committee on Financial Reform

In August 1991 the Government of India appointed three high level committees one each to suggest reforms in the financial sector, reforms in the tax structure and reforms in the trade regime. These committees started work on their respective assignments and the reports of the last two committees are awaited while the report of the first one was reported to have been submitted to the Finance Minister on Wednesday the 20th November 1991.

The Narasimhan Committee on the financial sector was headed by Shri. Narasimhan, a former Governor of the Reserve Bank of India and presently having a stint with the World Bank in Washington. The report expectedly bears the imprint of the ideological predilections of the IMF World Bank combine. The motive behind the appointment of this committee (and other committees for the matter) is to give the impression that the Reforms to be introduced in the various sectors are home made and not imported from Washington.

The reforms suggested in the report are structural adjustment measures on the implementation of which the fund bank aid depends. The main objective of the structural adjustment lending is to facilitate the restructuring of the country's economy so as to provide the best basis for economic growth on a sustainable level within 3-5 years. The loans support programmes that are intended to anticipate and avert economic crises through economic reforms and changes in investment priorities. The report on the financial sector is intended to serve as a basis for the financial adjustment programme.

When the parleys with the IMF officials about the loan were on, the IMF put forth several conditions on the fulfillment of which the loan would be made. One of them dealt with banking reform which is an euphemism for privatization (though the Government has emphatically ruled this out). This is part of the drift towards market oriented reform. Under this scheme sick banks have to be closed down. If this is allowed there arises the colossal problem of compensating million of rural and urban depositors; besides this it creates a crisis of confidence in the financial system. Considering the fact that 7 percent of bank lending is to large and medium sick companies and an equal amount to industries struggling on the verge of unavailability, the closure of banks will lead to the closure of these industrial and business units. Market oriented banking reform leading to privatization may not be appropriate when the financial health of most banks is poor though it is good in the best of all possible words.

It is suggested that the unviable banks should be merged or amalgamated with the strong banks. But this suggestion ignores the fact that strong banks are too few and the weak ones are too many. The policy being followed by the Reserve Bank of India of unleashing mutual funds, commercial paper, certificates of deposits etc., on the money market will reduce the scope of bank lending to the better class borrowers and would force them to take on risky business and window dress their accounts to hide their weakness from the public. This did happen in the US banking system in the 1980s. while structural reform of the banking system is necessary it should proceed at a slow pace.

Privatization of banks and the closure of unviable units have not found favour with the bank employees. It is their argument that privatisation will harm the cause of social obligation of the banks enunciated in 1969 when the banks were nationalized. They also fear that privatization would bring in accountability which has not been there since 1969. The industrial workers who apprehend unemployment caused by the closure of unviable and stick units have determined to go on an agitation against it; if the bank employees join them there will be a collapse of the economy at least partially. The Government has to consider whether it can face this situation with any degree of success.

The report recommends that new private sector banks will be allowed provided they start with Rs. 100 crore or more of capital. At the same time, the committee recommends re-grouping of the public sector banks for their efficient functioning and for avoiding duplicating operators. Allowing private sector banks to be opened is a welcome move as it exposes the existing banks to the bracing winds of competition and improve their operational efficiency.

The report recommends that foreign banks can open 100 percent owned subsidiaries in India. Earlier the Government followed the policy of reciprocity meaning thereby that for every branch of a foreign bank opened in India, India was entitled to open a bank branch in that country. Now this reciprocity clause is given a go-by while foreign banks can open their branches in India, Indian banks cannot open their branches in the foreign countries on a reciprocal basis. This is a case of "heads you win and tails I lose" policy of the Government of India. This recommendation might have been at the instance of the Fund Bank combine.

The foreign banks opening branches in India have to meet a differential capital base criterion which means that foreign banks which open branches in India have to provide a differential capital base criterion. This means that the capital of a foreign branch will vary according to the economic status of the zone in which it is located. The new private sector banks which are freely allowed have to provide a minimum capital base of Rs. 100 crore. There is thus a discriminatory treatment between the foreign banks and domestic private banks opening their branches in India.

The report mentions that of the 21 nationalised banks only five are viable. The Report recommends a two phased re-capitalization and reorganization of banks including mergers. The report understands that huge funds would be needed to recapitalize the nationalized banks. As this is beyond the capacity of the Government to generate, recapitalisation is possible only with loans from multilateral financing agencies like the World Bank and the Asian Development Bank. Here is the catch. The idea is to surrender our banking and financial systems to the World Bank and to enable it to handle them in the way it likes.

The report recommends the presence of the nominees of the Government and of the Reserve Bank of India on the boards of banks. This is to ensure government control over the operations of the banks. The Fund Bank combine can manipulate the operations of the banks through these nominees. These two nominees enjoy sweeping powers at Board proceedings. No decision gets through without their consent for they are vested with veto power. It would be ideal to free the banks from official fetters; competition and control do not go together.

The IMF had earlier hinted at the suggestion of slashing down the combined CRR and SLR ratio from the present 52 percent. The Narasimham Committee endorses this suggestion. In this respect the credit policy and the fiscal policy work at cross purposes. Normally the ratio is raised to contract credit supply and it is lowered to expand credit supply. Slashing down the ratio has the effect of expanding credit supply. This is bound to counteract the anti-inflationary effect of the expected reduction of the fiscal deficit to 5 percent of GDP. The extent to which the ratio should be slashed is not indicated. It is left to the judgment of the monetary authorities. It would have been perfectly in order if the reserve ratio was left at 52 percent while the fiscal deficit is reduced to 5 percent of GDP. Already, funds are being obtained by the borrowers from the parallel money market flooded by black money. This has rendered the weapons of credit control ineffective. To slash down the reserve ratio would be to make borrowing from the banking system cheap and to encourage borrowing from it in addition to borrowing from the parallel money market. This would be overly inflationary. This exercise points to the absence of an integrated perception of fiscal monetary management in an economy which requires an integrated perception. This is the fund bank model imposed on India.

It is true that the banks are to fulfill a social obligation. This was the ideological basis of bank nationalisation in 1969 and the earlier scheme of social control over banks. But with the passage of time this social obligation came to be exploited and misused by the politicians in power with the support of the complaint bureaucrats. Loan melas were organized throughout the country and funds were liberally distributed among the claimants ostensibly for productive purpose. But funds borrowed for productive purpose seeped into unproductive channels through an osmotic process and in consequence, the loans could not be repaid. Many banks which had made the loans under this scheme became sick and their profitability was considerably reduced. While the banks have to fulfill a social obligation, there should be no damage to the viability of the banking system especially in a competitive regime. Soundness of the banking system should take precedence over social obligation. Otherwise, with the entry of domestic private banks and foreign banks into banking business with no such social obligation to burden them, the existing banks will not be able to survive.

It is obvious that the report of the Narasimhan Committee is strongly influenced by the guidelines laid down by the fund bank combine. Possibly the forthcoming reports of the committee on tax reform and the committee on trade reform are also influenced by the same guidelines. One wonders whether Indian economic policy is formulated in Delhi or Washington. Loans from the fund bank combine are a painful necessity but this should not make us amenable to the imposition of external economic counsels. Unfortunately this is what had happened. The economic events of the past five months confirm this statement. The close surveillance of the fund bank combine over the economic policies of the Government of India speaks volumes for the ineptitude of Government which places the IMF loan over everything else.

The Government of India is already negotiating with the World Bank to get a structural reform loan of about $ 600 million for the financial sector. In order to get this loan the Government has to implement the recommendations of the Narasimhan Committee report. But the Government which is bent on implementing the reforms has taken its untoward consequences too lightly. The future will reveal what is there in store for the reforms. India, unfortunately, needs loans which are a painful necessity. But on this score India should not surrender its sovereignty to the Fund-Bank combine. They know that the foreign exchange crunch is India's Achilles' heel. But they cannot exploit it.

# 109

## The Finance Minister in a Cruel Dilemma

When the present Government assumed office in June 1991 India's foreign exchange reserves were of the order of rupees 2,600 crore in August they dropped to Rs. 1,000 crore. But now they are in the neighbourhood of Rs. 8,000 crore and one expected to reach the 10,000 crore mark by the end of December. In view of the comfortable foreign exchange reserve position there are pressures to lift import curbs. Though the relaxation of import curbs will increase customs revenue which was projected to cross Rs. 3,500 crore and will thus help to reduce the budget deficit, there is a gnawing worry that this step would reduce the foreign exchange reserves. For the sake of higher customs revenue resulting from relaxations of import curbs it is dangerous to allow the foreign exchange reserves to be depleted. It must be remembered that the foreign exchange reserves were replenished by the inflow of NRI funds and loan proceeds from the IMF and the World Bank. India's credit rating in the international financial markets is upgraded now. In the event of the foreign exchange reserves falling, the credit rating will decline. This is bound to harm India's interests. If as projected the foreign exchange reserves reach the Rs. 10,000 crore mark India's credit rating will be upgraded and this will be source of comfort to the Finance Minister as in that case it will be easy for him to approach the international financial institutions for loans as he cannot rely on export earnings to replenish the foreign exchange reserves. In fact, exports are declining. Thus the finance minister has to choose between garnering more customers revenue by relaxing import curbs and through it to reduce the budget deficit and suffering a depletion of foreign exchange reserves with unwelcome repercussions on India's credit rating. This is a cruel dilemma from which escape is not easy.

In India there is at present stagflation what with production being stagnant and the rate of inflation rising. There is a drop in exim scrip premium indicating the onset of a recession. The premium has fallen from 45 percent to 30 percent and is expected to fall further. If there is no release of foreign exchange reserves to pay for imports Exim scrips will be in great demand.

In the attempt to hold down the rate of inflation the Reserve Bank of India imposed a credit squeeze. This has slowed down economic activity with adverse consequences on revenue collection. The excise duty collection is bound to decline with the accentuation of recessionary trends. Traders are hard put to it get money to lift goods off the producing centers. The credit squeeze has boosted in recessionary trends in the economics.

The decline in customs revenue due to the maintenance of the present import curbs in the attempt to save foreign exchange and the decline in excise duty collection due to the recessionary trends caused by the credit squeeze are bound to make it difficult for the Finance Minister to contain the budget deficit in fulfillment of his assurances given to the IMF. This is a source of discomfort to him.

How can he get over this situation? One way out is the disinvestment of shares in the public sector units for the second time. In his speech presenting the Union Budget for 1991-92 the Finance Minister's proposed disinvestment of only 20 percent of shares. This generated a furore that the Government was trying to privatize public sector units. In view of this, the second installment of disinvestment may not be an easy task, especially after he has made the policy announcement that the public sector units would not be privatized.

The Finance Minister has to limit budget deficit to 5 percent of GDP in the 1992-93 budget as required by the IMF. It would be a miracle if this could be achieved. He has to depend upon reducing the quantum of non-plan expenditure, interest payment on the public debt. Subsidies and defense expenditure. But this is not an easy task. Interest payment on the public debt is a rigid item and it is irreducible. Abolition of subsidies will provoke resistance and the Government may not be prepared to risk popular resistance. In view of the deteriorating security environment in the neighbourhood, there is a case for increasing defence expenditure and not for reducing it. China's spending 10 percent of its GDP on defence, Pakistan is spending 7.8 percent of its GDP on defence, India is spending only 3.8 percent of its GDP on defence. In view of this it is nearly impossible to reduce defence expenditure. Unless these items of non-plan expenditure are reduced the IMF will not release future installments of loans. This, of course, is a tricky situation which is worrying the Finance Minister.

The IMF has to be persuaded not to insist on the reduction of the aforesaid three items of non-plan expenditure in addition to further devaluation of the rupee of the IMF has any plans of insisting on it. If they are not reduced the budget deficit cannot be brought down to 5 percent of GDP in 1991-93. In this case also the IMF will not release future installments of the loan.

In this situation there are two courses open to the Government to undertake a second disinvestment in public sector units convincing the parliament that this is inevitable in the context of the undertaking to reduce the budget deficit to 5 percent of GDP (2) to increase the progressivity of the tax structure and raising the rates of indirect taxes on luxury goods steeply despite protests from the affluent society. Besides this, there is another source of the revenue. It is reported that the income tax arrears of Rs. 9,000 crore are outstanding. If the whole of it is recovered, there will be no need for raising tax rates or reducing non-plan expenditure. The budget deficit can easily be brought down to 5 percent of GDP or even below it. It behoves the Finance Minister to initiate steps to recover the income tax arrears with no loss of time. It has to be understood that the interests of the nation are more important than the interests of a few income tax assesses in arrears. Those who are in arrears must be subjected to penal action of a drastic nature. This is the only way in which the Finance Minister can hope to escape from the cruel dilemma in which he finds himself to-day. His success in emerging out of the dilemma depends on his success in collecting the outstanding income tax arrears.

# 110

## Memorandum to the Prime Minister on Fertilizer Subsidy

The Finance Minister in his Budget speech on 24-7-1991 envisaged a 40% cut in fertilizer subsidy and a raising of the procurement price by way of compensation to the farmers. The idea was to reduce the budget deficit and through it to restrain the price level. It did not occur to the Finance Minister that the enhancement of the procurement price would also raise the price level and this would offset any reduction caused by the reduction of the budget deficit.

The small farmers are at the mercy of the large farmers as they stand obliged to them for help in times of dire need. The small farmers who purchase fertilizers at a lower price will be forced to sell them to the large farmers at that price. As a result, the large farmers prosper and the small farmers suffer as this results in a fall in farm productivity on the small farms.

The state Governments have not maintained records of small farmers. Even large farmers can call themselves small farmers, obtain certification from the local authorities by fraudulent means, get permits from the State Agricultural Departments and purchase fertilizers at a lower price for use on their farms. There is no mode of identifying them as large farmers. Even when they are identified as such, they may obtain permits by means of underhand dealings. While the New Industrial Policy is doing away with the permit license system for good, it is un-understandable that the Government introduces the system in respect of fertilizers without realizing that it leads, as it has done in the past to corruption and black marketing.

Under these circumstances the best course of action would be to scrap the cut in subsidy completely and to allow the farmers, large and small, to purchase fertilizers at the subsidized price and use them on their farms in order to increase farm productivity. India is yet to enter the unadulterated free market system though it is moving in that direction slowly. In a full blooded free market system, of course, subsidies have no place. Abolition of subsidies can take place in a gradual manner. If the IMF (pejoratively called the Imperial Monetary Fund) enforces the abolition of subsidy as a precondition for the loan, this must be resisted as it is bound to prove ruinous to Indian agriculture. There cannot be a total surrender. The state Governments in the country are vehemently opposed to the abolition of fertilizer subsidy and to the adoption of a dual pricing policy for good reasons. The farmers in the country are genuinely apprehensive of the fall in farm productivity and are threatening to organize agitations. These must be averted in the interests of peace.

Therefore, it is the essence of economic wisdom to scrap the cut in subsidies and to eschew the dual pricing policy. This will help to increase farm output, hold down farm prices and to assist the forces of macro-economic stabilization.

# 111

## Is the Soviet Model Relevant to India?

The Eighth Five Year Plan was launched on April 1, 1992. This plan is far different from the previous plans in that it was formulated in the context of the far-reaching economic reforms initiated by the Government and the historic development taking place in the world at large. The plan document is to reflect these developments at home and abroad.

The Deputy Chairman of the Planning Commission said that the Eighth Plan would involve the people in a big way in the plan process. The plan would turn the people into operations of the plan while the government would play the role of cooperator and facilitator. This is a welcome feature of the plan considering the fact that the people will be responsible for the plan process and plan execution. The burden of this song is that it is a plan of the people, by the people and for the people. This ideology will enthuse the people into active participation in the planning process for it is a plan for their own well being.

Domestic resources are too inadequate to meet the requirements of the plan for financing on the scale envisaged in it. The domestic rate of savings is 22 percent of GNP and it is too inadequate to reach the investment targets. There is, therefore, the need for external financing both foreign direct investment and NRI capital inflows. The conditions for the entry of direct foreign investment are liberalized and in the days ahead some more liberalization will be effected. Foreign investors assured as they are of the irreversibility of economic policy, are entering the Indian economy in a big way.

The Government has called for a shift of emphasis from commercial borrowing to direct foreign investment. It is examining suggestions for automatic approval of proposals with 51% equity provided imports are covered by foreign equity and dividends balanced by export earnings. The political and economic conditions are conducive to the implementation of the new liberalized regime. But many knowledgeable people have strong reservations about extending foreign investment to the consumer goods sector. Many in the country strongly believe that investment in the capital goods sector is more paying and necessary and consumer goods are of low priority. It is held by them that resources must be moved to the priority sector. Much of this thinking is influenced by the Soviet emphasis on capital goods in the earlier period of industrialization.

Growth theorists have built models which demonstrate that the investment in the capital goods sector generates a higher rate of growth than investment in the consumer goods sector. At the same time, investment in the capital goods sector also generates inflation. Investment in the capital goods sector generates income immediately but generates supply after a lag, the length of the lag depends on the capital intensity of investment. This generates inflation. This is Domar's "sigma effect". Thus, investment in capital goods sector generates a higher rate of growth and also a higher rate of inflation while investment in the consumer goods sector generates a lower rate of growth and also a lower rate of growth without much inflation.

It is a basic tenet of the Harrod-Domar Model of growth that the rate of growth is a function of the rate of net new investment which in turn is a function of savings. This means that higher the rate of savings, the higher the rate of investment and so higher the rate of economic growth. The assumption underlying the Soviet Model is that when investment is made in the capital goods sector income rises and as the consumption goods sector from which resources are shifted does not produce enough goods to absorb the rising income, savings increase to increase the rate of investment which would accelerate the rate of economic growth. But this line of reasoning seems to assume that there will be no inflation caused by the excess demand for consumption goods. This assumption is legitimate in the Soviet Model where consumers' freedom is curtailed and the consumption is held down by rationing and controls so that the consumers cannot demand more than the stocks of available. This is a command economy which prevailed in the Soviet Union during the period of industrialization. But this model cannot be implemented in India which, though not a free market economy is moving fast in that direction. If this is so, income generated by increasing investment in the capital goods sector beats against a limited stock of consumption goods and generates excess demand which, in a free market, causes a rise in prices. Furthermore, inflation causes a rise in consumption expenditure in money terms unless there is money illusion. Again a rise in prices in the current period, in the context of the Hicksian elasticity of expectation of greater than unity, generates expectations of a greater rise in future prices and causes an inter-temporal substitution of present goods for future goods. Inflation thus is the inevitable consequence. In a command economy these effects are no longer relevant. For this reason in the Soviet economy during the early period of industrialization there was no inflation for there was no excess demand. Controlled demand for goods just matched the available supply of goods and there was no occasion for inflation to raise its ugly head. The savings rate increased as consumption was held down and this caused a rise in the investment rate and the rise in the rate of economic growth. Thus, if savings are to rise there must be a forced reduction in the level of consumption. This goes against the philosophy of liberalization and market friendliness in the Indian democracy. The Soviet economic historians deserve in great detail the sufferings and sacrifices of the Soviet people in this period. But this cannot be imposed on the Indian people.

The Second Five Year Plan (1956-61) was based on the Mahalanobis Model which was based on the Feldman Model on which also the Soviet and the Chinese models were based. The emphasis in the Mahlanobis model was on heavy industry. As a result, the consumer goods industry was relegated to the secondary position. Agriculture was marginalized; the export sector was underplayed in importance. Investment in heavy industry generated income. But there was an acute shortage consumers' goods including food. The sigma effect came into operation and generated the inflation crisis. As the export sector was not given due importance exports did not rise in the same proportion as imports. This generated the balance of payment crisis. These two crises compelled the Government to prune the plan when it was half-way through. Even so, the core of the plan heavy industry remained almost intact. This provoked professor Colin Clark to say in his Hobart Paper : "Growthmanship".

It must be admitted that the structural adjustment policies prescribed by the International Monetary Fund have a built-in inflationary bias. It must be realized that IMF does not want them but India needs them in order to make the economy grow. It should be the object of policy that these structural adjustment policies do not impose a heavy burden on the poor and the destitute. The ideal should be growth for the sake of welfare and not growth for the sake of growth per se.

Foreign investment in the consumption goods sector is not bad after all so long as it is not in areas promoting kit culture. Emphasis should be placed on producing sufficient basic consumption goods on which the rising incomes of the people can be spent so that the expenditure of rising incomes does not generate inflation to the detriment of human welfare. The people of this country are sick and tired of relentless inflation since 1956 and are praying for a respite from it. They should not be goaded to believe in the Mao's philosophy of the "pie in the sky" and to make great sacrifices expecting the pie to fall. Thus, there is the need for diverting a part of the foreign investment into the consumption goods sector also i.e. for the production of consumption goods (including food) on which the middle class consumers spend their income. India should grow but grow without inflation. The common man is wondering whether we are planning for growth or for inflation. He should be convinced that we are planning for growth and that any inflation is only incidental.

# 112

## Need for Market Determined Interest Rate Structure

The Indian banking system is invaded by sickness with over- manning, low productivity and low profitability. One reason has been the large scale bank expansion in the 1970s and the 1980s to serve certain social objectives. When the ideology went out of fashion, the problem of overstaffing and uneconomic branches surfaced. All the ills of the banks which necessitated nationalization in 1969 do not obscure the fact that many of them had specific strengths both in terms of services as well as regional coverage. Along with other problems nationalization which introduced unwanted homogenization and uniformity discounted their achievements. For the public sector banks in particular the problem is one of adjusting to the changes in official polices which have, in many instances, been a complete reversal of the past. It is in this context that the reform of the banking system acquires relevance.

Economic reform is not an isolated process. An integrated approach covering all major sectors of the economy simultaneously can ensure success. Unfortunately, however, in the entire process of reforms an important area like the financial sector (which encompasses the banking sector) has not been as much stressed upon as it ought to have been.

The reforms in the financial sector are long overdue. The financial sector reform so ably elucidated in the Narasimham Committee Report has created an environment for change in the financial sector of the country. Committed as the government is to the philosophy of market driven economy in contrast to the earlier centrally controlled economic planning, it must assume a greater role in implementing the recommendations of the Narasimham Committee to speed up the reforms. Though the Report was submitted over two years ago no major recommendation has been touched upon either by the Government or by the Reserve Bank of India. The delay in reforming the financial sector can affect the growth of the real sector. Moreover, any inconsistent action unmindful of the pace and sequences in the financial sector reforms programme on the part of the Reserve Bank of India can lead to disaster.

The Government has successfully introduced the liberalization process in industry and trade and has introduced the process of fiscal consolidation, it owes to itself the duty of taking prompt action in the financial sector. The Reserve Bank of India has to initiate an action programme for the commercial banks for implementation. The first and foremost thing to do is to allow the market forces to determine interest rates as this happens to be the heart of the financial sector reforms. At present there are ceiling and floor rates of interest on bank deposit rate and lending rates. They have to be removed to make the reform meaningful. The task before the Reserve Bank is clear. All interest rates are to be left to be determined by the market forces. There should not be any discrimination between the commercial banking sector and the co-operative banking sector. This will facilitate the building up of a nexus between the risks and returns on investment for different purposes. In this scenario concessionary interest rate structures will disappear as the borrowers in the priority sector lending will prefer greater quantum of credit at higher interest rates and for this reason the cross-subsidization of interest rates will not be required. The larger credit will enable them to have a larger turnover and larger income. The borrowers prefer this type of economic scenario in the competitive environment rather than labouring under inadequate credit made available to them activity-wise in the past as this has left them at the mercy of the non-institutional credit agencies to meet the remaining part of their credit requirements.

There have been several authoritative studies on the rationalization of the interest rate structure. The Chakravarty Committee report on the working of the monetary system examined this issue as early as 1985. The committee observed: "Interest rates applicable to a substantial portion of a bank asset portfolio are either lower than or barely above the cost of funds. This is not a healthy situation". The committee further observed that the growth of the real sector will depend on the entire restructuring of our financial system which has become inefficient and weak. The committee notes:

"As the financial system has an important role to perform in the growth and development of the economy, it is essential that the system (a) functions at a high level of both allocation and operational efficiency, (b) stable and (c) introduces instruments and financing techniques to meet the ever changing preferences of the community of savers and investors".

Therefore, the need for restructuring and improving the financial system has been rightly underlined by the Narasimham Committee which states that "there is a need to improve the efficiency and effectiveness in order to improve the health of the present financial system." The committee observed that the banking system is almost collapsing, its efficiency is at a low ebb and its profitability is almost eroded. In this situation the committee recommends the restructuring of the banking system in order to enable it to face global challenges. According to the committee the banking industry during the 1990s should imbibe the spirit of competition; it must become aggressive in its marketing strategy and for enhancing its profitability and it should strengthen its internal management system.

In the realm of interest rate structure the committee suggested reduction in the number of lending and deposit interest rates. The World Bank Report on "India's Financial Sector" advocated the strengthening of the financial system by gradual reduction of Statutory Liquidity Ratio and the Cash Reserve Ratio, rationalization of interest rate structure, introduction of new prudential norms for income recognition, provision for bad debts, reclassification of health code systems and so on.

Although the growth of the financial sector has been creditable and its spread is broad-based the World Bank is not satisfied with its progress. It strongly feels that the country has to liberalize the financial sector if it is to achieve faster economic growth in the 1990s. In 1989 the World Bank Development Report observed that "In the past government's efforts to promote economic development by controlling interest rates, directing credit to priority sectors and securing expensive funding for their own activities has undermined the financial development". In the opinion of the World Bank, State intervention in the financial system has constrained its growth. The financial system in the 1990s can play a crucial role if it is left to develop along lines determined by the market forces. Such a financial system will accelerate the growth process in the country. The Chakravarty Committee earlier observed that the structure of administered interest rates in the past hampered the efficiency of the financial system. The committee stated : "The administered interest rate system has grown to be unduly complex and contains features which have reduced the ability of the system to promote the effective use of credit". In view of this the committee emphasized the rationalization of the interest rate structure.

Following the recommendations of the Chakravarty Committee Report, a beginning to rationalize the interest rate structure was made in April 1985. The Reserve Bank of India announced that the number of prescribed maturity period for fixed deposits be reduced from nine to five. Thereupon the Reserve Bank took further steps to fix a minimum lending rate for commercial banks. In September 1989 the Reserve Bank, in pursuit of the process of liberalization free the call money rate which had remained pegged at 10% for a long time. In September 1992, all sector-specific and programme-specific interest rate structure was discontinued. Again the Reserve Bank decided to link interest rates to the size of the loans with a fixed floor rate of interest. In March 1993 the interest rate slabs were reduced from 6 slabs in 1990, to 4 slabs in 1992 and then to 3 slabs in 1993. In this manner the Reserve Bank adopted several measures which had the effect of liberalizing the interest rate structure. The commercial banks were also allowed to charge higher interest rates to borrowers as no ceiling was prescribed. These steps towards gradual deregulation of the interest rate structure were in the right direction. But a lot more is to be done. There is urgent need for deregulating the entire interest rate structure. The Reserve Bank should also scrupulously desist from fixing the interest rates on deposits and the lending rates.

In the Union Budget for 1994-95 the Finance Minister announced the reduction of the bank lending rate from 15% to 14% in order to stimulate borrowing for consumption and investment to remedy the recession. This of course, assumes that the demand for borrowing is elastic to interest rate changes. Borrowing depends not just on the interest rate variable but on several other variables besides. A reduction of the lending rate and the deposit rate remaining constant will reduce the spread between the two rates and will thus reduce the profitability of banking operations. If the spread is to be kept constant, the deposit rate should be reduced. But his step will have adverse effects on deposit mobilization. The depositors will divert their savings to investing in gold or real estate whose value is appreciating with the passage of time. In this event the banks will not have sufficient resources to lend. Therefore, the purpose of reducing the lending rate will be defeated. If on the other hand the deposit rates are held constant the profitability of the banks will fall and the banks come to grief. This is the problem associated with administered interest rates. The Indian banks have gone some way in the direction of deregulating the interest rate structure but they have to go still further. The Reserve Bank should desist from fixing the interest rates on deposits and on lending rates.

Recently the Discount and Finance House of India was established indicating that the Indian money market has attained significant maturity. At the heart of the financial sector reform lies the liberalization of the interest rate structure. In many developed countries interest rates are market determined and these countries are doing well. They hold out valuable lessons for India in the sphere of financial sector reform.

The Narasimham Committee recommended the adoption of capital adequacy norms; making provision against non-performing assets/loans, new income recognition guidelines, asset reclassification, provisioning to put he banks on right lines. The committee also redefined the priority sectors and fixed the target for this sector at 10% of the aggregate bank credit. In the matter of providing credit to the priority sector the Reserve Bank should adopt a flexible policy. The priority sector cannot have both a large allocation of credit and at low interest rate. When the interest rate is market-determined and the priority sector can borrow any amount of credit likes there would be no problem. Credit is made available to the priority sector but it has to pay the market determined interest rate. The priority sector cannot have it both ways. Hence the case of liberalizing the interest rate structure.

The commercial banks have to raise capital in order to satisfy the capital adequacy norms by the end of 1996. After the necessary legislation is passed they will be able to offer to the public upto 49% of their equity. It has been freely admitted that the next 2-3 years would be very difficult for most of the banks. Prior to 1991-92 the issue was one of declining profitability. But the problem was substantially aggravated by the introduction of the new income recognition and provisioning norms which represents a fundamental shift in the way Indian banks have been asked to treat their accounts. Not surprisingly, therefore, many banks reported losses and would continue to do so for the next few years at least. Adding urgency to the issue is the requirement to meet international standards of capital adequacy. Already more than seven nationalized banks have entered the capital market to meet the target of capital adequacy norms. The provision of Rs. 5700 crore made in the budget for 1993-94 and of Rs. 5600 crore made In the budget for 1994-95 is not sufficient. For this reason the banks have to enter the capital market. If the banks are sure of adequate profitability the amount of capital they have to raise in the capital market is reduced. The profitability depends inter alia on the spread between the deposit rate and the lending rate. If the rates of interest are allowed to be market determined profitability is assured. Hence the need to have the market determined interest rates structure.

# 113

## Agricultural Planning

While replying to the heated debate in the import of wheat in the last week of November in the Lok Sabha the Prime Minister stated that the import of wheat was necessary to build up stocks of food grains which were fast declining and through it to hold down the rate of inflation. He also threw light on the possible decline in food output in the coming years due to the farmers' desire to shift from food crops to the more remunerative cash crops. In saying so he underlined the response of the cropping pattern to the price incentives.

The importance of adequate food supply in a growing economy like India cannot be overemphasized. India's population is growing at the rate of 2.2% per annum and at present it is 870 million. Every year sees the addition of 17 million to India's population. At present the per capital consumption of food grains (cereals and pulses) is far below the minimum nutritional standards. According to Government statistics the per capita consumption of pulses in India is 13.3 kg per year against the world average of 6.2 kg per year; the per capital cereals consumption stands at 175.9 kg per annum as against the world average of 187.7 kg per annum. Even if the target production of 183 million tonnes of food grains is produced it will not be able to reach the world average of consumption of pulses and cereals. Food production and procurement have been declining already. It is held in knowledgeable quarters that the food grains production target of 183 million tones cannot be reached. In fact this target was fixed for 1991-92 but was not reached as the food grains production was 6 percent less than expected. Between October 1991 and January 1992 the Government rice procurement was only 7 million tonnes which was 18 percent less than the procurement during 1990-91.

Wheat procurement was down by 30%. The wheat stock fell to 2.4 million tonnes. This was one million tonnes less than the minimum buffer stock prescribed by the Government. This was sufficient for two months. With wheat procurement short by 2 million tonnes and higher off-take by the public distribution system the stock of food grains has declined by more than third in 1991-92. The food situation between now and the end of the decade is most uncomfortable.

During the planning era which began in 1951 the Government fostered the growth of the agricultural sector. But the costs and procurement prices bore no relation to reality. The subsidization of the agricultural sector in terms of low prices of fertilizers, water and electricity has consumed a large part of the Government's resources. The agricultural sectors in the different states were not uniformly developed. The country depends on a few states for its supply of food. These states account for the bulk of the money spent on agricultural progress. But these states especially Haryana and the Punjab have reached the peak in the production of wheat and rice. In these states the productivity growth has reached its peak and no further growth is in evidence. For instance the Punjab which accounts for one-fourth of the country's wheat production and 10% of rice production has reached its peak in the 1980s as the yields have reached their maximum with no scope for a further rise. Furthermore, the states where the "green revolution" occurred have begun to experience a switch over from food crops to cash crops. This tendency, if allowed to go unchecked will further reduce food supply. In the Punjab the area under wheat cultivation fell from 247 lakh hectares in 1983-84 to 235 hectares in 1989-90 and this trend is continuing albeit at a slower pace. The other states also exhibit a similar trend. Andhra Pradesh and Kerala are switching over from rice to red palm cultivation.

There is substantial evidence to show that India's performance in the area of agricultural growth is poor when compared with the areas which have similar agro-climatic conditions. The study by the World Bank staff shows that the agricultural growth in Pakistan was higher than that in North India that in Sri Lanka was higher than that in South India and that in Burma was higher than that in East India. Barring spices and oils seeds the growth of other crops was similar in the 1980s to that in the 1970s. This calls for a reallocation of resources from the areas where the fields have reached a peak to the areas where the growth potential is high. This is what a market friendly country should do. This is what the Neo-classical paradigm taught us.

The National Council of Applied Economic Research has made an authoritative study of the comparative advantage of production in different states. On the basis of this study it is recommended that the Government should increase wheat production in Uttar Pradesh and Madhya Pradesh. The states of Bihar, Orissa, Uttar Pradesh and Madhya Pradesh have low yields of rice at present and resources should be reallocated in favour of theses states in order to enable them to realize greater yields of rice. This will help to increase the production of food and to check the shift to cash crops. But these areas are labouring under inadequate investment. They do not have adequate irrigation facilities which are necessary to increase food production. They also lack adequate supplies of high yielding varieties of seeds. Some states get plentiful supplies of subsidized fertilizers while others are starved of it. This calls for a reallocation of fertilizers also. If fertilizers are redistributed from the high use to low use areas total production will increase. The reduction of supply of fertilizers to the states where there is overuse of fertilizers will not reduce food output there while an increase in their supply to states which lack adequate supply of it will increase food output. This results in an increase in food output for a constant input of fertilizers in the country as a whole.

This is easier said than done. The Government finds it difficult to reduce the resources in the high production states and it is short of resources to be pumped to the other areas. The aggregate of subsidies on water, electricity and fertilizers is estimated to absorb Rs. 15,000 crore a year. The use of this colossal sum for subsidies has been crowding out investment. A reduction in subsidies can alter the product mix of Indian agriculture. If the agriculture inputs are realistically priced i.e., if the subsidies are withdrawn there is likely to be fall in the output of rice in Punjab by 20% and in wheat output in Haryana by 10-12%. This would reduce food supply and give an upward thrust to the rate of inflation. It is argued that a reduction of subsides will free resources for investment in agriculture which will provide the infrastructure necessary to accelerate agricultural growth. But this is possible in the long run with the outcome being uncertain.

The Government can of course, shift crop patterns to new areas. But the lack of irrigation facilities will frustrate such a move. Irrigation potential in the country has increased from 22.6 million hectares during the pre-plan period to about 81.2 million hectares at the end of 1991-92 against the ultimate irrigation potential estimated at 113.5 million hectares. But as the investment in irrigation is tardy it is not possible to exploit the entire irrigation potential. Real investment in irrigation in 1981-82 reached a peak of Rs. 1125 crore (at 1980-81 prices) and since then there has been no significant rise. As a consequence in the 6th and 7th plans expenditure on irrigation and capacity expansion fell below target by 25-30%. This is due to the fact that the State Government are investing less in irrigation in real terms than they should as they believe that the Government would dot it. The farmers are not constructing field channels in the 3-4 million hectares where there are main water arteries. This inspite of the fact that the Government is paying an irrigation subsidy of Rs. 500 crore. Even the built up capacity has remained unutilized. Between 1980 and 1987 public investment in irrigation fell by 18% in real terms. As a consequence private investment in irrigation during this period remained constant at Rs. 2,800 crore. Therefore, there is need to step up public investment in irrigation to serve as a catalytic agent for the private investment so that the two investments together can help to exploit the irrigation potential in the country.

A second input to agricultural progress is electricity. At present electricity is subsidized so that the farmers can use it to pump water from irrigation wells. If the electricity rates are exorbitant there will be a decline in pump irrigation in areas where canal or tank irrigation is not available. This will adversely affect agricultural production. This calls for a step up of investment in power generation. This will purely be a public investment as private investment is not forthcoming for power generation.

The last but not the least input is fertilizers. The price of fertilizers was low but in September 1991 the Parliament constituted the Joint Parliamentary Committee (JPC) on fertilizer pricing. The JPC recommended decontrol of fertilizer prices. In the Union Budget for 1991-92 the fertilizer price was hiked by 30%. In July 1992 in the wake of the JPC report on fertilizer pricing the Government announced the decontrol of prices of phosphatic and potassic fertilizers. This decision was in pursuance of the commitment made to the IMF in the context of the need to borrow the third tranche of the loan from the IMF under the Extended Fund Facility (EEF). As a result of the decontrol of fertilizer prices the farmers are compelled to pay a overly high price for fertilizers.

The price of fertilizers in India is far higher than that in our neighboring countries Pakistan and Bangladesh. At present the fertilizer consumption in India is considerably low. The farmers in India use an input of 73 kg of fertilizer per hectare; the farmers in Pakistan use 82 kg of fertilizer per hectare. Consequently the rate of agricultural growth and the yield per acre in Pakistan are higher than in India. Due to a hike in the price of fertilizers in the aftermath of the Union Budget of July 1991 by 30% India produced 19 million less of. food grains. India has to produce 240 million tonnes of food grains to feed 1000 million mouths by the year 2000. This is possible if the per acre yield in increased by at least 30%. But the enhanced price of fertilizer which causes a reduction of the per acre input of fertilizers renders the target impossible of attainment.

Those who oppose the continuance of subsidies have to ponder over the logic of their argument. The per capital subsidy in the farm sector on which 75% of the population depends is a meager $6. In the United States where 2% of the population depends on agriculture the per capital subsidy is $22000 and in the European Community Countries it is $16000. The IMF overly dominated by the United States has no reason to demand that the subsidies should be withdrawn in the Indian case.

When compared with Indian agriculture which is even now backward the European or American agriculture is high technology or high profile. The demonstration by farmers in the European community rocked European capitals early in December 1992. In fact, it was Paris that blazed their trail. The French Vineyard community in particular was opposed to the European Community's agreement with the United States on hefty reduction in subsidies on the continent. The French Minister of agriculture denounced this as "agricultural imperialism." The move to cut down subsidies is perceived as a conspiracy to protect the interests of American agriculture at the expense of the European farmers. The same idea may be prompting the US dominated IMF when it prescribed the reduction / abolition of subsidies now being paid to Indian agriculture. The price of imported wheat is put at Rs. 5174 per tonne including ocean freight, insurance, port handling, bagging and distribution cost as against an estimated economic cost of Rs. 4550 per tonne of domestic wheat. This means that the difference between the economic cost of imported wheat and the economic cost of domestically procured wheat is a meagre Rs. 624 per tonne. This amounts to a difference of 62 paise of price between imported wheat and domestic wheat. This is because of the low support price offered to domestic producers of wheat. If the support price is raised the difference between the price of imported wheat and the price of domestic wheat vanishes and the imported wheat becomes cheaper than the domestic wheat. When this happens in a market-friendly economy the consumers prefer imported wheat to domestic wheat. This will be ruinous to Indian farmers.

The Indian farmers, despite their being tradition bound have displayed a remarkably high degree of responsiveness to price incentives and market signals. If a higher level of remunerative prices is fixed they will increase production and stop from switching over to cash crops. In view of this the case for fixing a higher level of remunerative prices is strong and unassailable. This price should take due note of the prices of fertilizers, water and electricity and the relentless rise in agricultural wages. If this is done the food output increases and renders food imports unnecessary. This will ensure considerable saving in foreign exchange. In 1992 the Government imported wheat at a cost of Rs. 1500 crore or $50 crore. This will be the saving in foreign exchange.

It is true that the IMF and the World Bank are jointly underwriting India's transition to a market economy. When compared with India the economies of the United States and of the European Community are more sophisticated market economies responding efficiently to market signals as they are free from socio-cultural cobwebs. When these economies have retained agricultural subsidies, there is no logic in asking the Government of India to do away with these subsides. Without subsides, the prices of food articles rise; with subsidies also they rise as they increase the fiscal deficit. But the rise in prices due to the increase in fiscal deficit is less dangerous than the rise in prices occasioned by the abolition of subsides. This strengthens the case for retaining subsidies on food and fertilizers.

If the Government is sincere about ensuring adequate food supply in the country an agricultural policy incorporating the following suggestions has to be formulated: (a) a study should be undertaken of the comparative cost advantage of each region or sub-region for a particular food crop and those regions of sub-regions which enjoy comparative cost advantage in rice or wheat should be earmarked for that crop.

It would be futile to do away with subsidies at this stage as they would raise the cost of production and hence the prices of food grains. When the countries of the west which have high technology, high profile agriculture are giving subsidies to farmers it would not stand to reason to suggest that the Government of India should do away with subsidies in keeping with the market friendly dispensation.

Considering the fact that Pakistan where the farmers use greater fertilizer input has registered a higher rate of agricultural growth than India, it is necessary to encourage the Indian farmers to increase their input of fertilizers in their farms. This calls for a policy of restoring controls in fertilizer prices which results in lower fertilizer prices and greater fertilizer inputs and through them higher yields of food crops.

Irrigation is necessary to increase food production. At present the vast irrigation potential is left untapped. For this reason there should be a step up of both public and private investments in irrigation.

The suggestion that the vast sum of Rs. 15000 crore presently spent on subsidies on fertilizers, irrigation and electricity could be diverted to public investment is well taken. But it is too early to resort to this exercise as it would raise the rate of inflation to incredibly high levels. This exercise could be undertaken when the Indian economy adjusts itself to the operations of the market mechanism.

At present wheat is imported at a price higher than the domestic price of wheat. This calls for a policy of (1) either importing wheat at a price equal to the domestic price of wheat or (2) the price paid to the domestic wheat producers must be equal to the price paid for imported wheat. The latter alternative is better for it acts as an incentive to domestic producers of wheat to increase production.

At present there is a switch from food crops to commercial crops. This tendency can be reversed by making food production remunerative. This calls for the payment of higher remunerative prices to farmers. This suggestion is founded on the fact that the farmers respond to price incentives and market signals in designing their cropping pattern.

In Britain a team of experts under the direction of the late Professor Dudley Stamp identified and demarcated agro climate zones and reported on which zone is suited for which crop. The cropping pattern in that country is designed accordingly. In like manner in India also a team of experts should be put in a committee to determine, identify and demarcate the agro-climatic zones and the crops which could be grown most productively in each agro-climatic zone should be grown there. This requires a thorough restructuring of the agricultural practices in the country so as to make it highly productive.

At present there are restrictions on the inter-state movement of food grains. This has resulted in disparity in prices for the same product in different states. In the surplus states prices of food grains are low and in the deficit states they are high. This has resulted in hoarding and black marketing. If, instead the restrictions on the inter-state movement of food grains are removed there will be a tendency towards price equalization in different states, automatic disappearance of hoarding and black marketing activities of traders and middlemen and both the consumers and producers stand to benefit.

At present, there are clear warning signals about the inadequacy of food supply to feed the growing population. If no action is taken to remedy the situation one has to witness rising prices, starvation deaths and social turmoil. The adoption of the foregoing suggestions will go a long way in averting the impending food scarcity.

# 114

## The Case for a Uniform Lending Rate

In the context of stagflation plaguing the Indian economy at present the Finance Minister in his budget speech on February 27, 1993 announced a cut in the bank lending rate by 1% from 18% to 17% and a similar cut by 1% in the deposit rate from 12% to 11%. This is in conformity with the theory of the policy-mix meant to maintain macroeconomic stability. According to this theory there should be two instruments to reach two targets. The two targets are reduction of the rate of inflation and remedying recession. The reduction of the fiscal deficit as committed to the IMF in the Government's Memorandum is meant to reduce the rate of inflation; the reduction in the lending rate is meant to encourage borrowing and investment and thus to remedy recession. Thus the fiscal-monetary mix is employed to remedy inflation and recession in the Indian economy. The two targets and two instruments matrix is satisfied.

The reduction in the bank lending rate has, of course, a salutary effect on recession. But one must see the other side of the picture. The banks complain that their profitability will come under pressure following the cut in the lending rate. This will be on top of the burden the banks have to bear due to the implementation of the new income recognition and provisioning norms. This is because while the lending rate has already come into fore banks will not have the benefit of raising fresh deposits at the reduced deposit rate in the immediate future. The bankers feel that it would take at least 4-5 months for new deposits to come in. The advances made by the banks in the meanwhile will cut profit margin by 1%.

The Reserve Bank of India has announced that the one percent cut in the advance rate would be applicable to advances above Rs. 2 lakh. Simultaneously, it announced a cut in the deposit rate by 1%. This dual decision was intended to ensure that the profit margins (the difference between the lending rate and the deposit rate) of banks do not shrink. However, the bankers feel that they have to bear the burden of the 1% cut in the advance rate in the short run.

The Reserve Bank of India has administered strict instruction to the banks to pass on the interest rate concession to the borrowers with immediate effect. During the busy season of October 1992 the Reserve Bank of India announced a credit policy under which the lending rate was cut by 1%. Simultaneously, the Reserve Bank announced a cut in the deposit rate by 1% from 13 to 12% in order to protect banks' profitability. However, the Reserve Bank allowed the banks to use their discretion in fixing interest rates for borrowers depending on the cost of funds. But at present, the banks do not have the option of exercising their discretion as they are under strict instructions to pass on the lending rate cut with immediate effect. This means that the banks have to make advances of above Rs. 2.0 lakh at the interest rate of 17 percent per annum. Banks normally charge different rates depending on the creditworthiness of the borrowers. But at present the 1% reduction in the lending rate has to be passed on to all the borrowers on loans above Rs. 2.0 lakh. If earlier a borrower was charged 20% he has now to be accommodated at 19% for fresh loans now.

The presumption of lending rate of 17% for advances above Rs. 2.0 lakh and of 18% for advances below Rs. 2.0 lakh is patently discriminatory. There are many small and medium scale industries which operate on borrowed funds. Many of them are on the verge of unavailability if not actually sick. Their profitability is low and their employment and export potential is remarkably high. If a relief was absolutely necessary it was for these industries borrowing less than Rs. 2.00 lakh. Even the big industrial units borrow by them. This apart, the large industrial units which borrow less than Rs. 2.0 lakh have to pay an interest rate of 18%. The discrimination is not on the basis of size of the industrial units but on the size of borrowing by them. This apart, the large industrial units enjoy all the economies of scale, an advantage which the small units do not enjoy. If any relief is needed it is for the small units rather than for the larger units. For a small unit borrowing Rs 2.00 lakh at 17% interest instead of at 18%, the saving on interest rate is only Rs. 2000 which is not much. For this reason, it would be of some help to the industrial units big or small, to make loans available to them at a uniform interest rate whatever be the size of the loan. It is hoped that the Finance Minister and the Reserve Bank of India will change their present stance and make the lending rate 17% irrespective of the size of the borrowing units and the size of the loan borrowed.

The reduction in the deposit rate by 1% from 12 to 11% is intended to make good any loss the banks may incur on their loan portfolio. This on the assumption that their deposit mobilization programme remains intact. But the depositors are sensitive to the interest rate on their deposits. If the deposit rate falls they may divert their deposits to speculative activity in the real estate market and the gold bullion market. As the prices of real estate in urban centres and of gold continue to rise investment in these assets appears profitable. For this reason the depositors may not deposit their savings in the banks and may also divert their deposits to the purchase of urban property and gold. This reduces the inflow of deposits to the banks and increases the outflow leaving the banks with a smaller volume of deposits. Thus, while banks make a loss in their income due to the cut in the lending rate, they may not make good this loss by a cut in the deposit rate.

However, there is good news to the banks. The reduction in the statutory liquidity ratio (SLR) will have a larger amount of resources at the disposal of the banks and enable them to lend more to the commercial sector. This will reduce the impact of a cut in the lending rate on their profitability. In this event the banks could be asked to lend at 17% whatever be the size of the borrowing units or whatever be the size of the loans advanced. Charging an interest rate of 18% for advance below Rs. 2.0 lakh does not appear to be appropriate. The case, therefore, is strong for charging a uniform lending rate irrespective of the size of the loan. The present Rs. 23.0 lakh limit is arbitrary and is not founded on any acceptable reasoning.